MW01224906

Computer Supported
Co-operative Work

TRENDS IN SOFTWARE

User Interface Software
ed. Len Bass and Prasun Dewan

Configuration Management
ed. Walter Tichy

Software Fault Tolerance
ed. Michael Lyu

Software Process
ed. Alfonso Fuggetta and Alexander Wolfe

Formal Methods for Real-Time Computing
ed. Constance Heitmeyer and Dino Mandrioli

Data Visualization Techniques

ed. Chandrajit Bajaj

Computer Supported Co-operative Work

Edited By

Michel Beaudouin-Lafon
Université Paris-Sud, France

JOHN WILEY & SONS
Chichester · New York · Weinheim · Brisbane · Singapore · Toronto

Copyright ⓒ 1999 by John Wiley & Sons Ltd,
Baffins Lane, Chichester,
West Sussex PO19 1UD, England

National   01243 779777
International (+44) 1243 779777

e-mail (for orders and customer service enquiries): cs-books@wiley.co.uk

Visit our Home Page on http://www.wiley.co.uk
or
http://www.wiley.com

All rights reserved. No part of this publication may be reproduced, stored in a
retrieval system, or transmitted, in any form or by any means, electronic, mechanical,
photocopying, recording, scanning or otherwise, except under the terms of the Copyright,
Designs and Patents Act 1988 or under the terms of a licence issued by the Copyright
Licensing Agency, 90 Tottenham Court Road, London, W1P 9HE, UK, without the
permission in writing of the publisher.

Other Wiley Editorial Offices

John Wiley & Sons, Inc., 605 Third Avenue,
New York, NY 10158-0012, USA

WILEY-VCH GmbH, Pappelallee 3,
D-69469 Weinheim, Germany

Jacaranda Wiley Ltd, 33 Park Road, Milton,
Queensland 4064, Australia

John Wiley & Sons (Asia) Pte Ltd, 2 Clementi Loop #02-01,
Jin Xing Distripark, Singapore 129809

John Wiley & Sons (Canada) Ltd, 22 Worcester Road,
Rexdale, Ontario M9W 1L1, Canada

Library of Congress Cataloging-in-Publication Data

Beaudouin-Lafon, Michel.
    Computer supported co-operative work / Michel Beaudouin-Lafon
        p.   cm. — (Trends in software ; 7)
    Includes bibliographical references and index.
    ISBN 0-471-96736-X (alk. paper)
    1. Teams in the workplace — Computer networks.   I. Title
    II. Series.
    HD66.2.B4   1999
    658.4′02 — dc21   98-42699
                                                          CIP

British Library Cataloguing in Publication Data

A catalogue record for this book is available from the British Library.

ISBN 0-471-96736-X

Produced from Postscript files supplied by the author.
Printed and bound in Great Britain by Biddles, Guildford, UK.
This book is printed on acid-free paper responsibly manufactured from sustainable
forestry, in which at least two trees are planted for each one used in paper production.

Contents

Series Editor's Preface   ix

Preface   xi

List of Authors   xv

1 Designing Groupware Applications: A Work-Centered Design Approach   1
K. Ehrlich

  1.1 Introduction   1
  1.2 Requirements   4
  1.3 Design   14
  1.4 Deployment and Adoption of the Application   18
  1.5 Case Study: TeamRoom   20
  1.6 Summary   23
  Acknowledgements   24
  References   24

2 Workflow Technology   29
C.A. Ellis

  2.1 Overview   29
  2.2 Workflow Concepts and Architecture   30
  2.3 Historical Perspective and Related Work   36
  2.4 Workflow Models and Modeling   38
  2.5 Workflow Meta-Model   40
  2.6 Example Systems   43
  2.7 Research Directions and Issues   46
  2.8 Summary   51
  References   51

3 Media Spaces: Environments for Informal Multimedia Interaction 55
W.E. Mackay

3.1 Introduction 55
3.2 Early Media Spaces 57
3.3 RAVE: EuroPARC's Media Space 58
3.4 Other Major Media Spaces 67
3.5 WAVE: A Detailed Case Study 71
3.6 Ethical Issues 77
3.7 Conclusion 79
Acknowledgements 79
References 79

4 Integration of Shared Workspace and Interpersonal Space for Remote Collaboration 83
H. Ishii

4.1 Introduction 83
4.2 TeamWorkStation-1 and Seamless Shared Workspaces 86
4.3 TeamWorkStation-2 for N-ISDN 89
4.4 Seamless Integration of Interpersonal Space and Shared Workspace 92
4.5 Design of ClearBoard-1 93
4.6 Design of ClearBoard-2 95
4.7 Summary and Future Work 97
Acknowledgements 99
References 100

5 Group Editors 103
A. Prakash

5.1 Introduction 103
5.2 Examples of Group Editors 104
5.3 Group Editor Architecture 107
5.4 Concurrency Control 109
5.5 Undo in a Group Editor 117
5.6 Supporting Collaboration Awareness 123
5.7 Design of Document Structure 126
5.8 Other Design Issues 127
5.9 Future Work 131
References 131

6 Groupware Toolkits for Synchronous Work 135
S. Greenberg and M. Roseman

6.1 Introduction 135

6.2   Run-Time Architectures   136
6.3   Programming Abstractions   144
6.4   Groupware Widgets   150
6.5   Session Management   158
6.6   Conclusion   161
Acknowledgements   164
References   164

7   Architectures for Collaborative Applications   169
P. Dewan

7.1   Introduction   169
7.2   Collaboration Model   170
7.3   Generic Architecture   172
7.4   Design Space   174
7.5   External Modules   185
7.6   Rules   187
7.7   Classifying Existing Systems   188
7.8   Conclusions and Future Work   189
Acknowledgements   191
References   191

8   Software Infrastructures   195
P. Dourish

8.1   Introduction   195
8.2   Infrastructure Elements in CSCW   196
8.3   Communication   199
8.4   Coordination   202
8.5   Storage   205
8.6   Infrastructure and Specialization   207
8.7   Summary   216
Acknowledgements   217
References   217

9   Expanding the Role of Formal Methods in CSCW   221
C. Johnson

9.1   Introduction   221
9.2   Starting From the Ground Up: The Application of Formal Methods to CSCW   228
9.3   Dialogue Sequences   230
9.4   Formalizing the Presentation of CSCW Systems   236
9.5   Working Environments   243
9.6   Representing Workstation Layout   245
9.7   Using Ergonomic Guidelines to Inform CSCW Design   246
9.8   Prototyping   248
9.9   Conclusion   252

References   254

Index   **257**

Series Editor's Preface

During 1990, the twentieth anniversary of *Software Practice and Experience*, two special issues (one on UNIX Tools and the other on the X Window System) were published. Each issue contained a set of refereed papers related to a single topic; the issues appeared a short time (roughly nine months) after the authors were invited to submit them. The positive experience with the special issues resulted in *Trends in Software*, a fast turn-around serial that devotes each issue to a specific topic in the software field. As with the special issues of *SP&E*, each issue of *Trends* will be edited by an authority in the area.

By collecting together a comprehensive set of papers on a single topic, *Trends* makes it easy for readers to find a definitive overview of a given topic. By ensuring timely publication, *Trends* guarantees readers that the information presented captures the state of the art. The collection of papers will be of practical value to software designers, researchers, practitioners and users in that field.

Papers in each issue of *Trends* are solicited by a guest editor who is responsible for soliciting them and ensuring that the selected papers span the topic. The guest editor then subjects each paper to the rigorous peer review expected in any archival journal. As much as possible, electronic communication (e.g. electronic mail) is used as the primary means of communication between the series editor, members of the editorial board, guest editor, authors, and referees. A style document and macro package is available to reduce the turn-around time by enabling authors to submit papers in camera-ready form. Papers are exchanged electronically in an immediately printable format.

Trends will appear roughly twice a year. We now have issues in interactive data visualization techniques and computer supported cooperative work. Topics to be covered in forthcoming issues include other novel aspects of software.

The editorial board encourages readers to submit suggestions and comment. You may send them via electronic mail to **bala@research.att.com** or by postal mail to the address given below.

I would like to thank the editorial board as well as the staff at John Wiley for their help in making each issue of *Trends* a reality.

Balachander Krishnamurthy
Room D-229
AT&T Labs–Research
180 Park Avenue
Florham Park NJ 07932
USA

Preface

Computer Supported Cooperative Work, or *CSCW*, is a rapidly growing multi-disciplinary field. As personal workstations get more powerful and as networks get faster and wider, the stage seems to be set for using computers not only to help accomplish our everyday, personal tasks but also to help us communicate and work with others. Indeed, group activities occupy a large amount of our time: meetings, telephone calls, mail (electronic or not), but also informal encounters in corridors, coordination with secretaries, team workers or managers, etc. In fact, work is so much group work that it is surprising to see how poorly computer systems support group activities. For example, many documents (such as this book) are created by multiple authors but yet no commercial tool currently allows a group of authors to create such shared documents as easily as one can create a single-author document. We have all experienced the nightmares of multiple copies being edited in parallel, format conversion, mail and file transfers, etc.

CSCW is not recent. Back in the late 1960s, Doug Engelbart created the NLS/Augment system that featured most of the functions that today's systems are trying to implement such as real-time shared editing of outlines, shared annotations of documents, and video-conferencing. The field really emerged in the 1980s and has been growing since then, boosted in the recent years by the explosion of the Internet and the World Wide Web. The Web itself is not a very collaborative system: pages can be easily *published* but it is impossible (or very difficult) to *share* them, e.g. to know when someone is reading a particular page or when a page has been modified. The range and complexity of the problems to solve to support cooperative activities is rapidly overwhelming: data sharing, concurrency control, conflict management, access control, performance, reliability, the list goes on.

A large part of this book is devoted to the exploration of these problems and the state of the art of their solutions. In fact, CSCW is challenging most of the assumptions that were explicitly or implicitly embodied in the design of our current computer systems. CSCW tools, or *groupware*, are by nature distributed and interactive. To succeed in the marketplace, they must be safe (authentication), interoperable (from network protocols to operating systems and GUI platforms), fault-tolerant and robust (you don't want to be slowed down or loose your data if another participant in the session uses a slow connection or experiences a crash).

In addition to these technical difficulties, there is another, maybe harder, problem in implementing groupware: people. For a medium to work, there must be an audience that accepts using it. Usability issues have stressed the need to take the users into account when designing, developing and evaluating an interactive software. For groupware, usability issues go beyond the now well-understood (if not always well-applied) methods from psychology and design. They involve social sciences to understand how people work together, how an organization imposes and/or adapts to the work practices of its workers, etc. In many CSCW projects, ethnographic studies have been conducted to better understand the nature of the problem and the possible solutions. A large body of the research work in CSCW is conducted by social scientists, often within multidisciplinary teams. Computer scientists often ignore or look down upon this aspect of CSCW and almost always misunderstand it. User-centered design is essential to ensure that computer scientists solve the right problems in the right way. Traditional software works as soon as it "does the job"; Interactive software works better if it is easy to use rather than if it has more functions; Groupware works only if it is compatible with the work practices of its users.

Overview of the book

This book attempts to cover the broad field of CSCW and to give an overview of the history, state of the art and research issues of this exciting field. It is divided into two parts: the first part covers *groupware tools* while the second part covers *tools for groupware*.

The first chapter by Ehrlich focuses on a category of groupware for asynchronous group work such as the well-known Lotus Notes. More importantly, it provides an in-depth analysis and a set of recommendations to help design, develop and deploy groupware in an organization. Ehrlich emphasizes that groupware is for group work and therefore all aspects of group work must be well understood for the software to be accepted.

Chapter 2 by Ellis covers workflow systems. Since the 1960s, businesses have been converting their manual or mechanical information systems into computerized systems. Workflow systems go beyond traditional information systems by embodying a description of the work processes of the organization. The system therefore can be proactive, e.g. by automatically circulating documents or by reminding users of their duties when they are late. Ellis analyzes the promises, realities and problems of this category of groupware.

Chapter 3 by Mackay describes media spaces, i.e. communication systems that combine audio, video and computers to provide distant users with a means for social interaction and informal communication. Unlike videoconferencing rooms which require reservations and inevitably lead to formal meetings, media spaces attempt to broaden the bandwidth among users in order to support "real-life" human communication. Mackay covers the underlying design rationale of the existing systems and raises awareness on ethical and privacy issues of groupware.

Chapter 4 by Ishii describes systems that allow small groups to work in a tightly-coupled way at a distance, such as an instructor and a student or a group of designers. The chapter is illustrated by a description of a series of prototypes developed by Ishii and his group. While the prototypes are technically more and more complex, the chapter shows how the observation of the type of group work that was to be supported leads from one prototype to the next.

Chapter 5 by Prakash covers shared editors, editors that can be used by several users simultaneously to edit, in real-time, a single document. It marks the division between the two parts of the book: the concepts of shared editor are introduced and some examples are presented. The chapter then goes into an in-depth description of the techniques used to implement shared editors, focusing on issues such as managing the consistency between several copies of the document being edited and implementing multi-uscr undo.

Chapter 6 by Greenberg and Roseman describes groupware toolkits. In the same spirit as user interface toolkits, groupware toolkits provide programmers with predefined components that help implement groupware tools. The chapter covers toolkits for real-time (or synchronous) groupware, with components such as group widgets, awareness widgets, session managers, etc. Greenberg and Roseman use their own toolkit, GroupKit, to illustrate the design issues of such tools.

Chapter 7 by Dewan covers software architectures for CSCW. Since groupware applications must interact, by definition, with several users, they are in general distributed over a network. Dewan systematically examines the various ways in which an application can be decomposed into modules, threads and processes and the many tradeoffs that the various solutions incur. This leads to a set of measures for an architecture that help better understand this large design space.

Chapter 8 by Dourish covers software infrastructures, i.e. the types of services that are or could be provided by the operating system, network and other middleware to implement groupware applications. Given the varying needs of groupware applications, Dourish presents a particular approach, open implementation, as particularly promising since it combines flexibility, performance and openness.

Chapter 9 by Johnson provides an original perspective on the role of formal methods in CSCW, more particularly in the requirements phase of development. Johnson introduces several formal notations and models and uses examples to show how they can be applied to practical cases.

CSCW radically changes the status of the computer. Until now, the computer has been used as a *tool* to solve problems. With CSCW, the computer/network is a *medium*: a means to communicate with other human beings, a vector for information rather than a box that stores and crunches data. If we look at the history of technology, new media have been much more difficult to invent, create and operate than new tools. From this perspective, it is not surprising that CSCW has not yet realized its full potential, even in the research community. I hope this book will help readers to better understand the challenges and promises of CSCW and encourage new developments both in research and in industry.

Michel Beaudouin-Lafon
Laboratoire de Recherche en Informatique
Bâtiment 490
Université de Paris-Sud.
91 405 Orsay Cedex FRANCE
mbl@lri.fr

List of Authors

Prasun Dewan
Department of Computer Science
University of North Carolina
Chapel Hill, NC 27599
USA
dewan@cs.unc.edu

Paul Dourish
Xerox PARC
3333 Coyote Hill Road
Palo Alto, CA 94304
USA
dourish@parc.xerox.com

Kate Ehrlich
Lotus Development Corp.
55 Cambridge Parkway
Cambridge MA 02142
USA
kate_ehrlich@lotus.com

Clarence Ellis
Department of Computer Science
University of Colorado
Boulder, CO 90309-0430
USA
skip@cs.colorado.edu

Saul Greenberg
Department of Computer Science
University of Calgary
Calgary, Alta T2N 1N4
CANADA
saul@cpsc.ucalgary.ca

Hiroshi Ishii
MIT Media Laboratory
20 Ames Street
Cambridge, MA 02139
USA
ishii@media.mit.edu

Chris Johnson
Glasgow Interactive Systems Group
Department of Computer Science
University of Glasgow
Glasgow G12 8QQ
SCOTLAND
johnson@dcs.gla.ac.uk

Wendy E. Mackay
Department of Computer Science
Aarhus University
Aabogade 34
DK-8200 Aarhus N
DENMARK
mackay@daimi.aau.dk

Atul Prakash
Department of EECS
University of Michigan
Ann Arbor, MI 48109-2122
USA
aprakash@eecs.umich.edu

Mark Roseman
Department of Computer Science
University of Calgary
Calgary, Alta T2N 1N4
CANADA
roseman@cpsc.ucalgary.ca

1

Designing Groupware Applications: A Work-Centered Design Approach

KATE EHRLICH

Lotus Development Corp.

ABSTRACT

Group-ware is about group-work. It is about developing technologies that support the way people communicate and collaborate to accomplish work goals in the context of personal, managerial and organizational imperatives. In contrast to single user applications which support peoples' tasks, groupware supports peoples' work. Tasks are often explicit, observable and concrete. Work is often tacit, invisible and amorphous. The challenge in developing a groupware application lies in understanding, explicating and then supporting the invisible work. The chapter provides some insight into the process of developing groupware applications by first describing some new methodologies for generating requirements. It then outlines several themes — communication, awareness, anonymity — which have emerged as common across many groupware applications. The chapter also addresses the technical and social issues that emerge when deploying a groupware application in an organization. Application deployment is one of the most challenging aspects of developing a groupware application. The chapter concludes with a case study of an application designed to support coordination and communication in distributed teams. The case study brings together the topics of Methodology, Design and Deployment in a concrete setting.

1.1 INTRODUCTION

Group-*ware* is about group *work*. Group work is the work practice that evolves to get ordinary, daily work done. Group work includes the informal ad hoc communication that happens between people in adjoining offices or people in different countries and time zones. Group work happens in a context of personal, managerial and organizational imperatives that encourage people to share their work with others and reward them when they do.

The design of single-user applications translates users' tasks and needs into a functional description which directs the overall design and development of the application. When delivered, most single user applications can be used "right out of the box" — aside from time spent learning the application. Groupware applications, designed to support group work, require a different methodology to understand the tacit, invisible aspects of work practices. Translation into cogent, explicit requirements is not straightforward but requires extensive ongoing collaboration between researchers and application developers to translate descriptions of group work into application features. The functional requirements govern the technical development of the application. But adoption of the application is just as likely to be determined by organizational and managerial preparedness as by the design and technical implementation of the application itself.

This chapter draws on recent research and practical examples to examine groupware applications from three perspectives:

- *methodologies* for providing new product ideas or for extracting requirements from work practices
- common themes that emerge in the *design* of many groupware applications
- technical and social challenges in *deploying* an application.

The chapter concludes with a case study of the design, development and deployment of an application to support coordination in distributed teams.

1.1.1   Definitions and examples of groupware applications

Groupware, the applied side of CSCW (Computer Supported Cooperative Work), has been described by Cameron et al. [Cam95] in the Forrester report as:

> "Technology that communicates and organizes unpredictable information, allowing dynamic groups to interact across time and space."

And by Bob Johansen of the Institute for the Future as:

> "a generic term for specialized computer aids that are designed for the use of collaborative work groups. Typically, these groups are small, project-oriented teams that have important tasks and tight deadlines. Groupware can involve software, hardware, services and/or group process support." [Joh88, page 1]

Groupware applications provide computer support for group work. At a general level, group work includes *written and spoken communication, meetings, shared information*, and *coordinated work*. Some group work occurs when people interact with each other at the same time (synchronously). Face-to-face meetings are an example of people working together at the same time and often in the same place. People can also work together at different times (asynchronously). When people leave messages in electronic mail, the communication occurs over a period of time.

1.1.1.1   Communication

Perhaps the most common type of group work is communication between individuals or groups. Groupware applications to support *synchronous* communication includes videoconferencing, shared screens/applications, MediaSpaces, Chat (see Chapters 3, 4 and 5 in this book [Mac99, Ish99, Pra99]). These applications let people communicate with each other even though one person(s) is located at a different place than the other person(s), by using technology to link separate screens. For instance, when people communicate using videoconferencing a camera pointed at one person's face can relay that image and any sounds to the screen of someone sitting at another computer. That other computer could be located down the hall, or in another city or country. In this way people who cannot be physically in the same place at the same time can still communicate with each other.

Applications to support *asynchronous* communication include electronic mail, perhaps the most widely used groupware application. Electronic mail lets people leave messages for one or more other person at any time to be read by that person at any time and in any place.

Other things can emerge from communication such as the development of virtual communities whose continued communication/participation is then further supported by technology.

1.1.1.2   Meetings

One of the most common work activities in most organizations are face-to-face meetings. While it might seem that this is one place where there are no barriers of time or place, there is still opportunity for applications to support work. Groupware applications to support meetings include software that captures and organizes ideas for brainstorming, summarization and reporting. This software is most often used in specially equipped rooms with computers embedded in desks. People attending one of these meetings can enter ideas, comments, votes into the computer at particular times during the meeting. The software might simply display the written ideas, let someone, usually a meeting facilitator, group the ideas, or the software might tally votes. All of which supports the work of the meeting in a way that goes beyond what the people in the meeting could do on their own.

1.1.1.3   Information Sharing

When people work together, there is often a need not only to communicate with others but to share information. Information is commonly shared by leaving an electronic document in a database where it can be read by anyone with access to that database. This is different from electronic mail where a document is sent to a particular person or sometimes a group of people. Groupware applications include discussion databases, bulletin boards and electronic news groups where documents and their responses are often grouped together under a single heading or keyword making it easier to follow the thread of a discussion.

Applications for publishing documents have sometimes also been called groupware. However, this labeling is somewhat controversial. This chapter takes the position, that an application can be considered groupware only when more than one person has the opportunity to create documents or other responses. Applications that let one person publish documents to a wide audience of readers are not good examples of groupware.

1.1.1.4   Coordinating Work Processes

In many operational settings, people coordinate their work over time making sure that decisions made by one person are acted upon before being passed on to the next person. Commonly referred to as workflow systems, these applications often embody features such as privacy control, sequencing, notification, and routing (see also Chapter 2 in this book [Ell99]). Workflow systems may also include a decision support component as part of the overall process. Workflow systems are often thought of in the context of formal approval processes or large production settings. Systems designed to support coordination between people include project management, tracking systems, shared calendars. As defined here, workflow could also describe the kind of system used in medical settings where several people need to interact with the same data in handling administration of patient records. While not necessarily formally acknowledged as workflow or groupware, these kinds of applications meet the criteria of having multiple people interacting with the same application and hence the need on the part of the application developer to pay attention to issues of access, privacy and simultaneity of use.

Forrester [Bro97] gives this description of a groupware application built by a computer company to better manage projects:

> "We are the professional services division of a major computer company. Time is our enemy. The longer a project goes, the worse things are. We're building a project management system that puts the project plan on the Internet for feedback, updates, notation, and comments from all team members, including customers. Before, one person managed the project with relatively static plans, but with this program, project management becomes much more dynamic and fluid."

1.1.1.5   Groupware Solutions

In addition to applications designed to solve particular problems, there are also efforts such as digital libraries, electronic commerce, knowledge management and distance learning, all of which include some degree of groupware within a larger context. It is often the case that the scale of these efforts requires a stronger "solution"-based approach in which technology is embedded within technical and professional services such as training and management consulting. These "solutions" are often distributed through consulting and other service organizations who are best suited to adapt the solution to the customers' needs and to handle the larger scale effort.

1.2   REQUIREMENTS

This chapter assumes a phased approach in the development of a new groupware application. In broad terms, the first phase, called *requirements*, concerns the translation of the users' needs into a functional specification from which a detailed design can be made. The second phase, called *design*, focuses on what gets built and how. The third phase, called *deployment*, attends to the details of introducing and rolling out the application to the customer or user.

In gathering requirements for the development of a new groupware application, the focus should be on understanding the invisible work and work practices [Nar98a, Suc95] as well as the visible, and on understanding the physical and organizational context in which work is done. That work context is increasingly nontraditional — homes, airports, train stations, hotel rooms; anywhere where a laptop computer — or a fax or phone — can be carried and attached to a wide area network such as the Internet. If members of a group frequently work apart, both the technology and the culture of the group needs to accommodate a different style of interaction and coordination, as O'Hara-Devereaux and Johansen [OHa94] emphasize:

> "Global organizations cannot function without information technology. But the technology itself is not the answer to the myriad problems of working across geographical and cultural boundaries. The ultimate answers to these problems remain in the realm of human and organizational relations." [page 74]

It should be noted that the emphasis on groups, work, and work practices should not obscure the need for some level of task analysis within the application design. Workflow applications may have specific tasks embedded within them that are amenable to conventional task analysis methods. Similarly, applications originally designed for single users may be appropriated by the group. For example, spreadsheets, originally designed for individual use, were found to be part of an overall group collaboration (e.g. [Nar93]), especially in sharing expertise and generating alternative scenarios. Groupware applications also need to be deliberate about the design of the user interface so that each person interacting with the application understands how to *use* the application as well as understanding the meaning of the work that is being supported by the technology. Designing for ease of use is as much a part of the design of groupware as it is for single-user applications.

1.2.1 Work Practices

Before plunging into the methodological approaches toward collecting requirements, it is important to understand what is meant by work *practices* and how these might differ from what is thought of as work *processes* or routine work.

Most groups engage in some degree of routine work that appears predictable, is often thought to be tedious, may be time-consuming, and is often error-prone. Some organizations, such as insurance companies, make a business out of such routine work by, for instance, processing insurance claims. This would appear to be an area in which computer support could reduce the amount of uninteresting work that people do, reduce error rates, provide accurate, up-to-the-minute status information and save money. Because the work is routine, it should be relatively straightforward to write down the sequence of steps that make up these workflows.

However, it turns out that even in simple cases, the work is never simply "routine" (e.g. [Mul95]) even though the people doing it might describe it that way. When Suchman [Suc83] studied accounting clerks, they described their jobs in a way that corresponded to the formal procedures. However, when Suchman observed these clerks, it was clear that they relied on informal, locally determined practices to get their work done. These practices were not written down anywhere nor were they part of any explicit training that the clerks received. Rather these practices were learned on the job.

If the application fails to support local work practices, people will either stop using the application or develop workarounds so that they can continue to work in a way that has evolved to be effective and efficient. People may also resist adoption if the application is perceived as compromising core skills and competencies. The two examples below, from a rich literature of work practice studies (e.g. [Pyc96, Sta94, Hug92, Hea91]), illuminate what can happen when systems are designed and delivered based on externally generated processes rather than the actual work practices.

1.2.1.1   Printing

Bowers et al [Bow95] describe work done by a large printer with several offices around Britain. The organization used both traditional print technology, such as hot metal presses and offset lithography, as well as newer technologies, such as high-end photocopying and digital reprographics. From an outsider's point of view, printing might seem to be a well-known and somewhat routinized process that should be easily described in terms of the sequence of tasks and movement of materials. As such, the work of printers might be considered amenable to some level of automation through, for instance, a workflow application that would handle some of the administrative work by which jobs are categorized by type and assigned codes, customers, delivery dates and so forth. The application might further capture data about length of time and type of materials, as well as control some of the more routine operations so that the operator had more time to handle other parts of the job.

From the point of view of the people doing the work, however, the operations and their sequence are anything but routinized. In fact, close inspection of the work reveals that the print operators evolved numerous small but significant modifications to the normative sequence of operations to ensure a smooth and efficient flow of work. These practices included: prioritizing the work, anticipating the work, supporting each other's work, knowing the idiosyncrasies of the machines, identifying and allocating interruptible work. For instance, each print job, which often involved multiple processes and different people, was accompanied by a "docket" marking details of the job, such as materials required, cost code, and desired delivery date. This docket would get transferred with the print job from operator to operator. Operators were supposed to order these dockets in terms of delivery date and select the next print job with the earliest date. However, in practice the operators would ensure a smooth flow of work by sometimes juggling these jobs based on complexity of job, how long it would take and whether there were other time-consuming processes later on, as well as factoring in jobs remaining from the previous day. In fact, the digital reprographics technology used in the print industry meant that simply following date order would not utilize the equipment efficiently, requiring, for instance, frequent changes of paper type or size or long idle times following a short print job if the operator was busy with another part of the job.

The operators were very familiar with the competing demands on the equipment and other resources and had evolved practices which adapted the normative ordering to the situation enabling them to conduct their work smoothly and efficiently. Moreover, these variations on the explicit process were well understood by all the operators and the administrative staff and constituted, as it were, their shared and distributed cognition of the work.

This group had a contractual obligation to install and use a workflow application designed specifically for the print industry, although not necessarily for this particular group. The application was designed to automate many of the routine administrative tasks while also maintaining a record of time taken on a job, materials used etc. Such information was useful in preparing reports and maintaining stock control. By contrast with the efficient smooth flow of work that had evolved in practice, the imposition of the workflow application disrupted the smooth flow of work by requiring that all print jobs be handled only in a normative fashion. For instance, the application required that no job could be started until an order form had been submitted. While this is the correct procedure, in practice, the operators would often jump the gun and begin the work in order to utilize the equipment effectively. The method of recording jobs and time failed to take into account that an operator could be doing multiple jobs at the same time. Using the system generally demanded extra time by everyone.

Because the operators had a contractual obligation to use the application, ignoring it and returning to the familiar method of working was not an option. Instead, they responded to the system by either developing work arounds, or, in extreme cases, reorganizing the work itself to adapt the work to the system. In either case, the overall work was done less efficiently.

As Bowers et al [Bow95] expressed:

> "Workflow from within characterises the methods used on the shopfloor which emphasise the local and internal accomplishment of the ordering of work. Workers juggle their in-trays, jump the gun, glance across the shopfloor, listen to the sounds coming from machines, re-distribute the work in the here and now so that what to do next can be resolved. ... In contrast, workflow from without seeks to order the work through methods other than those which the work itself provides."

When technology makes things worse, not better, there are various approaches to the re-design: a) features in the application should have more flexible mappings between processes and operators; b) redesign the application with greater emphasis on awareness and mutual monitoring; c) acknowledge real management practices and pressures to adopt technology and adapt some of the practices.

1.2.1.2 Trouble Ticketing System

A similar example of a well intentioned groupware application failing to embody the actual work practices comes from Sachs [Sac95]. She describes a system intended to improve the efficiency of assigning work to telephone company workers who are called in when there is a problem with a phone line. The system acts as a general dispatcher routing job tickets to the office nearest to the person to whom the work has been assigned. The job ticket gets recorded and is available for the worker to pick up. When one job is finished the worker picks up the next ticket in the stack. This dispatch function was one part of a larger system which also handled scheduling, work routing and record keeping.

While this method would seem to make sense and help increase the efficiency of getting information to the workers in a timely fashion, in practice it failed to acknowledge critically important information. When a linesman picked up a ticket he/she would spend some time talking with the coworker. During the conversation, the linesman would pick up incidental in-formation such as useful phone numbers, prior history as well as a more detailed explanation, of the actual problem. These valuable "invisible" transactions were getting lost by the appli-cation. Where some level of diagnosis is involved, it helps if the person fixing the problem can converse with the person who detected it (see also [Ehr94, Ehr98]). What happened with the TTS system was that people reverted to their old habits and used the system after the fact to encode what happened rather than, as intended, to direct their work.

> "While TTS was designed to make job performance more efficient, it has created the op-posite effect: discouraging the training of new hands, breaking up the community of practice by eliminating troubleshooting conversations, and extending the time spent on a single job by segmenting coherent troubleshooting efforts into unconnected ticket-based tasks." [page 41]

1.2.2   Methodologies

Having emphasized the importance of studying groups at work, the question arises, what is the best method to use to study work practices and group behavior. The work is largely tacit, invisible and unarticulated, distributed across time and place and hence hard to observe, and involves multiple people.

This section outlines three methodologies commonly used to understand work practices and group behavior: Ethnography, Participatory Design, Action Research. Even a deep understanding of work practices does not automatically result in requirements for applications to support those practices. There is an additional and explicit step required to translate the results of empirical research into ideas for new applications. This step is explored in a discussion of "Applied Ethnography" which describes how empirical results might be used to a) identify new product opportunities; b) evaluate existing technologies; c) provide input to design specifications.

It should be noted that groupware applications are frequently developed in direct consultation with the user. In cases where the application is built by a consulting group or an internal IS department, the close relationship with the customer often means that the customer's problem is known ahead of time. In these cases, the challenge for the application developers and designers is to elicit requirements from the customer that get at the root of what the problem *really* is, rather than what the customer says it is. Methods such as focus groups (e.g. [Hol93]), brainstorming and scenarios (e.g. [Car95]) may be employed, along with an iterative development process using rapid prototyping techniques to elicit these requirements.

When a particular customer has not been identified ahead of time, as is the case with research projects and "shrink-wrapped" commercial applications that are not designed for a particular customer, then methods derived from research may be more appropriate. These methods can, of course, also be used in consulting and other settings. Three methods are described here which have been used by researchers and practitioners of CSCW and groupware.

1.2.2.1   Ethnography

Perhaps the most common methodology used in CSCW and groupware derives from ethnography as it was developed in anthropology, building on the recognition that workplaces are types of specialized cultures (see especially [Blo93a, Jor96]).

> "As practiced by most ethnographers, developing an understanding of human behavior requires a period of field work where the ethnographer becomes immersed in the activities of the people studied. Typically, field work involves some combination of observation, informal interviewing, and participation in the ongoing events of the community. Through extensive contact with the people studied, ethnographers develop a descriptive understanding of the observed behaviors." [Blo93a, page 124]

By focusing on observation and the study of people at work in their normal work setting, ethnographic methods can uncover and articulate the tacit, invisible work practices.

> "The ethnographic method, through participant observation, pays attention to how actors construct their understandings with others through a set of shared practices." [Ban96, page 14]

Asking people directly about their work won't reveal what is going on because even those who spend time reflecting on their own work — and they are in a minority — are too engaged in the work to be able to step back and explain the minutiae of what they do. However, some researchers have developed video-based observational and analysis methods in part to elicit post-hoc reflections from the users (e.g. [Jor95]).

Yet, as we saw in the examples from the print industry and the phone company, developers must pay attention to the minutiae of work practices in order to design and build an application that will be accepted, adopted and adapted by users to their work.

> "The purpose of ethnography is to carry out the detailed observations of activities within their natural setting. The aim is to provide details of the routine practices through which work is accomplished, identifying the contingencies that can arise, how they are overcome and accommodated, how divisions of labor are actually achieved, how technology can hinder as well as support activities, and so on." [Bly97b, page 40]

1.2.2.2 Participatory Design

A complementary method is one in which the users and other stakeholders of the software are involved in the design from a very early stage and throughout the design and development process. Often referred to as Participatory Design ([Sch93, Mul93]), this approach emerged from work by labor unions and others in Scandinavia acting as advocates for workers and for workplace democracy (see [Gre91] for review of work). A Participatory Design approach privileges the users in design decisions.

> "The focus of participatory design (PD) is not only the improvement of the information system, but also the empowerment of workers so they can co-determine the development of the information system and of their workplace." [Cle93, page 29]

1.2.2.3 Action Research

There are a number of methods from social psychology and related social sciences which seek to understand groups and group behavior (see especially, [McG84]). Of these, Action Research is distinguished for its emphasis not only on groups — especially teams — but for its desire to apply the results of the research to interventions that are designed to improve team performance (e.g. [Arg78, Arg82]).

A premise of Action Research is that organizations learn — and hence improve — by reflecting and reexamining the premises under which they are operating:

> "The ultimate purpose of action science is to produce valid generalizations about how individuals and social systems, whether groups, intergroups, or organizations can (through their social agents) design and implement their intentions in everyday life. The generalization should lead the users to understand reality and to construct and take action within it." [Arg82, page 469]

Action Research resembles ethnographic methods only in so far as both rely on observation and qualitative rather than quantitative descriptions. They diverge, in how the empirical results are used. Ethnographers prefer to take a neutral position on imposing any value judgment on what they observe; action researchers have it as a goal to change, for the better, the team's behavior and performance.

Historically, practitioners of Action Research have eschewed technology, preferring direct personal interventions to achieve organizational change. However, there is no *a priori* reason why the understanding and insights from Action Research methods could not be applied to the design of technologies which reflect organizational practices. Indeed it is not uncommon for people engaged in adapting, advising on or building groupware applications to describe their work as Action Research. Action Research and Participatory Design differ in whether the application should support or challenge the current status quo. Participatory Design privileges current users and current practices and seeks, by and large, to design applications to support and maintain those practices. Action Research enters into a study of a team with a belief in the value of bringing in interventions in order to assess patterns of activity.

Some potential points of synergy between these methodologies can be found in Snyder [Sny98] who combines theories of organizational learning with ethnographic research to yield insights and potential new interventions to communities of practice. Orlikowski and Hofman [Orl97] discuss strategies for introducing technology into organizations.

1.2.3   Applied Ethnography

There has, unfortunately, often been a disconnect between those who study work practices and those who develop groupware systems. On the one hand, research ethnographers have generally shied away from translating their empirical results into specific design recommendations lest their descriptive findings be misconstrued as being too prescriptive. On the other hand, developers have not delved into the details of the findings to extricate the implications for their particular application.

The gap between empirical results and application is due in part to the difficulty in translating from the specificity of the work environment being studied to the general and often unknown constraints and requirements of the application environment. Plowman et al. [Plo95] argue that the lack of translation from ethnographic studies to application design arises in part because the people who do the workplace research by and large do not also develop the applications. This, they argue, means that someone has to translate the results from the empirical to the technical domain — a problem compounded by the inherently descriptive nature of ethnographic findings. Some (e.g. [Rog97]) have taken the translation task to heart and arrived at various techniques such as creating a set of guiding questions, use of video clips and photos, highlighting breakdowns in the current process to convey the results of ethnographic studies to the development team. Others (e.g. [Ben92]) acknowledge the philosophical differences between ethnographers and system developers. The ethnographers are able to influence the design by working closely with the development team and showing a willingness to be flexible.

When properly applied, insights and results of ethnographic studies can: a) identify new product opportunities, b) evaluate the use of existing technologies, and c) provide input to design specifications [Bly97b]. Examples of this "applied ethnography" can be found in the proceedings of conferences such as the biannual CSCW and European ECSCW conferences.

1.2.3.1   Identify New Product Opportunities

Ideas for new, innovative applications won't come exclusively from ethnographic studies (see [Bro91] for extensive discussion on the source of ideas for innovative applications). However, ethnographic studies, because they focus so closely on the actual work being done, are well suited to generate insights into potential new software applications. When the result of an ethnographic study is used to identify new product opportunities, the group being studied are often different than the group targeted by the application. For instance:

1. In a study of a customer support organization, Ehrlich and Cash [Ehr94] observed that support analysts routinely shared references to previous cases and to printed or on-line material. Most of these references were shared as part of the normal dialog about a case. These and other observations of how people share recommendations led to the development of a collaborative filtering system for semi-automated personalized recommendations to on-line documents [Mal95]. Using the application, a person who finds a document that he/she believes will be of interest to a colleague can forward an e-mail link to the document along with a personal recommendation.

2. Nardi et al [Nar98b] report on the design of Apple Data Detectors, which are intelligent agents that analyze structured information and perform the appropriate operations. For instance, a user finding a meeting announcement could instruct the Detector to automatically add the announcement to a calendar. The development of this product emerged in part from observations made by Barreau and Nardi [Bar95] who, in a study of how people organize their desktops, found that users often complained of not being able to act on structured information found in common documents. The development of the product was also informed by a detailed ethnographic study of reference librarians [Nar96] who acted as agents on behalf of users looking for information. The results of that study translated into a design goal of having the software agent be unobtrusive and able to infer user needs.

1.2.3.2   Evaluation of Existing Technology

A variety of field methods can be used to evaluate how well existing applications are being incorporated into the work practice. If the application is not well suited to the setting, as we saw in the earlier example of the print shop, the failure will be readily apparent. Conversely, when technology has been successfully incorporated into the work practices, the application designer can consider extending the application or applying the application to other settings, but not without considering the consequences of transfer.

> In a recent ethnographic study of nurse reviewers who worked on disability and workers' compensation cases, Ehrlich and Cash [Ehr97] found that an administrative application with an embedded decision support component was well integrated into the nurse reviewers' work practice. They used the application to estimate the length of time that an injured worker should be away from work. The successful use by the nurse reviewers led to speculation that the application could be successfully deployed by physicians and physician assistants who were treating the patients. Although the physicians and nurse reviewers are linked in a type of extended enterprise, they nevertheless acted independently. The decisions made by the nurse reviewers were informed by their professional judgment and by their evolved work practices. Ehrlich and Cash argue that reallocating tasks to another part of an enterprise requires re-analysis of the overall context.

Lab rather than field methods can also be a useful way of evaluating applications, especially when the goal is to identify particular effects. For instance:

> Mark et al [Mar95] studied the effect of a hypermedia system, Dolphin, on the form, content and linkage amongst ideas created in a face-to-face meeting. Participants in the meeting were engaged in problem-solving exercises. Mark et al found that the people who used the application would group their ideas into networks rather than hierarchical structures and provide more

elaboration for their ideas. Those people not using the application generated less elaborated ideas. Thus, the technology had a qualitative effect on problem-solving behavior of the people in the meeting.

1.2.3.3   Input to Design Specifications

New applications often follow a process in which an initial concept — generated from marketing requirements or from the vision of a small group of people — is modified and elaborated into a richer functional specification. Ethnography and other field methods, *when used to study the intended user population,* can provide input to these design requirements. The examples below provide a diverse set of cases where ethnography had a direct influence on design directions.

1. In a study of air traffic controllers Bentley et al [Ben92] and Hughes et al [Hug92] found that seemingly routine work was coordinated through a sophisticated use of flight "strips". These pieces of paper carry static information about expected and current flights along with instructions to the aircraft being controlled by the center. However, the controllers had evolved a practice of manually organizing the strips on a visible flight progress board. The physical ordering of the strips provided implicit, tacit cues to help the controllers dynamically coordinate and allocate their work. Based on these observations the ethnographers could direct the design of an automated system for controllers away from an automatic assignment of strips and toward maintaining elements of the manual method. The study highlights one of the critical roles of ethnography which is to articulate and demonstrate to developers that "manual intervention and manipulation of information may be essential implicit methods of communication and cooperation".

2. Blomberg et al [Blo93b] offer brief descriptions of several studies done under the rubric of work-oriented design in which attention to the details of work is used to help guide the design of new applications. For instance, they studied the use of color and highlighting to distinguish the text annotations of different people on order forms as part of the coordination of activity across organizational boundaries. "By providing developers with visual representations of how the work of processing orders is supported by annotations, and by viewing videotapes of the people engaged in the work, we are exploring with developers and work practitioners how computationally active marks on paper might support this work."

3. In a different arena, Kukla et al [Kuk92] worked with Monsanto and Fisher Controls Inc. "to investigate and apply modern information technology" to Monsanto's integrated nylon facility in Pensacola, Florida. The goal was to optimize the use of raw materials and energy through the facility. An ethnographic approach, comprising interviews, observations and detailed information on one sector of the plant was used to "construct models of events, conversations and processes within that area of the plant. These models were to be used as a basis for developing software tools for use within the plant." At the beginning, work was characterized as routine and repetitive. But based on ethnography, a number of less visible aspects of work were uncovered. These included: the ability of people working in the plant to do ad-hoc juxtaposition of data screens (such as compare live process data to histograms or maintenance records); and the importance of manual, not automated, collection of data (e.g. by sensors of machines) by people to get the richness of the environment (e.g. noises, smells, comments by people working near and with machines). These and

other findings were translated into the design and development of specialized software for the process industry, linking realtime process data with desktop applications. The product, DEC@aGlance, was marketed in 1992.

4. Bly [Bly88] and Tang [Tan91] studied teams of people, working at distance, who need to work together to create drawings, designs and engage in general brainstorming. Ethnographic studies of people working together as well as people working apart led to many observations about such things as the use of gestures and marks to illustrate ideas, how control is passed from one person to another and how drawing and talking are combined. These observations led to the development of a prototype (e.g. [Min91]) for use in a research setting. That prototype subsequently influenced the development of products for synchronous shared collaboration from Sun Microsystems (e.g. ShowMe) and Xerox (e.g. LiveBoard).

5. Blythin et al [Bly97b] describe an ethnographic study at a bank of a service center which processed routine administrative details of accounts. Based on studying this group over time, the researchers uncovered limitations and problems imposed by the physical and organizational setting which impeded the effective and smooth flow of work. For instance, there was a physical separation between some supervisors and their teams which reduced the opportunity for informal awareness of the progress of work. Based on these and other findings, the researchers made recommendations for changes in management practices and processes, to provide better review and oversight and changes in (physical and functional) office assignments. These changes helped increase the supervisor's awareness of the group's work.

6. Katzenberg and Piela [Kat93b] used work language analysis combined with ethnography to study and verify "work language" in the form of names that different groups of people use to label computer systems, such as "compile, instantiate, create, build". The results of the ethnographic study were a set of guidelines for the continued development of a technology used in engineering and economic forecasting to analyze design alternatives.

Being able to use the results of ethnographic studies means that researchers and practitioners must be open to question their initial assumptions in the face of user data. For instance, in a field study of a distributed team, Bellotti and Bly [Bel96] observed that members of the team were rarely at their desks but instead could be found in the hallways or working in labs. Although Bellotti and Bly went to the site to gather requirements for a computer-based application to support distance collaboration, it was apparent that such an application would not be used if it was only available from the computer. Instead, the researchers were able to recommend alternative solutions based on mobile computing devices.

1.2.3.4 Working Together

These examples also draw our attention to the most important part of the design process, which is the collaboration between the ethnographers and the application designers. The results of ethnographic studies do not stand on their own but must be interpreted by both the ethnographer and the application designer. Just handing a report of the ethnography to the designers is not sufficient. The two groups must work together as a team when the data are being collected and analyzed. It is also crucial that there be reciprocal appreciation and respect of others' viewpoints. The need to overcome different world views, cultures and perspectives is a recurring theme in these studies.

An especially good example of a successful collaboration comes from a study by Linde, Pea and others at IRL (Institute for Research on Learning) for the design of an interactive multimedia communication device [Gog96, All93, deV91]. In a close examination of actual work sites, a multidisciplinary team of researchers representing application developers and ethnographers investigated the learning and work practices that emerged as new communication and computational technologies were integrated into ongoing activities. The design and development process was highly iterative. Outcomes of the studies would get translated into mock-ups which would be tested with users, modified and re-tested.

In one phase of this study, the ethnographers were videotaping a small group of graphic designers at work [Lin91]. The graphic designers organized their ideas using folders. But what the ethnographers observed was that during group meetings the folders were placed on the table in a particular way. The placement — close to the owner or toward the middle — was a form of non-verbal communication used to signal permission for others to talk. The ethnographers were able to point out this observation to the application designers who would not otherwise have been aware of the importance of the folders and their placement. Based on the ethnographers' analysis and their own observation, the application designers realized that the design of the software would need to include not just the ability to share folders but those folders would need to be marked as read only, private or open. This is a small example that was repeated many times in the course of the collaboration between the ethnographers and the application designers.

1.3 DESIGN

Part of the appeal of groupware lies in the promise of being able to eradicate barriers of time and place. Using technology, colleagues should be able to collaborate on projects whether their offices are next to each other or in separate countries, whether they work at the same time or different times of the day. Applications that help bridge barriers of time and place include videoconferencing, shared screens, media spaces, electronic mail, shared files/databases, shared authoring, and group calendaring systems. However, subtle social protocols influence the willingness of participants to communicate with others, the candor of their communication, the richness of information they are willing to impart, and the degree of their engagement in the process. If technology is going to mediate communication especially for people who lack opportunities for face-to-face meetings, it must support rather than ignore these protocols. Getting inside this notion of group *work*, a few themes emerge:

- communication is generally ad hoc, *informal* and unplanned
- there is a need to be *aware* of others for communication and in coordinating work
- issues of sharing often hinge on subtle notions of *anonymity*.

1.3.1 Informal Communication

Research on synchronous, informal communication emphasizes its importance and prevalence in most workplace settings [Kra90, Whi94]. These studies suggest that formal communication is used to coordinate routine tasks whereas brief, informal communication such as spontaneous hallway conversations can help to establish trust, promote social relationships and provide background information about the work environment. Moreover, these spontaneous conversations are more likely to occur amongst people who are physically located close to each other; as many as 91% of all conversations recorded in a particular study occurred among people on the same floor [Kra90].

One type of video-based system, known as MediaSpaces, has been developed to provide visual access and opportunity for conversation to people who are not located in the same place [Fis90, Man91, Dou92, Bly93, Fis93] (see also Chapter 3 in this book [Mac99]). These systems provide continuous visual access between sites through large video screens, often placed in public areas such as hallways or informal meeting places. However, despite their careful design, these systems cannot substitute for unmediated face-to-face conversations.

1.3.2   Awareness

Awareness, of the location and activity of other people, is a critical mechanism for regulating and coordinating our behavior with others. We use cues in the physical environment such as a colleagues' open door, the placement of a work-related document [Hug92] or the level of participation in an on-line discussion, to make decisions about whether to initiate a conversation, begin the next sequence of work or anticipate a meeting. The same social protocols still operate when the work is mediated through computer technology. Groupware applications designed to support coordinated work need to find new ways to represent what were physical cues, so that even when online, people can be aware of the activity of their colleagues. Awareness of others usually takes place when there is on-going or anticipated, direct, synchronous communication between people. But there is also a need to be aware of a general level of involvement and participation of a group over time. Both synchronous and asynchronous awareness are explored below.

1.3.2.1   Synchronous Awareness

The Montage desktop videoconferencing system (e.g. [Tan94a, Tan94b]) supports the kind of momentary, reciprocal glances that occur when one person peeks into another's office to see if that person can be interrupted. In Montage the person initiating the conversation selects the name of the person to be contacted, which causes the recipient to receive an auditory signal that a call is about to commence, followed by a gradual fade-in small video image of the caller. Either person can acknowledge the glance by pressing a button to open an audio channel followed by a 2-way audio-video connection. This mediated interruption can get translated into a more extended interaction supported by the full desktop videoconferencing system by pressing the Visit button. If the caller sees from the glance that the other person is not available, the caller can browse the person's calendar, send a short note or send an e-mail message. As in office-based social conventions, Montage users can set their system to display different levels of interruptibility. These range from "locked" which means no interruptions, to "out of the office" and "other", which lets the caller leave a message, to "do not disturb" which still lets the caller glance in to negotiate an interruption, to "available".

There are numerous other studies of awareness including those on awareness as a mechanism to support coordination (e.g. [Dou92]) and social awareness (e.g. [Tol96]). Products to support awareness include "buddy lists" (e.g. [Mic97]) which signal when someone from the list is on line and hence potentially available for an online "chat".

1.3.2.2   Asynchronous Awareness

We also develop awareness of the general work patterns of our colleagues based on cues left in public or semi-public places. If I want to schedule a meeting with my manager, I might ask his assistant about his availability or I might check online sources such as group calendars, e-mail or online discussions to pick up cues about up-coming meetings, trips and so forth. In the case of group calendars, availability of people's schedules is both a strength for scheduling meetings, and a source of noncompliance for those people who feel exposed (e.g. [Gru95]).

1.3.3   Anonymity

In face-to-face communication, whether direct or mediated by computer technology, the contributors to the conversation are known and visible or audible. However, when there is no visual component to the communication, as in the case of electronic mail and asynchronous communication in general, the technology can hide the identity of the sender or the recipient of the message. This feature has interesting and often unexpected affects on the communication. For instance, people are much more likely to engage in antisocial behavior, such as "flaming" in electronic mail, where the sender's identity may be hidden by an obscure e-mail address and where the usual social protocols to discourage such behavior are absent. Sproull and Kiesler [Spr93] argue that social norms are not well established in computer mediated communication in part because social cues, which are normally present in the physical environment, are absent. For example, the physical appearance and dress code of someone we are about to meet clues us in to the level of formality expected.

On the other hand anonymity can have positive effects. Several researchers have observed that anonymity can reduce effects of power, status and attractiveness (e.g. [Zub88, Tur95]) enabling people who might not have participated in social engagements due to lower status or power to do so when they are anonymous. Similarly, Sproull and Kiesler [Spr93] report that junior members of an organization are much more likely to communicate with senior managers or executives using electronic mail than in a face-to-face meeting. As a classic cartoon in the New Yorker put it: "On the internet no-one knows you are a dog".

Similar effects of anonymity on people's social behavior in computer mediated settings have been observed with computer supported meetings (e.g. [Nun91]). Computer supported meetings typically take place in rooms which have been specially configured with computers embedded into desks or tables [Man89]. The software running on these computers support activities such as brainstorming by letting people freely enter their ideas. The software can then display the individual ideas or some aggregated version of those ideas on the individual terminals or on a large screen visible to all participants. These meetings are generally controlled by a trained facilitator who provides some degree of software support and training as well as handling the dynamics of the meeting itself.

The software portion of these systems can be easily configured to control when ideas get shared amongst the group and whether the ideas are marked with the name of the person who contributed them. Nunamaker and his colleagues have observed that in these kinds of settings, anonymity reduces the pressure to conform and reduces apprehension related to evaluation by one's peers. This, in turn, may encourage a more open, honest and freewheeling discussion. On the other hand, anonymity can increase "free riding". If nobody's comments are attributed, there is no way of checking that everyone in the meeting is actually participating.

1.3.4 Application of Design Themes

Themes such as informal communication, awareness and anonymity rightly belong to the category we have described as *group work* in that these features are not readily apparent from a task focused view. Yet, the presence of these features in an application can materially affect *how* the application is used and *whether* it is used. The inclusion of these and other themes into the design of the application depends in part on the type of application. Using the division of applications laid out in the introduction, those that focus primarily on communication such as e-mail, videoconferencing, media spaces and chat, may be designed around themes of informal communication and awareness. Applications designed to support meetings, on the other hand, need to pay attention to whether issues such as anonymity are needed in the design. In the case of applications that support information sharing, one of the main barriers to acceptance is the readiness of the organization in which the application is to be deployed. This topic will be addressed in Section 1.4.

1.3.5 Customization

We may think of groupware applications such as those that support communication, meetings and information sharing as general-purpose applications ready to be used by a wide range of users for a variety of purposes. This is true of individual "productivity applications" which are designed to be used out of the box with little or no customization. However, groupware applications are rarely ready to use "out of the box" but require some degree of customization. How much work is required depends in part on the type of application, whether it was developed for a particular customer and how the application is architected.

It is fair to say that while customization is not exclusive to groupware applications, in practice there are sufficient differences in work, culture and context from one customer to another that most groupware applications require some degree of customization. This is an important topic which has received little public discussion and hence is only covered briefly here and based largely on personal observations.

1. *Content-based customization.* This is a case where the application is merely a shell and doesn't really become useful until someone begins putting content in. Prime examples are discussion databases, news groups, e-mail etc. Examples from outside the realm of communication software include applications for distance learning where the instructor needs to add course material before the software is useful for the students. In all these examples, the "customization" is done by one or more end-users by supplying content. No specialized technical skill is required.
2. *Setting external parameters.* This is also end-user customization but is more intentional. Examples include TeamRoom (see description in Section 1.5) which is an application to support distributed team work through shared documents, etc. TeamRoom defines attributes such as document category and communication type whose values get set by the team. In this way, the team gets to customize the application to suit the way they intend to use it. A research group, for instance, may want to define categories for documents to represent different research projects while a product group may want to define documents in terms of product families. This is still end-user customization but this time it may involve an outside facilitator to guide the thinking of the group around the goals of the project, the group norms and expectations for the level of participation.
3. *Setting internal parameters.* This is where some degree of system administration or macro

level programming comes in. For instance, in an internally developed system to support on-line reviewing of papers submitted to conferences, the level of customization from one conference to the next ranged from inputting a new set of reviewer names to rewriting parts of the interface to recoding the rules that govern who sees which papers and at what stage of the reviewing process. Many of these changes reflected differences in the reviewing process from one conference to another.

4. *Totally customized solutions.* Applications that match the particulars of an organization's work practices, processes and culture often require that a customized application be built either by someone within the organization or by engaging external consultants.

Some issues of customization are addressed by the available development tools and environments which may provide the pieces out of which the customization is done. One example is the use of templates out of which new solutions can be fashioned. In an article on the use of templates for building business applications, Hofman and Rockart [Hof94] provide an example of a template developed by John Wiley, the publisher, to support internal business processes that allowed for customization by each business unit. This approach allowed them to share best practices, both applications as well as knowledge, aggregate data centrally, and "tailor the business process and system to local needs."

1.4   DEPLOYMENT AND ADOPTION OF THE APPLICATION

In addition to the challenges of building a good groupware application, there are significant challenges facing a developer who is trying to get the application adopted by an organization. Unlike single-user applications which can often be purchased by an individual, groupware applications are, be definition, for groups of people. Hence, enough copies of the application need to be purchased and installed at about the same time for the application to be available to more than one person. Moreover, groupware applications often require a sophisticated technology infrastructure which may in turn require skilled technical staff for the system's administration. In addition to the financial cost of purchasing, installing and maintaining a groupware application, there are also organizational implications of deploying the application. These implications vary with the type of application. For instance, deploying a video-conferencing system may require very little preparatory work within the group, assuming the application itself has been well designed and the infrastructure is in place. On the other hand, an application that depends on a high level of information sharing presumes an organization in which information sharing is already well established and rewarded. This section explores a few of the organizational and cultural barriers to successful deployment and adoption.

1.4.1   Organizational Preparedness

Technology can be introduced into organizations through a mandate imposed by senior management. This method has the advantage of ensuring continued financial and technical support through deployment and in helping disperse the technology through the organization to reach a critical mass of users (e.g. [Mar90]). However, this method of adoption can leave end-users feeling that a decision was forced on them. For instance, Orlikowski [Orl92] reports on the adoption by a large consulting company of groupware to support information sharing. Not only was the culture of the group one in which information sharing was not rewarded, but the technology was introduced to the group without sufficient explanation or training, thus giving these end-users no real understanding or motivation for wanting to expend the extra effort to learn and use the technology. As a result, the technology was poorly adopted and only gained in acceptance over time and with considerable investment and push on the part of senior management, who retained strong conviction in the benefits of the technology. An interesting side note is that the same technology was adopted more or less spontaneously by other groups in the same company where there had been no mandate by management.

Technology can also be introduced into an organization by someone within the organization seeing the potential of the technology. This method has the advantage of getting end-users involved early on. But it has the disadvantage of needing to get buy-in from senior management for continued support.

In a recent study, Grudin and Palen [Gru95] examined the adoption of shared calendar applications in two large organizations. They observed widely dispersed use of the application despite no clear mandate from senior management. They argued that

> "The features ... may attract a critical mass of users, after which technology-abetted social pressure by peers and others extends use" [page 277]

In at least one organization, the adoption was slow when the application was first introduced. Over time, what developed was a more consistent infrastructure that gave wider access to the application, improved functionality and ease of use and peer pressure. Once a critical mass of people begin using the application, there is strong peer pressure to bring others in line. Calendaring is an example of a groupware application that requires near universal adoption to be successful. Once someone uses the tool to schedule meetings with some colleagues, they will want to be able to use the tool to schedule meetings with other colleagues, and will apply pressure to those colleagues not yet using the application to begin to do so.

1.4.2   Incentives and Motivation

In a work setting, most people are persuaded to adopt a new technology by arguments that make it clear how that technology will improve their work. Such arguments may focus on the technology as enabling the person to do something that was previously very difficult or cumbersome to do. For instance, on-line discussions make it easier to share information with a number of colleagues simultaneously than it is to attend face-to-face meetings. This is especially true if colleagues are not all located in the same place or if it is hard to schedule a time when everyone can attend a meeting. New technology in general, especially groupware, will get adopted more easily if it fills a need rather than simply replaces an existing well understood, working process. For instance, videoconferencing technologies got a major push during a recent oil crisis when it got harder and more expensive for people to travel. The need to communicate and collaborate with colleagues didn't go away, but reaching those people got harder.

Convincing end-users of the benefit of any new technology is challenging — especially so for groupware applications for which there may be no visible examples of use. For example, several years ago, Wang introduced a multimedia communication system which bundled together image capture, voice recording, electronic mail, pen annotation and high-resolution graphics [Fra91]. The system was intended to be used to annotate and route documents through an organization. However, when the system was introduced into client sites it failed, in part because neither end-users nor management were ready to risk new unproven methods of working despite being told of the benefits of the system.

1.4.3   Critical Mass

Groupware applications are principally designed to benefit and reward the group rather than the individual. But most people are not altruistic. They want some personal benefit from using the application. Getting enough early adopters to use a new system is especially challenging for applications which rely on a large number of people to be effective. Many collaborative filtering systems recommend selections (e.g. of video, music, Net News) based on a statistical aggregate of individual ratings (e.g. [Hil95, Sha95, Res94, Gol92]). When the database has been seeded with enough ratings, users can query it to learn which selections are recommended. But where is the incentive for the early adopters to add their ratings? Resnick et al [Res94] argue that some people are altruistic, while others may be motivated by external rewards such as money to be an early adopter. Reaching a critical mass also proved to be the key factor in a study which systematically compared adoption rates of two similar video telephone systems [Kra94].

The potential asymmetry between those who contribute and those who get the benefit has been underscored by Grudin [Gru90]. He points out that with group-enabled systems such as group calendars and shared project management applications, the beneficiary is often the person scheduling meetings or managing the project, rather than the people contributing the information about their schedules or time.

1.5   CASE STUDY: TEAMROOM

To illustrate many of the points in this chapter, this section presents a brief case study of the design, development and deployment of a particular groupware application. The application, called TeamRoom, was initially developed for use by internal task forces at Lotus [Col96] to support discussion and coordination. It was then made available to outside customers as part of a consulting engagement, and is now sold as one of the family of Lotus/Domino applications.

1.5.1   Teams

Before building an application to support discussion and coordinating by members of a team, it is important to understand how teams work. At a very general level, teams of people work collectively and collaboratively to:

- make decisions
- share information
- coordinate actions.

Teams will be high performing, to the degree that they engage in these activities in a deliberate and persuasive manner to produce something of value to the organization such as a tangible product, a process or a service. There is a large amount written about teams and team performance, which will not be addressed here. As Katzenbach and Smith [Kat93a] expressed recently:

"Real teams are deeply committed to their purpose, goals, and approach. High-performance team members are also very committed to one another." [page 9]

However, there is increased pressure on teams to deliver more value in less time with few resources. Moreover, teams are often ad hoc (e.g. [Fin90]); formed "just in time" to solve a particular problem and then disbanded. And, members of the team may be dispersed throughout the organization as well as separately located due to travel or residence. Team members often come from different cultures in terms of professional training, background, tenure with the company, or nationality.

Technology cannot eliminate these barriers on time and place. However, in conjunction with judicious training, technology can help make the team, once formed, more effective and efficient. People working together need: shared context, shared language and shared objectives. They also need a "workplace" in which the majority of work will get done and where shared discussions as well as private conversations can take place. It is not the place of technology to help create the team, but rather, to support the team once it has formed. (An important and debatable question is whether the application is only as effective as the team or whether a well designed application can overcome limitations in the group dynamics.)

1.5.2   Requirements

TeamRoom was developed in response to a request from one of the senior vice-presidents at Lotus for an application that could support the work of internal task forces. Although all the people on a task force worked for the same company, they came from different parts of the organization and also traveled frequently. This meant that face-to-face meetings occurred only occasionally, necessitating the need to have a place to post documents, have discussions, plan meetings and share ideas. The development team was composed of people from development, design, internal information systems, Human Resources/Organizational Development, as well as the main customer and a representative group of users. Detailed user requirements and functional specifications were arrived at through discussions within this team and by exposing early prototypes to the users.

1.5.3   Design Features

Instead of having team members go to one application to retrieve shared documents, another for group e-mail and a third application for coordination, TeamRoom provides a single "place" for these activities by integrating all three functions in a single application.

TeamRoom builds on the Lotus Notes model of a threaded discussion database where messages can be posted and read by anyone who has access to the database. Documents can be entered to start a topic or as a response to an existing topic. In TeamRoom documents are keyed by communication type as well as by category. Common communication types include: discussion, action request, meeting announcement and reference document, and are used to signal the intent and type of communication. For instance, a discussion document signals that the author wants other people to respond, whereas a reference document may require little or no further discussion. These different document types reinforce and simplify communication. Documents can be viewed by topic, communication type and author as well as by date, so that a user can quickly see which documents have been added recently.

One of the distinguishing characteristics of TeamRoom is its embodiment in the software of the communication norms of a group. The translation of norms to features is handled through the *process* of having the group define its goals, mission, categories and communication types, and the *mechanism* of having these instantiated in the software by completing information about the team on a "Mission Page". This information includes: categories, communication types, participants and events. Once entered, this information becomes available to the team in the form of keyword lists, which a user selects when composing a document, and visible categories, which users see when viewing documents. Documents can also be automatically archived, which reduces the problem of information overload. The Mission Page is the place where the team records details of their processes and norms; such things as when to post documents to particular people rather than have the document default to be seen by everyone; and the meaning and intent of the different communication types and categories. Teams who have spent time filling out the mission page have found the information there to be invaluable as a source of group memory and an excellent vehicle for new members to get oriented. TeamRoom, especially the Mission Page, becomes a *work* space for *group* memory.

1.5.3.1   Relation to Design Themes

Section 1.3 identified three main group work themes: informal communication, awareness of others, and anonymity. Many of these themes can be seen in TeamRoom.

TeamRoom differs from both e-mail and discussion databases in that it is a place where all work — not just discussions — gets posted. Making each person's work visible to the rest of the team contributes to an awareness of other people's level of contribution and the current status of their work. By looking across the different categories, it is easy to see which documents are still in process and which are completed. An index view also shows the number of documents per author or communication type. An author view shows documents by type, which provides a view into whether a person is mostly commenting on other people's work or contributing their own.

TeamRoom supports informal communication by supporting loosely structured discussions. But it doesn't really support ad hoc informal communication since it is designed for teams that are not co-located (see Section 1.5.4 below).

TeamRoom does not let people participate anonymously, but it does support private, as well as public discussions, and personal as well as shared workspaces. When a document is posted in TeamRoom, the author is required to specify only the communication type and the document type. The author can optionally mark a document as private to be seen only by people who the author lists in the To: field. The To: field is also used to designate people who need to pay particular attention to a document, even if that document can be seen by the rest of the team. TeamRoom constructs personal workspaces for each member of the team, based on documents for which the person is listed in the To: or cc: field or documents that the member has authored. In this way, TeamRoom supports personalized as well as shared views.

1.5.3.2   Relation to Deployment

When it comes time to deploy the groupware application, organizational preparedness, incentive and motivation, and critical mass are some of the factors which influence the ultimate adoption of the application.

TeamRoom addresses issues of organizational preparedness by accompanying the introduction of the technology with a facilitated meeting during which the members of the team go through the exercise of deciding on their mission, communication and work styles as a team. In this way, all members of the team can participate in setting the goals. The mission and the technology can be seen as being in service of the core work of the team.

One of the ways in which TeamRoom addresses the problem of critical mass — that is making sure that there is enough activity to promote more activity — is by having a facilitator as one of the designated roles in the TeamRoom. This person, who is also a team member, monitors traffic in the TeamRoom and encourages participation if the discussion and postings are becoming reduced.

1.5.4   Lessons Learned

TeamRoom has been deployed in a wide range of companies and settings. Based on informal feedback there are several themes that emerge that are critical success factors: 1) strong leadership; 2) a distributed team who need TeamRoom to overcome barriers of time and place and for whom face-to-face meetings are often scheduled, rather than ad hoc; 3) a well defined team. Below are examples where these factors were *absent*.

Strong leadership. Strong leadership is needed, especially early on, to get people to submit postings. For some teams, collaboration and sharing was a new way of working and if the team leader didn't demonstrate and lead by example, the team generally did not take to it. This was lacking at one company where it seems the team leader set the tone/behavior for the group. In a few cases, the workers still took to the tool, seeing its value and needing the communication that it provided.

Geographically distributed team. TeamRoom is a good alternative to voice or videoconferences for teams whose members are far apart. Especially for complex projects, TeamRoom becomes an information repository to facilitate analysis. However, there can sometimes be delays in replicating TeamRoom to the different sites for these distributed teams. On the other hand, when team members were co-located, TeamRoom was just another thing to have to worry about and it wasn't used.

Well defined team. A well defined team has a common mission and a shared context, language and objectives. Team membership is limited and definable. Well defined teams are not about longevity; a team could be just forming or be together for a long time. One team that used TeamRoom that wasn't really a team, but just a department, failed in their use because there was no real team mission, team norms, or team deliverables. In this case, TeamRoom served as a place to communicate meeting agendas and some marketing announcements. TeamRoom is a mirror on the team. If the team is chaotic, then so it will appear in TeamRoom and people's experience with the tool will be frustrating. A well-organized team takes a lot of work.

1.6   SUMMARY

This chapter takes the position that whereas single-user applications are about *tasks*, groupware applications are about *work*. Tasks are generally explicit, observable, concrete. Work is generally tacit, invisible and amorphous. Work is about people, habits and culture.

Generating a product concept and design specifications for a groupware application demands a methodology that can capture these invisible work practices. The methods, derived from social and management sciences, that are most commonly used in groupware or CSCW

(Computer Supported Cooperative Work) are often descriptive rather than prescriptive, leaving it up to the design team to fashion requirements, functions and architecture themselves. A multidisciplinary team is essential for the design and development of groupware applications.

Getting inside the notion of group "work", a few themes emerge: communication is generally ad hoc, informal and unplanned. There is a need to be aware of others for communication and in coordinating work. Issues of sharing hinge on subtle notions of anonymity, which play out in different ways.

Finally, deploying a groupware application is perhaps the most difficult step in process. First, the application itself will need some level of customization to fit in each customer's work context. Second, groupware applications are rarely ready to go "out of the box" but need to be accompanied by some measure of training in organizational behavior to ensure a fit between the tool and organizational processes. Factors such as motivation, incentives and critical mass are potential show-stoppers when it comes to rolling out the application to the entire group.

The notion of work and translating it into an application is put into perspective by describing a Lotus Notes application that was designed to provide a "place" on line to support discussion and coordination of work amongst members of a distributed team.

Groupware and CSCW are still in their infancy compared with more established practices in the development of single-user applications. Yet, technological developments such as the World Wide Web seem to lead to more need for groupware applications where people spread across the globe, across the country, or just across the street can use technology to coordinate their work and communication with each other.

ACKNOWLEDGEMENTS

There are many people who have contributed to this chapter through discussions, especially those enlightening me on various methodological issues. For their time and patience in talking with me about methodology, I extend my appreciation to: Barbara Katzenberg, Charlotte Linde, Bonnie Nardi, Roy Pea, and Lee Sproull. My colleagues at Lotus Institute, especially Barbara Kivowitz, Linda Carotenuto, and Nicol Rupolo helped me understand many of the nuances and tacit features of TeamRoom. I extend a special thanks to my colleague Debra Cash with whom I have had many engaging and heated conversations and who took the time to read and comment on several drafts of this chapter. Thanks are due to Paul Cole, Sal Mazzotta and especially an anonymous reviewer who read and commented on an earlier version.

REFERENCES

[All93]   Allen, C., The reciprocal evolution of technology, work practice and basic research. In D. Schuler and A. Namioka (Eds.) *Participatory Design: Perspectives on System Design.* Lawrence Erlbaum Associates, Hillsdale, NJ, 1993.

[Arg82]   Argyris, C., *Reasoning, Learning and Action: Individual and Organizational.* Jossey-Bass, San Francisco, 1982.

[Arg78]   Argyris, C. and Schon, D., *Organizational Learning.* Addison-Wesley, Boston, 1978.

[Ban96]   Bannon, L. Ethnography and design. In D. Shapiro, M. Tauber, and R. Traunmuller (Eds.), *The Design of Computer Supported Cooperative Work and Groupware Systems*, pages 13–16. Elsevier Science, Amsterdam, 1996.

[Bar95]   Barreau, D. and Nardi, B., Finding and reminding: File organization from the desktop. *SIGCHI Bulletin*, July 1995.

[Bel96]   Bellotti, V. and Bly, S., Walking away from the desktop computer. Distributed collaboration and mobility in a product design team. In *Proceedings of the Conference on Computer Supported Work, CSCW '96 (Boston, MA)*, pages 209–219. ACM Press, New York, 1996.

[Ben92]   Bentley, R., Hughes, J.A., Randall, D., Rodden, T., Sawyer, P., Shapiro, D. and Sommerville, I., Ethnographically-informed systems designs for air traffic control. In *Proceedings of the Conference on Computer Supported Work, CSCW '92 (Toronto, Canada)*, pages 123–129. ACM Press, New York, 1992.

[Blo93a] Blomberg, J., Giacomi, J., Mosher, A and Swenton-Wall, P., Ethnographic field methods and their relation to design. In D. Schuler and A. Namioka (Eds.), *Participatory Design: Perspectives on System Design*, pages 123–154. Lawrence Erlbaum Associates, Hillsdale, NJ, 1993.

[Blo93b] Blomberg, J., McLaughlin, D. and Suchman, L., Work-oriented design at Xerox. *Communications of the ACM*, 36(4):91, June 1993.

[Bly88]   Bly, S., A use of drawing surfaces in different collaborative settings. In *Proceedings of the Conference on Computer Supported Work, CSCW '88*, pages 250–256. ACM Press, New York, 1988.

[Bly93]   Bly, S., Harrison, S., and Irwin, S., Media spaces: Bringing people together in a video, audio and computing environment. *Communications of the ACM*, 36(1):28–45, January 1993.

[Bly97a] Bly, S., Field work: Is it product work? *interactions*, pages 25–30, January+February 1997.

[Bly97b] Blythin, S., Rouncefield, M, and Hughes, J.A., Ethnography in the commercial world. *interactions*, pages 38–47, May+June 1997.

[Bow95]   Bowers, J., Button, G., and Sharrock, W., Workflow from within and without: Technology and cooperative work on the print industry shopfloor. In H. Marmolin, Y. Sundblad, K. Schmidt (Eds.), *Proceedings of the Fourth European Conference on Computer-Supported Cooperative Work, ECSCW '95 (Stockholm, Sweden)*, pages 51–66. Kluwer Academic, Dordrecht, 1995.

[Bro91]   Brown, J.S., Research that reinvents the corporation. *Harvard Business Review*, page 330, January-February 1991.

[Bro97]   Brown, E.G., Dolberg, S. Boehm, E.W. and Massey, C., Beyond groupware. *Forrester Report: Software Strategies*, 8(4), July 1997.

[Cam95]   Cameron, B., DePalma, D.A., O'Herron, R. and Smith, N., Where does groupware fit? *The Forrester Report: Software Strategies*, 6(3), June 1995.

[Car95]   Carroll, J.M., Introduction: The scenario perspective on system development. In J.M. Carroll (Ed.), *Scenario-Based Design: Envisioning Work and Technology in System Development*. John Wiley and Sons, New York, 1995.

[Col96]   Cole, P. and Johnson, E.C., Lotus development: TeamRoom - A collaborative workspace for cross-functional teams. In P. Lloyd and R. Whitehead (Eds.), *Transforming Organizations Through Groupware: Lotus Notes in Action.*. Springer-Verlag, New York, 1996.

[Cle93]   Clement, A and Van den Besselaar, P., A retrospective look at PD projects. *Communications of the ACM*, 36(6):29–37, June 1993.

[deV91]   de Vet, J. and Allen, C., *Picasso System Design Rationale*. IRL Technical Report, November 1991.

[Dou92]   Dourish, P and Bly, S., Portholes: Supporting awareness in a distributed work group. In *Proceedings of Human Factors in Computing Systems, CHI '92 (Monterey, CA)*, pages 541–547. ACM Press, New York, 1992.

[Ehr94]   Ehrlich, K and Cash, D., Turning information into knowledge: Information finding as a collaborative activity. In *Proceedings of the Conference on Digital Libraries (College Station, TX)*, pages 119–125, 1994.

[Ehr97]   Ehrlich, K and Cash, D., *Communication and Coordination in Workers Compensation Cases: Implications for Extended Enterprises*. Internal Report, 1997.

[Ehr98]   Ehrlich, K. and Cash, D., The invisible world of intermediaries: A cautionary tale. *Computer Supported Cooperative Work: An International Journal.*, In Press.

[Ell99]   Ellis, C.A., Workflow technology. In Beaudouin-Lafon, M. (Ed.), *Computer Supported Cooperative Work*, Trends in Software Series 7:29–54. John Wiley & Sons, Chichester, 1999.

[Fin90]   Finholt, T., Sproull, L., and Kiesler, S., Communication and performance in ad hoc task groups. In J. Galegher, R.E. Kraut, C. Egido (Eds.), *Intellectual Teamwork: Social and Technological Foundations of Cooperative Work*, pages 291–326. Lawrence Erlbaum, Hillsdale, NJ, 1990.

[Fis90]   Fish, R., Kraut, R.E., and Chalfonte, B., The videowindow system in informal communication. In *Proceedings of the Conference on Computer Supported Work, CSCW '90 (Los Angeles, CA)*, pages 1–12. ACM Press, New York, 1990.

[Fis93]   Fish, R., Kraut, R.E., Root, R., and Rice, R., Video as a technology for for informal communication. *Communications of the ACM*, 36(1):48-61, January 1993.

[Fra91]   Francik, E., Rudman, S.E., Cooper, D., Levine, S., Putting innovation to work: Adoption strategies for multimedia communication systems. *Communications of the ACM*, 34(12):53-63, December 1991.

[Gog96]   Joseph Goguen, J and Charlotte Linde, C., Techniques for requirements elicitation. In R. Thayer and M. Dorman (Eds.), *Software Requirements Engineering, Second Edition*. IEEE Computer Society, 1996.

[Gol92]   Goldberg, D., Oki, B., Nichols, D., Terry, D.B., Using collaborative filtering to weave an information tapestry. *Communications of the ACM*, 35(12):61-70, December 1992.

[Gre91]   Greenbaum, J and Kyng, M. (Eds.), *Design at Work: Cooperative Design of Computer Systems*. Lawrence Erlbaum, Hillsdale, NJ, 1991.

[Gru90]   Grudin, J., Groupware and cooperative work: Problems and prospects. In B. Laurel (Ed.), *The Art of Human Computer Interface Design*. Addison-Wesley, Reading, MA, 1990.

[Gru95]   Grudin, J., and Palen, L., Why groupware succeeds: Discretion or mandate? In *Proceedings of the Fourth European Conference on Computer-Supported Cooperative Work, ECSCW '95 (Stockholm, Sweden)*, pages 263–278. Kluwer Academic, Dordrecht, 1995.

[Hea91]   Heath, C. and Luff, P., Collaborative activity and technological design: Task coordination in London Underground control rooms. In *Proceedings of the Second European Conference on Computer Supported Cooperative Work, ECSCW '91*. Kluwer Academic Publishers, Amsterdam, 1991.

[Hil95]   Hill, W. Stead, L., Rosenstein, M., and Furnas, G., Recommending and evaluating choices in a virtual community of use. In *Proceedings of Human Factors in Computing Systems, CHI '95, (Denver, CO)*, pages 194–201. ACM Press, New York, 1995.

[Hof94]   Hofman, J.D. and Rockart, J.F., Application templates: Faster, better and cheaper systems. *Sloan Management Review/Fall*, pages 49–60, 1994.

[Hol93]   Holtzblatt, K. and Beyer, H., Making customer-centered design work for teams. *Communications of the ACM*, 36(10):93–103, October 1993.

[Hug92]   Hughes, J.A., Randall, D., and Shapiro, D., Faltering from ethnography to design. In *Proceedings of the Conference on Computer Supported Cooperative Work, CSCW'92, (Toronto, Canada)*, pages 115–122. ACM Press, New York, 1992.

[Ish99]   Ishii, H., Integration of shared workspace and interpersonal space for remote collaboration. In Beaudouin-Lafon, M. (Ed.), *Computer Supported Cooperative Work*, Trends in Software Series 7:83–102. John Wiley & Sons, Chichester, 1999.

[Joh88]   Johansen, R., *Groupware: Computer Support for Business Teams*. The Free Press, New York, 1988.

[Jor95]   Jordan, B. and Henderson, A., Interaction analysis: Foundations and practice. *J. Learn. Sci.*, 4(1):39-102, 1995.

[Jor96]   Jordan, B., Ethnographic workplace studies and CSCW. In D. Shapiro, M. Tauber, and R. Traunmuller (Eds.), *The Design of Computer Supported Cooperative Work and Groupware Systems*, pages 17–42. Amsterdam: Elsevier Science, Amsterdam, 1996.

[Kat93a] Katzenbach, J. R. and Smith, D. K., *The Wisdom of Teams: Creating the High-Performance Organization*. Harvard Business School Press, Boston, MA, 1993.

[Kat93b] Katzenberg, B. and Piela, P., Work language analysis and the naming problem. *Communications of the ACM*, 36(4):86–92, April 1993.

[Kra90]   Kraut, R.E., Fish, R.S., Rot, R.W., and Chalfonte, B.L., Informal communication in organizations: Form, function and technology. Reprinted in R.M. Baecker (Ed.), *Readings in Groupware and Computer-Supported Cooperative Work*, pages 287–314. Morgan Kaufmann, 1990.

[Kra94]   Kraut, R.E., Cool, C., Rice, R.E., and Fish, R.S., Life and death of new technology: Task, utility and social influences on the use of a communication medium. In R. Furuta and C. Neuwirth (Eds.), *Proceedings of Conference on Computer Supported Cooperative Work, CSCW '94 (Chapel Hill, North Carolina)*, pages 13–21. ACM Press, New York, 1994.

[Kuk92]   Kukla, C., Clemens, E.A., Morse, R.S. and Cash, D., Designing effective systems: A tool approach. In Paul Adler and Terry Winograd, (Eds.), *Usability: Turning Technologies into Tools*, pages 41–65. Oxford University Press, New York, 1992.

[Lin91]   Linde, C., What's next?: The social and technological management of meetings. *Pragmatics* 1(3), 1991.

[Mac99]   Mackay, W.E., Media spaces: Environments for informal multimedia interaction In Beaudouin-Lafon, M. (Ed.), *Computer Supported Cooperative Work*, Trends in Software Series 7:55–82. John Wiley & Sons, Chichester, 1999.

[Mal95]   Maltz, D. and Ehrlich, K., Pointing the Way: Active Collaborative Filtering. In *Proceedings of Human Factors in Computing Systems, CHI'95 (Denver, CO)*, pages 202–209. ACM Press, New York, 1995.

[Man89]   Mantei, M., Observations of executives using a computerized supported meeting environment. Reprinted in R.M. Baecker (Ed.), *Readings in Groupware and Computer-Supported Cooperative Work*, pages 695–708. Morgan Kaufmann, 1989.

[Man91]   Mantei, M.M., Baecker, R.M., Sellen, A.J., Buxton, W.A.S. Milligan, T., and Wellman, B., Experiences in the use of a media space. In *Proceedings of Human Factors in Computing Systems, CHI '91 (New Orleans, LA)*, pages 203–208. ACM Press, New York, 1991.

[Mar95]   Mark, G., Haake, J.M., Streitz, N.A., The use of hypermedia in group problem solving: An evaluation of the DOLPHIN electronic meeting room environment. In *Proceedings of the Fourth European Conference on Computer-Supported Cooperative Work, ECSCW '95 (Stockholm, Sweden)*, pages 197–213. Kluwer Academic, Dordrecht, 1995.

[Mar90]   Markus, M.L. and Connolly, T., Why CSCW applications fail: Problems in the adoption of interdependent work tools. In *Proceedings of Conference on Computer Supported Cooperative Work, CSCW '90*, pages 371–380. ACM Press, New York, 1990.

[McG84]   McGrath, J.E., *Groups: Interaction and Performance*. Prentice-Hall, 1984.

[Mic97]   Michalski, J., Conversation on the Net. *Release 1.0 newsletter*, January 1997.

[Min91]   Minneman, S.L. and Bly, S., Managing à trois: A study of multi-user drawing tool in distributed design work. In *Proceedings of Human Factors in Computing Systems, CHI '91 (New Orleans, LA)*, pages 217–224. ACM Press, New York, 1991.

[Mul93]   Muller, M.J. and Kuhn, S. (Eds), Special Issue on Participatory Design. *Communications of the ACM*, 36(6), June 1993.

[Mul95]   Muller, M.J., Carr, R., Ashworth, C., Diekmann, B., Wharton, C., Eickstaedt, C., and Clonts, J., Telephone operators as knowledge workers: Consultants who meet customer needs. In *Proceedings of Human Factors in Computing Systems, CHI '95 (Denver, CO)*, pages 130–137. ACM Press, New York, 1995.

[Nar93]   Nardi, B., *A Small Matter of Programming: Perspectives on End User Computing*. MIT Press, Cambridge, MA, 1993.

[Nar96]   Nardi, B and O'Day, V., Intelligent agents: What we learned at the library. *Libri*, 46(3):59–88, September 1996.

[Nar98a] Nardi, B., A web on the wind: The structure of invisible work. *Special issue of CSCW*, 1998.

[Nar98b] Nardi, B., Miller, J.R. and Wright, D.J., Collaborative, programmable intelligent agents. *Communications of the ACM*, In press.

[Nun91]   Nunamaker, J.F., Dennis, A.R., Valacich, J.S., Vogel, D.R., and George, J.F., Electronic Meeting Systems to Support Group Work. *Communications of the ACM*, 34(7):40–61, July 1991.

[OHa94]   O'Hara-Devereaux, M and Johansen, R., *Global Work: Bridging Distance, Culture and Time*. Jossey-Bass, San Francisco, 1994.

[Orl92]   Orlikowski, W.J., Learning from Notes: Organizational issues in groupware implementation. In J. Turner and R. Kraut (Eds.), *Proceedings of the Conference on Computer Supported Cooperative Work, CSCW'92, (Toronto, Canada)*, pages 362–369. ACM Press, New York, 1992.

[Orl97]   Orlikowski, W.J. and Hofman, J.D., An improvisational model of change management: The case of groupware technologies. *Sloan Management Review/Winter*, 38(2), 1997.

[Plo95]   Plowman, L. Rogers, Y, and Ramage, M., What are workplace studies for? In H. Marmolin, Y. Sundblad, K. Schmidt (Eds.), *Proceedings of the Fourth European Conference on Computer-Supported Cooperative Work, ECSCW '95 (Stockholm, Sweden)*, pages 309–324. Kluwer Academic, Dordrecht, 1995.

[Pra99]   Prakash, A., Group editors. In Beaudouin-Lafon, M. (Ed.), *Computer Supported Cooperative Work*, Trends in Software Series 7:103–133. John Wiley & Sons, Chichester, 1999.

[Pyc96]   Pycock, J. and Bowers, J., Getting others to get it right: An ethnography of design work in the fashion industry. In *Proceedings of Conference on Computer Supported Cooperative Work, CSCW '96 (Boston, MA)*, pages 219–228. ACM Press, New York, 1996.

[Res94]   Resnick, P., Iacovou, N., Suchak, M. Bergstrom, P., and Riedl, J., GroupLens: An open architecture for collaborative filtering of Netnews. In *Proceedings of Conference on Computer Supported Cooperative Work, CSCW '94 (Chapel Hill, North Carolina)*, pages 175–186. ACM Press, New York, 1994.

[Rog97]   Rogers, Y. and Bellotti, V., Grounding blue-sky research: How can ethnography help? *interactions*, pages 58–63, May+June 1997.

[Sac95]   Sachs, P., Transforming work: Collaboration, learning and design. *Communications of the ACM*, 38(9):36–44, September 1995.

[Sch93]   Schuler, D. and Namioka, A., *Participatory Design: Principles and Practices*. Lawrence Erlbaum, Hillsdale, NJ, 1993.

[Sha95]   Shardanand, U and Maes, P., Social information filtering: Algorithms for automating "Word of Mouth". In *Proceedings of Human Factors in Computing Systems, CHI'95 (Denver, CO)*, pages 210–217. ACM Press, New York, 1995.

[Sny98]   Snyder, W.M., Communities of practice: Combining organizational learing and strategy insights to create a bridge to the 21st century. *Organization Development and Change*, 1998.

[Spr93]   Sproull, L. and Kiesler, S., *Connections: New Ways of Working in the Networked Organization*. MIT Press, Cambridge, MA, 1993.

[Sta94]   Star, S.L. and Ruhleder, K., Steps towards an ecology of infrastructure: Complex problems in design and access for large-scale collaborative sytems. In *Proceedings of Conference on Computer Supported Cooperative Work, CSCW '94 (Chapel Hill, North Carolina)*, pages 253–264. ACM Press, New York, 1994.

[Suc83]   Suchman, L., Office procedures as practical action: Models of work and system design. *ACM Transactions on Office Information Systems*, 1(4):320-328, 1983.

[Suc95]   Suchman, L., Making work visible. *Communications of the ACM*, 38(9):56–64, September 1995.

[Tan91]   Tang, J.C., Findings from observational studies of collaborative work. *International Journal of Man-Machine Studies*, 34(2):143–160, February 1991.

[Tan94a]   Tang, J.C., Isaacs, E.A. and Rua, M., Supporting Distributed Groups with a Montage of Lightweight Interactions. In R. Furuta and C. Neuwirth (Eds.) *Proceedings of Conference on Computer Supported Cooperative Work (Chapel Hill, North Carolina)*, pages 23–34. ACM Press, New York, 1994.

[Tan94b]   Tang, J.C. and Rua, M., Montage: Providing teleproximity for distributed groups. In *Proceedings of Human Factors in Computing Systems, CHI '94 (Boston, MA)*, pages 37–43. ACM Press, New York, 1994.

[Tol96]   Tollmar, K. Sandor, O. and Schomer, A., Supporting social awareness@work: Design and experience. In *Proceedings of Conference on Computer Supported Cooperative Work, CSCW '96 (Boston, MA)*, pages 298–307. ACM Press, New York, 1996.

[Tur95]   Turkle, S., *Life on the Screen: Identity in the Age of the Internet*. Simon and Schuster, New York, 1995.

[Whi94]   Whittaker, S., Frohlich, D., and Daly-Jones, O., Informal workplace communication: What is it like and how might we support it? In *Proceedings of Human Factors in Computing Systems, CHI '94 (Boston, MA)*, pages 131–137. ACM Press, New York, 1994.

[Zub88]   Zuboff, S., *In the Age of the Smart Machine*. Basic Books, New York, 1988.

2

Workflow Technology

CLARENCE A. ELLIS
University of Colorado

ABSTRACT

This chapter is concerned with workflow, its systems, its models, its problems and promises. Workflow management systems assist in the specification, modeling, and enactment of structured work processes within organizations. These systems are a special type of collaboration technology which we describe as "organizationally aware groupware". Since the turn of the decade, over 200 new workflow products have been introduced into the world market. This chapter motivates and defines the concepts of workflow. Examples are presented from existing products and prototypes. Finally, we explore some of the current inhibitors and research issues in this fast growing domain.

2.1 OVERVIEW

Today, organizations find that there is global competitiveness in many areas, and a continual need to improve productivity. Problems plaguing organizations include increased administrative overhead, external pressures for increased efficiency, internal pressure for increased effectiveness, and desire by workers for more reward and less stress. Many organizations look to technology such as workflow management systems for help.

Contemporary organizations typically employ a vast array of computing technology to support their information processing needs. There are many successful computing tools designed as personal information aids (word processors, spreadsheets, etc.) but fewer tools designed for collaborating groups of people. One of the most popular recent types of group/organizational tool is workflow. Workflow management systems are designed to assist groups of people in carrying out work processes, and contain organizational knowledge of where work flows in the default case. This is in contrast to other group tools such as electronic mail or video-conferencing systems which contain no knowledge of work processes, and therefore are not organizationally aware. Workflow is defined as "systems that help organizations to specify,

---

Computer Supported Cooperative Work, Edited by Beaudouin-Lafon
© 1999 John Wiley & Sons Ltd

execute, monitor, and coordinate the flow of work cases within a distributed office environment" [Bul92]. The system contains two basic components: the first component is the workflow modeling component, which enables administrators and analysts to define processes (or procedures) and activities, analyze and simulate them, and assign them to people. This component is sometimes called the "specification module" or the "build time system". It also may be used to view work process statistics, and to make changes to processes.

The second component is the workflow execution (or enactment) component, sometimes called the "run-time system". It consists of the execution interface seen by end-users and the "workflow engine", an execution environment which assists in coordinating and performing the processes and activities. It enables the units of work to flow from one user's workstation to another as the steps of a procedure are completed. Some of these steps may be executed in parallel; some executed automatically by the computer system. The execution interface is utilized for all manual steps, and typically presents forms on the electronic desktop of appropriate workers (end-users.) The user fills in electronic forms with the assistance of the computer system. Various databases, personal productivity tools, and servers may be accessed in a programmed or ad-hoc fashion during the processing of a work step. Typically, a workflow system is implemented as a server machine which has and interprets a representation of the steps of the procedures and their precedence; along with client workstations, one per end-user, which assists the user in performing process steps. This is typically combined with a network and messaging system (or communication mechanism) to allow the server to control or interact with end-user workstations; also included is a database that stores the process representation, attributes of end-users, and other pertinent workflow information. Many of the workflow products are combined with imaging and/or document management systems [Bul92].

2.2   WORKFLOW CONCEPTS AND ARCHITECTURE

This section provides some basic workflow definitions in the context of an example office procedure. This is followed by an architectural specification which is typical of current workflow systems, and is in keeping with our definitions. The terminology generally follows the recommendations of the Workflow Management Coalition which is a non-profit, international organization of workflow vendors, users, and analysts. The coalition, founded in August 1993, has a mission to promote the use of workflow through the establishment of standards for terminology, interoperability, and connectivity between workflow products [WMC].

2.2.1   Definition Set

2.2.1.1   Definition (Workflow Management System)

A *workflow management system* is a system that defines, manages, and executes workflow processes through the execution of software whose order of execution is driven by a computer representation of the workflow process logic [WMC].

Many types of office work can be described as connected sets of structured recurring tasks (called *workflow processes* or *procedures*) whose basic work steps (called *activities*) must be performed by various people (called *actors*) in a certain sequence. The power of workflow systems lies in their computerized representation of these processes, and activities. This section describes the basic terminology and capability of workflow; much more power and utility is possible once this procedural representation is available within the computer system.

A particular workflow application is created by specifying to the workflow system a set of processes and activities which are performed within an organization or workgroup. This is the first step toward computerized workflow; the goal is to enhance the efficiency and effectiveness of the office work, while making the workplace a friendlier, more humane place to work.

2.2.1.2   Definition (Process)

A *workflow process* (or procedure) is a predefined set of work steps, and partial ordering of these steps. A work step consists of a header (identification, precedence, etc.) and body (the actual work to be done).

Examples include the "order processing procedure" within an engineering company, and the "claims administration process" within an insurance company. Both of these are relatively standardized and structured, and each can be described by a sequence of steps. Workflow also attempts to assist in less structured work tasks. Different steps of a process may be executed by different people or different groups of people. In some cases several steps of a process may be executed at the same time or in any order. In general, we therefore define a process to be a partially ordered set of steps rather than a totally ordered set. We also define workflow processes in such a way that loops are allowed. Processes typically have attributes, such as name and responsible person, associated with them.

2.2.1.3   Definition (Activity)

An *activity* is the body of a work step of a process. An activity is either a compound activity, containing another process, or an elementary activity.

An *elementary activity* is a basic unit of work which must be a sequential set of primitive actions executed by a single participant. Alternatively, an elementary activity may be a non-procedural entity (goal node) whose internals we do not model within our structure. An activity is a reusable unit of work, so one activity may be the body of several work steps. For example, if "order entry" and "credit check" are (sub-)processes, then the activity "send out letter" may be an activity in both of these processes. In this case, these are two distinct steps, but only one activity. An activity instance associated with the body of a particular work step is called a work step activity.

Activities typically have attributes such as description and mode associated with them. An activity has one of three modes. Some work step activities may be automatically executed (automatic mode), some completely manual (manual mode), and some may require the interaction of people and computers (mixed mode). For example, if the process is "order equipment" then there may be work steps of:

1. order entry
2. credit check
3. billing
4. shipping.

Order entry in some companies is totally automatic; but credit check is frequently done completely by people (manual mode.) This level of detail of description is typically adequate for an engineering manager, but is not enough detail for a credit clerk. The credit clerk would like to look inside of the work step called credit check, and see a process that requires steps of logging each new credit request, gathering data, evaluating a customer, and filling out of a report form. Thus, the body of this step is itself a process with work steps of:

2.1. log request
2.2. gather data
2.3. evaluate
2.4. fill out report form.

Furthermore, the step 2.4 of filling out the report form may itself consist of work steps to fill out the various sections of the form. This example shows that it can be useful to multiply nest processes within processes. Thus, a work step body has been defined to possibly contain a process. Work steps typically have attributes, such as unique identifier and executor, associated with them.

By definition, a workflow system contains a computerized representation of the structure of processes and activities. This also implies that there is a means for someone (perhaps a system administrator) to specify and input descriptions of processes, activities, and orderings into the computer. These specifications are called scripts. An ongoing research issue is to develop better, more end-user compatible scripting languages.

2.2.1.4   Definition (Script)

A *script* is a specification of a process, an activity, or an automatic part of a manual activity. The composition or building of this script from available building blocks is called scripting.

Once processes and activities have been defined, the workflow system can assist in the execution of these processes. We separate the concept of the static specification of a process (the template) from its execution.

2.2.1.5   Definition (Work Case)

A *work case* (or *process instance*) is the locus of control for a particular execution of a process. In some contexts, the work case is called a job; if a process is considered a Petri net, then a work case is a token flowing through the net. If the process is an object class, then a work case is an instance. In our example, if two customers submit two orders for equipment, then these would represent two different work cases. Each work case is a different execution of the process. If both work cases are currently being processed by the order entry department, then the state of each work case is the order entry state. Work cases typically have parameters such as state, initiator, and history associated with them.

Because of the ever changing and sometimes ad-hoc nature of the workplace, it is important for workflow systems to be flexible, and have capabilities to handle exceptions. Many processes which appear routine and structured are, in reality, highly variable, requiring problem solving and creative exception handling. Another workflow concept that partially helps address these issues is the indirect association of people (called actors) with activities via the concept of roles. Numerous other advantages accrue by the use of roles.

2.2.1.6   Definition (Role)

A *role* is a named designator for a workflow participant, or a grouping of participants which conveniently acts as the basis for access control and execution control. The execution of activities is associated with roles rather than end-users. Thus, instead of naming a person as the executor of an activity, we can specify that it is to be executed by one or more roles. For example, instead of specifying that Michael executes the order entry activity, we can specify that

1. the order entry activity is executed by the order administrator, and
2. Michael is the order administrator.

There may be a very large number of activities in which Michael is involved. When Michael goes on vacation, it is not necessary to find and change all processes and activities involving Michael. We simply substitute Michael's replacement in the role of order administrator by changing step 2 to

2. Robert is the order administrator.

A role may be associated with a group of actors rather than a single actor. Also, one actor may play many roles within an organization. If there are many order administrators within our example, then these can be defined as a group, and it is easy to send information to all order administrators. In this case, an option may be available to "send to all" or alternatively, "send to any" administrator, and the system might use some scheduling algorithm to select one. Other flexible scheduling algorithms are possible, including the notification of all members of the group that a job is available, and allowing the first responder to handle the job. In this chapter, we use the term *participant* to refer to a person, a group, or an automated agent as further defined below. For example, the credit check activity in our example is really executed by the credit department, not by any single person. And the printing operation is really executed by one of many print servers that might be participants with the role of "printer".

2.2.1.7   Definition (Participant)

A *workflow participant* is a person, program, group, or entity that can fulfill roles to execute, to be responsible for, or to be associated in some way with activities and processes. A human participant is called an *actor*.

Access attributes or capabilities may be associated with participants and with roles. Other attributes, parameters and structures can be associated as needed. For example, the role of manager is perhaps only played by Michael within the order entry department. Thus a parameter of the role may be the group within which this role applies.

In summary, this section has briefly presented a definition of workflow together with explanations of the concepts of process, step, activity, work case, script, role, actor, and participant. These are basic concepts upon which many workflow systems are built. Other concepts (e.g. data repository) will be introduced in this chapter as needed.

2.2.2   Conceptual Architecture

This subsection presents the conceptual architecture of a generic workflow system using the entity-relationship model [Che76]. The architecture builds upon the general concepts intro-

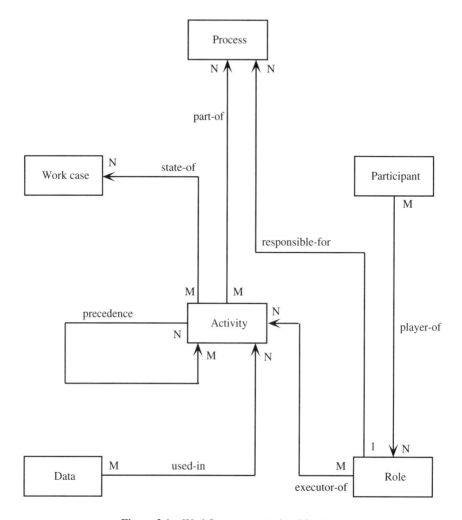

Figure 2.1   Workflow conceptual architecture

duced in the previous subsection. It lays out some workflow system basic conceptual entities and their relationships.

The entity-relationship (abbreviated E-R) model is a high-level semantic model using nodes and arcs; this model has proven useful as an understandable specification model, has been implemented within E-R databases, directly parallels some object-oriented concepts, and has a well-known direct mapping into a relational database.

In the E-R model, objects of similar structure are collected into entity sets. The associations among entity sets are represented by named E-R relationships which are either one-to-one, many-to-one, or many-to-many mapping between the sets. The data structures, employing the E R model, are usually shown pictorially using the E-R diagram. An E-R diagram depicting the conceptual architecture of a workflow system is shown in Figure 2.1. A labeled rectangle denotes an entity set; a labeled arc connecting rectangles denotes a relationship between the corresponding entity sets.

In Figure 2.1, the box labeled *process* denotes an entity set of processes that may actually be a table of process names and their attributes. Likewise, *activity* may be a table of activity names and their attributes. There is an arc connecting these two boxes because there is a relationship called *part-of* between these two entity sets. Some elements in the activity set are steps of (or parts of) some processes. This arc is labeled with the relationship name, and a denotation of M and N indicates that this is a many-to-many relationship. Therefore, a process can contain many activities, and an activity can be part of more than one process. The arc joining the activity box to itself labeled *precedence* tells which activities may precede which others.

Since the diagram specifies that this is a many-to-many relationship the process scripting facility supports the specification of conjunctive and disjunctive precedence relations. For any activity labeled conjunctive, any specification of immediate successors denotes activities which all directly follow the completion of the given activity; specification of immediate predecessors denotes activities which must all complete before the given activity can begin. Some activities will be labeled disjunctive. OR-out from some activity means that out of the many immediate successor activities, we select only one to actually execute. Similarly, OR-in means that only one of the activities which immediately precede the given activity must complete before it can begin. Thus, any partial ordering of activities using sequencing and these AND/OR constructs, can be specified and supported using workflow.

Other entities shown in Figure 2.1 are jobs and data. A job, or work case, which can be considered to be flowing through a process, has a state at any instant which is denoted by the set of current activities being executed by the job, and the job's history. The relationship "state-of" captures this state. This relationship gets updated by the system each time that a job moves from one activity to another. This is a many-to-many relationship, so one job may be executing within several activities in parallel, and one activity may be simultaneously serving several jobs. Similar considerations hold for the data entity which refers to the application data which are accessed by the various activities. People are connected into the system directly if they are listed in the "participant" entity set. Thus, people are players of roles, and roles are designated as the executors of activities.

In summary, the conceptual architecture described in this subsection builds upon the general concepts introduced in the previous subsection. It lays out some workflow system basic conceptual entities and their relationships. Other entities (e.g. goals) and relationships (e.g. manager-of) can usefully be built upon, or added to, this base.

2.2.3   Concrete Architecture

The distributed technology underlying a workflow system typically is a server–client architecture with a large powerful computer designated as the server, and smaller client machines on participant work desks at various locations throughout the organization. These are all interconnected, along with other file systems, databases, and servers, via a local area/wide area networking configuration. See Figure 2.2 for a typical structure. We note that, depending upon a vendor's history, different workflow systems are built upon different implementation bases such as electronic mail base, relational database, or document processing system.

At the server, there is typically a database to store the process specification and related organizational information, and there is a workflow engine which uses this information to coordinate the execution of activities at various client workstations. The server thus knows about roles and participants, and uses this information to do scheduling and dispatching. The server ships appropriate information at the appropriate time to the appropriate user machine

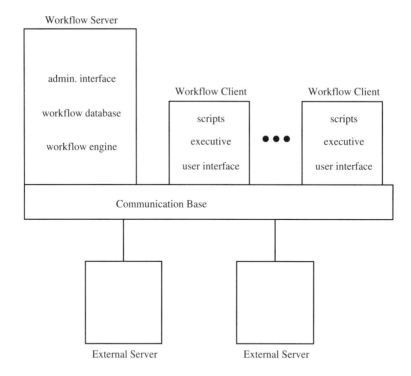

Figure 2.2   Workflow concrete architecture

for activity execution. It also implements security and concurrency control, monitors these executions, logs statistics and backup/recovery information, and as necessary sends reminders and time-out information. Occasionally, the server may itself execute an automated activity. It is also typical for the server to supply an administrative user interface to allow administrators and analysts to define processes and activities, to gather work performance statistics, to do analysis and simulation, and to make changes and adjustments to processes.

The client machines are the locus of work activity at enactment time. A client machine typically serves one end-user (secretary, clerk, ...) who we call a participant. Frequently this is an IBM PC class of machine running a Windows operating system, and using a package such as Visual Basic to present a familiar electronic desktop working environment for the end-user. This environment may include local scripts so that some activities can be executed automatically or interactively, allowing the local computer to do some of the information processing work for the user. It should also allow the user to invoke personal productivity tools such as editors and spreadsheets on a programmed or ad-hoc basis. Finally Internet interconnectivity and access to non-local resources such as a customer database or a mainframe routine, are useful functions that should be available to the user.

2.3   HISTORICAL PERSPECTIVE AND RELATED WORK

The term workflow was in use at the turn of the century when the industrial revolution was taking place. There was much efficiency gain, and much profit associated with areas such as factory automation [Bae93]. It was also assumed in the mid-1900s that the same techniques (e.g. time and motion studies to optimize office work) would be very successful in bringing automation to the office. In fact, the history of workflow application in corporate America has been mixed; more systems have silently died than been successful [Bai81, Whi94]. The 1970s were the years of introduction of the first sophisticated Office Information Systems. Some of these systems were indeed workflow management systems embedding complex specifications of the corporation's office procedures, detailing which procedure steps must precede which, and what data must be used in which steps [Zis77]. The 1970s were a time of wild optimism about the great beneficial effects upon productivity and effectiveness of this new technology. However, much of this optimism was unfounded. It was observed that organizations succeed only if people creatively violate, augment, or circumvent the standard office procedures when appropriate. When these electronic coordinators were introduced into offices, people could no longer blatantly disobey the office procedures. In many cases, these systems led to ineffective organizations and technology rejection. Thus, the rigid systems of the 1970s tended to interfere with work routines rather than expedite them. Workflow was also unsuccessful in the 1970s because sufficient technology was not available, because personal computers in the office were not socially accepted, because vendors were unaware of the requirements and pitfalls of group technology, and because networking was not commonly available.

There has been considerable published work which addresses workflow systems. Some of the beginnings in this area come from the author's early work on Officetalk/ICNs in the 1970s [Ell80]. Also, GMD has implemented several versions of Domino [Kre84], a Petri net based prototype office information system. Usage reports detail numerous problems and reasons for user rejection of the system — this typifies problems of current workflow. Other workflow efforts include the Xerox "Collaborative Process Model" [Sar91], Polymer at the University of Massachusetts [Cro88], Prominand [Kar91], Role Interaction Nets [Rei92], and the WooRKS workflow prototype within the ITHACA ESPRIT project [Ade92]. There has been a flood of new workflow systems in the 1990s, and a flood of papers describing them. See for example, the yearly proceedings of the Workflow 9x vendor conferences.

Considerable effort has been put into workflow studies. Many of these have transpired in the Information Systems field and the Organizational Design field within business schools. Examples include Bair's TUMS [Bai82], Woo's SACT [Woo90], Hirshheim's model [Hir85], the Society model [Ho86], Hammer's BDL and OAM [Sir84], and the OSSAD model [Dum91]. Several office models have emerged from concepts of discrete mathematics. These include Petri net based workflow models [Zis77, Hol88, Li90], and graph theory based models [Luq90]. There is also a set of models which have emerged out of the software engineering community. These could be classified as extended flowchart/state machine notations [Har90], project management models [Kel91], and process programming models [Ost88]. Office models are reviewed and contrasted in several articles including [Ell80], [Bra84], and [Leu92].

An interesting statistic published by the Gartner group, is that in the decade from 1980 to 1990, manufacturing productivity in the USA increased 40%, partly due to technology investment, and office productivity declined by 2% despite an estimated one trillion dollars of office automation spending. In the 1980s, there was a swing away from the workflow belief. The thrust of much of this work was to better understand the working of small groups, and to provide very flexible tools for people to use within unstructured work, and to *not* attempt to capture organizational knowledge within the computer system [Ell91]. Some groupware products saw success within their limited domains. It was apparent that a huge amount of leverage could be attained if we could successfully understand groups and organizations enough to produce organizationally aware groupware. It was also apparent that this is not an easy task. One of the lessons learned stems from the social situated nature of office work; this implies the need for a user-centered interdisciplinary approach. The 1990s saw the enthusiastic rebirth of interest in workflow; customers have been requesting workflow within all document handling and imaging and electronic mail systems. Unfortunately, it seems that many of the bitter lessons experienced in the 1970s and 1980s are still not heeded by many of the greater than 200 workflow products on the market today.

As an early example, Officetalk was an experimental office information system developed in the Office Research Group at Xerox PARC in the 1970s [Ell80]. Officetalk was the first system that we know of that provided a visual electronic desktop metaphor across end-users' personal computers. It also provided a set of personal productivity tools for manipulating information, a forms paradigm, and a network environment for sharing information. This family of systems was created, evolved, and used extensively within the Xerox PARC research lab, and was also tested in selected sites outside of PARC. During the 1970s and 1980s, the author participated in design, evaluation, enhancement, and significant extensions to Officetalk. This included work on Backtalk [Nut79], an interactive workflow simulator, Officetalk-D [Ell82], a database oriented workflow system, and Officetalk-P [Ell79b], an intelligent forms oriented workflow system.

However, it sometimes happened that an Officetalk system that was loved and worked wonderfully in the research laboratory, was hated and worked terribly when installed in a typical production office setting. We observed, as others have observed (see Chapter 1 in this book [Ehr99]), that workflow systems are *people* systems, and must take into account the situated, frequently unstructured nature of office work. Many workflow systems have failed because they did not adequately take into account the social and organizational setting into which they were being placed.

2.4   WORKFLOW MODELS AND MODELING

Models of workflow have spanned the gamut from very informal to very formal. Informal modeling has been reported by Suchman [Suc83]. Early work to formalize workflow models was presented in the thesis of Michael Zisman [Zis77] where he developed APNs (Augmented Petri Nets) that attached production rules to specify semantics within Petri nets. These concepts were implemented in the SCOOP system. The model UBIK represents an organization by "configurators" which perform actions by sending messages to each other [DeJ90]. The OFS model represents the flow of forms within an office; within this model, all messages, documents, letters, etc., are defined to be forms [Tsi82]. Another alternative is to model the office as a database with transactions. TEMPORA is an integrated architecture for doing business design and analysis within a database environment [Lou92]. This is a small sampling of the large number of models which have been used for the modeling of offices and workflow.

Our research group at the University of Colorado is (and has been for many years) actively researching the Information Control Net model (abbreviated ICN) for information systems analysis, simulation, and implementation. The ICN is a simple, but mathematically rigorous formalism created and designed in the 1970s specifically to model office procedures [Ell79a]. ICNs are actually a family of models which have evolved to incorporate control flow, data flow, goals, actors, roles, information repositories, and other resources [Ell83]. ICNs have been studied in universities [Dum91] and applied in industry [Bul92]. They have been shown to be valuable for capturing office procedures, for mathematical analysis, for simulation, and for systems implementation. Some of the documented analyses of ICNs include throughput, maximal parallelism, reorganization, and streamlining [Coo80]. As a comprehensible, generic, and extensible process model, the basic ICN is described next.

2.4.1 Mathematical Definition

The ICN family of models are structured around the fundamental observation that organizations encompass goals, resources, and constraints. Some organizations are very highly structured, with precisely defined processes and rules; others are very loosely constructed with predominantly unstructured activities. Owing to the variety of organizations, and owing to the variety of questions that models may be employed to investigate, we have seen that no one model adequately addresses all aspects. Thus, we derive a family of models by selecting different types of resources and different levels of structure to incorporate in any particular member of the family. For example, an organizational model which focuses upon informal interpersonal communication must incorporate the very important resource of people, and the roles that they play in the organization. For the thrust of this chapter, we use the basic "control ICN" which models partial orderings of activities and their control structures; this explanation does not include the data structure component.

Definition: A Marked Control ICN is a marked graph specified as a 4-tuple, $G = (C, r, l, m)$ where

(1) C is a finite set of nodes, $\{c_1, c_2, ..., c_n\}$.

(2) r is a relation over $C \times C$ which defines edges of the graph G. If (c_1, c_2) is a member of r, then there is an edge from c_1 to c_2. We say that the edge is an output of c_1, and an input of c_2.

(3) l is a function from C into $\{0, 1\}$ denoting the input–output logic of nodes. $l(c_i) = 0$ denotes conjunctive logic and $l(c_i) = 1$ denotes disjunctive logic. By convention, we separate activity nodes (single-input, single-output) from AND nodes (conjunctive input and output) from OR nodes (disjunctive input and output).

(4) m is a marking for the graph G which associates a set (of tokens) with each node and each edge of G. If x is a member of $C \cup r$, then m associates with x a set $M(x)$ such that if $M(x)$ is nonempty, then x is said to be marked. The elements of $M(x)$ are the tokens residing on the graph component x. A token is a marker that may cause a node to fire. If a graph component x contains a token t, then we say the component x is marked with the token t.

We are now in a position to describe how a marked ICN executes:

A node, c_i, with $l(c_i) = 1$ is pseudo-enabled if there is at least one input edge, $r(c_j, c_i)$ such that $M(r(c_j, c_i))$ is not empty (OR logic). A node, c_i, with $l(c_i) = 0$ is pseudo-enabled if $M(r(c_j, c_i))$ is not empty (AND logic) for every input edge of c_i, $r(c_j, c_i)$.

A node c_i can fire if it is pseudo-enabled; initiation of firing results in a change of marking such that if $l(c_i) = 1$, then some token t in $M(r(c_j, c_i))$ is deleted from one $M(r(c_j, c_i))$, and added to $M(c_i)$. If $l(c_i) = 0$, then some token is deleted from each $M(r(c_j, c_i))$, and a single token is added to $M(c_i)$.

When a node terminates an execution at some finite time after its initiation of firing, then some t in $M(c_i)$ is deleted from $M(c_i)$. If $l(c_i) = 1$, then t is added to $M(r(c_i, c_j))$ for some successor node c_j; if $l(c_i) = 0$, then t is added to $M(r(c_i, c_j))$ for all successor nodes c_j.

2.4.2   An ICN Example

Frequently ICNs are manipulated in their graphical form. Figure 2.3 shows the graphical form for an Information Control Net depicting a procedure for order processing within a corporation. When a customer request for goods arrives, the first step is the order entry activity in which an order administrator fills out an order form. This is graphically depicted by the first (top) circle in Figure 2.3. The large hollow circles thus denote activities. Arcs denote precedence, so for example, the shipping activity must complete before the billing activity can begin. After order entry is completed, inventory check and compile references activities can proceed concurrently, indicated by the black dot labelled "and". A corresponding second black dot denotes the "and join" of activities. After the order evaluation activity, either shipping or rejection processing occurs. Thus, the small hollow dot labelled "or" denotes choice or decision making. There is a corresponding "or join" hollow circle, so that the archive activity occurs after either the rejection or the shipping activity is completed.

2.5   WORKFLOW META-MODEL

An important aspect of a successful work environment is that people have the capability and resources to act as effective problem solvers and exception handlers. In one case study, a worker commented: "The boss in New York says to do it that way, but we do it this way because we're in Jamaica. We change the procedure here, and this worked fine until the computer system was installed." Thus an important observation emerged from these office studies: Workflow models must not be so prescriptive that they are a barrier to the office worker. Models must somehow span a large *conformance* spectrum; likewise, experience has shown that within a single process, there is a need to model different parts in different amounts of detail, and different levels of operationality.

   Given the observations concerning the failure of workflow systems and models to adequately recognize the situated unstructured nature of work, this section explains a useful 3-dimensional meta-model that captures some of the human dimensions of workflow. The CDO meta-model (CDO abbreviates conformance, detail, operationality) distinguishes parts of the process that must be strictly performed for the process to be acceptable (mandatory parts), from parts that can be freely altered (e.g., a mechanism to describe a recommended way of accomplishing the work). The meta-model is also intended to distinguish parts of the process described at very abstract levels from very detailed levels. Along a third dimension, the meta-model supports representations that are either highly declarative or highly operational. For example, goals and intentional specifications are considered to be highly declarational; in contrast, a C encoding of a sorting algorithm is considered to be highly operational. The dimensions of the model space are shown graphically in Figure 2.4. A point in the 3-D space represents a part (task) of a workflow.

   The model space is intended to represent processes according to the way the workflow model is to be used, as defined by three different criteria: the amount of conformance that is required by the organization for which the process is a model, the level of detail of the description, and the operational (versus declarational) nature of the model (see Figure 2.1). The model is normalized to the unit cube, so strict total conformance is at $x = 1$, and maximum detail is at $y = 1$. The third dimension, operationality, attempts to quantify the degree to which the model describes *what* is required rather than *how* the process works. A *what*

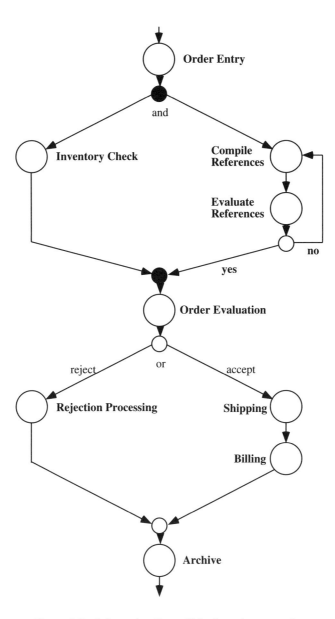

Figure 2.3   Information Control Net for order processing

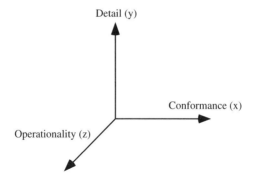

Figure 2.4   CDO model dimensions

model is highly declarative (near $z = 0$); a *how model* is highly operational (near $z = 1$). In this domain space, systems that represent only structured work, fully specified, codified, and required, are at $x = 1$, $y = 1$, and $z = 1$; this is the typical workflow point in the space. Workflow models and systems frequently do not provide assistance below this point. On the other hand, groupware systems intended to address unstructured work are in a space closer to $x = 0$, $y = 0$, and $z = 0$. Fully automated workflow enactment systems could be (ideally) characterized as a point in the space with x near to 1, y near to 1, and $z = 1$. Systems that focus on exception handling are in a space where $x << 1$. Goal-based systems typically operate in a domain in which z is near to 0, but x and y vary according to the specifics of the model.

The extended ICN model, used in some of our recent studies, is intended to address the full space, with different parts of the model addressing different subspaces according to the need for that part of the model. For example, if part of the work is highly structured, operationally specified, and required to be accomplished according to the specification, then it should be modeled differently from work for which only the goal is known. The model should allow one to represent a process for which parts are operational and required, while the way that other parts are executed is arbitrary, provided that the executions satisfy the intent. The extended ICN model allows different parts (or sub-tasks) of a process to be modeled at different points in the 3-D space; all within the same ICN model.

One aspect of an ICN specifies activities (or tasks, or process steps) and their attributes in the process; each activity belongs to a region whose type is (informally) defined by a point or region in the space in Figure 2.1. For example, a type "R" (for required work) region might be represented by a point in the $(1, y, z)$ plane; the model can be represented as a conventional ICN subgraph composed entirely of required (mandatory) steps.

A type "A" region (for assisted work) may use an operational or declarational style specification, but the submodel in the region can be interpreted as one approach to accomplishing the work. This type of specification is a point in the $(0, y, z)$ plane; it is used when a process designer has one notion of how to accomplish the work, but realizes that different situations require different variations on the specification. The A-region work can be used directly, or it can be used to (manually) infer the intent of this part of the work. This is typically a much healthier way to view a workflow specification than to consider it the immutable total specification that must be followed exactly.

A type "D" region (for declaration region) represents a part of the model that defines what the region is intended to accomplish, rather than a description of how the work must/might be conducted. This type of region occurs at points such as $(0, 1, 0)$ and $(.5, .5, 0)$. Thus, points in the $(x, y, 0)$ plane are "non-operational" specifications.

Ongoing research work at the University of Colorado focuses on exploring new models to explicitly distinguish among policy, process, and regulations in different regions of our 3-D space. The dimensions of this model are not totally orthogonal, and they obviously do not totally span the space of all human dimensions. Note, for example, that a workflow process description which has a very high degree of detail is also likely to have a high degree of operationality, so these dimensions seem to be not totally independent in general. There are, however, cases in which process descriptions are detailed, but not operational. This occurs in rule-based systems which have huge numbers of rules (constraints), but are not operational because the rules are not adequate to completely specify the process.

Indeed, some researchers assert that in numerous *human* situations, there is no such thing as a "complete and explicit" account of the process because all process instances are situated and implicit [Suc87]. Indeed, Brown points out [Bro93] that abstraction from process instance to process class (i.e. modeling) is itself an imperfect situated social practice that is developed in the social context of an ongoing meta-process. An example is learning to ride a bicycle — books give tips, but not an algorithm. You cannot simply learn from a book.

In the case of driving an automobile, some of the "official rules of the road" books are quite thick manuals articulating auto driving distances and courtesies and places not to park and so forth. Many of these books list more "don't do" constraints than "do" steps. These manuals contain enormous detail, but they do not give you an algorithm for driving. Thus they do not, and are not intended to be, operational.

Conversely, there exist many process descriptions that are operational, but not detailed. The statement within an order processing process: "All orders must be routed to credit check, then billing, then shipping" is operational but not detailed. It is operational because a workflow system can automatically coordinate the electronic forwarding of the order forms to the correct departments from these specifications. However, the above statement is not detailed — it gives us no information about what is supposed to happen *inside* of credit check or billing or shipping.

Although the CDO meta-model does not span the space of all human dimensions, and its dimensions are not totally orthogonal, the model nevertheless is quite useful to present a novel process analysis perspective, and to illustrate gaps in the space of previous models. We believe that this new perspective might be particularly useful in understanding the role that various models should play in large enterprise re-engineering efforts.

2.6 EXAMPLE SYSTEMS

2.6.1 IBM FlowMark

The IBM workflow management product is FlowMark, a system which was beta-tested in 1993, and first released as a product in 1994. FlowMark clearly distinguishes workflow build-time (modeling and analysis) from run-time (enactment). The run-time system is useful when actors (end-users of the system) at their workstations are doing the process work steps (activities) that have previously been specified. Run-time functions coordinate and oversee the execution of activities within the distributed system, while maintaining backups, and audit trails. Run-time allows those participants with proper access rights to start and terminate processes and activities, to view their up-to-date to-do lists, and to access application data as needed.

The build-time system is useful for creating and changing the specification of processes. Build-time functions include facilities to allow the drawing, editing, and compilation of process graphs. The creator or analysts during build-time can create, test, simulate, and animate process specifications, can assign staff to activities, and can associate programs (scripts) with activities. The diagrammatic process graphs allow one to create and manipulate activity icons, data icons, and connector arcs. Criteria for control flow branching and decision making are specified via conditions attached to arcs. Data flow is specified via containers, data structures, and data arcs. Aggregates of activities called blocks and bundles allow diagrams to remain small and comprehensible via activity nesting. Properties associated with activities include actors, I/O data, scripts, who is responsible, time, manual/automatic switch, starting conditions, and completion conditions.

The FlowMark organizational model is interesting. Notions of roles and actors are captured within the staff specifications, and relationships. The staff specification can include participants (end-users), levels, roles, organizations and relationships. People have attributes such as userID, absent flag, and level. Levels are integers between 0 and 9 inclusive which can be locally interpreted by different applications. For example one company may decide that 0 denotes novice, 1 through 3 is associate, and above 3 denotes expert. Organizations are defined as groups with managers, and they are related by a tree structure. Each participant is involved in two types of relationships. They can be the *player of* multiple roles, and they *belong to* exactly one organization.

The above concepts and definitions are stored in a FlowMark database after they are created. For distribution and interoperability, FlowMark definitions can be described in an ASCII text file in an external format called FlowMark definition language (FDL). The FlowMark workflow management system provides import and export utilities so that process graphs and other specifications can be ported from one location to another via FDL.

2.6.2   Action Workflow

The Action Workflow product by Action Technologies Inc., provides a workflow model, and architecture based upon the philosophical notions of Heidegger, and the linguistic speech act theory. These notions and theory are well explained in publications by Winograd and Flores [Flo88, Med92], who are the founders of the company. The creation of this framework based upon a multi-disciplinary theory is unique and potent. Winograd and Flores point out that all interactions (or conversations) are composed of communication acts which must be interpreted, and that are subject to mis-interpretation by the receiver. Speech act theory suggests that there are a finite number of categories of speech that characterize all communications. Computer systems can help to avoid mis-interpreted communications by clearly displaying the category of each communication to the receiver.

The theory can be applied to workflow by considering each work case as a conversation between a "customer" who wants the task to be done, and a "performer" who takes on enactment of the task or process. In Figure 2.1 we saw an example where someone wants to buy goods — this person is the customer to whom the goods (and the bill) will be delivered. The performer in this case is the company that will supply the goods to the customer. Every workflow, under this model, is drawn as a loop with four phases:

1. the customer formulates the request
2. the customer and performer negotiate the terms of agreement
3. the performer does the task
4. the performer and customer negotiate the customer satisfaction.

The analysts at Action Technologies provide a convincing argument that the negotiation phases are very important, but that all too often the fourth phase (customer satisfaction) is ignored. In their product usage, no phase is ignored because a loop is not closed (completed) until all four steps have been completed, implying that the customer has said "I am satisfied." Of course, loops most often have sub-loops nested within the different phases, allowing delegation, subcontracting, or simply the specification of various levels of detail. Frequently the performer of a loop becomes the client of a sub-loop.

Action Technologies also has a client–server architecture which can execute on several different platforms. Like the FlowMark system, there exists an intermediate workflow specification language and a workflow language interpreter that enables compilation to/from the graphical nested loops diagram. The speech act theory has been the basis of other products also, and the source of much lively debate in the research community.

2.6.3   Polymer

Polymer is an experimental goal-based workflow system constructed at the University of Massachusetts [Cro88]. As Professor Bruce Croft, leader of the Polymer project explained: "Polymer is intended to assist in tasks that are loosely structured, multi-agent, under-specified, and complex." The potential utility of this approach can be understood by noticing statements that have been made concerning human work behavior: "People do not follow every step of a work procedure specification; rather they know the goal of their task and do whatever is necessary to attain that goal." Doing this invokes the creative and unstructured activities that help an organization to flourish. Many organizations have voluminous procedures manuals, but almost no employee sits down and reads these in all of their detail.

It is well known that many successful managers work in this mode. It is also the case that many office tasks that seem very structured and simple, frequently have unstructured problem solving tasks imbedded. Consider the difficult sub-task done by the order entry clerk of interpreting the signature of a customer on a piece of paper. At times this can be quite a challenge. Thus, instead of building an over-structured workflow system that forces the users into unnatural, inefficient and ineffective step-by-step processing, a workflow system might allow workers to work via goals. Furthermore, the work of Croft and team attempts to create a workflow system that knows the goals and works with the humans to help achieve them.

Polymer uses concepts and technologies from the artificial intelligence literature to do goal-based planning [Cro89]. It attempts to satisfy the goals that are specified in a top-down depth first traversal fashion. Polymer allows the specification of tasks, agents, objects, goals, and plans. Within an activity description, there can be goals, preconditions, postconditions, and also subgoals. Besides this application description module, there is also a planner, an execution monitor, a truth maintenance module, and user interaction module. Other research projects are also investigating goal based approaches to workflow [Ell95]. This is an area of great promise which is still in the research phase. The next section discusses workflow research directions further.

2.7   RESEARCH DIRECTIONS AND ISSUES

Workflow systems have been categorized into a) administrative workflow systems, b) production workflow systems, and c) ad-hoc workflow systems. An administrative system typically has complex administrative types of processes to administer. There may be many diverse and complex sub-processes, and a lot of dependency is placed on the system to monitor and remind people. Examples include billing and order processing. Some research issues prominent within the administrative category include integration, interoperability, and efficient triggering mechanisms. In contrast, a production workflow is very structured, and high volume. Thus, many parts of this can be and are relatively highly automated, and the number of work cases per unit time is high. For example, customer inquiry processing within a large telephone company has millions of diverse inquiries per month [Dav91]. Many of the tasks and process steps are done wholly by computer, and a good transaction management system is an important part of this. Research issues of efficient extended transaction mechanisms, concurrency control, recovery, and distributed architecture are important within this category. Finally, the ad-hoc workflow is one in which there is much unstructured work, and in which much of the planning of which steps to take cannot be done in advance. Much of the work of managers has been described [Min79] as "fire fighting and crisis management", and is very unplanned in its detail. Ad-hoc workflow is frequently a relatively small workflow in terms of the number of transactions incoming, and in terms of the complexity of the mainline people and process specifications. There is need for people to be creatively involved, and for group problem solving to be supported. An example in this category is document routing which is dependent upon the content of the document, and human judgement about who in the organization it should be routed to next. Given these distinct workflow types one might suspect that their problems are disjoint. This is not the case. Note that these categories are actually *all* present in many workflow situations. Areas in which very similar problems arise include exception handling and dynamic organizational change. These two exemplary research challenges, and others, are examined next in this section.

2.7.1   Exception Handling

One attribute which distinguishes workflow systems from many other kinds of computer systems is *people*. Typically workflow involves people in non-trivial ways. People are not simply the consumers of output, but are intimately involved in the processing. Several studies of offices have been done with an express interest in observing and categorizing the exception processing. These studies have found that there is a large amount of exception handling in all three of the categories of workflow. And the creativity and problem solving abilities of humans, rather than just computers, are strongly needed. Thus, successful workflow designs need to think beyond the computer as a tool to automate and replace people, to computer as collaborator and communication vehicle to help people in problem solving and exception handling.

In a recent Ph.D. dissertation by Heikki Saastamoinen [Saa95], he analyzed exceptions by performing an 8 month study at a large paper handling company in Finland. He looked at the frequency of exceptions, their scope, complexity, type, amount of delay, and amount of repair work. He found that exceptions are consuming a huge amount of the time of the people in organizations. These findings are consistent with other studies, and statistical analysis using a large number of questionnaires to a sampling of companies [Saa94, Str89] that have been published. Saastamoinen finds that it is useful to separate exception detection from exception handling from exception prevention. He also notes that some people use the term "error" for exception, and that this is sometimes inappropriate because it is frequently not a mistake, but a "freak occurrence of nature" that is a fault. He interestingly also found several examples of "positive exceptions" which helped raise awareness of people, and led to a better organization. He classified exceptions into three types:

1. Established Exceptions: they are not the normal case, but there are rules to handle them; they are anticipated.
2. Otherwise Exceptions: no rule to handle, but these are local bounded exceptions where scope and goal are known.
3. True Exceptions: no precedent, non-local (span multiple people/activity domains), goal unclear, unanticipated.

In established exceptions, techniques like UNDO, REDO, compensation and rollback may apply from database theory. An example of this type of exception is "external tax paid for internal order". There is a standard compensation process which compensates for this, and this exception was anticipated by the system designers. The important point that was made convincingly by Lucy Suchman, is that it is impossible for the system designers to *a priori* think of all exceptions [Suc87]. So, for example in a trip planning system, the designers may implement an exception handler for the case of "airplane full" (an established exception), but may not have implemented any exception handler for "airplane crashes" (a true exception). Saastamoinen found that the exception detection, prevention, and handling take up more than 50% of the work time in many companies. He found that true exceptions were the most expensive in terms of delay, complexity, and usage of the most time of the most expensive people within an organization. The older workflow systems were especially bad offenders. First they would regularly insult the users by printing a message for each exception that was worded to make it seem like an "error!". These systems were so rigid that they did not allow humans to do reasonable work-arounds. And they frequently hindered rather than helped the creative people to solve problems.

Thus, an important issue is the question of how workflow systems can be designed for unexpected exceptions, to help rather than hinder the knowledge workers. The work folders concept of Karbe tried to provide exception handling facilities for the top ten exceptions [Kar91], but found that this was inadequate for true exceptions. The FlowPath workflow product introduced the capability for any user at any time to send a work case to another activity, role, or participant with parameters to specify further routing, time of delivery, return to sender afterwards, etc. A problem of access control and general control of the process then emerges. Lucy Suchman gives an excellent example of a true exception within an accounting office in which somehow one page of a two page billing statement is missing [Suc83]. It takes quite a lot of creativity and problem solving to crack this one, and to stay within the rules of the organization.

2.7.2 Interoperability

One of the complaints that is very high on the list for workflow customers is that their workflow systems cannot adequately interact with their legacy data processing systems. Frequently some inputs, outputs, and intermediate results of the workflow system must go to and from other previously existing computer systems. The workflow typically needs to interact with a number of other databases, file systems, and applications. In many organizations it is not feasible to throw away the large mainframe systems simply because there is a new workflow system in house. Thus, pragmatically speaking, a strong requirement of workflow management systems is to communicate and interact well with a variety of other data processing and information systems within an organization. Owing to the proliferation of different types and styles of these systems, workflow vendors face a significant challenge. Vendors must seek solutions that offer quick, low effort programming of varied interfaces to varied legacy systems. This requirement also extends to interaction with varied applications, databases, and personal productivity tools.

Another type of interoperability that is becoming more and more in demand is interoperability between different workflow systems. The workflow management coalition is trying to address this and other interfacing problems within their standards work [WMC]. For example, if a large corporation is buying expensive goods, they may use their workflow management system to execute the equipment purchase process. Preferably, their purchase orders and other relevant workflow outputs can be automatically and electronically input to the workflow system of the supplier. The work of Eder and group [Ede95] explores issues of workflow on the Internet; inter-organizational interoperability can be obtained by using the extended HTTP and HTML protocols, and EDI. There are now a number of workflow systems whose transport medium is strictly the Internet technology [W4].

2.7.3   Dynamic Change

Change is a way of life in most organizational and personal settings. There are many different types of change, scales of change, and timeframes for change. Workflow systems must support rather than hinder this changeability. Those organizations in the modern business world which refuse to change are typically headed toward rapid obsolescence because they cannot compete. Organizations must frequently make structural changes such as:

- adding a new employee
- adjusting procedures for a new tax law
- filling in for a manager on vacation.

There are also important issues concerned with change of application data, evolution of organizational objectives, change of social communication structures, etc. In order to make structural changes as above within a workflow system context, it is typically and unfortunately necessary to suspend or abort the work in progress within the execution module, and start up the specification module to make the changes to the specification. Then after the change, the specification module is terminated, parameters are re-initialized, the specification is re-compiled, and once again, the execution module is started. This is an inefficient, error prone, and ineffective process because many organizations find it very unproductive, and sometimes impossible, to shut down all activity in order to make changes. From pharmaceutical factories to software engineering houses, this is a nagging problem — the bigger the organization, the more complex are the processes, and the more painful the change process. Today, organizations usually do not solve this problem, they cope, evade, or "muddle through".

By combining the first and second components of workflow, the model is constantly available and process change can potentially occur dynamically if the correctness and consistency problems of dynamic change can be solved. Thus, even with these components combined, we do not know how to smoothly and correctly handle the myriad of changes which are constantly happening. Although there is considerable literature addressing workflow, office modeling, and business re-engineering, the problem of dynamic structural change has not been generally solved. In this section, we see an example of one type of incorrect behavior that can accidentally occur within dynamic structural change. The conclusion is that in large organizations around the world, dynamic change is an ad-hoc and risky event.

Change to the values of application data items is a normal type of activity that occurs in administrative information processing. However, structural change to the procedures and processes is not considered "normal" by most organizations. Dynamic means that the change to the process occurs while the process is executing. Static change, in the ICN context, means that the execution of the process is halted, all tokens are removed, and the change is applied at quiescence. Static correctness means that certain assertions or constraints are not violated — it implies that we have a set of correctness criteria that hold for all tokens flowing through the ICN before the change, and also for all tokens that enter the ICN after the change is completed.

Dynamic change correctness is concerned with tokens which enter the net prior to the change and do not exit the ICN until some time after the change. Anomalous behavior can be exhibited by these tokens even if we know that the change maintains static correctness. A simple example of this is the change that includes swapping of the billing and shipping activities in the example ICN of Figure 2.5. Notice that Figure 2.5 is simply a sub-ICN of the previously explained ICN of order processing (Figure 2.3). Tokens that are currently within the shipping node when the swap change occurs never encounter the billing activity, so the company never gets paid for the goods that are shipped. Suppose that the correctness criterion is that all customer orders must pass through shipping and billing in some order. This anomaly occurs although the ICN before the change is correct, and the ICN after the change is correct. Similarly, an anomaly occurs if we simply try to enhance the efficiency of the procedure by changing to perform billing and shipping in parallel. This example depicted in Figure 2.5 is small and obvious; other examples which occur in ICNs of hundreds of nodes are not at all obvious, and difficult to find and correct. By combining some techniques of Petri nets and graph grammars, Keddara [Ked95] has been able to characterize situations in which this behavior is non-problematic.

2.7.4 Workflow Transactions

Many notions such as transactions, that have been studied within the database community, are not present in today's typical workflow products. Concepts of archival storage (data mining), efficient retrieval, transparency (e.g. of distribution), concurrency control, and reliability/recovery have been conceived within the database community, studied in research labs, and implemented in database management products, but have mostly not made their way into workflow management systems [Sh95]. This is partly due to thinking of workflow as equivalent to control flow, and ignoring data flows. This is also partly due to the origins of many workflow products and companies being non-database companies. Finally, this is partly due to the need to rethink these concepts within the workflow context, and to not simply copy the database implementations of these concepts. Sometimes the database expert does not have sufficient knowledge or sensibilities about the workflow needs of organizations.

For example, there are clearly multiple people needing to access the workflow information and system concurrently. Both within a single workflow, and among different workflows, we must enable parallelism. Thus, the database transaction has been suggested because it

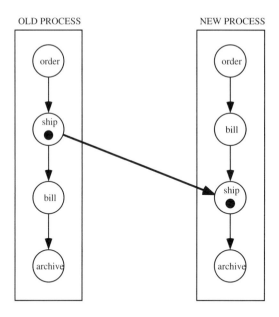

Figure 2.5   Dynamic structural change

allows concurrent access while maintaining atomicity and serializability. However, the people working on a workflow are typically collaborating, for example, on a customer work case. The transactions are thus not executing on the order of microseconds, but on the order of minutes, days, or even months. The standard solutions lock up too much of the information for too long. Thus we must be concerned with long transactions; concepts such as nested transactions may be applicable here [ElM92]. Furthermore, we know that the system must enhance, not destroy, the ability of people to work tightly together as teams to do decision making and problem solving. The underlying database philosophy of guaranteeing to users that their work is independent and isolated from others' is basically an incorrect perspective for the workflow domain. There need to be facilities that allow a distributed team to work together unfettered on a dataset by all having read and write access to all data, and all to see instantaneously the work and changes of all others. This is the real-time interaction mode that can be very useful, but that is hindered by the locks that are created, and the firewalls that are created within conventional transaction mechanisms. Serializability turns out to be an inadequate correctness criterion in this application area. New creative solutions are needed.

In workflow there is a need to anticipate the unexpected. Frequently after some amount of working on a work case, the customer calls and says to cancel their case, significantly alter their case, or to expedite it. This suggests a need for undo, cancel, abort, and rollback mechanisms. Once again these concepts are not adequate if they are blindly adopted from database implementations. Different threads of the workflow may have been executed in parallel in such a way that it is impossible to undo some parts, but possible for others if parts have, for example, been delegated to a subcontractor. If the tree has already been chopped down, then it is impossible to undo; if the plane trip has already been flown, then it is impossible to just cancel it [Jab96].

There have been numerous proposals to use database-like techniques that have been developed for "non-standard transactions". For example, undo, redo, compensation, sagas, nested transactions, and abort mechanisms [ElM92]. These mechanisms are good innovations for established exceptions, but are much less useful for true exceptions where the detection point may be totally disjoint from the cause point, and where it may be totally impossible to undo.

2.7.5 Further Research Directions and Issues

This chapter has introduced only a few of the workflow research areas. Other areas include distributed workflow, workflow benchmarking, combining workflow and groupware, real-time interactions, incorporation of goals into workflow systems, incorporation of multimedia, learning and evolving workflow systems, organizational sub-models, social sub-models, and group user interfaces. Also, numerous deep problems exist concerning end-user programmability by secretaries, clerks, and other non-computer people. Many of these problems remain as inhibitors to successful workflow implementations.

2.8 SUMMARY

This chapter has presented a tour of workflow issues, technology, and challenges. Workflow management systems consist of two components: a modeling component used for the definition, analysis, simulation and restructuring of processes, and an enactment component, called the "run-time system" which has a workflow engine to coordinate process steps, and an execution interface for use by the distributed end-users.

Besides presenting workflow definitions, architectures, and models, this chapter has presented a historical perspective that suggests that the human and social factors are very important, and have frequently been ignored in the past. Workflow systems are foremost people systems. This leads to consideration of a meta-model attempting to capture some of the human dimensions of workflow, and the description of some workflow systems and research prototypes which are attempting to solve some of the hard problems that are still plaguing the field. A few of these hard problems have been described, including exception handling, interoperability, dynamic change, and workflow transactions.

It is hoped that the work presented herein will raise awareness of work and considerations that are paramount for workflow success, and also that this will stimulate good researchers to take up the banner of doing needed research in this fast growing area.

REFERENCES

[Ade92]   Ader, M. and Lu, G., The WooRKS Object Oriented Workflow System. *OOPSLA92 Exhibition*, booth 712–714, October 19–21, 1992. Developed as part of the ITHACA Research project within the ESPRIT Program.

[Bae93]   Baecker, R. (Ed.), *Readings in Groupware and Computer Supported Cooperative Work.* Morgan Kaufmann Publishers, January 1993.

[Bai81]   Bair, J. (Co-editor), Office automation systems: Why some work and others fail. *Stanford University Conference Proceedings*. Stanford University, Center for Information Technology, 1981.

[Bai82]   Bair, J., Methods for success with new workflow systems. In D. Coleman (Ed.), *GroupWare'92*, pages 160–164. Morgan Kaufmann Publishers, San Mateo, CA.

[Bar83]   Barber, G., Supporting organizational problem solving with a workstation. *ACM Transactions on Office Information Systems*, 1(1), 1983.

[Bra84]   Bracchi, G. and Pernici, B., The design requirements of office systems. *ACM Transactions on Office Information Systems*, 2(2):151–170, April 1984.

[Bro93]   Brown, J.S. and Duguid, P., Stolen knowledge. *Educational Technology*, March 1993.

[Bul92]   Bull Corporation, *FlowPath Functional Specification*. Bull S. A., Paris, France, September 1992.

[Che76]   Chen, P., The entity-relationship model – Toward a unified view of data. *ACM Transactions on Database Systems*, 1(1), 1976.

[Coo80]   Cook, C., Office streamlining using the ICN model and methodology. In *Proceedings of the 1980 National Computer Conference*, June, 1980.

[Cro88]   Croft, W. and Lefkowitz, L., Using a planner to support office work. In *Proceedings of ACM COIS'88*, pages 55–62, March 1988.

[Cro89]   Croft, W. and Lefkowitz, L., Planning and execution of tasks in cooperative work environments. *IEEE AI*, 1989.

[CSCW92]   *Computer Supported Cooperative Work (CSCW), An International Journal*. Kluwer Academic Publishers, Vol. 1, 1992.

[Dav91]   Davis, D. B., Software that makes your work flow. *Datamation*, 37(8):75–78, April 1991.

[DeJ90]   De Jong, P., Structure and action in distributed organizations. In *Proceedings of ACM COIS'90*, pages 1–10, April 1990.

[Dum91]   Dumas, P., *La Méthode OSSAD*. Les Editions d'Organisation, 1991.

[Dys92]   Dyson, E., Workflow. *Release 1.0*, EDventure Holdings, New York, September 1992.

[Ede95]   Eder, J. and Groiss, H., Interoperability with world wide workflows. *Integrated Design and Process Technology*, IDTP Vol.1, December 1995.

[Ehr99]   Ehrlich, K., Designing groupware applications: A work-centered approach. In Beaudouin-Lafon, M. (Ed.), *Computer Supported Cooperative Work*, Trends in Software Series 7:1–28. John Wiley & Sons, Chichester, 1999.

[Ell79a]   Ellis, C. A., Information control nets: A mathematical model of office information flow. In *Proceedings of the 1979 ACM Conference on Simulation, Measurement and Modeling of Computer Systems*, pages 225–239, August 1979, .

[Ell79b]   Ellis, C., OfficeTalk-P: An office information system based upon migrating processes. In Najah Naffah (Ed.), *Integrated Office Systems*. INRIA, France, 1979.

[Ell80]   Ellis, C. A. and Nutt, G. J., Office information systems and computer science. *ACM Computing Surveys*, 12(1):27–60, March 1980.

[Ell82]   Ellis, C., OfficeTalk-D: An experimental office information system. In *Proceedings of the First ACM Conference on Office Information System*, June 1982.

[Ell83]   Ellis, C., Formal and informal models of office activity. In *Proceedings of the IFIP International Computer Congress*, Paris, 1983.

[Ell91]   Ellis, C. A., S. J. Gibbs, and G. L. Rein, Groupware: Some issues and experiences. *Communications of the ACM*, 34(1):38–58, January 1991.

[Ell95]   Ellis, C. and Wainer, J., Goal-based models of collaboration. *Collaborative Computing Journal*, 1(1), 1995.

[ElM92]   ElMagarmid, A. (Ed.), *Database Transaction Models for Advanced Applications*. Morgan Kaufmann, 1992.

[Flo88]   Flores, F., Graves, M., Hartfield, B. and Winograd, T., Computer systems and the design of organizational interaction. *ACM Transactions on Office Information Systems*, 6(2):153–172, April 1988.

[Gas86]   Gasser, L., The integration of computing and routine work. *ACM Transactions on Office Information Systems*, 4(3):205–225, July 1986.

[Geo95]   Georgakopoulos, D. , Hornick, M., and Sheth, A., An overview of workflow management: From process modeling to workflow automation infrastructure. *Distributed and Parallel Databases*, 3(22):119–154, April 1995.

[Gru88]   Grudin, J., Why CSCW applications fail, In *Proceedings of the Conference on Computer Supported Cooperative Work (CSCW'88)*, pages 85–93. ACM Press, New York, 1988.

[Har90]   Harel, D., et. al., STATEMATE: A working environment for the development of complex systems. *IEEE Transactions on Software Engineering*, 16(4), April 1990.

[Hir85]   Hirschheim, R. A., *Office Automation: A Social and Organizational Perspective*. John Wiley & Sons, 1985.

[Ho86]   Ho, C., Hong, Y. and Kuo, T. A., Society model for office information systems. *ACM Transactions on Office Information Systems*, 4(4):104–131, April 1986.

[Hol88]   Holt, A., Diplans: A new language for the study and implementation of coordination. *ACM Transactions on Office Information Systems*, 6(2), 1988.

[Jab96]   Jablonski, S., Bussler, C., *Workflow Management*. Thomson Computer Press, 1996.

[Joh94]   Johansen, R., and Swigart, R., *Upsizing the Individual in the Downsized Organization*. Addison-Wesley, 1994.

[Kar91]   Karbe, B., Ramsperger, N., Concepts and implementation of migrating office processes. *Verteilte Kunstliche Intelligenz und Kooperatives Arbeiten*, page 136, 4, Internationaler GI-Kongress Wissensbasierte Systeme, Munchen, Germany, October 1991.

[Ked95]   Keddara, K., and Rozenberg, G., Dynamic change within workflow systems. In *Proceedings of the ACM SIGOIS Conference on Organizational Computing Systems*, August 1995.

[Kel91]   Kellner, M., Software process modeling support for management planning and control. In *Proceeding of the First International Conference on the Software Process*, pages 8–28. IEEE Computer Society, October 1991.

[Kre84]   Kreifelts, T., Licht, U., Seuffert, P. and Woetzel, G., DOMINO: A system for the specification and automation of cooperative office processes. In Wilson and Myrhaug (Eds.), *Proc. EUROMICRO'84*, pages 3–41, 1984.

[Kre87]   Kreifelts, T. and Woetzel, G., Distribution and exception handling in an office procedure system. In Bracchi and Tsichritzis (Eds) *Office Systems: Methods and Tools*, pages 197–208, 1987.

[Kre91a]   Kreifelts, T., Coordination of distributed work: From office procedures to customizable activities, *Verteilte Kunstliche Intelligenz und Kooperatives Arbeiten*, page 148, 4, Internationaler GI-Kongress Wisensbasierte Systeme, Munchen, Germany, October 1991.

[Kre91b]   Kreifelts, T., et.al., Experiences with the DOMINO office procedure system, In *Proceedings of the ECSCW'91*, pages 117–130. Kluwer, Dordrecht, 1991.

[Leu92]   Leung, Y., Workflow products market report. *B.S.A. Technical Memorandum*, Bull Corporation, 1992.

[Li90]   Li, Jianzhong, *AMS: A Declarative Formalism for Hierarchical Representation of Procedural Knowledge*. Ph.D. Thesis, Ecole Nationale Supérieure des Télécommunications, Paris, France, December 1990.

[Lou92]   Loucopoulos, P. and Katsouli, E., Modelling business rules in an office environment. *SIGOIS Bulletin*, 13(2). ACM, August 1992.

[Lut88]   Lutze, R. and Triumph-Adler, A., Customizing cooperative office procedures by planning. In *Proceedings of ACM COIS'88*, pages 63–77, March 1988.

[Luq90]   Luqi, A., Graph model for software evolution. *IEEE Transactions on Software Engineering*, 16(8), August 1990.

[Mal94]   Malone, T. and Crowston, K., The interdisciplinary study of coordination. *ACM Computing Surveys*, 26(1):87–120, March 1994.

[Mar91]   Martial, F.V., Activity coordination via multiagent and distributed planning. *Verteilte Kunstliche Intelligenz und Kooperatives Arbeiten*, page 90, 4, Internationaler GI-Kongress Wissensbasierte Systeme, Munchen, Germany, October 1991.

[Med92]   Medina-Mora, P. et. al., The Action Workflow approach to workflow management technology. In *Proceedings of ACM CSCW'92*, pages 281–288, November 1992.

[Min79]   Mintzberg, H., *The Structure of Organizations*. Englewood Cliffs, 1979.

[Nut79]   Nutt, G. J. and Ellis, C. A., Backtalk: An office environment simulator. In *ICC '79 Conference Record*, pages 22.3.1–22.3.5, June 1979.

[Nut83]   Nutt, G. J., An experimental distributed modeling system. *ACM Transactions on Office Information Systems*, 1(2):117–142, April 1983.

[Nut89]   Nutt, G. J., Beguelin, A., Demeure, I., Elliott, S., McWhirter, J., and Sanders, B., Olympus: An interactive simulation system, In *Proceedings 1989 Winter Simulation Conference (Washington, D.C.)*, pages 601–611, December 1989.

[Nut90]   Nutt, G. J., A simulation system architecture for graph models. In Rozenburg, G. (Ed.), *Advances in Petri Nets '90*. Springer Verlag, 1990.

[Ost88]   Osterweil, L., Automated support for the enactment of rigorously described software processes. In *Proceedings of the Third International Process Programming Workshop*, pages

122–125. IEEE Computer Society Press, 1988.

[Pan84]   Panko, R., 35 Offices: Analyzing needs in individual offices. In *Proceedings of the Second ACM-SIGOA Conference on Office Information Systems*, June 1984.

[Rei92]   Rein, G., *Organization Design Viewed as a Group Proces Using Coordination Technology*. Ph.D. Thesis Dissertation, Department of Information Systems, University of Texas at Austin, May 1992.

[Rei93]   Rein, G., Singh, B., and Knutson, J., The grand challenge: Building evolutionary technologies. In *Proceedings of the HICSS93 Conference*, pages 5–8, January 1993.

[Roo68]   Roos, L., and Stark, F., Organizational roles. In Lindzey, G., and Aronson, E. (Eds.), *Handbook of Social Psychology*, 2nd Edition, 1968.

[Saa94]   Saastamoinen, H.T., Markkanen, M.V., Savolainen, V.V., A survey of exceptions in information systems. *University of Colorado Technical Report*, CU-CS-712-94, April 1994.

[Saa95]   Saastamoinen, H.T., *On the Handling of Exceptions in Information Systems*, Ph.D. Thesis Dissertation, University of Jyvaskyla, November 1995.

[Sar91]   Sarin, K. S., Abbott, K. R. and McCarthy, D. R., A process model and system for supporting collaborative work. In *Proceedings ACM COCS'91*, pages 213–224.

[Sh95]   Sheth, A., and Rusinkiewicz, M., Specification and execution of transactional workflows. In W. Kim (Ed.), *Modern Database Systems: The Object Model, Interoperability and Beyond*, pages 592–620. ACM Press, New York, 1995.

[Sir84]   Sirbu, M., Schoichet, S., Kunin, J. S., Hammer, M. and Sutherland, J., OAM: An office analysis methodology. *Behaviour and Information Technology*, 3(1):25–39, 1984.

[Str89]   Strong, D.A. and Miller, S.M., Exception handling and quality control in office operations. *Boston University School of Management Working Paper*, #89-16. Boston, MA, 1989.

[Suc83]   Suchman, L., Office procedure as practical action: Models of work and system design. *ACM Transactions on Office Information Systems*, 1(4):320–328, October 1983.

[Suc87]   Suchman, L., *Plans and Situated Action: The Problem of Human–Machine Communication*. Cambridge University Press, Cambridge, England, 1987.

[Tsi82]   Tsichritzis, D., Forms management. *Communications of the ACM*, 25(7):453–478, July 1982.

[Woo90]   Woo, C., SACT: A tool for automating semi-structured organizational communication. In *Proceedings of ACM COIS'90*, pages 89–98, April 1990.

[Whi94]   White, T. and Fisher, L., *The Workflow Paradigm: The Impact of Information Technology on Business Process Reengineering*. Future Strategies, Inc., Alameda, CA, 1994.

[WMC]   Workflow Management Coalition, *Coalition Overview, Reference Model, and Glossary*. See Internet home page http://www.aiai.ed.ac.uk/WfMC/

[W4]   *The W4 World Wide Web Workflow product features*, 1997. http://www.w4.fr

[Zis77]   Zisman, M. D., *Representation, Specification, and Automation of Office Procedures*. Ph.D. Thesis Dissertation, Wharton School, University of Pennsylvania, 1977.

3

Media Spaces: Environments for Informal Multimedia Interaction

WENDY E. MACKAY
Aarhus University

ABSTRACT

Distributed organizations, with distributed cooperative work, are a fact of life. How can new technologies help? Distributed video is an appealing choice, carrying more contextual information than voice alone and, arguably, better at conveying subtle cues, such as the emotional states. Although new commercial systems are being introduced, they focus primarily on providing new technology. Most are based on relatively simple extensions of two existing models of communication: formal meetings become videoconferences and telephones become videophones. However, research in computer-supported cooperative work has tried to emphasize the user, with models based on Shared Workspaces (to support shared work on a common task), Coordinated Communication (to support structured communication to serve a specified purpose), and Informal Interaction (to support informal, unplanned and unstructured interactions). Although mediaspaces can incorporate all three, they emphasize informal communication, providing people working together at a distance with interactions that they take for granted when they are co-located. This chapter describes some of the pioneering work in media spaces, with more detailed descriptions of our own work at Rank Xerox EuroPARC (RAVE for our own use in the laboratory and WAVE, to support engineers working collaboratively between facilities in England and the Netherlands), concluding with a discussion of the technical, user interface and social issues involved in designing media spaces.

3.1 INTRODUCTION

Telephones, faxes, electronic mail and the World Wide Web have transformed work, enabling people to work together, even when they live in different countries and in different time zones. Yet long-distance projects are still difficult, even when cultural and organizational differences are taken into account. Why? One important reason is the lack of informal social contact that people have when they work in the same physical location [Hea91]. People who are co-located benefit from chance encounters in hallways or chats before and after meetings, resolving problems before they become critical. Working in the same physical environment helps people discover shared interests and develop a sense of community. Implicit knowledge about the state of each other's work can prevent misunderstandings or resentment: If I see that my colleague's report is sitting in her "out" basket, ready to send, I can avoid asking her about it and thus avoid offending her. When people are separated geographically, much of their informal knowledge about each other disappears and communication becomes much more formal. Attempts to address this with additional meetings and reports often serves to exacerbate the situation and emphasizes the differences between groups.

Moran and Anderson [Mor90] identify three fundamental approaches to supporting co-operative work at a distance: Shared Workspaces [Tan90, Min91, Ish92, Ols91a, Ols91b], which emphasize people working cooperatively on a common task, Coordinated Communi-cation [Win89, Ell99], in which people communicate in a structured fashion for some purpose (such as decision-making), and Informal Interaction, in which people engage in unplanned and unstructured interactions. Chapters 4 and 5 in this book [Ish99, Pra99] address shared workspaces and Chapters 1 and 2 [Ehr99, Ell99] address coordinated communication. This chapter is most concerned with informal interaction, providing people working at a distance with the kinds of informal interactions they enjoy when working in close proximity to each other.

The explosion of networked computing through the World Wide Web and the decreasing cost of video technology have made distributed video a popular choice for addressing the problem of providing distributed social context. However, whenever new technology is cre-ated, it usually begins as an imitation of something that already exists. Not surprisingly, then, most commercial distributed video systems are modeled after one of two familiar forms of communication: telephone calls and formal meetings. Videophones are based on the model of a telephone call in which a caller establishes a video and audio link to a second party. When the call is initiated, the phone rings in the other location; if the other person is available, he or she decides whether or not to accept the call and complete the connection. The call continues as long as both parties participate; when one hangs up, the connection is broken. Videoconfer-encing is the other common model, usually involving specially-designed conference rooms. A common arrangement uses one video camera to capture people sitting at a table and a second, overhead camera, to capture documents or slides. Live video images are sent to one or more remote video conference rooms, via telephone or satellite and projected onto wall screens. Often, a separate speaker phone is used to enhance the quality of the voice. Desktop video-conferencing is a low-cost alternative, designed to be used with computers in the office. A small video camera is usually placed on top of the monitor and digitized images are sent to a window on another participant's screen. Some of these systems can handle several video images at once, although the computer monitor quickly runs out of screen space. Audio can be a problem if it is delayed and people often use telephones or speaker phones in addition to the on-line video.

Telephone and conferencing models represent a limited subset of the ways in which video can support distributed cooperative work. The purpose of this chapter is to describe the con-cept of a media space, which attempts to extend distributed video to include a variety of forms of communication, ranging from informal encounters and peripheral awareness to focused, formal meetings. The difference between media spaces and most commercial distributed video systems has little to do with technology and everything to do with the way in which the technology is embedded into the social environment. Understanding these social issues is essential for understanding how to design and introduce effective media spaces. As Moran and Anderson [Mor90] explain in their description of EuroPARC's RAVE media space:

> "EuroPARC's concern is not simply with artifacts and their enabling technologies, but with understanding the processes and relationships which such artifacts support, including the processes by which they are designed. The discipline of design must involve a constant movement back and forth between the design and use of technologies and reflection upon those activities."

3.2   EARLY MEDIA SPACES

The idea of a videophone has been around for a long time. In the early 1960s, AT&T demonstrated a prototype "PicturePhone" at the Seattle World's Fair, which allowed callers to view each other on small video monitors, set up in expanded telephone booths. The set-up optimized lighting conditions and video camera position to simulate face-to-face contact. (Note that callers could not actually call someone they knew; they had to wait for a stranger at another PicturePhone booth to arrive before having a conversation.) Although touted to be the phone of the future, it never really caught on and was ultimately deemed a failure [Nol92]. Another interesting experiment was the Hole-In-Space by video artists Galloway and Rabinowitz [Gal80]. They created a real-time video/audio connection between two sites in Los Angeles and New York. Pedestrians walking by could see full-size images of people walking in the corresponding location 3000 miles away. People not only stopped and stared, but often would respond to the remote conversation and begin talking to the passersby at the other end.

The term "Media Space" was coined by Stults and his colleagues at Xerox PARC [Stu86], who developed what was probably the first real media space. The cost of video had begun to drop in the 1980s, making it possible to link a laboratory in Palo Alto, California with a related laboratory in Portland, Oregon. Stults defined a media space as:

> "An electronic setting in which groups of people can work together, even when they are not resident in the same place or present at the same time. In a media space, people can create real-time visual and acoustic environments that span physically separate areas. They can also control the recording, accessing and replaying of images and sounds from those environments."

The Xerox Media Space was originally designed to model the informal types of communication that occur in hallways and in common areas, re-establishing the possibility of informal communication for people located apart from each other. The goal was to create a technology-supported analog to the mailroom or cafeteria; places where people naturally congregate informally and chat, with one conversation leading into another. An important aspect of this media space was that the connections were always there: only the people came and went. Conversations or meetings did not have a formal start or stop; they simply represented ongoing interactions among people. Subsequent media space research has emphasized the role of informal interaction as its key goal, although many have been extended to include facilities for shared workspaces and coordinated communication.

The period of the late 1980s and early 1990s was an active period in media space research. Several laboratories embarked on major long-term projects in which members of the laboratories both developed and lived in their media spaces. Although they share a number of characteristics, each media space was clearly shaped by the particular social and physical environments in which they were established and reflect different research goals. Some of the groups collaborated closely, with researchers moving back and forth between laboratories. In particular, Xerox PARC, EuroPARC, University of Toronto and Université de Paris-Sud shared researchers, software and numerous design discussions.

Bly et al [Bly93] describe their experiences with the Xerox PARC Media Space, including the three-year experiment linking their laboratory with Portland and the on-going evolution of the Media Space even after the Portland laboratory was closed. In the beginning, they used physical buttons to establish or replace video connections. Lab members experimented with different configurations and handled privacy in a very mechanical way, by turning off the microphone or turning the video camera towards the wall. They examined how their own social and work relationships changed as they used the Media Space and highlighted the need for additional research in user tailorability of the interface and support for managing privacy issues [Ols91b]. Over time, the Media Space was expanded from four offices, several public areas and the link to Portland, to include multiple offices in both sites and a variety of video devices attached to the network. This pioneering work at Xerox PARC influenced the development of the next major media space, created at PARC's sister lab in England, EuroPARC.

3.3   RAVE: EUROPARC'S MEDIA SPACE

Rank Xerox EuroPARC was founded in 1987 as a laboratory of Xerox PARC, located in Cambridge, England. The building, Ravenscroft House, has 27 rooms with five open areas spread over four floors. Each floor has two "pods" separated by a central stairwell, which causes a surprising degree of isolation among lab members. The layout of the lab simulates some of the problems people face when they must work together, but are physically separated. The lab decided to encourage cooperative work and foster social interaction by offering lab members ubiquitous audio, video and data interconnectivity within the building [Bux90]. The small size of the laboratory (approximately 30 staff and researchers) made it possible for everyone to have a media space node: everyone lived and worked in both the physical space and the media space. This global participation enabled EuroPARC to explore a variety of social as well as user interface and technical issues and provided insights into how to provide similar levels of social contact for people working together but at a distance.

RAVE (the Ravenscroft Audio Visual Environment) was not designed to replace face-to-face communication but rather to support work and social interactions, ranging from informal casual encounters to formal planned cooperative tasks [Gav92b]. RAVE was built with off-the-shelf analog audio and video technology, using several kilometers of coaxial cable to connect all analog devices to a computer-controlled 64×64 analog switch. This approach provided very high- quality video images and stereo sound; but was limited to a single building (extending it further would have been prohibitively expensive) and required a major recabling effort whenever nodes were moved. Figure 3.1 shows the basic set-up of EuroPARC's RAVE media space.

Each office and many of the common areas were equipped with media space "nodes" with a PAL video camera, a monitor, a microphone, a mixer to handle multiple audio inputs, stereo speakers and an optional foot pedal for controlling audio (Figure 3.2). Audio and video connections were managed from client applications running on either LISP machines or, later,

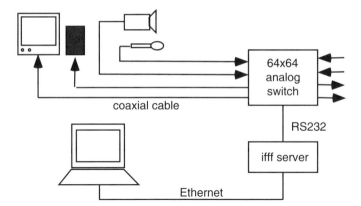

Figure 3.1   The RAVE media space consists of individual nodes connected via coaxial cable to a computer-controlled analog switch

Figure 3.2   A typical configuration for an analog media space node, with a video camera, microphone, video monitor and workstation

Unix workstations. Users had complete control over the position of the equipment, including location of cameras and microphones. They could turn equipment on or off, either electronically or physically (e.g. putting on a lens cap or unplugging it). Some nodes were equipped with additional video picture-in-picture (PIP) hardware, which permits simultaneous connections with up to four video sources on the same monitor. Connections to remote media spaces were created by connecting digital codecs to the analog switch via ISDN lines.

The *iiif* server [Bux90], running on Unix, controlled the analog switch and managed audio and video connections among media space nodes, as requested by client applications. In addition to allowing easy point-to-point connections within the building, *iiif* also guaranteed privacy and security. Different versions of the *iiif* server were used to set up media spaces at Xerox PARC, the University of Toronto and the Université de Paris-Sud, with individualized client applications designed according to the technical and social needs at each location.

Figure 3.3 Lab members can glance at each other or maintain long-term connections, such as this one between two administrative staff members

3.3.1   The RAVE User Interface

The RAVE user interface enabled users to display views from different video cameras located around the building and, if given permission, set up a two-way audio-video connection with any other node connected to the analog switch. Figure 3.3 shows one of the longest-running connections, between the reception desk on the first floor and the personal assistant to the director on the top floor. They established a permanent "Office Share", with continuously-available video of the other person. Audio connections were made only when a foot pedal was pressed, to increase privacy. When the participants wanted to glance at others in the building or make other video connections, they did so directly and then returned to the default Office Share. Other members of the lab came to rely on their Office Share connection, using it to talk to each other and avoid running up and down the stairs. The effect was of a permanent "hole-in-space", changing everyone's psychological perception of the physical layout of the lab.

The user interface to RAVE evolved over the years, as users requested new functionality and when the entire lab shifted from a LISP-machine-based to a Unix-based environment. The original RAVE interface was based on user-tailorable on-screen buttons that accessed different functionality. Tailorability was particularly important, allowing users to explore different kinds of connectivity and express individual differences, ensuring everyone a choice in how they were represented within the media space.

The Buttons interface grew out of research at Xerox PARC [Hen86] and EuroPARC [Mac90]. Instead of typing commands or selecting from a menu, users could interact with an on-screen graphical object that ran relevant commands. They could look inside the button and tailor its functionality, as well as change its appearance, copy or even e-mail it to other users. Since buttons could be parameterized, users could change application specific variables and edit the encapsulated code. This flexibility allowed lab members to explore the RAVE media space and develop the services that were most useful to them. The earliest buttons provided relatively low-level functionality, such as making or breaking a specific connection. Over

Figure 3.4   RAVE buttons provide users with services that reflect varying degrees of engagement

time, buttons evolved higher-level functions, providing encapsulated services, with built-in assumptions about handling issues such as privacy.

One of the most interesting features of RAVE is the ability to shift easily from peripheral to focused views. The five buttons shown in Figure 3.4 offer different levels of interaction based on the level of engagement required: from *Background* views operating at the periphery of attention, to the unobtrusive presence of a *Sweep* through the building or an informal *Glance*, to the shared awareness enjoyed by participants in an *Office Share*, to the full engagement of a *Vphone* conversation.

Vphone: A highly-focused form of interaction with two-way audio and video connections. Like telephone calls, one party must explicitly initiate the call and the other must explicitly accept the connection. The call ends when one party hangs up. Participants used this when they wanted to discuss a specific topic.

Office Share: The physical connection is technically identical to a Vphone call; the difference is that the participants decide on the connection in advance, after which they do not explicitly initiate or terminate individual calls. Participants choose whether or not to include permanent audio as well as video connections. Office Shares facilitated a range of communication, from passive awareness to highly-focused interaction. Long-term Office Share users, with connections lasting for months or even years, claimed it was like sharing a physical office without many of the annoyances.

Glance: A brief (three-second) one-way video connection to another node. The person being glanced at first hears an audio cue (or the name of the person), then the connection is established, after which another audio clue indicates that the Glance is complete. Lab members define in advance who has permission to glance at them. Glances provided a quick and unobtrusive method of determining whether or not someone was around or currently busy, similar to glancing into someone's physical office.

Sweep: A brief (one-second) one-way view of a series of pre-authorized nodes, local or distant. Users could customize their sweep patterns to include the most useful public (and, if authorized, private) nodes, in order to find out who was around and generally what was going on in the lab.

Background: A long-term view of a particular location that acts as the default view of the media space. Technically, Background is indistinguishable from an Office Share. However, most Background connections are of public areas that do not require specific permission, unlike the pre-arranged connections to a particular office. Although the view from the roof was popular with people in windowless offices; the most popular Background was the EuroPARC

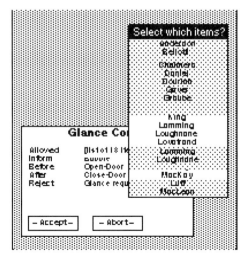

Figure 3.5   Users can select who has the right to glance at them through the RAVE media space

commons. Since everyone in the lab visited the commons regularly to check mail or get a cup of coffee, it provided everyone with a low-level consciousness of who was in the building and when informal gatherings (such as afternoon tea) had started.

Godard [Dou91a] defined and controlled these and other services, directing all connections made by the *iiif* server. Based on preferences expressed by users (such as who had permission to glance at them), Godard would determine whether or not to perform specific requests for services, requesting additional input when necessary. Before performing an authorized connection, Godard would record the previous connection (such as an Office Share or Vphone call), ensuring that the user would return to the correct state after the service was performed.

One of the primary benefits of this architecture is that participants can interact with RAVE in terms of high-level services rather than low-level physical connections. Each service includes a representation of the user's intentions and makes it possible to embed information used to protect privacy. Participants can decide in advance who has the right to perform each service, as opposed to making on-going decisions about low-level connections, which helps to balance the tradeoff between privacy and access. Figure 3.5 shows an example of a service control panel. In this case, the user looks at a list of lab members and indicates those who have the right to establish a Glance connection.

In practice, the default settings of such lists are very important. If the default is that everyone has the right to glance unless explicitly deleted from the list, a refused Glance request can be taken as an explicit, personal rejection. However, if the default is that no one has the right to glance unless specifically added to the list (as at EuroPARC), then refused Glance requests may simply indicate a non-updated Glance list, which is less likely to be viewed as an insult. This poses particular problems for new members of the lab. Since people rarely update their Glance lists, even during project and group changes, newcomers will find themselves unable to glance at many of their colleagues and feel excluded from the media space. The result is that long-term members may have much greater access to the media space than newer members, often without realizing it. Seemingly-innocuous decisions about default settings may have long-term effects on the ultimate acceptance of a media space within an organization.

3.3.2   Notification with Auditory Cues

Lab members not only wanted control over the types of connections they made, but also wanted feedback about when and what kinds of connections were in use. Because Godard had some understanding of the participants' intentions, it could not only distinguish among physically identical connections such as Vphone, Office Share and Background, but it could also determine and deliver the appropriate feedback. Users could request a variety of notification types, such as presenting a message on their workstations. However, the most popular notifications were more subtle. Gaver's work on auditory icons [Gav86] and the affordances of audio [Gav91b] was incorporated into RAVE, providing real-world auditory cues that indicated what was going on. For example, when someone glanced at another person, Godard triggered a sound (the default was that of a door opening) as the connection was being made. Three seconds later, when the Glance was terminated, another sound was triggered (usually a door closing). Other sounds were associated with other kinds of connections, indicating the corresponding intent. A knock or telephone ring signaled a Vphone, footsteps indicated a sweep and a camera whir flagged when a single-frame snapshot had been taken. Gaver [Gav92a] explains why real-world sounds are particularly effective:

- Sound indicates the connection state without requiring symmetry; providing information without being intrusive.
- Sounds do not require the kind of spatial attention that a written notification would.
- Non-speech audio cues often seem less distracting and more efficient than speech or music (although speech can provide different sorts of information, e.g., who is connecting).
- Sounds can be acoustically shaped to reduce annoyance [Pat89]. Most sounds involve a gradual increase in loudness to avoid startling listeners.
- Finally, caricatures of naturally-occurring sounds are an intuitive way to present information. The sound of an opening and closing door reflects and reinforces the metaphor of a glance and is thus easily learned and remembered.

A number of other researchers have explored the role of audio in distributed collaborative work and media space settings. Researchers at PARC [Mor97] and MIT [Kob97] explored the problem of browsing for audio data. Seligmann et al [Sel95] examined the cues that people use to understand ordinary telephone calls and then looked at the more complex information needs required in multi-party, multimedia conversations. They found that needs for "assurance" became more complex and that users needed information about connectivity, presence, focus and ways of distinguishing between real and virtual activities.

Godard, with auditory cues, provided control, feedback and intentionality, three prerequisites for privacy, at very little cost in terms of intrusiveness. Godard used a system called Khronika [Lov91] to handle auditory events. Khronika is an "event notification service" that supports selective awareness of planned and electronic events, announcing when a video connection has been made, reminding people about upcoming meetings, providing information about visitors and even gathering people to go to the pub.

Khronika was based on three fundamental entities: *events, daemons and notifications*, as shown in Figure 3.6. Events were organized within a class hierarchy, each with a class, start time and duration. Specific events included meetings, visitors, arriving e-mail and RAVE Glances. Events could also be manipulated as more abstract classes, such as "professional", "electronic" and "entertainment". Event daemons produced notification events when they detected specified event types. Users could constrain daemons, enabling them to select only the

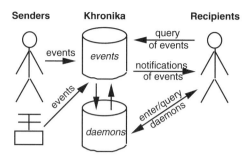

Figure 3.6 Khronika maintains an event database entered both by people and on-line systems. Daemons watch for specified events and post notifications when they are detected

events they wished to hear about. For example, a user could create a daemon to look for all EuroCODE project meetings in the conference room and generate a notification five minutes prior to the meeting. Users could also specify different notifications, such as an e-mail message a day prior to an important meeting, with a pop-up screen message an hour before and a synthesized speech message five minutes before the start time.

General-purpose non-speech audio cues were also popular. For example, the sound indicating the start of a meeting began with sound of people murmuring at low-volume, followed by a gavel sound to indicate the precise start time. Such sounds provided low-level peripheral awareness of events, enabling people to shift their attention to them when necessary and ignore them otherwise. Gaver et al [Gav91a] found that non-speech audio feedback changed both participants perception of the system and their tendency to collaborate while using it.

A button interface to Khronika let users browse the event database as well as create new events and daemons. Another interface, *xkhbrowser*, showed a calendar with events spanning different periods of time. Events could be displayed according to their level of specificity, enabling users to quickly view the kinds of events they were interested in. We compared the use of two EuroPARC calendar systems [Dou93]: Khronika's and the paper-based system managed by the administrative staff. We discovered that even though the information was ostensibly identical, users were influenced by their knowledge of the source of the information, with correspondingly different levels of trust in different kinds of information. If there was a conflict between the two systems, users would try to determine which calendar system was more likely to be accurate, given the particular piece of information. (For example, the person in charge of the brown bag lunch seminar series was known to input the events into Khronika, so users tended to believe the Khronika-based information. In contrast, the administrative staff would track people's travel schedules, thus the paper-based calendar was assumed to be more accurate for that kind of information.) Thus the social context played as important a role as technological functionality in determining how users interacted with each system.

3.3.3 Long-Distance Awareness

EuroPARC maintained a close association with her sister laboratory in the United States, Xerox PARC. Maintaining live video connections was too expensive, so members of the lab investigated different ways of linking the two media spaces.

Polyscope [Bor91] distributed low-resolution (200×150 bits) digitized images captured approximately every five minutes from each media space (assuming the owner had given

Figure 3.7 Portholes presents a collection of recently-captured still images from the media spaces at EuroPARC and Xerox PARC

permission). A simple animation facility looped several images in sequence, to provide a jerky, but usually effective, sense of motion and a way to disambiguate scenes. The button interface allowed users to select an image and immediately establish a Glance or Vphone connection.

Portholes [Dou91b] was developed to help lab members stay in touch by sharing more-frequently captured still images from the respective media spaces (Figure 3.7).

Both Polyscope and Portholes allowed multiple nodes from several remote locations to be presented simultaneously, providing passive awareness of distributed workgroups without making explicit video connections. They offered spatially-distributed but asynchronous functionality, which complemented the synchronous but single-channeled video services from each media space.

3.3.4   Observations of Use

Users define the social protocols surrounding the use of their electronic communications. For example, people try to avoid annoying each other. In the early days of electronic mail, outsiders were surprised that people working physically next to each other would still send each other electronic mail. This was not due to a preference for technology-based rather than human-based communication; it was simply a matter of courtesy. Calling over the wall or telephoning is an interruption, whereas sending e-mail allows the recipient to respond at their convenience.

Similar social protocols developed in response to the media space. Over time, media space users began to change it, creating uses not originally anticipated by the system's creators. Subtle characteristics in the technology suggested new uses or resulted in changes in how the system came to be understood [Suc91]. An interesting example was the use of the RAVE media space for "projecting" presence, taking advantage of the knowledge that members of the lab had a shared peripheral awareness of the EuroPARC commons. People usually waited until a critical mass of people had assembled in the commons before appearing in person. People thus showed up in two waves: the first few arrived. When three or four were there, suddenly everyone else appeared. People took advantage of their ability to work until the last minute (and avoided "wasting time") and were still assured of arriving when the meeting actually started.

Sitting in the commons, in view of the camera, is a way for a researcher to broadcast his or her availability, letting colleagues know that it is acceptable to come up and chat. For example, I had about an hour before I needed to catch a plane and five people I needed to talk to before I left. I decided to sit in the commons and found that, one-by-one, all five came to talk. Each person monitored my meetings on their monitors and came up when they could see I was ready to talk to someone else. Everyone coordinated their activities, managing to find appropriate times to meet, without wasting their time waiting for me or wasting my time waiting for them [Mac92].

Interestingly, when members of the administrative staff sat in the commons, their message was the opposite. They were on a break and it was not acceptable to ask them to do something (although it was fine to have a chat). The commons had an explicitly "video free" section, so that people who wanted to avoid being seen could do so easily and naturally. The overall effect was that of having the common area right outside one's door, but without the noise. Whenever the link to the commons broke down, such as when the equipment was being upgraded or there was work on the building, members of the lab reported the sense of being slightly disoriented and feeling out of touch.

Sharing the same physical office with someone can be annoying, especially if you have different tastes in music or are prone to talking all the time. Office Shares, particularly for people who worked late at night, proved to be extremely comforting. Without listening to each other, we could still sense each other's presence (and when the other person was ready for a break). To a somewhat lesser extent, the Portholes connection to PARC provided a similar sense of comfort, since someone was always there no matter how late the EuroPARC crowd worked (given the nine-hour time change from England to California).

Heath and Luff [Hea91] observed lab members using long-term RAVE connections and found that video sometimes undermined the effectiveness of subtle communicative gestures. For example, since the camera and monitor are offset, a person looking at the monitor will appear to be looking down slightly when displayed on the other monitor. Experienced media space users learned to shift their gaze back and forth between the "natural" view for them (i.e. looking at the person on the monitor) and the "effective" view (i.e. creating the appearance of eye-contact by looking directly into the camera). Visitors entering an office with an Office Share would sometimes be confused, thinking the person on the other end of the media space connection was looking at them when they were in fact looking elsewhere.

Gaver et al [Gav93] examined the effect of giving users a choice among four different views, rather than the usual single-camera, face-to-face view. The additional views included an "in context" view, showing people and objects in relationship to their workspace, a "desk view", using a high-resolution monochrome camera to view documents and either a "dollhouse" view specific to the experimental task, or a "birds-eye" view showing most of the room. They found that face-to-face views were rarely used when people were actively involved in a collaborative task; the exception was when participants engaged in negotiation about task strategy. This study suggests that the camera setup for media spaces should change when users want to engage in collaborative tasks.

3.4   OTHER MAJOR MEDIA SPACES

Several other media spaces were developed in the same time frame as RAVE. The US West Advanced Technologies Telecollaboration project [Bul89] was similar to the PARC/Portland link, supporting a small group of people sharing several projects who were located in Denver and Boulder, Colorado. The media space included several offices, a conference room and public areas at both sites. Users could "call" to get a private office-to-office audio/visual connection, "look around" to get a video-only connection, and "videoconference" to support multiple participants in the conference rooms. Public areas were continuously connected, as at PARC.

BellCORE was also very active in media space research at this time, creating Cruiser [Roo88] and the VideoWindow [Fis90], both controlled by a system called Rendezvous [Hil94]. In contrast to the Xerox PARC approach, which emphasized letting the users evolve the characteristics of the media space, BellCORE researchers followed a theoretical approach, focusing on the role of informal communication [Kra88, Fis93]. Cruiser was based on the model of walking down a hallway and glancing into open offices to see who was there. All connections were reciprocal, in that the person doing the glancing was always seen by the person being glanced at. Participants could control the access to their images and could also establish two-way connections in the course of a "cruise". Cruiser was designed to encourage spontaneous, informal communication, but often resulted in longer-term Office Share. Cooperstock [Coo92] reports on the iterative design of Cruiser, describing how users and designers influenced the design of the system over four iterations.

VideoWindow was more similar to the PARC/Portland Media Space link, with two large-screen displays located in two public areas on different floors of the research building. The link was available continuously for three months and was designed to support informal communication among the 50 researchers and staff in the area. People would arrive to get their mail or have a cup of coffee and engage in conversation with the people physically present as well as the people located at a distance.

The Montage system from SunSoft [Isa93] explored how to use video to help members of distributed groups develop a sense of "teleproximity", helping collaborators find opportune times to interact with each other by using reciprocal glances to "peek into someone's office". The system also provided access to an on-line calendar, e-mail and on-screen note facility. As with Cruiser, video connections appeared in a small window on the computer screen, rather than on a separate monitor. Researchers found that most glances did not result in interactive communication [Tan94]. Issacs [Isa95] reports on their experiences using video in a broadcast setting, as opposed to in a smaller forum with a local audience. They found that the audiences preferred watching the multimedia presentations by speakers in the broadcast setting, while the speakers themselves preferred the intimacy of local talks.

The University of Toronto engaged in two major media space projects, in collaboration with researchers at Xerox PARC and EuroPARC. CAVECAT [Man91, Gal91] was implemented with software from EuroPARC's RAVE system and supported approximately ten offices within a single building. In addition to the media space features from RAVE, researchers explored the problem of integrating shared drawing facilities with shared presence [Pos92]. Sellen [Sel92a] studied the speech patterns in video-mediated conversations. She

Figure 3.8 Hydra incorporates a video camera, monitor and directional microphone into a small table-top unit that can act as a proxy for distant participants of a meeting

compared same-room and video-mediated conversations, using two interfaces, including a system called Hydra [Sel92b]. Figure 3.8 shows three Hydra units, each with a small video camera, monitor and directional microphone, which act as proxies for distant meeting participants. Real and video-mediated participants could react to each other as they would if all were co-present in the same room. Sellen found quantitative differences between face-to-face conversations and the two video-mediated interfaces. Although there were no significant quantitative differences between the two video-mediated interfaces, there were significant qualitative differences, with users preferring the Hydra interface. Olson and Olson [Ols95] studied the role of adding video to remote-collaborations. They found that users of audio-only connections had more difficulty communicating but that there were no basic differences between the quality of work performed in face-to-face settings and in settings with both high-quality audio and high-quality video.

The University of Toronto's follow-on project, called Telepresence, experimented with media spaces outside of a laboratory setting and included studies of the ways in which media spaces changed the social relationships among people working at a distance [Har94]. Both Toronto media spaces used an icon of a door, displayed in various states to indicate the user's level of accessibility (Figure 3.9). A fully-open door indicated that anyone could make a full two-way audio/video connection, whereas a door ajar enabled people to glance, but required a ring or further interaction from the user in order to make a full two-way audio/video connection. When the door was shut, glances were not authorized and further interaction was required to establish a two-way audio/video connection. When the door was locked, no video connections were possible. Yamaashi et al [Yam96] describe another extension in which users were given two views: a wide-angle view to show the context of the office and a more detailed shot linked seamlessly together. They also explored the use of sensors placed in the physical environment to provide contextual cues to remote users of the media space. For example, the state of the physical door to the office (i.e. open, ajar, closed or locked) controlled the state of the on-screen door icon.

A later Xerox PARC media space, called Kasmer [Bly93], was created to support a much

Figure 3.9 The original doors interface allowed users to select from four different door states: open, ajar, closed and locked

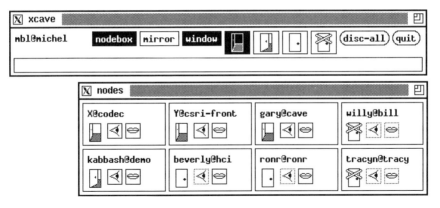

Figure 3.10 The interface to the Kasmer media space. The upper control panel allows users to select services. The lower display panel shows other users and their current level of accessibility

larger group of people in different groups within the laboratory, as well as offering codec links to external sites (Figure 3.10) . The underlying software was borrowed from CAVECAT, University of Toronto's system, and RAVE, from EuroPARC. The system was designed to balance frequent, easy communication within groups, while also providing less frequent communication to distant or external groups. Each working group included 10–25 participants and media space nodes; each with their own social conventions and models of use. Adler and Henderson [Adl94] describe their experiences with a 9-month Office Share connection within this environment. Mynatt et al [Myn97] explore the differences between on-line and physical space, arguing that media spaces reinterpret physical space through the positioning of audio and video elements and argue that activities derived from one space do not translate well into other spaces.

Another extension of the media space work is on-going at the Université de Paris-Sud, based on work the authors did at EuroPARC, PARC and University of Toronto. Mediascape

Figure 3.11   The Mediascape media space, with the standard user interface (left) and an electronic Post-It note (right)

[Rou98] was originally built with the *iiif* server, but has since been reimplemented with a set of custom HTTP servers, enabling users to embed access to the media space into any document on the World Wide Web. Unlike the numerous "webcams" that have appeared, which show a single view from a fixed camera, Mediascape is a full media space, with facilities for managing connections among multiple sites, notifying users and controlling access. The user interface is highly customizable since it is a plain HTML document. The standard interface is shown in Figure 3.11 (left). Images are updated every few minutes as in Portholes. Passing the cursor over an image initiates a Glance. A double-click establishes a Vphone connection, according to both users' expressed availability. Mediascape uses the same door metaphor as CAVECAT. In the figure, one user has locked his door (bottom left) and another has left his door ajar (bottom right). Additional services include Post-It, to leave a message on someone's computer screen, Grab, to grab a still image from the media space, and Dvideo to send pre-recorded or live digitized video. Electronic Post-It notes are implemented by remotely controlling the recipient's Web browser (in this case Netscape Navigator). The image in the note has the same capabilities as in the interface: it updates every few minutes and can be used to establish other media space connections.

3.4.1   Building Upon the RAVE Media Space

The RAVE media space provided an infrastructure for other research projects as well. As part of a European ESPRIT project, called EuroCODE [Mac95a, Mac98], we were responsible for designing a multimedia communication system for engineers building a bridge across Denmark's Great Belt (Storebaelt) Waterway. This project developed a radically-different interface to the media space: a paper engineering drawing. We developed Ariel (Figure 3.12) which detects individual engineering drawings via their barcodes. In the prototype shown, the drawing was placed over a large (A0 size) graphics tablet. A projector on the ceiling projected menus and other computer-generated information, including media space images, onto the paper. Here, the user is establishing a Glance connection with the author of the drawing, in order to discuss possible changes. The user could also associate any audio, video or text information with any part of the drawing and capture handwritten notes which could be sent to colleagues.

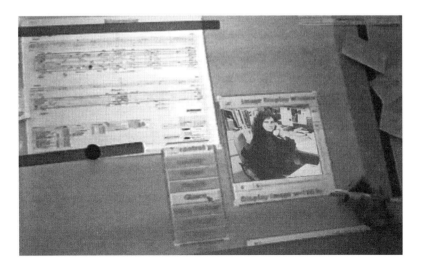

Figure 3.12 Ariel lets construction engineers access the media space and a hypermedia annotation system via paper engineering drawings. The user selects the media space option from the control section of the paper engineering drawing (upper left). Ariel projects a menu and the user selects Glance with the graphics tablet pen, which establishes a three-second connection

3.5 WAVE: A DETAILED CASE STUDY

WAVE [Pag93] was an attempt to test the media space concepts learned from RAVE in a real-world setting: a distributed product development organization within a large multinational corporation. WAVE differed in several important respects from the RAVE media space. RAVE existed within a single building and was designed to encourage communication among people who had other forms of informal and formal communication available to them. WAVE was more similar to the original PARC Media Space and Portholes, in that the participants were distributed in both space and time. (However, Portholes had to span eight, sometimes nine, time zones, whereas WAVE involved a one-hour difference between England and the Netherlands.)

RAVE was able to take advantage of point-to-point analog video connections, with an analog video switch and kilometers of coaxial cable, to provide high-quality images and sound with no delay. Portholes was restricted to still images displayed on a computer screen, with occasional dial-up links with a low-resolution video link and a rather annoying audio delay. The distances between the WAVE sites caused us to consider different technical solutions for distributing video, which had a corresponding impact on the user interface and social use of the media spaces. One research goal was to find out the acceptable thresholds for video quality under various media space conditions, given the bandwidth and cost constraints of international long-distance links. Another critical difference from RAVE and Portholes was that the participants were not researchers, but engineers creating a product. For them, the media space was like a telephone or fax, a technology to be used only if it supported the work at hand.

We studied an engineering design center in England, which took designs created in Japan or the United States and localized them for the European market. The organization was subject to the typical pressures of any high-tech company in a highly innovative, competitive and turbulent market: They had to increase customer satisfaction, maintain a technological edge and improve quality while decreasing costs. Product development had to reduce time-to-market, streamline processes, adapt to rapid technological change, while making efficient use of resources.

The organization had a sophisticated telecommunications infrastructure: a corporate telephone system based on leased lines (users need only dial an extension to reach other sites); voice conference calls; answering machines; beepers; electronic mail; fax; and sophisticated (and expensive) satellite videoconference facilities. All engineers and administrative staff had either a workstation or a computer terminal on their desks. Yet, in spite of this infrastructure, engineers spent a great deal of their time traveling; travel accounted for over 10% of the product development budget. At the time of our study, the travel budget was being cut and managers were interested in finding ways to reduce the need for face-to-face meetings. We met with the director of the division and interviewed all of his senior managers and many of their staff, who often took us on tours of their work areas after the interview. Interviews were generally open-ended, although each began with a set of standard questions, including the person's role in the organization, a description of his or her work (either a project or a function), as well as any communication breakdowns and strategies for addressing them. We also attended regularly-scheduled live and video-mediated meetings [Pag93].

We chose a major product development project in a critical stage within its two-year life cycle. The product was designed in England and was being assembled in a factory in the Netherlands, requiring complex communication and coordination between the two sites. The English engineers understood the product design, whereas the Dutch engineers understood the manufacturing problems and maintained the relations with the local suppliers. We identified two situations with serious coordination and communication needs: cooperation between design and manufacturing engineers and configuration management. After further analysis of their work patterns, we installed two media space connections: a dial-up video phone between the desktop of an engineer in England and the shop floor of the factory in the Netherlands, and an Office Share between the desktops of two people sharing administrative tasks across the two sites.

3.5.1   Analyzing the Existing Videoconference System

Early forecasts of the success of videoconferencing and video telephony were wildly optimistic. Egido [Egi88], in her analysis of why videoconferencing systems fail, cites an early 1970s prediction that a full 85% of meetings would be conducted by videoconferences by the end of the decade. Yet, videoconferencing has been slow to be accepted, despite major financial investments by corporations. Because people easily equate media spaces with videoconferencing, we were interested in how the people in the organization we studied felt about their existing satellite-based videoconferencing system.

Each site (in Europe and the United States) had a special meeting room set up to accommodate six people at a table, with two video cameras to capture each group of three. A ceiling-mounted camera was used to transmit images of objects or documents. Images of colleagues at remote sites were projected on two large video monitors opposite the table, with images of documents presented on a third monitor in the middle. One user likened it to being on a television quiz show, with opposing teams lined up, facing each other.

The videoconference room was designed for highly-stressful project checkpoint meetings, which had priority over everything else. Others could schedule meetings when the room was not already booked, usually to address critical problems that arose. Such meetings generally involved technical people who made use of the ceiling cameras to discuss design documents. (They had no facilities for bringing hardware prototypes into the meeting room, nor did they have facilities for sharing electronic documents.)

Like Egido, we found mixed, mostly negative reactions to the videoconferencing system. High-status managers were most likely to find it useful: they controlled the meetings and appreciated the reduction in travel costs. For example, during a period in which cross-Atlantic travel was eliminated, one manager said "It really came into its own during the Gulf war; [its] use has really increased since then." Another found it "good for sharing problems and project status; [although not] for general information exchange".

Interestingly, most others found it to be divisive, increasing the adversarial nature of the relationship among the participants. These users were individual contributors who used the system to negotiate issues and solve problems. Several people described their concerns as follows: "There is lots of friction. If people [already] have positions, being able to see them doesn't help to bridge the gap. You see a panel of people; it's a stand-off situation. It encourages antagonism" and it "is not good for problem solving ... you react differently to body language on it versus face-to-face. The etiquette changes." One person described his weekly Friday meetings: "It would end the week horribly ... it was pretty bloody. Emotions fly across the airwaves."

In summary, most people viewed face-to-face meetings as the optimal form of communication. Telephones were useful, but only for certain kinds of communication. The video conference system was viewed as useful by upper-level management, but created adversarial relationships among the participants. We were interested in whether or not a media space, with its emphasis on informal interaction, would provide better communication and reduce the adversarial quality of the interactions found with the videoconference system.

3.5.2   Design Center – Shop Floor Link

Since stopping the production line was very expensive, the engineers had a basic rule of thumb: if a problem arose that they did not think could be solved with telephone or fax in less than four hours, the design engineer got on a plane and flew to the Netherlands. The media space was seen as a way to reduce the latter.

One end of the link was on the desktop of a system integration engineer in England, responsible for ensuring that all sub-systems worked together. He knew most of the designers on the project and could quickly contact the appropriate person whenever a problem arose on the shop floor. The other end of the link was the shop floor itself. We installed equipment on a cart which could be moved to any part of the manufacturing line. We used two codecs, based on the H.272 standard (designed for desktop videoconferencing using public ISDN networks), connected by a 64 Kb/s data line (Figure 3.13). The codec in England was connected to an ISDN telephone via an X.21 interface; the ISDN telephone was used for dialing and for displaying line status messages. Unfortunately, the Netherlands did not have ISDN available at the time, so we used a switched 64 Kb/s IDN line. This made the set-up on the Dutch side a bit more complicated. We connected a 64 Kb/s modem to an X.21 controller, which was connected to the codec and to a VT100 terminal. In order to dial and disconnect the line, the Dutch users had to type several commands on the VT100 terminal.

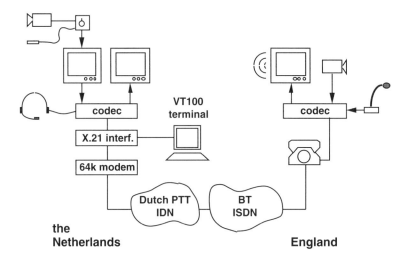

Figure 3.13   WAVE link between the design center in England and the factory in the Netherlands

Figure 3.14   Image captured from the WAVE link. Note the use of the small hand-held camera to show a close-up view of the problem

In England, we installed a single camera, a monitor with built-in speakers and a directional microphone. We also installed a videotape recorder to capture video from the Netherlands and audio in both directions. On the Dutch side, we installed two cameras: a standard-sized camera was clamped to the cart to provide an overview, and a miniature camera (1cm×5cm) with a flexible cable to show small details (i.e. 2mm size type). We also installed two monitors, for incoming and outgoing video. Since there was a great deal of background noise on the shop floor, we provided headphones with a built-in microphone.

The link on the shop floor was up for two weeks; during this period, we spent two days at each site sitting next to the equipment and observing what users did. For the remaining time, we collected videotapes of the video and audio going through the link and later interviewed the people who used the link (Figure 3.14). Users complained about the poor audio quality, poor video resolution and the lack of reliability. Yet they were elated when they were able to solve problems without traveling. As one manager said, "This technology is a pain ...However yesterday we used it and it saved us a trip, therefore I will let my people spend more time on it. I would rather have this lousy link than nothing. There are many things here which are not perfect that we have to cope with, this will be another one." The following examples show how they used the system:

Show a problem: A manufacturing engineer shows something going wrong on the production line and asks designers for explanations, solutions, or changes. Video is very important, not only to improve communication, but also to overcome the initial skepticism and mistrust. Looking at the problem together and jointly working on the solution helps to overcome cultural differences (not only between Dutch and English, but also between manufacturing and design roles), fostering a cooperative attitude towards solving the problem and "getting things done", rather than arguing an abstract problem over the phone to "pass the ball".

For example, following a part change, the packaging also had to be changed, making a new cut into the cardboard and assembling the pieces so they would fit together. A packaging engineer was able to use the video link to show, step-by-step, how to make the cut and assemble the pieces, while the Dutch engineers repeated each step. In half an hour, a problem which would have required a trip was solved. The engineers were enthusiastic about the video link, saying that it had been particularly useful to do each step of the assembly at both sites, watching each other's actions.

Show a solution: A design engineer demonstrates the correct way of doing something on the shop floor. The video link allows the engineers to go through each step of the process, performing it simultaneously at both sites to ensure that everyone understands the solution and its consequences. The video link is much faster and more direct; allowing participants at both sites to see the solution, which increases confidence in the solution and trust between the two sites.

For example, a manufacturing engineer showed a programmer in England a software bug by pointing the camera at the display and keyboard of the product so that the programmer could see what was going wrong. The programmer told the manufacturing engineer which keys to press and they found another, related bug. The problem might have been described over the telephone, but the manufacturing engineer felt that the programmer was skeptical about the bug and assumed the manufacturing engineer was doing something wrong. Using the video link allowed him to actually see the problem and try things out; it also allowed him to locate the bug precisely.

Cooperative problem-solving: A problem is shown and engineers at both ends of the link brainstorm solutions, discuss ideas, point at causes and try out experiments on the machine. Unlike a standard videoconference, the participants rarely look at each other's faces and concentrate on the technical problem to be solved.

For example, the paper feed mechanism worked well on the prototypes, but did not work reliably on the units coming off the manufacturing line. Although it seemed to be a manufacturing problem, the manufacturing engineers were interested in suggestions from the designers. Six Dutch engineers showed the problem to three English engineers, who were able to brainstorm and test various solutions. Because there was only one set of headphones on the shop floor, the Dutch engineers passed around the miniature camera to show things and let one person handle the audio communication to England.

The management made a cost/benefit evaluation of effectiveness of the link and concluded that the system was useful for solving problems on the shop floor and that the link saved at least two trips during the course of the experiment. They were not happy with the unreliability of the link, but said, "when it works and is used for the right application, it is a very powerful tool".

3.5.3 Configuration Management Link

The second media space link was installed between two planner analysts, located in England and the Netherlands. The planner analysts were responsable for configuration management, including tracking design changes, evaluating the cost of parts and changes and maintaining the inventory of the thousands of parts which make up a product acting as a bottleneck for all design changes. They registered each change, evaluated the cost and submitted them to the weekly Change and Control Board (CCB), held at the videoconference facility. Senior management at both sites would review and approve change requests, based on cost, timing, quality and technical issues. The planner analysts spent a great deal of time on the phone (10–30 calls per day) and managed 30–50 change requests per week.

We installed an Office Share type of link with a continuous video connection, active throughout the day. Because a continuously-available ISDN line would have been too expensive, we used the corporate TCP-IP network, using existing 128 Kb/s leased lines. We installed a Videopix video digitizing board on each of their Sun workstations, using two software packages: *vfctool*, which came with the Videopix board, and IVS, a public domain software developed at INRIA (Figure 3.15).

Vfctool grabbed frames from a video digitizing board shared over a LAN, without compression. With the network traffic between the Netherlands and England, it took up to six minutes to update an image with a size of 320×240 pixels and 8 gray levels. IVS [Tur93] was designed to support video and audio conferences over the Internet and achieved higher refresh rates by compressing the images according to the H.261 standard. IVS transmitted the compressed data stream over an IP network using the User Datagram Protocol (UDP) and took about 20 to 30 Kb/s of bandwidth. We used QCIF images (176×144 pixels) with eight gray levels and obtained a refresh rate of one frame every two to four seconds, according to network traffic. IVS was very robust to packet loss and network overload; the only problem was that sometimes the video window was closed down. However the software never crashed and the user could restore the link with a couple of mouse clicks.

The link to support configuration management ran for a full six days, spread over a period of about one month. We spent several hours observing users while the link was up and interviewed them periodically. We abandoned Vfctool, because the refresh rate was too slow and it was unreliable as a source of information. Although they enjoyed putting up messages such as "Good morning", "I'll be back at 3pm" or "I am on holiday today", the planner analysts were frustrated that the image was usually out-of-date and that the person in the image was often no longer there. We switched to IVS, with a smaller video window and lower image resolution, but a much higher refresh rate. The planner analysts regularly checked the IVS image before calling each other (at least ten times per day). They particularly enjoyed the Office Share on Monday nights, when they would often work until midnight preparing for the Change and Control Board meeting the next morning. They said that the link provided them with "remote solidarity", encouraging them to drink coffee together and keep working until they were done. Another, more subtle aspect was how they communicated that they did not

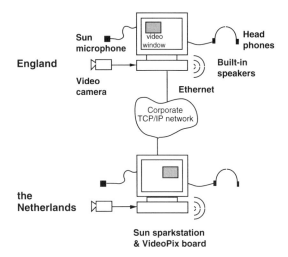

Figure 3.15   Office Share between planner analysts located in England and the Netherlands

want to be disturbed, by explicitly holding the phone, actively working through a large pile of papers or by moving out of the range of the camera. Their informal ways of communicating were encoded and decoded with no effort or attention; in most of the cases they were unaware that they were communicating. In one case, a planner analyst said: "Yesterday I saw you were talking with …", but was later unable to remember that he had seen the person via the Office Share. Other people in the building also used the Office Share. Passersby would wave at the remote planner analyst and sometimes used it to find someone or talk to someone at the other site. People adapted easily to the link; after an initial period of self-consciousness they quickly forgot about the camera and responded to the other person.

3.6   ETHICAL ISSUES

Video is a very powerful medium, perhaps too powerful. One of the biggest issues is privacy: how do we balance the benefits of a relatively open media space with individuals' needs for privacy? Privacy issues are multi-dimensional and are greatly affected by the culture of the organization in which the media space is placed and the purposes for which it was created. Gaver [Gav92a] identifies four issues that must be disentangled when thinking about privacy:

- *Control:* Users want to control who can see or hear them at any time.
- *Knowledge:* Users want to know when somebody is in fact seeing or hearing them.
- *Intention:* Users want to know what the intention of the connection is.
- *Intrusions:* Users want to avoid connections that disturb their work.

Fish et al [Fis93] point out that the tradeoff between privacy and functionality involves a conflict between the desirability of control and knowledge and the intrusion implied by activities needed to maintain them. Explicitly acknowledging every connection provides control, but the requests themselves would be intrusive. Similarly, if every glance results in seeing someone's face on the monitor, it demands some sort of social response and may well disrupt previously-existing connections. If users must specify and be informed of the exact intention of every connection, the media space is no longer lightweight and is bogged down with continuous demands for the user's attention. The challenge is to provide users with control and notification, but in a lightweight and unobtrusive way.

Since privacy issues are affected by the social context in which the media space is embedded, it is not possible to simply create an "ideal technology" that is appropriate in every setting. The Xerox PARC Media Space, RAVE and WAVE media spaces worked within an atmosphere of trust because the participants knew each other and worked together. From a management perspective, it was also very important to enforce the idea that "turning off the media space" was acceptable behavior; allowing people at all levels of the organization to feel comfortable. (Contrast this to the experiences of users of the videoconferencing system in the WAVE study, in which high-level managers were very satisfied with the system, but everyone else found it to be disruptive.) Larger media spaces, such as Kasmer, have had some problems, when people suddenly found themselves being glanced at by people they don't know. Web-based media spaces such as Mediascape have world-wide reach, with correspondingly lower levels of trust among the users and require greater levels of privacy protection.

The organizations that created the media spaces in this chapter each developed their own safeguards to privacy, making judgments about how to balance privacy concerns while still making the media space worthwhile. In Cruiser [Roo88], all connections had to be symmetrical; such that hearing or seeing someone implied that that person could also see or hear you. The Media Space [Bly93] took the opposite extreme; all video connections were fully open with both audio and video links. This worked well when the media space involved close-knit members of a small work group, but eroded when others from other parts of the organization joined the media space and were seen to be "voyeurs". RAVE was based on the notion of services, such as Glance, in which the user's intention was incorporated into the service. Users decided in advance who had permission to glance at them; letting them avoid giving permission each time. RAVE specified access levels per person, which were rarely updated over time, whereas CAVECAT used the door metaphor to establish dynamic access levels, but did not distinguish who requested which type of access. Mediascape combines the two models: users can customize access rights according to the current state of the door as well as the origin of the call. This is especially important since Mediascape is accessible through the World Wide Web.

Media space designers need to explicitly consider a set of ethical issues when handling video [Mac95b]. People should be informed of the presence of live cameras. (Unfortunately, most of us are largely unaware of the myriad security cameras that capture and record video of us every time we use a bank teller, shop in a store or even walk down the street. Such uses of video increase our insecurity when contemplating media spaces.) At EuroPARC, a mannequin with a sign around his neck was a light-hearted way of letting people know they were in the range of the cameras. Displaying the camera's image on an adjacent monitor is also effective. People should be able to easily detect when a camera is left on all the time, such as in commons areas. People should be able to figure out when they are on camera and have the opportunity to avoid it by moving out of range. Recording video is especially problematic, since video taken out of context can be used in ways that may cause viewers to completely misinterpret what happened. People should know when video is being recorded and be given the opportunity to stop. Once recorded, people should have the ability to view the recorded material and consent to any further use of the material, by giving their informed consent.

3.7 CONCLUSION

Distributed video is not a single, unitary phenomenon that can understood simply at the level of the technology it incorporates. What is important is the way in which the video (and associated technologies) are set up and used within a social setting. Media spaces, with their emphasis on informal and open-ended as well as formal communication, are an important new approach for supporting distributed cooperative work groups. Media space designers must consider the context in which their technology will be used and ensure that uses can easily adapt them to meet the specific needs of their users. Media spaces are still in their infancy with much research to be done. However, as video costs continue to drop and as the Web becomes ubiquitous, media spaces promise to provide an effective means for supporting distributed, collaborative work.

ACKNOWLEDGEMENTS

The RAVE media space at EuroPARC and its extensions were a collaborative effort of many people, including Bob Anderson, Victoria Bellotti, Michel Beaudouin-Lafon, Bill Buxton, Kathy Carter, Ian Daniel, Paul Dourish, Bill Gaver, Christian Heath, Lennart Lvstrand, Allan MacLean, Tom Milligan, Mike Molloy, Tom Moran, Toby Morrill, Daniele Pagani, Gary Olson, Judy Olson and Randy Smith. Our collegues at Xerox PARC in Palo Alto also contributed research ideas, particularly Annette Adler, Sara Bly, Steve Harrison, Austin Henderson, Scott Minneman and John Tang.

REFERENCES

[Adl94]   Adler, A. and Henderson, A., A room of our own: Experiences from a direct office share. In *Proceedings of Human Factors in Computing Systems, CHI '94* (Boston, MA), pages 138–144. ACM Press, New York, 1994.

[Bly93]   Bly, S., Harrison, S. and Irwin, S., Media spaces: Bringing people together in a video audio and computing environment. *Communciations of the ACM* special issue, 36(1): 29–47, January, 1993.

[Bor91]   Borning, A. and Travers, M., Two approaches to casual interaction over computer and video networks. In *Proceedings of Human Factors in Computing Systems, CHI '91* (New Orleans, LA), pages 13–19. ACM Press, New York, 1991.

[Bul89]   Bulick, S., Abel, M., Corey, D., Schmidt, J. and Coffin, S., The US WEST Advanced Technologies Prototype Multimedia Communications System. GLOBECOM '89: In *Proceedings of the IEEE Global Telecommunications Conference* (Dallas, Texas), 1989.

[Bux90]   Buxton, W. and Moran, T., EuroPARC's integrated interactive intermedia facility (iiif): Early experiences. In *Proceedings of the IFIP WG8.4 Conference on Multi-User Interfaces and Applications* (Herakleion, Crete), pages 11–34. North-Holland, 1990.

[Coo92]   Cool, C. Fish, R., Kraut, R., Lowery, C., Iterative design of a video communication system. In *Proceedings of the Conference on Computer-Supported Cooperative Work, CSCW '92* (Toronto, ON), pages 25–32. ACM Press, New York, 1992.

[Dou91a] Dourish, P., Godard: A flexible architecture for AV services in a media space. *EuroPARC working paper*, 1991.

[Dou91b] Dourish, P. and Bly, S., Portholes: Supporting awareness in a distributed work group. In *Proceedings of Human Factors in Computing Systems, CHI '92* (Monterey, CA), pages 541–547. ACM Press, New York, 1992.

[Dou93]   Dourish, P., Bellotti, V., Mackay, W. and Ma, C., Information and context: Lessons from a study of two calendar systems. In *Proceedings of COCS '93* (San Francisco, CA). ACM Press, New York, 1993.

[Egi88]   Egido, C., Videoconferencing as a technology to support group work: A review of its failure. In *Proceedings of the Conference on Computer Supported Cooperative Work, CSCW '88* (Portland, OR), pages 13–24. ACM Press, New York, 1988.

[Ehr99]   Ehrlich, K., Designing groupware applications: A work-centered approach. In Beaudouin-Lafon, M. (Ed.), *Computer Supported Cooperative Work*, Trends in Software Series 7:1–28. John Wiley & Sons, Chichester, 1999.

[Ell99]   Ellis, C.A., Workflow technology. In Beaudouin-Lafon, M. (Ed.), *Computer Supported Cooperative Work*, Trends in Software Series 7:29–54. John Wiley & Sons, Chichester, 1999.

[Ens92]   Ensor, J., Ahuja, S., Connaghan, R., Pack, M. and Seligmann, S., The Rapport multimedia communication system. Demo in *Conference Companion: Human Factors in Computing Systems, CHI '92* (Monterey, CA), pages 49–59. ACM Press, New York, 1992.

[Fis90]   Fish, R., Kraut, R. and Chalfonte, B.L., The VideoWindows system in informal communications. In *Proceedings of the Conference on Computer-Supported Cooperative Work, CSCW '90* (Los Angeles, CA), pages 1–13. ACM Press, New York, 1990.

[Fis93]   Fish, R., Kraut, R., Root, R. and Rice, R.E., Video as a technology for informal communication. *Communciations of the ACM* special issue, 36(1): 48–61, January, 1993.

[Gal80]   Galloway, J. and Rabinowitz, S., Hole-In-Space: *Mobile image videotape*. Santa Monica, CA. 1980.

[Gal91]   Gale, S., Adding audio and video to an office environment. In *Studies in Computer Supported Cooperative Work*. Bowers and Benford (Eds.), pages 49–62, Elsevier Science Publishers B.V., 1991.

[Gav86]   Gaver, W.W., Auditory icons: Using sound in computer interfaces. *Human-Computer Interaction*, 2:167–177. 1986.

[Gav91a] Gaver, W.W., Smith, R.B. and O'Shea, T., Effective sounds in complex systems: The ARKola simulation. In *Proceedings of Human Factors in Computing Systems, CHI '91* (New Orleans, LA), pages 85–90. ACM Press, New York, 1991.

[Gav91b] Gaver, W.W., Sound support for collaboration. In *Proceedings of the European Conference on Computer Supported Cooperative Work, ECSCW '91* (Amsterdam, the Netherlands), pages 293–308. ACM Press, New York, 1991.

[Gav92a] Gaver, W., Moran, T., MacLean, A., Lövstrand, L., Dourish, P., Carter, K. and Buxton, W., Realizing a video environment: EuroPARC's RAVE system. In *Proceedings of Human Factors in Computing Systems, CHI '92* (Monterey, CA), pages 27–35. ACM Press, New York, 1992.

[Gav92b] Gaver, W.W., The affordances of media spaces for collaboration. In *Proceedings of the Conference on Computer-Supported Cooperative Work, CSCW '92* (Toronto, ON), pages 17–24. ACM Press, New York, 1992.

[Gav93]   Gaver, W., Sellen, A., Heath, C. and Luff, P., One is not enough: Multiple views in a media space. In *Proceedings of Human Factors in Computing Systems, InterCHI '93* (Amsterdam, the Netherlands), pages 335–341. ACM Press, New York, 1993.

[Har94]   Harrison, B., Mantei, M., Beirne, G. and Narine, T., Communicating about communicating: Cross-disciplinary design of a media space interface. In *Proceedings of Human Factors in Computing Systems, CHI '94* (Boston, MA), pages 124–130. ACM Press, New York, 1994.

[Hea91]   Heath, C. and Luff, P., Disembodied conduct: Communication through video in a multimedia office environment. In *Proceedings of Human Factors in Computing Systems, CHI '91* (New Orleans, LA), pages 99–103. ACM Press, New York, 1991.

[Hen86]   Henderson, D.A. and Card, S., Rooms: The use of multiple virtual workspaces to reduce space contention in a window-based graphical user interface. *ACM Transactions on Graphics*, 5(3): 211–243, 1986.

[Hil94]   Ralph Hill, Tom Brinck, Steven Rohall, John Patterson and Wayne Wilner. The RendezVous architecture and language for constructing multiuser applications. *ACM Transactions on Computer Human Interaction*, 1(2):81–125, June 1994.

[Isa93]   Isaacs, E. and Tang, J., What video can and can't do for collaboration: A case study. In *Proceedings of ACM Multimedia '93* (Anaheim, CA), pages 199–206, 1993.

[Isa95]   Isaacs, E., Morris, T., Rodriguez, T. and Tang, J., A comparison of face-to-face and distributed presentations. In *Proceedings of Human Factors in Computing Systems, CHI '95* (Denver, CO), pages 354–361. ACM Press, New York, 1995.

[Ish92]   Ishii, H. and Kobayashi, M., Integration of interpersonal space and shared workspace: Clearboard design and experiments. In *Proceedings of the Conference on Computer-Supported Cooperative Work, CSCW '92* (Toronto, ON), pages 33–42. ACM Press, New York, 1992.

[Ish99]   Ishii, H., Integration of shared workspace and interpersonal space for remote collaboration. In Beaudouin-Lafon, M. (Ed.), *Computer Supported Cooperative Work*, Trends in Software Series 7:83–102. John Wiley & Sons, Chichester, 1999.

[Kob97]   Kobayashi, M. and Schmandt, C., Dynamic soundscape: mapping time to space for audio browsing. In *Proceedings of Human Factors in Computing Systems, CHI'97* (Atlanta, GA), pages 194–201. ACM Press, New York, 1997.

[Kra88]   Kraut, R. and Egido, C., Patterns of contact and communication in scientific research collaboration. In *Proceedings of the Conference on Computer-Supported Cooperative Work, CSCW '88* (Portland, OR), pages 1–13. ACM Press, New York, 1988.

[Lov91]   Löstrand, L., Being selectively aware with the Khronika system. In *Proceedings of the European Conference on Computer Supported Cooperative Work, ECSCW '91* (Amsterdam, the Netherlands), pages 265–278. ACM Press, New York, 1991.

[Mac90]   MacLean, A., Carter, K., Moran, T. and Lövstrand, L., User-tailorable systems: Pressing the issues with Buttons. In *Proceedings of Human Factors in Computing Systems, CHI '90* (Seattle, WA), pages 175–182. ACM Press, New York, 1990.

[Mac92]   Mackay, W.E., Spontaneous interaction in virtual multimedia space: EuroPARC's RAVE system. *Imagina '92*, Monte Carlo, Monaco. 1992.

[Mac95a] Mackay, W.E., Pagani D.S., Faber L., Inwood B., Launiainen P., Brenta L. and Pouzol V., Ariel: Augmenting paper engineering drawings. Video in *Conference Companion: Human Factors in Computing Systems, CHI '95* (Denver, CO), pages 421–422. ACM Press, New York, 1995.

[Mac95b] Mackay, W.E., Ethics, lies and videotapes. In *Proceedings of Human Factors in Computing Systems, CHI '95* (Denver, CO), pages 138–145. ACM Press, New York, 1995.

[Mac98]   Mackay, W.E., Augmented Reality: linking real and virtual worlds. In *Proceedings of ACM Conference on Advanced Visual Interfaces, AVI '98* (L'Aquila, Italy), pages 13–21. ACM Press, New York, 1998.

[Man91]   Mantei, M., Baecker, R., Sellen, A., Buxton, W., Milligan, T. and Wellman, B., Experiences in the use of a media space. In *Proceedings of Human Factors in Computing Systems, CHI '91* (New Orleans, LA), pages 203–208. ACM Press, New York, 1991.

[Min91]   Minneman, S.L. and Bly, S.A., Managing a trois: A study of a multi-user drawing tool in distributed design work. In *Proceedings of Human Factors in Computing Systems, CHI '91* (New Orleans, LA), pages 217–224. ACM Press, New York, 1991.

[Mor90]   Moran, T.P. and Anderson, R.J., The workaday world as a paradigm for CSCW design. In *Proceedings of the Conference on Computer-Supported Cooperative Work, CSCW '90.* (Los Angeles, CA), pages 381–393. ACM Press, New York, 1990.

[Mor97]   Moran, T., Palen, L., Harrison, S., Chiu, P., Kimber, D., Minneman, S., van Melle, W. and Zellweger, P., "I'll get that off the audio": A case study of salvaging multimedia meeting records. In *Proceedings of Human Factors in Computing Systems, CHI'97* (Atlanta, GA), pages 202–209. ACM Press, New York, 1997.

[Myn97]   Mynatt, E., Adler, A., Ito, M. and O'Day, V., Design for network communities. In *Proceedings of Human Factors in Computing Systems, CHI'97* (Atlanta, GA), pages 210–217. ACM Press, New York, 1997.

[Nol92]   Noll, A., Anatomy of a failure: Picturephone revisited. *Telecommunications Policy*, pages 307–316. May-June 1992.

[Ols91a] Olson, G. and Olson, J., User-centered design of collaboration technology. *Journal of Organizational Computing*, 1:61–83, 1991.

[Ols91b] Olson, M.H. and Bly, S., The Portland experience: A report on a distributed research group. *International Journal of Man–Machine Studies*, 34, 1991.

[Ols95]   Olson, J and Olson, G., What mix of video and audio is useful for small groups doing remote real-time design work? In *Proceedings of Human Factors in Computing Systems, CHI'95*

(Denver, CO), pages 362–368. ACM Press, New York, 1995.

[Pag93]   Pagani, D. and Mackay, W.E., Bringing media spaces into the real world. In *Proceedings of the European Conference on Computer-Supported Cooperative Work, ECSCW '93* (Milan, Italy). ACM Press, New York, 1993.

[Pat89]   Patterson, R.D., Guidelines for the design of auditory warning sounds. In *Proceedings of the Institute of Acoustics 1989 Spring Conference*, 11(5):17–24, 1989.

[Pos92]   Posner, I. and Baecker, R., How people write together. In *Proceedings of the Twenty-fifth Hawaii International Conference on Systems Sciences* (Kauai, Hawaii), volume IV, 1992.

[Pra99]   Prakash, A., Group editors. In Beaudouin-Lafon, M. (Ed.), *Computer Supported Cooperative Work*, Trends in Software Series 7:103–133. John Wiley & Sons, Chichester, 1999.

[Roo88]   Root, R.W., Design of a multi-media vehicle for social browsing. In *Proceedings of the Conference on Computer-Supported Cooperative Work, CSCW '88* (Portland, OR), pages 25–38. ACM Press, New York, 1988.

[Rou98]   Roussel, N., Towards a toolkit for building media spaces. *LRI Technical Report*, Université de Paris-Sud, Orsay, France, 1998. http://www-ihm.lri.fr/˜roussel/Mediascape.

[Sel92a] Sellen, A., Speech patterns in video-mediated conversations. In *Proceedings of Human Factors in Computing Systems, CHI '92* (Monterey, CA), pages 49–59. ACM Press, New York, 1992.

[Sel92b] Sellen, A., Buxton, W. and Arnott, J., Using spatial cues to improve videoconferencing. Video in *Conference Companion: Human Factors in Computing Systems, CHI '92* (Monterey, CA), pages 651–652. ACM Press, New York, 1992.

[Sel95]   Seligmann, D., Mercuri, R. and Edmark, J., Providing assurances in a multimedia interactive environment. In *Proceedings of Human Factors in Computing Systems, CHI'95* (Denver, CO), pages 250–256. ACM Press, New York, 1995.

[Stu86]   Stults, R., Media space. *Xerox PARC technical report*, 1986.

[Suc91]   Suchman, L. and Trigg, R., Understanding practice: Video as a medium for reflection and design. In *Design at Work: Cooperative Design of Computer Systems*, Greenbaum and Kyng (Eds), Lawrence Erlbaum, Hillsdale, N.J., 1991.

[Tan90]   Tang, J. and Minneman, S., VideoDraw: A video interface for collaborative drawing. In *Proceedings of Human Factors in Computing Systems, CHI '90* (Seattle, WA), pages 313–320. ACM Press, New York, 1990.

[Tan94]   Tang, J. and Rua, M., Montage: Providing teleproximity for distributed groups. In *Proceedings of Human Factors in Computing Systems, CHI '94* (Boston, MA), pages 37–43. ACM Press, New York, 1994.

[Tur93]   Turletti, T., H.262 Software codec for videoconferencing over the Internet. *INRIA Technical Report* No. 1834, Sophia Antipolis, France, 1993.

[Wel93]   Wellner, P., Interacting with paper on the DigitalDesk. In *Communications of the ACM*, 36(7):86–96, July 1993.

[Win89]   Winograd, T. and Flores, F., *Understanding Computers and Cognition: A New Foundation for Design*. NJ: Ablex, 1986.

[Yam96]   Yamaashi, K., Cooperstock, J., Narine, T. and Buxton, B., Beating the limitations of camera-monitor mediated telepresence with extra eyes. In *Proceedings of Human Factors in Computing Systems, CHI '96* (Vancouver, BC), pages 50–57. ACM Press, New York, 1996.

4

Integration of Shared Workspace and Interpersonal Space for Remote Collaboration*

HIROSHI ISHII
MIT Media Laboratory

ABSTRACT

Computer-based groupware and video telephony are the major technological components of remote collaboration support. However, integration of these two components has been a big design challenge. This chapter introduces the research effort to integrate the shared workspace created by groupware technology and the interpersonal space supported by video communication technology. TeamWorkStation and ClearBoard will be introduced as example systems which were designed to support focused real-time collaboration by distributed group members.

4.1 INTRODUCTION

"Groupware" is a label for computer-based systems explicitly designed to support groups of people working together. It is growing rapidly as a new application category in the computer industry [Ell91, Col93].

Most of the current groupware such as workflow systems and collaborative authoring tools are devoted to computational support and are designed under the constraint of limited communication bandwidth. However, the deployment of broadband digital networks opens a new future for multimedia collaboration environments that integrate real-time audio and video

---

* This chapter is based on an article "Iterative design of seamless collaboration media" originally published in *Communications of the ACM*, Special Issue on Internet Technology, Vol. 37, No. 8, August 1994, pp. 83–97, with the permission of ACM.

Computer Supported Cooperative Work, Edited by Beaudouin-Lafon
© 1999 John Wiley & Sons Ltd

communication links with computer-based shared workspaces [Bri92, Lyl93]. Especially, the integration of two functional spaces, shared workspace (e.g. electronic shared whiteboard) and interpersonal space (e.g. videophone), is a critical interface design issue.

4.1.1   Shared Workspace and Interpersonal Space

One major focus of groupware development has been the creation of virtual "shared workspaces" in distributed computer environments. Some groupware definitions take this workspace-oriented view, such as:

> "Groupware . . . the computer-based systems that support groups of people engaged in a common task (or goal) and that provide an interface to a shared environment." [Ell91]

Whiteboards and overhead projections of transparencies are examples of shared workspaces in face-to-face meetings. Participants can see, point to, or draw on a whiteboard simultaneously. An overhead projector makes handwritten or computer-generated documents visible to all participants in a room while permitting the speaker to point or draw. Shared workspace activities include sharing information, pointing to specific items, marking, annotating, and editing.

In a distributed, real-time collaboration, these activities can be supported by computer-based groupware, including

- shared screen systems such as Timbuktu [Far91]
- shared window systems such as VConf and Dialogo [Lau90], and
- multi-user editors such as Cognoter [Fos86], GROVE [Ell91], Commune [Bly90], Cave-Draw [Lu91], Aspects [Gro90], GroupSketch [Gre92], GroupDraw [Gre92], We-Met [Wol92], and TeamPaint (described later). Use of hand gestures in a shared workspace can be supported by shared video drawing media such as VideoDraw [Tang91] and Team-WorkStation [Ish90].

In face-to-face meetings, we speak, make eye contact, and observe each other's facial expressions and gestures. These verbal and non-verbal channels are important in building confidence and establishing trust [Arg75, Bux92, Man91]. The focus of telecommunication technologies such as the video-phone and videoconferencing has been the creation of "interpersonal spaces" that maintain a sense of "telepresence" or "being there" [Hol92] through the visibility of gestures and facial expressions of distributed group members. "Media Space" is an example of such technologies. Originated by Xerox PARC [Bly93], it is an environment that integrates video, audio, and computer technologies, allowing individual and groups to work together despite being distributed geographically and temporally (see also Chapter 3 in this book [Mac99]). Recent developments include Cruiser (Bellcore) [Fis93], VideoWindow [Fis90], RAVE (Rank Xerox EuroPARC) [Gav92], and CAVECAT/Telepresence (University of Toronto) [Man91]. ("Media space", originally the name of a specific system [Bly93], is used here in the sense of Mantei et al [Man91] as a general term to represent computer-controlled video environments.)

4.1.2   Limitations of Existing Support Technologies

Both shared workspace and interpersonal space are present in ordinary face-to-face meetings and may be essential for remote real-time collaboration. Several media space technologies support both spaces.

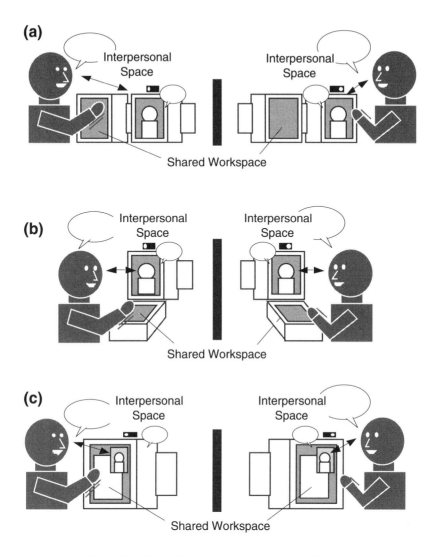

Figure 4.1 Typical screen arrangements in media space

Figure 4.1 illustrates three typical display arrangements of media spaces. In (a), a display providing a live video image of the partner's face adjoins a display showing the shared work. The ARKola simulation [Gav91] in the IIIF environment [Bux90a] and some nodes of CAVECAT [Man91] adopt this arrangement. SEPIA-IPSI media space [Str92] locates small custom-built desktop video devices (small monitors and cameras) on top of the computer screen. In (b), the displays are repositioned to resemble the situation of interacting across a table. VideoDraw [Tang91] and Commune [Bly90, Min91] adopt this arrangement. In (c), the live video images and the shared workspaces are incorporated into different windows of a single screen. TeamWorkStation, PMTC [Tan91], MERMAID [Wat90] and most of the recent PC-based desktop conferencing products employ this desktop-video technology.

4.1.3 Iterative Design of Seamless Collaboration Media

We have been exploring the future of collaboration media that make good use of real-time video through the iterative design of various groupware systems. Our research started in 1988 and was motivated by the study on shared drawing space [Tang91] in the Media Space environment [Bly93]. While most of the current video telephony has been designed to see "talking heads", our goal is to go beyond this model and demonstrate new usage of video-mediated communication technologies. Video is powerful media for not only seeing talking heads, but also for creating shared workspaces and shared visual context for remote collaboration.

The following sections introduce the progression of iterative media design from Team-WorkStation to ClearBoard. These systems were designed to support focused real-time collaboration by distributed group members. The key concept behind our iterative design is "seamlessness". Seamless design pursues the following two goals:

- *Seamlessness (continuity) with existing work practices:* People develop their own work practices after using a wide variety of tools and interacting with a large number of people. We believe the continuity with existing work practices and everyday skills is essential. Groupware that asks users to abandon their acquired skills and to learn a new protocol is likely to encounter strong resistance [Gru88].
- *Seamlessness (smooth transition) between functional spaces:* Collaboration requires us to shift among a variety of functional spaces or modes. Seamless design undertakes to decrease the cognitive load of users as they move dynamically across different spaces. For example, TeamWorkStation was designed to enable smooth transition between individual workspaces and shared workspaces by allowing users to keep using both familiar desktop tools and computer tools. ClearBoard realizes seamless integration of interpersonal space and shared workspace allowing people to use various non-verbal cues such as a partner's gaze direction for smooth focus switching between these two spaces.

4.2 TEAMWORKSTATION-1 AND SEAMLESS SHARED WORKSPACES

People do a lot of their work without computers, or using different tools on different computer systems, and have developed their own work practices for these situations. Even in a heavily computerized individual workplace, users often work both with computers and on the physical desktop. Neither one can replace the other. For example, printed materials such as books and magazines are still an indispensable source of information. Therefore, when designing real-time shared workspaces, depending on the task and the media of the information to be shared (paper or computer file), co-workers should be able to choose either computers or desktops, and to switch between them freely. One person's choice should be independent of the other members' choices. Group members should be able to use a variety of heterogeneous tools (computer-based and manual tools) in the shared workspace simultaneously. To realize such a seamless shared workspace, we designed TeamWorkStation-1 (TWS-1) [Ish90, Ish91].

The key design idea of TWS-1 is a "translucent overlay" of individual workspace images. TWS-1 combines two or more translucent live-video images of computer screens or physical desktop surfaces using a video synthesis technique. Translucent overlay allows users to combine individual workspaces and to point to and draw on the overlaid images simultaneously. We chose video as the basic medium of TWS because it is the most powerful for fusing presentations of traditionally incompatible visual media such as papers and computer documents.

Figure 4.2   Overview of TeamWorkStation-1 prototype

4.2.1   System Architecture of TWS-1

Figure 4.2 shows an overview of the first prototype, TWS-1. Two CCD video cameras are provided at each workstation: one for capturing live face images of the group member, and the other for capturing the desktop surface images and hand gestures. TWS-1 provides two screens. The individual screen (private workspace) is on the left and the shared screen is on the right. These two screens are contiguous in video memory, and this multi-screen architecture allows users to move any application program window between the individual and shared screens by merely mouse dragging. Therefore, it is easy to bring your own data and tools from each personal computer into the shared workspace to use in remote collaboration. Hardcopy information can also be shared easily by placing it under the CCD camera (i.e. on the physical desktop). Figure 4.3 shows an image of a shared screen where two users are discussing the system configuration by annotating and pointing electronic diagrams in a drawing editor by hand.

The first prototype TWS-1 was implemented on Macintosh computers to provide small work groups (2–4 members) with a shared workspace. The system architecture of TWS-1 is illustrated in Figure 4.4 [Ish91]. The video network is controlled by a video server that is based on a computer-controllable video switcher and video effecter. The video server gathers, processes and distributes the shared computer screen images, desktop images, and face images. Overlay of video images is done by the video server. The results of overlaying are redistributed to the shared screens via the video network.

4.2.2   Experience of TWS-1

Through experimental use of TWS-1, we found that users liked the feature which allowed them to keep using their favorite individual tools, especially papers and pen, while collaborating in a desktop shared workspace. That is, there was no need to master the usage of new sophisticated groupware. The drawback of this overlay approach is that the results of collab-

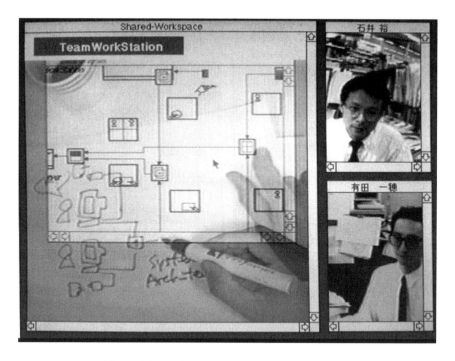

Figure 4.3   A shared screen of TeamWorkStation-1

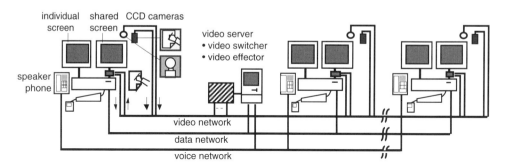

Figure 4.4   System architecture of TeamWorkStation-1 prototype

oration cannot be shared directly. Since individual workspaces are overlaid as video images, the marks and the marked documents occupy different "layers" in the shared screens. They are actually stored separately in different places in different media (in computer files or on paper). We mainly used a video printer or video tape recorder to record the results and the collaboration process.

"Shared workspace" is taken by many computer scientists to mean "data sharing". However, we think it is not required that all the outcomes of the work-in-progress be directly "manipulable" by all the participants. We seldom felt the necessity to edit the other's diagrams directly. If a diagram was to be changed, usually the originator would change it according to the comments made by the other. One reason appears to stem from the respect paid to the ownership of the outcomes. This seems to be a very natural feeling, even in a close collaborative session.

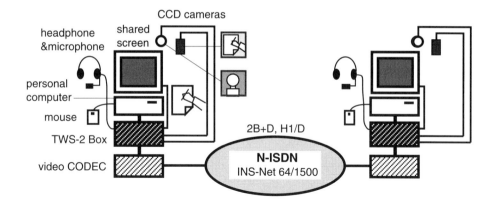

Figure 4.5   System architecture of TeamWorkStation-2 prototype

The overlay solution provides us with a comfortable work environment, because the overlaid layers keep the person's own layer of work intact.

Since TWS-1 was designed for laboratory experiments to verify the concept of seamless shared workspaces, we did not pay much attention to the number of cables or the communication bandwidth. As a result, the system configuration became complex and difficult to maintain. This complexity prevented us from conducting the field tests using publicly available digital networks, and motivated us to start designing a completely new system, TeamWorkStation-2.

4.3   TEAMWORKSTATION-2 FOR N-ISDN

TeamWorkStation-2 (TWS-2) was designed to provide a shared workspace over narrowband ISDN (N-ISDN) Basic Rate Interface (2B+D) and the Primary Rate Interface (H1/D) using the CCITT H.261 standard of moving picture transmission [Ish93a]. We chose N-ISDN Basic Rate Interface as the target network because of its widespread availability in Japan.

We devised a new multi-user interface called ClearFace for TWS-2. ClearFace superimposes translucent, movable, and resizable face windows over a workspace image to enable more effective use of the normally limited screen space. We found users had little difficulty in selectively viewing either the facial image or the workspace image.

4.3.1   System Architecture of TWS-2

We radically simplified the system architecture. Figure 4.5 shows the system architecture of TWS-2. We targeted dyadic communication to make the centralized video server unnecessary and to eliminate complexities that would arise from multipoint connection. The two TWS-2 terminals are connected by one ISDN link. Each terminal is composed of three major components: a TWS-2 box, a video codec, and a PC-9801™ personal computer. All video processing functions (e.g. translucent overlay, picture-in-picture) are supported at each terminal. All the hardware for video processing, camera control units, audio amplifiers, and power units were encapsulated into a single TWS-2 box.

The PC-9801™ computer is mainly used to control the video processing hardware in the TWS-2 box and the video codec. If direct sharing of information stored in the computer is

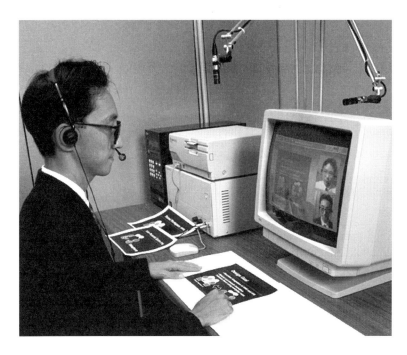

Figure 4.6   Appearance of TWS-2 terminal

required, we can use screen-sharing software while overlaying desktop video images with the shared computer screen.

Figure 4.6 shows the appearance of a TWS-2 terminal in use. A headphone with a small microphone is provided for voice communication. Like TWS-1, TWS-2 provides two CCD cameras, one to capture the user's face image and another to capture the physical desktop image. The TWS-2 box also provides an external video input port that can be used to show recorded video clips by connecting a video player.

TWS-2 provides only one screen instead of the two screens (individual and shared screens) of TWS-1. The experimental use of the previous system, TWS-1, led us to observe that most work was done in the "desktop-overlay" mode in which only the video images of physical desktop surfaces are overlaid. We decided to make "desktop overlay" the basic service of TWS-2, and to make "computer screen overlay" an option. This decision led to the one-screen architecture of TWS-2.

Figure 4.7 shows a typical screen image of TWS-2 in use. In Figure 4.7, users are discussing the system architecture using hand drawing and gestures. This example demonstrates the important TWS feature that all of the collaborators share not only the results of drawing, but also the dynamic process of drawing and gesturing.

4.3.2   Experimental Use of TWS-2

We have tested TWS-2 since 1992 by connecting our offices in Tokyo, Yokosuka, and Osaka by INS-Net 64. (The latest version of TWS-2 is available via Ethernet as well as N-ISDN.) We conducted several controlled laboratory experiments as well as tests of real work outside of laboratories [Ish93a]. Before we started the TWS-2 experiments, many people felt

Figure 4.7   Design session via TWS-2

dubious about the ability of INS-Net 64 to support real-time activities because of their previous experience with the jerky displays of video phones. However, the subjects generally commented that they could smoothly interact with their partner and that they were absorbed in the task. Although the subjects noticed some delay and jerkiness in the remote desktop video image, these did not hinder subjects from concentrating on their work. However, all the subjects noted that they could not clearly see their partner's desktop image. This confirmed that the CIF (Common Intermediate Format) (352 pixels/line × 288 lines/picture) standard is definitely insufficient to see small characters or fine drawings in the remote documents.

4.3.3   Beyond the Video Phone

Video phones and videoconferencing are the most typical video applications that use N-ISDN, and they represent the effort at imitating "being there" which has long been the goal of telecommunication technologies [Hol92]. Real-time video is used only to see the remote partners' facial expressions, postures and gestures in these applications.

   In contrast to these "talking head" applications, TWS-2 demonstrates a new direction for the usage of real-time video: the creation of a virtual shared workspace. The main focus of TWS-2 is not the imitation of face-to-face communication but rather the sharing of overlaid desktop images for collaboration.

   The experiments to date confirm that TWS-2 has one large advantage over ordinary video phones as the pre-eminent N-ISDN service. The advantage is due to the bandwidth limitation and human perception. People are especially perceptive to changes in facial expressions. If facial expression is the main means of communication, even slight asynchronism between the voice and the movement of eyes and lips is immediately noticed, and makes smooth conversation difficult. Since the facial expression is always changing and the face and body are always moving, delay in transmitting the partner's image increases perceived discontinuities and hence increases the negative impression of users.

The main difference between the desktop and face images is that the desktop images are relatively static. Images of papers and the marks drawn on the papers do not change quickly. Only the hands move on the desktop when users gesture or draw. Thus the total amount of motion is far less than that experienced with video phone displays. This more static nature of the desktop surface increases the effective video frame rate. Although quick hand motions look jerky, TWS-2 users can be more productive than their video phone counterparts since they can visually share objects and work on them.

4.4   SEAMLESS INTEGRATION OF INTERPERSONAL SPACE AND SHARED WORKSPACE

One major focus of groupware development has been the creation of virtual "shared workspaces" in distributed computer environments. Shared workspace activities include sharing information, pointing to specific items, marking, annotating, and editing. These activities can be supported by computer-based groupware, including shared screen systems, shared window systems, and multi-user editors [Ell91] (see also Chapter 5 in this book [Pra99]).

In face-to-face meetings, we speak, make eye contact, and observe each other's facial expressions and gestures. These verbal and non-verbal channels are important in building confidence and establishing trust [Bux92]. The focus of telecommunication technologies such as the video phone and videoconferencing has been the creation of "interpersonal spaces" that maintain a sense of "telepresence" or "being there" [Hol92] through the visibility of gestures and facial expressions of distributed group members.

Both shared workspace and interpersonal space are essential for remote, real-time collaboration. Many desktop multimedia conferencing systems such as TeamWorkStation, PMTC [Tan91], and MERMAID [Wat90] support both spaces, but they have a major limitation: an arbitrary seam exists between the shared workspace and the face images. We realized that this problem was not just the superficial physical discontinuity of spatially separated windows. Absent are the non-verbal cues that would enable a smooth shift in attention between the shared workspace and the partner's face image. Current groupware and videoconferencing technologies do not support these cues.

Lack of eye contact is another problem of TWS. Camera positioning prevents one person from knowing the direction of the other's gaze; it could be directed toward the face image, toward objects in the shared workspace window, or elsewhere. A shift in focus is not apparent until accompanied by a visible gesture or an audible remark. Awareness of gaze direction and mutual eye contact are impossible.

ClearBoard is designed to overcome these limitations by seamlessly integrating interpersonal space and shared workspace (Figure 4.8). A design goal of ClearBoard is to allow a pair of users to shift easily between interpersonal space and shared workspace using familiar everyday cues such as the partner's gestures, head movements, eye contact, and gaze direction.

4.4.1   ClearBoard Metaphor

The key metaphor of ClearBoard design is "talking through and drawing on a big transparent glass board". Figure 4.9 shows "ClearBoard-0" which is the simple mock-up of this ClearBoard concept for co-located pairs of users. ClearBoard-0 consists of a glass board positioned between the partners on which they draw or post objects. ClearBoard requires less eye and

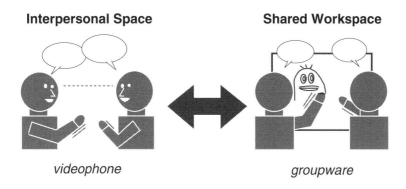

Figure 4.8 Seamless integration of interpersonal space and shared workspace

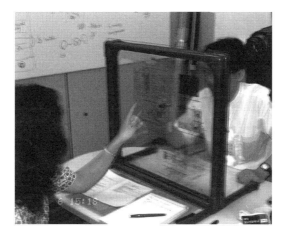

Figure 4.9 A simple mockup of the ClearBoard metaphor: ClearBoard-0

head movement to switch focus between the drawing surface and the partner's face than is needed in either the whiteboard or the desktop environment. However, a real glass board has the problem that written text appears reversed to one's partner; we were able to solve this problem by mirror-reversing video images in ClearBoard-1 and 2 as described below.

4.5   DESIGN OF CLEARBOARD-1

Figure 4.10 shows ClearBoard-1, our first prototype to support remote collaboration [Ish92a]. Two users are discussing a route by drawing a map directly on the screen surface. Both users can share a common map orientation. The partner can read all the text and graphics in their correct orientation.

In order to implement the remote version of ClearBoard, we devised the system architecture called "drafter-mirror" architecture illustrated in Figure 4.11. Each terminal is equipped with a tilted screen, a video projector and a video camera. Users can write and draw directly on the surface of the screen using color paint markers. The video camera located above the screen captures the drawings and the user's image as reflected by the half-mirror as a continuous

Figure 4.10   ClearBoard-1 in use

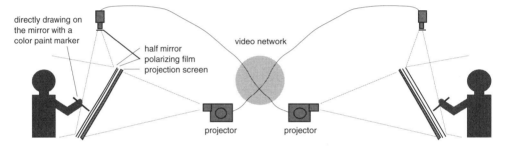

Figure 4.11   System architecture of the ClearBoard-1 prototype

video image. This image is sent to the other terminal through a video network and projected onto the partner's screen from the rear so that both users can share a common orientation of the drawing space. The partner can draw directly over this transmitted video image. This shared video drawing technique, which allows remote partners to draw directly over the video image of their co-workers' drawing surface, was originally demonstrated in VideoDraw [Tang91].

4.5.1   Experimental Use of ClearBoard-1

Since 1990 this prototype has been used in experimental sessions. We observed effortless focus switching between the task and the partner's face. Users could read their partner's facial expression, achieve eye contact, and utilize their awareness of the direction of their partner's gaze. Easy eye contact even during drawing-intensive activities increased the feeling of intimacy and co-presence. No subjects reported difficulty with the mirror-reversal of the partner. This may be because our faces are quite symmetric, or our own images are reversed in mirrors.

We found that ClearBoard provides the capability we call "gaze awareness": the ability to monitor the direction of a partner's gaze and thus his or her focus of attention. A ClearBoard user can tell which screen objects the partner is gazing at during a conversation more easily and precisely than is possible in an ordinary meeting environment with a whiteboard.

To understand the implication of gaze awareness, we conducted a collaborative problem solving experiment on ClearBoard using the "river crossing problem." [Ish93b]. This experi-

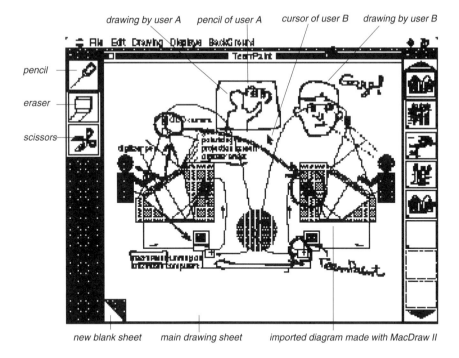

Figure 4.12   A screen of TeamPaint

ment confirmed that it is easy for the instructor to say which side of the river the student was gazing at. This information was quite useful in understanding the student's thinking process and in providing advice. The importance of eye contact in the design of face-to-face communication tools is often discussed. However, we believe the concept of gaze awareness is more general and more important. Eye contact can be seen as a special case of gaze awareness.

An interesting and less critical confusion manifested itself when users directly drew over their partner's image, playfully adding eye glasses or a mustache, for example. Clearly they had a "WYSIWIS" (what you see is what I see) expectation, not realizing that although the drawing is shared, the facial images are not, with each person seeing only the other's image. Thus, the metaphor of the ClearBoard is not always entirely assimilated.

4.6   DESIGN OF CLEARBOARD-2

In using this ClearBoard-1 prototype, we found several problems. The projected video image of a drawing was not sufficiently clear. Lack of recording capabilities was an obstacle to re-using the work results. To overcome these problems in ClearBoard-1, we decided to design a new computer-based prototype, "ClearBoard-2" [Ish93b]. Instead of using color paint markers, ClearBoard-2 provides users with "TeamPaint", a multi-user computer-based paint editor and digitizer pen.

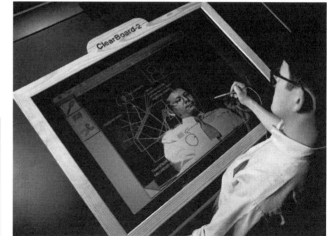

Figure 4.13   ClearBoard-2 in use

4.6.1   TeamPaint

TeamPaint is a groupware application for shared drawing. It runs on networked Macintosh™ computers, and it is based on a replicated architecture. TeamPaint offers several functions: recording of working results, easy manipulation of marks, and the use of data held in computer files. TeamPaint provides an intuitive interface based on the metaphor of drawing on a sketch pad with a color pencil as shown in Figure 4.12.

Each user is provided with individual layers and can only modify his or her own layers by default. All members see the composite image of all the layers. Because each layer is isolated from the others, no access control is necessary. TeamPaint has no floor control mechanisms but enables simultaneous gesturing and drawing by multiple users. Gestures, in the form of cursor movements, and through them the drawing process, are visually shared by all members.

4.6.2   The ClearBoard-2 System and Its Use

Using TeamPaint, transparent digitizer sheets, and electronic pens, we implemented a computer-based prototype, ClearBoard-2. Figure 4.13 shows the ClearBoard-2 prototype in use, and Figure 4.14 shows the system architecture of the prototype. The composite drawing image of TeamPaint is made to overlay the face images with a special video overlay board. The mixed RGB video image is projected onto the screen's rear surface. TeamPaint makes it easy to get a new blank sheet and the drawing marks are easier to see. The lower screen angle decreases arm fatigue, but gives the impression that the partner is under the screen, rather than behind it as in ClearBoard-1.

The use of RGB video and the chroma-keying overlay technique does increase image clarity. Furthermore, the capability of recording results and re-using the data produced in previous sessions or from any other application program promises to add tremendous value to an already practical tool. Through the use of ClearBoard-2, it was often observed that the user's gaze follows the partner's pen movements. We confirmed that "gaze awareness" is as well supported in ClearBoard-2 as it was in ClearBoard-1. One can easily tell which object on the TeamPaint screen the partner is looking at.

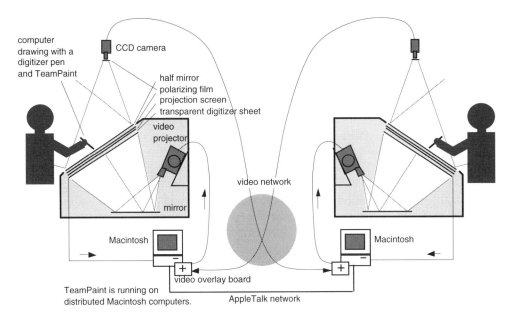

computer
drawing with a
digitizer pen
and TeamPaint

CCD camera

half mirror
polarizing film
projection screen
transparent digitizer sheet

video
projector

video network

mirror

Macintosh

Macintosh

video overlay board

TeamPaint is running on
distributed Macintosh computers.

AppleTalk network

Figure 4.14   System architecture of ClearBoard-2 prototype

We see the evolution from ClearBoard-1 to ClearBoard-2 as being very important. Computer and video-communication technologies have, until now, evolved independently. Although they have been loosely coupled using arbitrary multi-window interfaces in many desktop multimedia conferencing systems, they have never been integrated seamlessly from the users' cognitive point of view. ClearBoard-2 succeeds in naturally integrating the user interfaces of computer-based groupware with that of videoconferencing. We expect that the seamless integration of computer and video communication technologies will be an integral part of the next generation of collaboration media.

Moreover, ClearBoard-2 can be seen as an instance of the paradigm shift from traditional HCI (Human–Computer Interaction) to HHI (Human–Human Interaction) mediated by computers. We are interacting not *with* computers, but *through* computers.

We believe that the ClearBoard design is not only beyond the traditional desktop metaphor based on a multi-window interface, but also suggests a direction of "beyond being there" [Hol92]. We expect ClearBoard to be useful both as a collaboration medium and as a vehicle to investigate the nature of dynamic human interaction.

4.7   SUMMARY AND FUTURE WORK

This chapter has discussed the integration of shared workspace and interpersonal space for real-time remote collaboration, and has introduced an evolution of our seamless collaboration media design. TeamWorkStation (TWS) demonstrates a new usage of real-time video for collaboration, by providing distributed users with a seamless shared workspace. Using a translucent video overlay technique, real-time information such as hand gestures and handwritten comments can be shared, as can information contained in printed materials and computer files. Users can continue to use their favorite application programs or desktop tools, so there is only a minor cognitive seam between individual workspaces and shared workspaces. TWS-2, a redesigned version which uses N-ISDN Basic Rate Interface, demonstrated the advantage of this application over ordinary videophones given the same bandwidth limitation.

In order to integrate the shared workspace and the interpersonal space seamlessly, we designed ClearBoard. ClearBoard-1 permits co-workers in two different locations to draw with color markers while maintaining direct eye contact and the use of natural gestures. Through experiments, we discovered that ClearBoard also supported the important feature of "gaze awareness". In order to offer new functions, such as recording of working results, easy manipulation of marks, and the use of data held in computer files, we designed a computer-drawing version, ClearBoard-2. ClearBoard-2 supports shared drawing with TeamPaint and electronic pens.

Through the iterative design of these collaboration media, we believe it is most important to respect the skills that people use in everyday life [Bux90b]. The design focuses on basic skills such as drawing, gesturing, talking, gaze reading, and using computers. We believe skill-based design will lead to cognitive seamlessness.

We are now very much interested in how the next generation of collaboration media may augment the process of collaborative creation by people such as artists, musicians, designers and children. NTT's vision video, "Seamless Media Design" [NTT93], illustrates our expectation of future collaboration media based on the ClearBoard concept.

4.7.1   Broadband Digital Network

Although all these prototype systems except for TWS-2 were implemented using hybrid (analog video + digital data) networks, it is obvious that hybrid networks have serious limitations in extending their scale.

We expect that the new international telecommunication standard B-ISDN (Broadband Integrated Services Digital Network) and ATM (Asynchronous Transfer Mode) [Lyl93] will provide a universal and scalable infrastructure for various collaborative applications including TeamWorkStation and ClearBoard. ATM is expected to be a common technology for both LAN (Local Area Networks) and WAN (Wide Area Networks). ATM also provides "bandwidth-on-demand" to meet the requirements of many applications.

Although N-ISDN provides users with fixed communication bandwidth, we expect that ATM technology will provide users with the flexibility to dynamically change the appropriate bandwidth and the balance between the frame rate and resolution of motion pictures on demand (based on the contents and the usage of video). For example, a TWS session using a detailed blueprint of a new building may require more bandwidth for higher resolution of shared documents compared with a TWS meeting with shared sheets of blank paper for freehand drawing. Competitive negotiation tasks may require both higher frame rate and resolution to read your colleague's subtle facial expression rather than documents. ClearBoard requires much more communication bandwidth (higher resolution, higher frame rate, and less delay) than TWS since ClearBoard presents a life-size partner's image and users want to read subtle and quick changes of a partner's gaze.

Since required bandwidth changes dynamically both within a single application depending on the contents and usage of video, and among various applications, rapid reassignment of bandwidth on demand will be a critical feature to support seamless transitions among various collaboration modes.

4.7.2   From Multimedia to Seamless Media

"Multimedia" is now becoming a big buzz word in the computer and communication indus-
tries. As a result, the number of cables behind a computer, the number of features users need
to understand, and the number of incompatible data formats are increasing beyond the limits
of human cognitive capability. A variety of media (such as text, video, audio, graphics) and
services (on-demand video, videoconferencing, electronic newspaper) are becoming available
through a single powerful computer on the desktop and a broadband communication network
named the "information super highway". However, each medium and service are still separated from each other and they are not seamlessly integrated from a user's cognitive point of
view.

The communication channels of human beings are inherently multi-modal and seamless.
It does not make much sense to decompose the representation of information into primitive
data types such as text, video, audio, and graphics, and stress the "multi-ness" of the media.
For example, we are speaking, gesturing, and drawing simultaneously in a design meeting.
We have great skills to express ideas and understand each other in everyday contexts using
all these media as a whole. We believe the multi-ness of media is not the main issue; how to
integrate them into a seamless media, hiding the various low-level representations, discontinuities among primitive media, and complexity of underlying technologies is the core issue
in designing new applications. "Multi-media" sounds like a premature label that represents a
stage of media evolution from the mono-media to the seamless media.

4.7.3   Toward Ubiquitous Media and Augmented Reality

We hope that ClearBoard will change our concept of a wall from being a passive partition
to being a dynamic collaboration medium that integrates distributed real and virtual spaces.
We are now exploring a vision of new architectural spaces where all the surfaces including
walls, ceilings, windows, doors and desktops become active surfaces through which people
can interact with other spaces, both real and virtual. In these spaces, both computers and
video must be inherently ubiquitous media [Bux94, Wei91]. Many challenges exist to achieve
a seamless extension of spaces and their interconnections. Nevertheless, our design will be
based on the natural skills and social protocols people are using in everyday life to manipulate
and interact with information, artifacts and each other.

ACKNOWLEDGEMENTS

I would like to thank Masaaki Ohkubo, Kazuho Arita, and Takashi Yagi at NTT for their contribution to building the TWS prototype, and Minoru Kobayashi at NTT for his contribution
to implementing ClearBoard. I appreciate the contribution of Prof. Naomi Miyake at Chukyo
University and Prof. Jonathan Grudin at University of California Irvine to the observational
and experimental phase of this research. I thank George Fitzmaurice and Beverly Harrison
at the University of Toronto for their careful comments on an early version of this chapter.
Finally, the stimulating discussions with Prof. William Buxton at the University of Toronto
on the principles of skill-based design and the ubiquitous media were greatly appreciated.

REFERENCES

[Arg75]   Argyle, M., *Bodily Communication*. Methuen & Co. Ltd., London, 1975.

[Bae93]   Baecker, R. (Ed.), *Readings in Groupware and Computer-Supported Cooperative Work*. Morgan Kaufmann, San Mateo, 1993.

[Bly90]   Bly, S.A. and Minneman, S.L., Commune: A shared drawing surface. In *Proceedings of COIS '90*, pages 184–192. ACM, New York, 1990.

[Bly93]   Bly, S.A., Harrison, S.R. and Irwin, S., Media spaces: Bringing people together in a video, audio and computing environment. *Communications of the ACM* 36(1):28–47, January 1993.

[Bri92]   Brittan, D., Being there: The promise of multimedia communications. *MIT Technology Review*, pages 42–50, May/June 1992.

[Bux90a]   Buxton, W. and Moran, T., EuroPARC's Integrated Interactive Intermedia Facility (IIIF): Early experiences. In *Proceedings of the IFIP WG8.4 Conference on Multi-User Interfaces and Applications*, pages 11–34. North-Holland, Amsterdam, 1990.

[Bux90b]   Buxton, W., Smoke and mirrors. *Byte*, pages 205–210, July 1990.

[Bux92]   Buxton, W., Telepresence: Integrating shared task and person spaces. In *Proceedings of Graphics Interface '92*, pages 123–129. Morgan Kaufmann, Los Altos, 1992.

[Bux94]   Buxton, W., Living in augmented reality: Ubiquitous media and reactive environment. (unpublished paper).

[Col93]   Coleman, D. (Ed.), *Proceedings of Groupware '93*. Morgan Kaufmann, San Mateo, 1993.

[Ell91]   Ellis, C.A., Gibbs, S.J. and Rein, G.L., Groupware: Some issues and experiences. *Communications of the ACM* 34(1):38–58, January 1991.

[Far91]   Farallon Computing Inc., *Timbuktu 4.0 User's Guide*. Farallon Computing Inc., Emeryville, CA, 1991.

[Fis90]   Fish, R.S., Kraut, R.E. and Chalfonte, B.L., The VideoWindow system in informal communications. In *Proceedings of the Conference on Computer-Supported Cooperative Work, CSCW '90*, pages 1–11. ACM, New York, 1990.

[Fis93]   Fish, R.S., Kraut, R.E., Root, R.W. and Rice, R.E., Video as a technology for informal communication. *Communications of the ACM* 36(1):48–61, January 1993.

[Fos86]   Foster, G. and Stefik, M., Cognoter, theory and practice of a collaborative tool. In *Proceedings of the Conference on Computer-Supported Cooperative Work, CSCW '86*, pages 7–15. ACM, New York, 1986.

[Gal90]   Galegher, J., Kraut, R. and Egido, C., *Intellectual Teamwork: Social and Technological Foundations of Cooperative Work*. Lawrence Erlbaum Associates, Hillsdale, NJ, 1990.

[Gav91]   Gaver, W., Smith, R. and O'Shea, T., Effective sounds in complex systems: The ARKola simulation. In *Proceedings of Human Factors in Computing Systems, CHI '91*, pages 85–90. ACM Press, New York, 1991.

[Gav92]   Gaver, W., The affordance of media spaces for collaboration. *Proceedings of the Conference on Computer-Supported Cooperative Work, CSCW '92*, pages 17–24. ACM, New York, 1992.

[Gre91]   Greenberg, S. (Ed.), *Computer-Supported Cooperative Work and Groupware*. Academic Press, London, 1991.

[Gre92]   Greenberg, S., Roseman, M., Webster, D. and Bohnet, R., Issues and experiences designing and implementing two group drawing tools. In *Proceedings of HICSS '92*, pages 139–150. IEEE Computer Society, Los Alamitos, CA, 1992.

[Gre88]   Greif, I. (Ed.), *Computer-Supported Cooperative Work: A Book of Readings*. Morgan Kaufmann, San Mateo, CA, 1988.

[Gro90]   Group Technologies, Inc., Aspects: The first simultaneous conference software for the Macintosh. *Aspects User's Manual*, Group Technologies, Inc., Arlington, VA, 1990.

[Gru88]   Grudin, J., Why CSCW applications fail: Problems in the design and evaluation of organizational interfaces. In *Proceedings of the Conference on Computer-Supported Cooperative Work, CSCW '88*, pages 85–93. ACM, New York, 1988.

[Gru91]   Grudin, J., CSCW introduction, *Communications of the ACM*, 34(12):30–34, December 1991.

[Hol92]   Hollan, J. and Stornetta, S., Beyond being there. In *Proceedings of Human Factors in Computing Systems, CHI '92*, pages 119–125. ACM, New York, 1992.

[Ish90]   Ishii, H., TeamWorkStation: Towards a seamless shared workspace. In *Proceedings of the Conference on Computer-Supported Cooperative Work, CSCW '90*, pages 13–26. ACM, October 1990.

[Ish91]   Ishii, H. and Miyake, N., Toward an open shared workspace: Computer and video fusion approach of TeamWorkStation. *Communications of the ACM*, 34(12):37–50, December 1991.

[Ish92a] Ishii, H. and Kobayashi, M., ClearBoard: A seamless medium for shared drawing and conversation with eye-contact. In *Proceedings of Human Factors in Computing Systems, CHI '92*, pages 525–532. ACM Press, May 1992.

[Ish92b] Ishii, H., Arita, K. and Kobayashi, M., Toward seamless collaboration media: From TeamWorkStation to ClearBoard. *SIGGRAPH Video Review*, CSCW '92 Technical Video Program, Issue 87, Item 6. ACM, New York, 1992.

[Ish93a] Ishii, H., Arita, K. and Yagi, T., Beyond videophones: TeamWorkStation-2 for narrowband ISDN. In *Proceedings of European Conference on Computer-Supported Cooperative Work, ECSCW '93*, pages 325–340. Kluwer Academic Publishers, Dordrecht, the Netherlands, September 1993.

[Ish93b] Ishii, H., Kobayashi, M. and Grudin, J., Integration of interpersonal space and shared workspace: ClearBoard design and experiments, *ACM Transactions on Information Systems (TOIS)*, 11(4):349–375, October 1993. (a previous version of this paper was published in the *Proceedings of CSCW '92*, pages 33–42, ACM, November 1992).

[Lau90]   Lauwers, J.C., Joseph, T.A., Lantz, K.A. and Romanow, A.L., Replicated architectures for shared window systems: A critique. In *Proceedings of COIS '90*, pages 249–260. ACM, New York, 1990.

[Lu91]   Lu, I. and Mantei, M., Idea management in a shared drawing tool. In *Proceedings of European Conference on Computer-Supported Cooperative Work, ECSCW '91*, pages 97–112. Kluwer Academic, Dordrecht, the Netherlands, 1991.

[Lyl93]   Lyles, B., Media spaces and broadband ISDN. *Communications of the ACM*, 36(1):46–47, January 1993.

[Mac99]   Mackay, W., Media spaces: Environments for informal multimedia interaction In Beaudouin-Lafon, M. (Ed.), *Computer Supported Cooperative Work*, Trends in Software Series 7:55–82. John Wiley & Sons, Chichester, 1999.

[Man91]   Mantei, M., Baecker, R., Sellen, A., Buxton, W. and Milligan, T., Experiences in the use of a media space. In *Proceedings of Human Factors in Computing Systems, CHI '91*, pages 203–208. ACM Press, New York, 1991.

[Min91]   Minneman, S.L. and Bly, S.A., Managing á trois: A study of a multi-user drawing tool in distributed design work. In *Proceedings of Human Factors in Computing Systems, CHI '91*, pages 217–224. ACM Press, New York, 1991.

[NTT93]   NTT, Seamless Media Design (video). Presented at TED4 KOBE, May 1993. Also presented at CSCW '94 formal video session.

[Pra99]   Atul Prakash, Group editors. In Beaudouin-Lafon, M. (Ed.), *Computer Supported Cooperative Work*, Trends in Software Series 7:103–133. John Wiley & Sons, Chichester, 1999.

[Str92]   Streitz, N., Haake, J., Hannemann, J., Lemke, A., Schuler, W., Schuett, H. and Thuering, M., SEPIA: A cooperative hypermedia environment. In *Proceedings of Conference on Hypertext, ECHT '92*, pages 11–22. ACM Press, New York, 1992.

[Tang91] Tang, J.C. and Minneman, S.L., VideoDraw: A video interface for collaborative drawing. *ACM Transactions on Information Systems (TOIS)*, 9(2):170–184, April 1991.

[Tan91]   Tanigawa, H., Arikawa, T., Masaki, S. and Shimamura, K., Personal multimedia-multipoint teleconference system. In *Proceedings of INFOCOM '91*, pages 1127–1134. IEEE Communications Society, 1991.

[Wat90]   Watabe, K., Sakata, S., Maeno, K., Fukuoka, H. and Ohmori, T., Distributed multiparty desktop conferencing system: MERMAID. In *Proceedings of the Conference on Computer-Supported Cooperative Work, CSCW'90*, pages 27–38. ACM, New York, 1990.

[Wei91]   Weiser, M., The computer for the twenty-first century. *Scientific American*, pages 94–104, September 1991.

[Wol92]   Wolf, C. and Rhyne, J., Communication and information retrieval with a pen-based meeting support tool. In *Proceedings of the Conference on Computer-Supported Cooperative Work, CSCW '92*, pages 322–329. ACM, New York, 1992.

5

Group Editors

ATUL PRAKASH
University of Michigan

ABSTRACT

This chapter focuses on group editors, an important class of collaborative tools that allow multiple users to view and edit a shared document simultaneously. Building group editors requires solving non-trivial problems such as providing adequate response time for edit operations, ensuring consistency with concurrent updates, providing adequate per-user undo facilities, and providing collaboration awareness. Design choices are presented for implementing these facilities as well as examples of implementations from several group editors.

5.1   INTRODUCTION

A group editor is a system that allows several users to simultaneously edit a document without the need for physical proximity and allows them to synchronously observe each others' changes. Group editors are a way to enhance collaboration by providing a shared workspace in which users can organize ideas, work jointly on papers, do brainstorming, etc. A group editor should have most of the functionality of single-user editors, such as being able to open, edit, and save documents.

In addition, group editors must usually be designed to have the following features:

- *Collaboration awareness:* A group editor should provide sufficient context information so that users are aware of other active participants in the group session. It should also facilitate sharing of views and sufficient idea of the work each participant is doing so as to encourage communication and avoid conflicting work.
- *Fault-tolerance and good response time:* A group editing session should continue to run smoothly despite machine crashes and people joining or leaving a session. Also, the editors should provide interactive response time for frequently done operations, such as browsing and a sequence of updates by a particular user.

Computer Supported Cooperative Work, Edited by Beaudouin-Lafon
© 1999 John Wiley & Sons Ltd

- *Concurrency control:* Concurrency control is needed to ensure consistency of data being edited when parallel editing is going on. Concurrency control protocols should be designed to minimize the impact of network latency on response times experienced by users, so that group work using the editor is not an inconvenience.
- *Multi-user undo:* A group editor should allow users to individually undo their changes. This is important because users may use a group editor to work in parallel on different parts of a document. Users should be able to use an undo command to reverse their own mistakes even if their change was not the last one carried out in the editor.
- *Usable as a single-user editor:* Group editors should provide good support for single-user use. Users should not have to switch to a different editor when they are working alone or asynchronously.
- *A rich document structure to serve as a medium of collaboration:* Some group editors use the document as a medium for brainstorming, organizing ideas, or as a means of communication among users. An important factor in the design of such group editors, as a result, is providing an appropriate document structure that facilitates group communication.

The rest of the chapter is organized as follows. It first gives examples of several group editors, illustrating how they can be used to support collaborative activities. Then, it presents the high-level architecture of typical group editors so that fault-tolerance and response time requirements can be met. Next, it suggests several approaches to addressing concurrency control requirements and supporting undo in group editors, and the tradeoffs between the approaches. Then, it discusses the collaboration awareness features that can be useful to provide in group editors. After that, it presents the structure of content in group editors that are designed to support specific collaborative tasks such as brainstorming activities. Then, it briefly highlights other design issues that arise in building group editors. Finally, it presents some directions for future work in group editors.

5.2 EXAMPLES OF GROUP EDITORS

5.2.1 Group Graphical Editors

Dolphin [Str94] is an example of a graphical group editing environment for supporting joint work and brainstorming by users who are not co-located. In Figure 5.1, four users are using a shared document in Dolphin as the medium to support brainstorming. Users can sketch, type, or create links to other pages to communicate their ideas. Audioconferencing tools, such as MBone's *vat*, are often used with Dolphin so that users can conveniently discuss the contents of the document.

The rich hyperlink-based structure of documents in Dolphin allows different kinds of collaborative tasks to be supported. Simple brainstorming tasks may use the system only as a graphical sketch pad. More involved, decision-making discussions can choose to take advantage of the hyperlink-support to organize the discussions into IBIS-like decision tree structures [Rei91]. The system does not have most of the formatting features of commercial (single-user) word-processing systems such as Word or LATEX, though, in principle, it could be extended to support more extensive formatting features.

Many of the graphical operations, such as dragging or resizing objects, require high interactivity, independent of network latencies. Dolphin provides immediate feedback on such

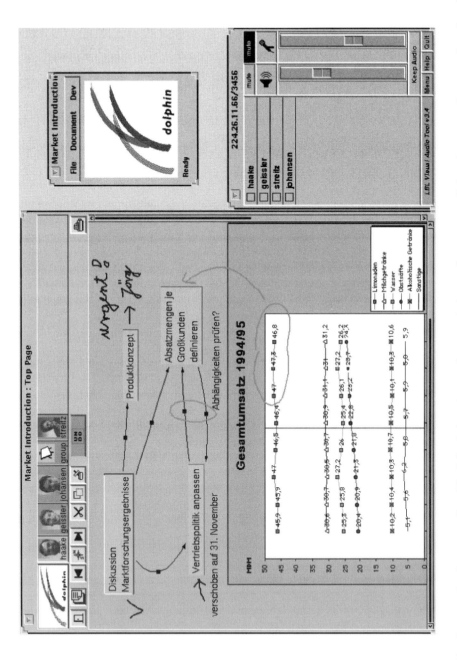

Figure 5.1 An example of a group editor. The left window shows a document being used to support collaboration among four users in a shared window. An audioconferencing tool (shown on the bottom right) is also used to facilitate interaction. © 1996 by GMD-IPSI, reprinted by permission.

operations. At the same time, Dolphin guarantees that all users will see a consistent state at quiescence, even if several users edit the document simultaneously.

Temporary anomalies may arise when several users attempt to modify the same object. For example, if two users drag the same object to different places simultaneously, they will initially see the object being dragged in their own direction. However, when the changes are propagated to other users, one of the operations is undone by the concurrency control algorithm. As a result, one of the users may see the object suddenly move back to its old location (undoing the user's change) and then move to the location selected by the other user (executing the other user's operation).

A Dolphin window shows the list of users who are looking at the same document. As users open or close the document window, the list is automatically updated. This is a form of group awareness that can be critical to the successful use of group editors. Users often need to know if other users are also looking at the same document, in order to have a meaningful discussion about the document. Audio communication among group members can provide additional context and awareness.

Dolphin allows users to have one shared public window and multiple private windows for a given document. Navigation in the public window (e.g. following links to other pages of the document) is visible to all the users. Navigation in a private window is private to a user. Editing changes to the document itself, however, are not private.

Multi-user whiteboards, such as MBone's *wb* and those in Netscape's Cooltalk and Intel's ProShare system, provide basic sketching facilities for brainstorming, as in Dolphin. These systems do not, however, provide the ability to create links to other parts of a document, or the ability to use both private and shared windows into a document.

5.2.2 Group Text Editors

All the above editors are primarily graphical editors. The support for text is generally limited to placing simple textual objects at a selected location in the graphical document. Text is usually treated as a graphical object that can be placed at a selected coordinate on the document canvas. Simultaneous update of a text object is usually not supported. Thus, these editors are not really appropriate for creating large text documents jointly.

Several group editors, such as GROVE [Ell88], DistEdit-based Emacs [Kni90], MACE [New91], and SASSE [Bae93] have explored issues in providing support for joint editing of text. In these editors, simultaneous editing of text objects is allowed, even within the same sentence or paragraph.

Allowing simultaneous editing of a related sequence of characters raises interesting concurrency control issues. Consider the following example:

> A document contains a string *ompute*. Suppose user A attempts to insert the character r after character e. In many text editors, this would be carried out using an operation $InsChar(7, r)$ on the document, inserting r at position 7 in the document. But, now suppose that between the time the operation is generated by A's input and the time it is executed, another user's operation $InsChar(1, c)$ is executed, in order to insert a c before the o. If the operations are simply executed in the order $InsChar(1, c)$ followed by $InsChar(7, r)$, the resulting string would be *computre*, rather than the intended result of *computer*.

Such a problem of unintended results rarely arises in graphical editors because most operations are with reference to absolute coordinates on a canvas. Intended results can usually

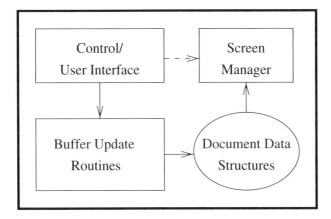

Figure 5.2   Typical structure of a single-user editor

be achieved by executing the operations in the same order at all sites. Furthermore, simultaneous operations often commute; when they do not, the differences in the results may not be significant enough for users to care [Gre94].

In a text editor, on the other hand, users usually intend their operations to be relative to positions of existing characters. However, internally, editors often represent operations using offsets from beginning of the text object. As illustrated in the above example, this can lead to unintended results. Some of the techniques for dealing with this problem are discussed later in the chapter.

Another class of group editing environments are those that support more asynchronous or non-real time styles of interaction. Examples are editors such as CES [Gri76], Quilt [Fis88], and Prep [Neu90]. Prep, for instance, introduced a novel interface in which multiple columns are used, with the first column displaying the editor's text, and subsequent columns showing the comments on the text by the collaborators in the group. These editors allow users to work on the same document but typically on different sections and at different times. As a result, interactions are over a much longer duration, even up to several days. Many of the issues of concurrency control, fault tolerance, and real-time propagation of updates are less relevant to such systems. This chapter does not discuss these systems.

5.3   GROUP EDITOR ARCHITECTURE

The high-level structure of a typical single-user editor is shown in Figure 5.2. A user interface and control section waits for input; when input is received, it is translated into a set of calls which update the document or update the interface.

Group editors, in order to provide interactive response times on browsing operations, usually use a fully replicated architecture in which the document state is replicated at each site (see Chapter 7 in this book [Dew99]). As an example, Figure 5.3 shows the replicated architecture of DistEdit-based group editors. DistEdit is a toolkit that allows existing text editors to be converted to group editors with minimal changes to their code as well as to ease development of new group text editors. Several editors, including MicroEmacs, Xedit, and Gnu Emacs, have been modified to make use of DistEdit. In DistEdit, modifications to an editor's document state are done using a set of standardized update primitives. Each editor's update

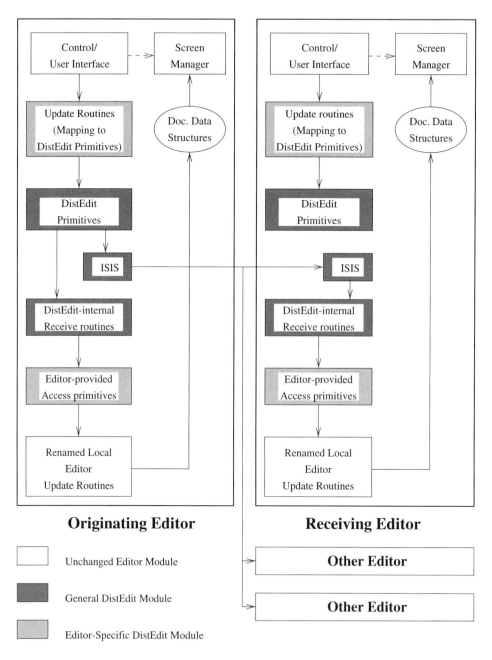

Figure 5.3   Replicated architecture of group editors built using the DistEdit toolkit

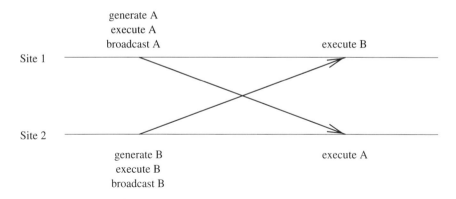

Figure 5.4   A scenario of the document state becoming inconsistent at different sites. Without concurrency control, the two operations A and B are executed in different orders at different sites, possibly leading to different states

operations are mapped to one or more calls on the DistEdit primitives. Those DistEdit primitives are multicast to all the editor copies, using the ISIS communication package[Bir90]. All the editors then apply the updates to their local copies. This general idea of replicating state and propagating changes is used in many group editors, though different editors differ in the choice of update primitives, document type, user-interface features, and algorithms for concurrency control.

As we will see in Sections 5.4 and 5.5, selection of a core set of update primitives that directly update the document state in a group editor is helpful in the implementation of concurrency control and multi-user undo. Usually, implementing concurrency control algorithms and undo is simpler if this core set of update primitives is kept small. Additional update operations can be defined in terms of the core set of update primitives, without substantially complicating concurrency control and undo algorithms.

5.4   CONCURRENCY CONTROL

Concurrency control techniques are required to ensure that a document's state in a replicated architecture remains consistent even when users attempt to modify the document simultaneously in a group editing environment. Consider a case where the state, S, of the document is initially consistent (identical) at the various sites. Let us consider the simple case that two users attempt to modify the document simultaneously via operations A and B. If each operation is executed locally first and then broadcast for execution at other sites (Figure 5.4), the operations would be applied in different orders at different copies of the document, potentially leading to inconsistent states — an undesirable situation in general.

One solution to the data consistency problem is to use ordered broadcast protocols to ensure that all broadcasts are received in the same sequence at all sites [Bir87, Cha84]. However, in this case, the sender of a broadcast has to wait to receive its own message from the network before it can execute the operation. In fact, it may receive other sites' messages prior to receiving its own message owing to message ordering requirements (Figure 5.5). This waiting can lead to poor interactive response-times in multi-user use. Unfortunately, it can also lead to poor interactive response times when one user is primarily interacting with the editor because

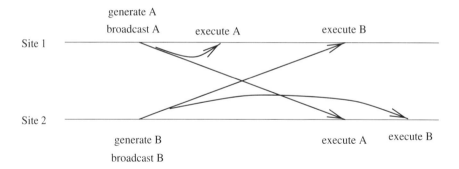

Figure 5.5   The use of ordered broadcast protocols to achieve data consistency. Delivery and execution of message B must be delayed at site 2 so that delivery/execution order is consistent with that at site 1. Also, B is executed in a different state than when it was generated, possibly leading to an unintended document state

ordered broadcast protocols usually rely on a central site to determine the order of delivery of messages. Another problem with this solution is that operations received from other sites may be done on the application's state between the time that the operation was generated and the time it is actually executed; executing the operation in the modified state may not lead to correct or intended results, as we will see later.

Another solution to the data consistency problem is to use a centralized data architecture, where the copy of the data resides only at one site. Without the use of any other concurrency control scheme, this is essentially equivalent to the use of a replicated architecture that uses ordered broadcast protocols. In particular, it has similar response time problems. It can have much worse performance for browsing if sites do not cache the document state locally. Also, the possibility of unintended results remains because the centralized site may execute parallel operations in an arbitrary order, perhaps leading to unintended results.

There are thus two key aspects of ensuring consistency that group editors must deal with:

- consistency of state among the various document copies, assuming that a replicated architecture is used in order to enhance response time
- consistency of the resulting state of a document with respect to a user's intention when doing an update, in cases where other participants' operations are applied to the document between the time the user's operation is generated and the time it is executed.

Techniques for maintaining consistency among copies of a document are largely based on algorithms that have been proposed in the work on replicated databases. However, performance tradeoffs are different between group editors and database systems, and that leads to different choices of concurrency control algorithms. Group editors must provide interactive response times; impact of network latencies on response time to user input must be minimized. The concurrency control strategies in databases, on the other hand, must usually maximize transaction throughput, rather than the response time of individual transactions.

Another difference from database systems is that group editors usually do not use a transaction-based approach to updates because of the complexities involved in developing support for transactions in a general-purpose programming language and for systems requiring highly-responsive, interactive graphical interfaces. However, some recent systems, such as COAST [Sch96] and DECAF [Str97], provide transaction-based support for building groupware systems.

There are two broad classes of concurrency control techniques: *pessimistic* and *optimistic*. Pessimistic techniques ensure that inconsistencies among copies do not arise by requiring that any update operations acquire appropriate locks to prevent conflicting updates from occurring. Optimistic techniques do not prevent inconsistencies from occurring, but use mechanisms to detect and correct inconsistencies if they occur.

Almost all practical databases use lock-based pessimistic techniques because they usually provide a better transaction throughput. Many group editors, on the other hand, use optimistic or special pessimistic techniques, with the goal of reducing interactive response times. The following first discusses strategies for applying pessimistic and optimistic strategies to group editors and then discusses enhancements to the strategies to avoid inconsistency among documents with respect to users' intentions.

5.4.1 Pessimistic Concurrency Control

To ensure consistency among copies of a shared document, one strategy is for operations to acquire network-wide locks before updating the various document copies. Thus, in the earlier example of two users doing operations A and B in parallel, the operations can be executed on all the copies in the order in which the operations acquire locks.

If acquiring or releasing locks requires going over the network, users may still perceive substantial increase in interactive response times because each user's update operation will involve acquiring some locks over the network, doing the operation, and then releasing the locks. In fact, if in a group session only one user is interacting with the application, the same overhead could occur. Such a situation is clearly undesirable.

To improve performance of lock-based schemes, one technique is to use a token-based locking scheme. DistView [Pra94b], a general-purpose toolkit for building groupware applications, uses a token-based locking scheme. When a site acquires a lock, it gets a lock-specific *token*; only one site can have the token at a time. When a site releases the lock, it is treated as a *hint* that the lock is no longer needed. The site still retains the token, but marks it as *available* for other users. If the same site wishes to reacquire the same lock, the lock can be granted immediately without going over the network by simply marking the token as *unavailable*. If another site wishes to acquire the lock, it sends a message out to the entire group, requesting the lock. The sites without the token ignore the message. The site with the token transfers the token if it is marked *available*; otherwise it denies the lock request.

The performance impact of the above token-based scheme is that network latencies in acquiring locks occur only if the lock has to be acquired from some other site. If only one user is repeatedly acquiring and releasing locks, no network messages need to be sent except for the first lock request (Figure 5.6). This can be an efficient locking strategy in practice because usage patterns in group editors are often such that one user does most of the interactions, while others observe the changes. A complication in the token-based scheme is that, for fault-tolerance, a distributed token recovery algorithm is needed to deal with situations where a site crashes while holding a token.

Another technique to reduce impact on response time is to support multiple, fine-grain locks on the document. Different users may hold different locks, so the likelihood of waiting on locks can be reduced. In DistEdit-based text group editors [Kni90], the granularity of locks can be as small as one character. A lock covers any contiguous region of text. Inserting a string requires obtaining a lock on the character which precedes the point of insert. Deleting a string requires a lock covering the characters of the string.

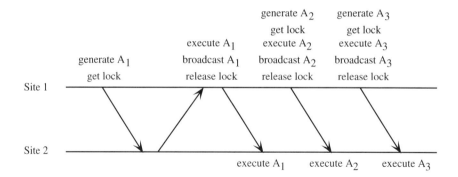

Figure 5.6 The DistView toolkit uses a token-based locking scheme to help improve response time for typical usage patterns. Site 1 needs to acquire a token from a remote site for the first operation A_1. For subsequent operations that require the same lock, no token needs to be acquired over the network, leading to good response times

As insertions or deletions are performed within a region, the associated lock in DistEdit expands or shrinks automatically, without re-acquiring fresh locks over the network. Thus, for insert operations (perhaps the most frequent operation in text editors), network latencies impact response time only for the first insert at a new position; subsequent characters are inserted with similar response times as in single-user editors.

Browsing operations in group editors normally do not need to acquire any locks (unless the editor supports synchronized browsing). Thus browsing can be done interactively, independent of updates initiated at other sites.

Locking, as described above, is largely intended to be hidden from users. Locks are automatically acquired or released as users interact with the editor. Several group editing systems, including MACE [New91] and DistEdit, also support *explicit* locking, where a user deliberately selects and locks a region of the document. A user may chose to acquire an explicit lock to work on a region in order to indicate to others that they should not work on that region until the lock is released. Techniques for handling explicit locks are similar to those used for handling automatic locks, except that explicitly-acquired locks are kept until released by the user.

5.4.2   Optimistic Concurrency Control

Another technique to ensure consistency is to use optimistic concurrency control. An operation is executed on the local copy immediately and then broadcast to other sites for execution. All update operations are first time-stamped so that any two operations can be consistently reordered at all the copies, even if they are received in different orders. To reorder operations, each site has to maintain a *history list*. The history list is a sequence of operations that have been performed on the document. The operations on the history list are stored in the order in which they were performed. For instance, if the history list is

$$B\ C\ D$$

then, starting from the state prior to B, carrying out the operations B, C, and D in sequence should lead to the current state of the document.

Consider the situation now if operation A is received by the above copy, where A has lower

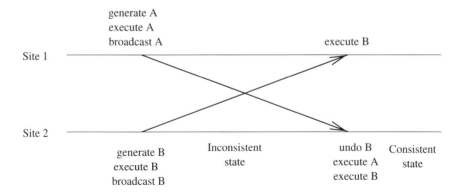

Figure 5.7   The use of undo/redo strategy for optimistic concurrency control. At site 2, execution order is made consistent with that at site 1 by undoing execution of B and then executing A and B. Site 2 is temporarily in an inconsistent state with respect to site 1

time-stamp than B, C, and D. In such a case, the operations can be reordered by *undoing* D, C, and B (in that order), performing A, and then performing B, C, and D. The resulting history list will be

$$A\ B\ C\ D$$

For this scheme to work, inverses need to be defined for all operations so that they can be undone. Figure 5.7 shows the use of optimistic concurrency control to achieve data consistency for the example in Figure 5.4.

Karsenty and Beaudouin-Lafon [Kar93] describe an algorithm that improves the performance of the above undo/redo scheme by taking advantage of commutativity among operations, when the commutativity information is provided to the editor. The following example illustrates the use of undo/redo in their scheme. Suppose that two operations A and B should be executed in the order A followed by B. However, one of the sites in a groupware system receives the broadcast of operation B first, executes it, and then receives the broadcast of operation A. Their algorithm will allow out-of-order execution of A at the site if A and B commute. The algorithm will in fact not execute A at all if B *masks* the effect of executing A; i.e. executing A followed by B gives the same results as just executing B. If commutativity or masking does not occur, the algorithm will undo A, execute B, and then redo B to correct the execution order. This algorithm is used in several systems including Dolphin and COAST [Sch96].

Note that the undo/redo in the above optimistic concurrency control scheme is internal to the system and is used only for ensuring consistency. No undo/redo capability is provided to end-users. In particular, support for undoing an operation that is executed in the correct order is not addressed by the above scheme.

Unlike in lock-based pessimistic schemes, optimistic schemes suffer from a window of opportunity where a user can interact with the editor while the user's copy of the document is in an inconsistent state. For instance, in Figure 5.7, the user at site 2 could issue editing operations immediately after broadcasting B. These operations would also execute optimistically at site 2. The problem is that these operations may be generated based on a state that is later going to be undone. Unlike in databases, the optimistic (inconsistent) state is visible to the users, since the goal of using an optimistic algorithm is to reduce response time. Currently, there does not appear to be a good solution to this problem. Most editors that use optimistic schemes simply assume that such a possibility does not arise too often, and when it does, users can deal with any unintended effect.

5.4.3   Consistency with Users' Intentions

A group editor must not only provide a consistent document state at each site, but must attempt to perform operations with effects that are consistent with users' intentions. The algorithms, as discussed above, need to be enhanced to address this. Consider the example given in Section 5.2.2, which is repeated below:

Example 1

A text editor's document contains the string *ompute*. User A attempts to insert the character r after character e. In many text editors, this would be carried out using an operation $InsChar(7, r)$ on the document, inserting r at position 7. But, now suppose that between the time the operation is generated by A's input and the time it is executed, another user's operation $InsChar(1, c)$ is executed, in order to insert a c before the o. If the operations are simply executed in the order $InsChar(1, c)$ followed by $InsChar(7, r)$, the resulting string would be *computre*, rather than the intended result of *computer*.

The above problem is not a replicated data inconsistency problem because all the copies of the data will have the same string. However, it is an inconsistency with the user's intention of inserting the character r after the e in the string. The inconsistency arose because another user's action was carried out on the document between the time the user initiated the action and the time it was executed. Thus the user's operation, which used positional offsets, was applied in a different location than intended, leading to unintended results.

The reader may think that the above scenario of two users modifying the same word is not very likely. However, the same problem arises if users are modifying different parts of a long document (a more likely scenario) as long as references used in the operations change as a result of other editing operations.

The solution commonly used in group text editors to address the problem is to *detect* the possibility of an undesirable result, *modify* the operation so that it leads to the intended, desirable result, and then execute the modified operation.

In Example 1, this scheme would transform the second operation from $InsChar(7, r)$ to $InsChar(8, r)$ so that it leads to insertion at the correct point, given that the first operation has already been executed.

The use of transformations requires the definition of a *transformation matrix* Tr [Ell89]. $Tr(A, B)$ tells how an operation A should be transformed to give the intended effect, given that another parallel operation B has already been executed. For instance, if A and B are generated in parallel by different users and

$$Tr(A, B) = A' \text{ and } Tr(B, A) = B',$$

then A' should be executed instead of A if B has already been executed. Similarly, B' should be executed at a site instead of B if A has already been executed.

Transformations can be used in several ways in optimistic schemes. Figure 5.8 shows the original use of it in the GROVE editor [Ell88, Ell89]. Site 1 executes the parallel operations A, B as A followed by B', whereas site 2 executes the operations as B followed by A'. Data consistency obviously requires that the transformation matrix satisfy the *transform property* that executing A followed by B' results in the same state as executing B' followed by A.

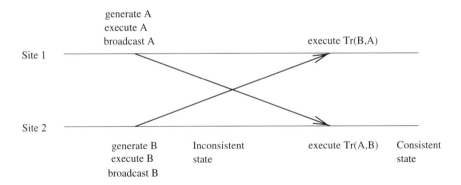

Figure 5.8 The use of transformations to achieve data consistency and consistency with users' intentions in an optimistic manner, without the use of undo/redo. Sites may do operations in different order and transformations must satisfy constraints that ensure consistency

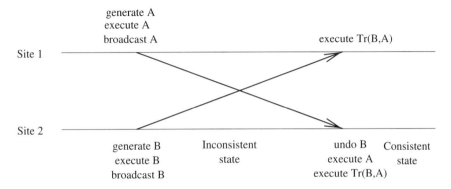

Figure 5.9 The use of transformations to achieve data consistency and consistency with users' intentions in an optimistic manner using undo/redo. In this case, all sites execute operations in the same sequence, if necessary after reordering operations

Figure 5.9 shows the use of transformations with the undo/redo concurrency control scheme. In this case, site 1 executes the operations as A followed by B'. Site 2 executes them in the same order, after undoing B to achieve the same order. This has the slight advantage that data consistency is achieved even if the transformation matrix fails to satisfy the transform property. The disadvantage is that the undo/redo-based strategy can be somewhat slower.

Transformations can also be useful in pessimistic schemes. For instance, if an ordered broadcast protocol is used, transformations can be applied to achieve the same results as in the undo/redo scheme shown in Figure 5.9.

With lock-based schemes, transformations can be used for mapping lock requests to correct regions in the document, even when parallel lock requests are made. Operations do not need transforms in that case, because operations can use positions that are relative to the positions specified in the locks. This simplifies transformations considerably, because the number of operations can be much larger than the types of lock requests.

A second approach to the handling inconsistency with user's intentions is to simply do nothing. The assumption is that users can correct any unintended results manually. This may be an acceptable approach in some cases. It is not an acceptable solution, however, if the problem is likely to occur frequently during group editing, if it could have a hard-to-correct effect on the document state, or if the users are unlikely to notice the problem when it occurs. For simple graphical editors, such as shared whiteboards, this can be a reasonable approach, because most operations can be designed so that transformations are not required.

A third approach to the problem is to *detect* the possibility of an undesirable result and to *abort* the second operation on all copies of the document (i.e. not execute the operation, or undo it if it has already been executed). This is somewhat better than doing nothing because undesirable results are prevented and the user who initiated the aborted action can be notified (e.g. via a beep) that the operation was not carried out.

Designers of sophisticated group editors may find it practical to rely on all the three approaches for different aspects in the same editor. The approach of modifying operations may be used in the same editor to deal with commonly-occurring situations that are easy to detect and correct, such as changes in the positional offsets of an operation as a result of parallel operations.

The second approach of doing nothing may be best for situations where the system cannot easily determine, usually owing to difficult data semantics, whether the results will be considered to be unintended by users. For example, if given the word *helo* in a document copy, if one user attempts to insert an *l* after the *e*, and another user attempts to insert an *l* before the *o* simultaneously, the resulting string would be *helllo* in most text group editors — perhaps an unintended result if the users expected the result to be *hello*. However, this result is difficult to avoid if the editor treats its document state as simply a string of characters — the concept of words and perhaps even spellings would have to be introduced in the editor to result in the intended string *hello*. And even that could be an unintended effect to some users because they may have expected both letters to be inserted. A more practical solution in this case is to design the editor to provide *predictable* behavior that will be compatible with users' intentions in *most* cases, and to provide collaboration-awareness features so that users are less likely to make updates that lead to unintended results.

The third approach of aborting operations may be useful in the same editor when operations conflict so severely that only one can be done meaningfully. For example, in editors that provide locking, if two users attempt to lock an overlapping document region simultaneously — obviously, only one operation can be allowed to succeed, and the other has to be aborted.

5.4.4   Alternatives to Concurrency Control

Another way to deal with concurrency control is to ensure that parallel editing operations always commute. In that case, neither pessimistic, nor optimistic concurrency control is needed. Operations can be executed by sites as they are received.

The MBone-based whiteboard, *wb*, used such a strategy. In *wb*, users could only modify their own work on the whiteboard — not that of others. This restriction ensured that parallel updates from different users modified different objects on the canvas, thus removing the need for a concurrency control algorithm. Such a strategy was useful in *wb* because in an MBone session, thousands of participants were often expected. Attempting to do concurrency control among such a large group was likely to be inefficient.

In a graphical editor that does not use any concurrency control, it is possible to get some inconsistencies. For instance, if two users move different filled objects, say *A* and *B*, simultaneously to the same location on the canvas, it is possible that one user's display shows *A* as being above B while the other user's display shows B as being above A. If such inconsistencies are acceptable to users, then the two operations can be considered to commute. Otherwise, a concurrency control algorithm is likely to be needed.

5.5 UNDO IN A GROUP EDITOR

The ability to undo operations is a useful standard feature in most interactive single-user applications. For instance, the availability of an undo facility in editors is useful for reversing erroneous actions [Han71]. It can also help reduce user frustration with new systems [Fol74], particularly if those systems allow users to invoke commands that can modify the system state in complex ways.

Compared with single-user applications, performing undo in groupware applications provides technical challenges in the following areas [Pra92, Pra94a]:

- *Selecting the operation to be undone.* In a group editing environment, there may be parallel streams of activities from different users. When work on a shared document occurs in parallel, users usually expect an undo to reverse their own last operation rather than the globally last operation, which may belong to another user. An undo framework for groupware systems needs to allow selection of the operation to undo based on who performed it.
- *Determining what operation will result in a correct undo.* Once the correct operation to be undone is selected, the operation to execute to effect an undo has to be determined. Simply executing the inverse of the operation to be undone may not work because of modifications done by other users.
- *Dealing with dependencies between different users' operations.* If multiple users interleave their work in the same region of a document, it may not be possible to undo one user's changes without undoing some of the other users' changes. In this case, there are dependencies between the changes which need to be taken into account during an undo.

Supporting undo in group editors requires a *history list* — which was previously used in Section 5.4.2 for doing optimistic concurrency control. If the editor uses a replicated architecture, a concurrency control scheme should be used that results in the history lists being consistent (i.e. operations added to the history list in the same sequence) at all sites.

In addition to maintaining a history list, supporting undo requires that all operations that modify the state of the document are *reversible*; i.e. for every operation A, we can determine an inverse operation $\overline{A}$ that will undo the effect of A, assuming A was the most recent operation executed. For instance, in an editor, an *INSERT* operation can be undone by a *DELETE* operation.

We next look at design strategies to address the above three issues.

5.5.1 Selecting Operations

In a group editor, a user may wish to undo his last operation, but that operation may not have been the globally last operation executed on the document (other users may have done operations subsequently). We therefore need to allow undoing of a *particular user's* last operation from the history list.

To allow such selection of the operation to undo based on user identity, each operation on the history list needs to be *tagged* with the *user-id* of the user who invoked the operation [Pra92]. For example, consider the following history list, where A_i's refer to operations done by one user, say Ann, and B_i's refer to operations done by other users:

$$A_1 \; B_1 \; A_2 \; B_2 \; B_3.$$

Now, suppose Ann wishes to undo her last operation. The selection mechanism would choose to undo A_2, the last operation on the list that is tagged with Ann's user-id.

In the above example, the operation to be undone, A_2, is selected based on the identity of the user. More generally, the operation to undo could be selected based on any other attribute, such as region, time, or anything else. To allow selection on other attributes, tags could include additional information such as the time at which the operation was carried out or the document region in which it was carried out.

In DistEdit, we have found undo that is restricted to a particular region of a document (e.g. paragraph) to be particularly useful, in addition to an undo based on user identity.

The above scheme has been termed *selective undo* [Pra92, Ber94, Pra94a], since the operation to be undone is not necessarily the last one, but is selected using some attributes attached to the operation.

5.5.2   Executing the Undo

Once the correct operation to be undone is selected, the operation to execute to effect an undo has to be determined. We look at several strategies for executing the operation.

5.5.2.1   Direct Selective Undo Strategy

One potential solution for undoing any operation in the history list is simply to execute its inverse, provided the inverse is executable in the current state [Ber94]. So, given the following history list:

$$A_1 \; B_1 \; A_2 \; B_2 \; B_3$$

operation A_2 is undone by simply executing A_2's inverse, $\overline{A_2}$, resulting in the history list:

$$A_1 \; B_1 \; A_2 \; B_2 \; B_3 \; \overline{A_2}.$$

This approach essentially assumes that any operation in the history list can be undone simply by executing its inverse from the current state (provided the inverse can be executed), irrespective of the other operations on the history list.

Unfortunately, not taking into account dependencies among operations can lead to unexpected or hard-to-predict undo behavior in certain situations. To see some of the problems that arise when operations have dependencies among them, consider the following example.

Example 2
Let's say that a graphical document contains a circle of size 6 and that the following two operations are done, leading to a circle of size 4:

- *Operation 1:* double the radius of the circle
- *Operation 2:* set the radius of the circle to 4.

Assume that the inverses of the above operations are chosen to be:

- halve the radius of the circle
- restore the radius of the circle to 12 (the size prior to doing operation 2).

Suppose the first user now issues a command to undo operation 1. To undo operation 1, using the above undo strategy, the inverse of operation 1 is executed, resulting in a circle of radius 2. Unfortunately, since the circle was never of size 2, this may be a result that is difficult for the users to understand.

Another problem with the strategy is that the result of undoing a set of operations may depend on the *order* in which the operations are undone. In the above example, one can end up with a circle of size 12 or a circle of size 6, depending on the order in which the above two operations are undone. Note that one of the possible results is different from 6, the initial size of the circle.

This strategy, despite the above problems, may be useful in some cases. First, if operations on the editor are carefully designed to always commute, then this strategy will give expected results. For instance, in the above example, if the second operation was replaced by an operation that reduces the radius of the circle by a factor of 3 (and its inverse being an operation that increases the radius of the circle by a factor of 3), then this strategy, as can be verified, would give expected results. Second, as suggested in [Ber94], if the users are presented with the list of operations that have been done and explicitly select one to be reversed with the understanding that the system will simply execute the inverse of the operation in the present state, then the results can be better understood by users.

5.5.2.2   Undo–Redo Strategy

Another strategy for undoing an operation is to bring the document to a state prior to an operation A by undoing all operations executed since A (in reverse order), then undoing A, and then redoing all the undone operations except A [Cho95]. This strategy is similar to that used in undo-skip-redo (US&R) strategy [Vit84] for single-user editors. For example, given the history list:

$$A_1 \; B_1 \; A_2 \; B_2 \; B_3$$

to undo A_2, first inverses of B_3 and B_2 are executed, then the inverse of A_2 is executed, and finally B_2 and B_3 are re-executed. This results in the history list:

$$A_1 \; B_1 \; A_2 \; B_2 \; B_3 \; \overline{B_2} \; \overline{B_3} \; \overline{A_2} \; B_2 \; B_3$$

or its equivalent, in terms of the effect on the document state:

$$A_1 \; B_1 \; B_2 \; B_3.$$

For Example 2, if operation 1 is to be undone, the effect would be to undo both operations and then redo the second operation, resulting in a circle of size 4. This is a reasonable result in the sense that the circle would have been of size 4 if operation 1 had never been done. On the other hand, a problem remains that this may not be what the user intended to happen because the undo will appear to have no effect and no error will be reported [Ber94].

Both this strategy, as pointed out by its authors [Cho95], and the direct selective undo strategy, do not account for the need for transformations. Consider the following example from a text editor.

Example 3

Let's say that a text document contains only the string *omputr*. The following two operations are done in sequence by two users, leading to the string *computer*:

- *Operation 1: InsChar(1, c)* to insert *c* before *o*, the first position in the string, resulting in the string *computr*.
- *Operation 2: InsChar(7, e)* to insert *e* between *t* and *r*, the seventh position in the string.

Reasonable inverses for the above operations are:

- *DelChar(1)* and
- *DelChar(7)*.

If now, the first user attempts to undo operation 1, we would like the result to be *omputer*, the string that would have resulted if operation 1 had not been executed by the first user. However, the undo/redo strategy would first restore the string to *omputr* by undoing both operations and then re-execute operation 2, leading to the string *omputre*. The direct selective undo strategy works for this example, but does not work if operation 2 had been done prior to operation 1.

The problem that occurred with Example 3 is that the second operation would have executed as *InsChar(6, e)* — at a different position — if the first operation had not occurred, assuming that the intended effect of the operation was to insert *e* between *t* and *r*. Unfortunately, this basic strategy does not take such needs of modifications to operations into account [Abo92, Pra92].

Despite the above limitations, the undo/redo strategy can be a useful one, especially when transformations are not required and users accept its semantics. Results after multiple undo commands, unlike the direct selective undo strategy, are independent of the order in which they are carried out.

5.5.3   Transformation-Based Selective Undo

The basic problem illustrated by Examples 2 and 3 is that to undo an operation other than the last one on the history list, one cannot simply execute the inverse of the operation (or use the undo/redo strategy) because subsequent operations could have shifted the location at which the operation was originally performed.

Another problem with implementing selective undo is the the possibility of *dependencies*, or *conflicts*, between operations. Suppose an operation B has modified the same region of the document as an earlier operation A. It may then not be possible to undo A without first undoing B. A general solution to undo needs to be able to detect when an operation cannot be undone because of later conflicting operations that have not been undone.

A general solution to the problem of dealing with transformations and conflicts is presented in [Pra94a]. Here we examine an intuitive description of the solution used. To allow an arbitrary operation on the history list to be undone, the solution in [Pra94a] requires that the application supply functions which can detect *conflicts* between operations, *re-order* non-conflicting operations, and create *inverse* operations. More specifically, besides the inverse function, the application must provide the following two functions:

- *Conflict(A, B)* that returns *true* if the operations A and B performed in sequence cannot be reordered, and *false* otherwise.
- If A and B do not conflict, a function *Transpose(A, B)* that returns (B', A'), a reordering

of operations A and B such that executing A and B in sequence has the same effect as executing B' and A' in sequence. Also, B' must be the transformed operation that should have been executed by the editor if A had not been executed earlier.

The notion of conflict is just a formal way of capturing the requirement that the operations should not be reordered because of semantic dependencies — typically the operations modify the same objects or region in the document. For instance, if operation A inserted a string and operation B modified the inserted string, there would be a conflict between the two operations. Also, note that the Transpose function above applies to operations that have already been executed with correct results, unlike the transformation function for the Transformation matrix, which is used to determine the operation to execute for getting correct results.

If an operation A is undone, we assume that the users want their document to go to a state that it would have gone to if operation A had never been performed, but all the following non-conflicting operations had been performed. For example, suppose that on a document in state S, operations A and B are performed in sequence, and then A is undone. Let's assume that $Transpose(A, B) = (B', A')$. Therefore, by the definition of the Transpose function, if A had never been performed, the system would have performed operation B' in place of B. Therefore, after undoing A, the selective undo algorithm should result in the document's state being as if only B' had been performed in state S.

The basic idea behind the algorithm is to *shift* the operation to be undone to the end of the history list by transposing it with subsequent operations. If the operation cannot be shifted to the end of the list owing to a conflict, then the operation cannot be undone without also undoing the conflicting operation. If the operation can be shifted to the end, then it can be undone by simply executing its inverse. As an example, suppose that we want to undo A given the history list:

$$A \ B \ C.$$

Suppose A conflicts with B. Then $Conflict(A, B)$ will be true, and the undo of A will fail, as it should, because A cannot be undone unless B is also undone. If A does not conflict with B, the result after one iteration of shifting will be:

$$B' \ A' \ C$$

where $(B', A') = Transpose(A, B)$. Note that the history list need not be actually altered because only the new A' is used in the next iteration. We show the altered list here for clarity.

Next, if $Conflict(A', C)$ is true, the undo will fail. Otherwise, another shift will occur, resulting in:

$$B' \ C' \ A''$$

where $(C', A'') = Transpose(A', C)$. It follows from the definition of the Transpose function that B' and C' are the operations that the system would have executed, instead of operations B and C, if operation A had not been executed earlier.

Now that A has been shifted to the end of the list, $\overline{A''}$ can be performed giving the list:

$$B' \ C'.$$

Performing $\overline{A''}$ in the present state therefore correctly cancels A, giving the same document state as executing B' and C' in the original state — the operations that would have executed had A never been performed; the undo has succeeded.

The Transpose and Inverse functions need to satisfy several formal properties for a correct undo algorithm. For more details on the properties the reader is referred to [Pra94a]. The paper also presents a generalization of the above scheme to handling undo of previously undone operations and undo of operations restricted to a region. Below, we only illustrate the Conflict and Transpose functions that would be defined for Examples 2 and 3 and the resulting behavior on undo.

In Example 2, $Conflict(Operation1, Operation2)$ is best declared to be true because they both change the same attribute of the circle; also there is no simple way to reorder the two operations with the same resulting effect on the state and satisfying all the properties that are given in [Pra94a]. Thus, $Operation1$ cannot be undone by this algorithm without also undoing $Operation2$. An implementation can either report a conflict error, undo both operations automatically, or give an option to the user to either undo both operations or to leave the document state unchanged, in view of the subsequent change by another user.

In Example 3, operations 1 and 2 need not be declared to conflict. The history list would contain:

$$InsChar(1, x) \; InsChar(5, y).$$

To undo the first operation, the algorithm would shift it to the end of the list by (temporarily) reordering the list as follows:

$$InsChar(6, e) \; InsChar(1, c))$$

It will then execute its inverse, DelChar(1). This results in the string *omputer*, the intended result that deletes e from the first position, leaving the effect of the second operation in the correct place.

5.5.4   Undo–Redo Strategy with Transformations

Another possible algorithm for selective undo is to use the undo/redo strategy for selective undo, augmented with transformations. This does not appear to have been described in the literature, so we only sketch the ideas here. To undo an operation A, one can assume that its inverse $\overline{A}$ is a late arriving operation that should have executed immediately after A. To execute $\overline{A}$, we can reverse all the operations that were done after A, then execute $\overline{A}$, and then redo the operations after A after transforming all the operations, using the Transformation Matrix described in Section 5.4.3.

5.5.5   Relation of Concurrency Control and Undo

An interesting question is whether the choice of concurrency control algorithm and the undo algorithm are dependent. There are some obvious similarities between the schemes, such as the use of transformations, undo/redo, etc. There are also some differences. Undo, like other operations, should behave identically at all sites in a replicated architecture and provide intended results.

Ensuring consistent behavior of the undo operations can be challenging for several reasons. First, the history list may not be identical at each site, particularly if the transformation-based scheme illustrated in Figure 5.8 is used. In Figure 5.8, undoing the command B at site 1 may not necessarily have the same effect as undoing the command B' at site 2, unless additional requirements are placed on the transformation matrix. And, in general, it is not clear if it is always possible to find a transformation matrix that satisfies the requirements for both consistency and undo. An elegant discussion of the properties that transformations need to satisfy so that operations can be selectively undone can be found in the work by Ressel et al [Res96].

Second, conflicting operations may be issued in parallel and the system may pick an execution order that achieves consistency but makes it later difficult to undo one of the operations with reasonable results.

Third, with optimistic concurrency control, the undo command itself may be issued and executed optimistically in an inconsistent state; it is not obvious what operation, if any, should be undone by an undo command that is issued from an inconsistent state.

In DistEdit [Kni93, Pra94a], some of these problems are addressed as follows. First, the undo commands are not broadcast, only the operation executed. Thus, even if history lists are not identical (but equivalent), data consistency is maintained. Second, locks are used so that only non-conflicting operations are allowed to be executed in parallel. Third, because of pessimistic concurrency control, the undo commands can only be issued in consistent states.

In [Cho95], several other issues in the design of an undo framework are considered, including the problem of undoing commands that are executed only at a subset of sites and undoing commands that affect more than one site.

5.6   SUPPORTING COLLABORATION AWARENESS

Collaboration awareness features can be critical in a group editor in order to provide better context regarding the environment in which collaborative activity is taking place. Below we look at examples of collaboration awareness features from various group editors. Additional examples can be found in Section 6.4 (page 150) and some implementation issues can be found in Section 7.4.2 (page 177) in this book [Gre99, Dew99].

5.6.1   Participant Context

Group editors often display the list of users in the group editing session, so as to provide context regarding the participants when group editing is not face-to-face. Examples of this can be found in the user interface provided by DistEdit [Kni90] and by Dolphin [Str94] (Figure 5.1). The list of participants is updated as participants leave or join a session.

The list of participants can be useful in several ways. It can be used to allow users to send electronic mail to individual participants (for example, by clicking on their name or icon). It can also be used to give additional information about the participants — such as the contact information from their business card, and their role in the session (observer, participant). Some recent systems, such as Habanero from NCSA, use the list of participants in the above ways.

Keeping the list automatically updated in the presence of network failures requires some support from the underlying communication system. In particular, if a user's editor crashes or the connection to the editor is lost, other editors need to be able to determine that and drop the user from the list. It is well known, though, that distinguishing a crash or lost connectivity from a very slow connection is not possible in typical networks. The standard solution in such cases is to drop a very slow connection, treating the editor at the end of the connection as effectively being out of the collaboration session. If the user's editor later attempts to communicate, it is forced to rejoin the session as a new member.

One difficulty with providing participant context is that showing a user as a member in a membership list normally only shows that the user has the group editor open. It does not guarantee that the user is paying attention to the group editing session. In face-to-face meetings, eye contact and other bodily cues indicate whether a particular participant is paying attention.

Several potential solutions exist or are being tried out to provide more information than just membership lists. One solution is to show idle time for each user — the period for which they have not interacted with the group editor. This is not a perfect indicator either because it could be that a user is idle but is paying attention; or perhaps the user could have stopped paying attention very recently.

Another solution is to use additional media, such as video, to provide awareness (see also Chapters 3 and 4 in this book [Mac99, Ish99]). Use of video can provide relevant participant context more rapidly than idle time. However, this solution also has limitations: 1) bandwidth and computing cycles may be limited to provide good quality video; 2) screen real-estate can be an issue if the group consists of more than two people; and 3) video is potentially more invasive of privacy than other solutions.

In general, providing good participant context in a non-obtrusive way and in a scalable manner is an open research problem. A more in-depth discussion of various aspects of awareness can be found in [Ben93, Rod96, Tol96].

5.6.2   View Context

People often find it natural to use references such as "top-line of the window" or "the node in the top right corner" to refer to objects being edited. Unfortunately, such references can be confusing in a group editing environment if users do not have their windows or views of the document synchronized. Many group editors, thus, usually attempt to provide an ability to synchronize their views of the document.

Group editors, however, differ in the extent to which they provide synchronized views. In DistEdit-based text editors, for instance, support is available for synchronization of cursor positions and highlighted selections, but no support is provided for synchronization of window sizes, position of lines within a window, etc.

In Suite [Dew91], facilities are provided for closer synchronization of views, including selection of fonts, scrolling, etc. — application designers are provided substantial controls on the editor attributes that they wish to synchronize, but the programmers must implement the attributes.

Supporting view synchronization is usually done by introducing additional shared state variables, besides the document itself. As an example, for implementing synchronized scrolling, the position of the scrollbar can be made a shared variable, with a copy at each site, and updated with the concurrency control techniques described earlier. Response time can be even more critical for operations such as scrolling that update views — since users expect browsing to be fast — so judicious use of concurrency control techniques is essential.

The above strategy of using shared state variables to capture the view state can sometimes be non-trivial to use for programmers. Graphical views of documents often consist of multiple user-interface widgets (e.g. scrollbars, windows, buttons, canvas), each of which can require a large number of state variables to represent completely. For example, state variables required to share the visual representation of a simple button can include its label, font of the text, size of the button, its shape, whether it is active or disabled, etc. It can, in general, be quite tedious for programmers to determine what state variables are required to be shared for a particular widget and then doing the programming to keep the state variables consistent with each other and with the visual state of the button.

In DistView-based groupware tools [Pra94b] on the NeXT systems, the task for implementing synchronized views is considerably simplified. *Groupware-enabled widgets* corresponding to each of the standard GUI widgets, but with built-in replication support using state variables, are provided by extending the standard set of NextStep widgets. These groupware-enabled widgets are made available in the NextStep's Interface Builder so that users can build applications with window replication and sharing using the standard NextStep's drag-and-drop graphical environment. More recently, a Java-based version of DistView is attempting to provide a similar drag-and-drop functionality for building groupware applications using the Java Beans component model.

5.6.3 Activity Context

While using a group editor on a large document, a participant may need to know the regions of the document that other participants are working on. Such information can help avoid conflicting work and facilitate interactions. SASSE [Bae93] (and its earlier version SASE) are examples of group editors that provided this information particularly well. In SASE, continuous feedback was provided to users about other collaborator's working locations in the document with color-coded text selections and multiple scrollbars (one per user). In SASSE, multiple scrollbars were replaced by two scrollbars in order to save screen real-estate: the normal scrollbar of the local user and another scrollbar with multiple color-coded indicators to show the locations of other users.

Activity context is also often provided by the use of audioconferencing tools or multi-user chat tools. This additional conferencing channel can be used by users to coordinate or discuss the document contents while it is being edited. Figure 5.1 shows the MBone audioconferencing tool, *vat*, being used along with the Dolphin group editor.

Use of other generic tools for communication to provide activity context is an attractive strategy because such tools can be useful for a variety of group editing environments. A key challenge however is providing a seamless integration among these tools and the group editing system. If each of the tools and the group editor requires its own set-up and provides its own interface for joining/leaving a group session, then the system can become tedious to use. Several strategies for integrating multiple tools seamlessly in a single system are centered around the *room* metaphor; participants join an editing session by entering a room. The rooms contains various tools, such as editors, chat, and audio, and all these automatically become available to a new participant upon entering the room. Systems that integrate multiple groupware tools based on the room metaphor include wOrlds [Tol95], Collaboratory Builder's Environment [Lee96], and TeamRooms [Ros96b].

One significant challenge with providing activity context is determining what is the appropriate context that users need. A system could show to each user what everyone else is looking at. However, that has screen real-estate implications (besides privacy concerns which we ignore here). In addition, it could probably overload users with too much unnecessary context information.

In general, there is a tradeoff between the extent of common view context and the extent of need for activity context. If views of the document for all users are synchronized, then less activity context may be needed — actions of one user are going to be visible to all other users because of view synchronization. On the other hand, if views are not synchronized, actions of one user may not be visible to other users. Thus, more *a priori* and on-going coordination among users may be needed in order to avoid conflicting or overlapping work.

5.6.4   Telepointing

Telepointing can be a useful collaboration awareness feature in group editors that provide synchronized views. In telepointing, a user's mouse movements can be tracked by the system and displayed on everyone's synchronized window.

Different editors provide varying levels of telepointing capability. DistEdit-based text editors only provide synchronized cursor capability. A user's cursor is tracked by cursors of other users when they are in a *lockstep* editing mode. Selections of regions of text are also tracked. No mouse-based telepointing is supported, primarily because close synchronization of views in a window is not supported owing to heterogeneity of the user-interfaces and platforms of DistEdit-based editors. Mouse-based telepointing makes little sense unless the pointer can be displayed in the same position with respect to the data being viewed in all the windows.

Editors such as Dolphin and SASSE support mouse-based telepointers. Both systems use a standard underlying platform (Smalltalk in Dolphin's case and Macintosh in SASSE's case) so that they are able to provide *group windows* that are identically-sized and have the same contents to all the users. This facilitates displaying a mouse-based telepointer at the same position with respect to the data in the group window.

Supporting multiple telepointers can also be useful, with a different telepointer assigned to each user [Hay94]. If multiple telepointers are provided, they should be assigned different colors or shapes so that users can identify who is manipulating a particular telepointer.

The main challenge with implementing telepointers is dealing with performance. Moving a pointer can generate a large number of mouse-move events. To reproduce the pointer movement at other sites with low latency, these events have to be broadcast over the network *as they are generated*. In low-bandwidth situations, the originating site can potentially be slowed down by the network bottleneck, leading to jerky mouse movement at the originating site. The movement of telepointers at receivers can also be unsatisfactory because of jitter introduced by the network in delivering the broadcast messages. The behavior can be worse than trying to use a window system such as X over a slow network.

Potential strategies to deal with the above performance problems include only broadcasting a subset of mouse-move events. Recent studies show that transmitting ten mouse-events per second is usually adequate to get continuity in pointer movements [Ste96]. With judicious sampling of pointer movements, by using non-blocking protocols, and by incremental painting of screen when remote pointers move, group editors can be designed to support telepointers adequately, even in low-bandwidth situations.

5.7   DESIGN OF DOCUMENT STRUCTURE

Some group editors have focused on not just supporting simultaneous editing of documents, but on the design of document structures that support collaboration activities such as brainstorming. The assumption is that brainstorming is a major use of group editors, and thus group editors need to provide appropriate document structures to support brainstorming.

The simplest kind of group editors to support brainstorming are simply little more than group drawing editors. They provide a graphical canvas on which users can draw shapes (such as rectangles, arrows, lines, etc.) to represent objects of conversation, type in text for labeling, and use one or more telepointers to draw attention to objects represented on the canvas. The shared whiteboard tools such as MBone's *wb*, Cooltalk in Netscape 3.0, and several public-domain programs are examples of such editors.

A much richer document structure for group editing is provided by the Dolphin system [Str94], whose interface is shown in Figure 5.1. Dolphin provides a *hypermedia* document structure, in which users can not only draw shapes and type in text, but also create *nodes* and *links*, where nodes can represent substructures within a document and links can be used to jump from one part of a document to another related part of the document. Recent experiments with Dolphin have shown that such hypermedia-based document structure can lead to more effective brainstorming than the standard shared whiteboard tools [Str94].

Supporting richer document structures is facilitated by richer support for object replication because a document may be represented using a large number of objects with distinct types (e.g. nodes, links, text, graphics), and not all objects may be shared among the entire group at a given time. The use of object replication for view synchronization is discussed in Section 5.8.3. In the case of Dolphin, the COAST system [Sch96] provides the necessary object replication support.

5.8   OTHER DESIGN ISSUES

5.8.1   File Management

Several problems arise when users share document files in order to do group editing. First, when a user requests a file be opened for editing, a group editor must determine whether anyone else is currently editing that file and, if so, load from the active group session rather than from the file. Second, a user should not be allowed greater editing access rights using a group editor than the file system would allow. Third, care must be taken should several users attempt to save a shared file at the same time.

In determining whether several users wish to edit the same particular file, it is not possible to simply examine the path names of the files; because of network file systems, a file can potentially be referenced by different paths. In DistEdit, this problem is solved as follows. When a user attempts to open a file from within an editor, DistEdit searches in the directory containing the file for an auxiliary file of the same name prefixed by '#de.'. For instance, when opening */aprakash/de/testfile*, DistEdit will search for the auxiliary file *#de.testfile* in the directory */aprakash/de*. This auxiliary file contains a unique identifier to be used as the group session name for the particular file. If no such file exists, DistEdit creates it so other users will be able to join the session. If the file exists, DistEdit attempts to join the session identified in the file.

Another solution to the file path problem is for the group editor to provide its own small file-server where files belonging to groups are stored. The group editor can then ensure that their file system presents a common view of files to all users. Several PC-based editors, such as ShrEdit [McG92], use this solution, primarily because network file systems were not commonly available in PC environments.

A group editor needs to be designed to enforce access control. Enforcing access control is more important than in single-user editors because a user can potentially modify not only his own documents, but also documents owned by other users in the same group session. The access control permissions may be inherited from the file system or the group editor can be designed to provide its own access control policies.

The normal file save routines of single-user editors can basically be used as-is in group editors. There is, however, a potential problem. If multiple users were to save slightly different versions (due to network message latency) at approximately the same time, care has to be taken that the resulting file saved is not corrupted owing to parallel save operations.

5.8.2   Screen Updates

The screen update code in group editors needs to be carefully designed with the following goals:

- *Minimize full screen redraws on updates:* Full screen redraw of the user-interface is the simplest strategy for displaying updates to the document, but can be annoying to users. We experienced this problem when converting *xedit* to a group editor using the DistEdit toolkit. Xedit's screen update code handled local updates well, but remote updates caused flickering because an assumption was made in the original Xedit code that updates can only occur at the user's cursor position. Changing the cursor position, applying a remote update, restoring the cursor position, and then displaying the screen caused flickering. Xedit's assumption was acceptable for a single-user version of Xedit, but caused us problems when making it a group editor. A similar problem occurs in most shared-X systems when *expose* events on one client's window cause the X server to redisplay the windows of everyone in the group [Abd91]. We did not have this problem with converting Emacs to a group editor using DistEdit, primarily because the single-user version of Emacs was already well-designed to handle updates from multiple windows into the same document buffer.

- *Manage cursor/pointer position and scrolling:* To the extent possible, applying updates from remote sites should not cause a user's cursor/pointer position to change or the display to scroll. If a user's window starts scrolling because of updates in earlier parts of a document by other users, the user is likely to find the behavior annoying — especially if the document parts that are changing are not even in the user's display.

5.8.3   Use of Object-Replication

The shared state of some group editors can sometimes be naturally represented using multiple encapsulated objects such that not all objects are necessarily of interest to all users. Toolkits such as DistView [Pra94b] and COAST [Sch96] provide support for managing multiple replicated objects in such editors. These toolkits require applications to be built using techniques similar to the Model–View–Controller paradigm; the application consists of *model* objects and *view* objects. Model objects represent the underlying application data, such as the document state, that must always be kept consistent at all sites. View objects usually correspond to the visual representation of the model objects using user-interface widgets, such as windows, scrollbars, etc. Using these toolkits, an application, such as an editor, can provide both synchronization of document state and that of the views of that state. To allow simultaneous work on the same model object, the model object is replicated at the various sites. If a subset of users wish to get identical views of model objects in their windows, they can also replicate a view object so that their views are consistent.

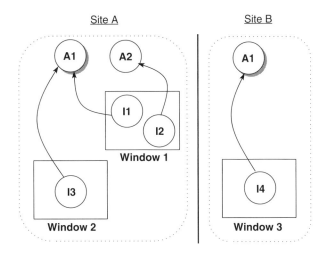

Figure 5.10 The state of a multi-user application at sites A and B before sharing of Window 1 in a DistView-based application. $A1$ and $A2$ are application objects, and $I1$, $I2$, $I3$, and $I4$ are interface objects

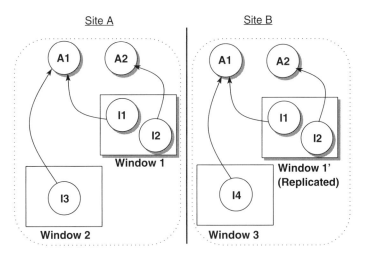

Figure 5.11 The state of the multi-user application at sites A and B after the user at site B imports Window 1 in the DistView-based application. Appropriate objects necessary for sharing windows efficiently are replicated and maintained consistent on subsequent updates

Figures 5.10 and 5.11 illustrate the use of an object replication infrastructure in DistView to facilitate synchronized views of the underlying document. Figure 5.10 shows the objects at two sites when they are not sharing any window (though they are sharing data corresponding to object $A1$). Figure 5.11 shows the objects that are automatically replicated upon demand after Window 1 is *exported* by the user at Site A and *imported* by the user at site B for exact view synchronization. Concurrency control techniques, discussed in Section 5.4, are then used to keep object copies consistent as windows/data are interacted with by the users.

5.8.4   Transactions

Concurrency control, transformations, and undo algorithms are greatly simplified if a group editor uses only a small set of core update primitives. However, any other editing action to be provided by an editor then must be mapped to a sequence of these operations.

In single-user editors, treating a group of simple operations as one larger, user-level action is important primarily for implementing undo; a user, upon doing an undo operation, usually expects all the changes associated with the last single-user-level action to be undone, rather than just some of them.

In a group editor, grouping operations into a larger action is also important for undo. In addition, it is an important issue from the perspective of atomicity because users may expect the operation to behave as a single atomic (indivisible) action even when concurrent updates are being applied by other users.

Supporting the undo of multi-operation actions requires that operations on the history list be tagged with a *transaction-id* so that all operations belonging to a transaction can be undone together. DistEdit uses this scheme. An issue remains as to whether to allow partial undo of a transaction when a complete undo is not possible (say, due to inability to acquire locks or due to conflicts with subsequent updates), but this is largely a policy issue and either choice can be implemented in a straightforward manner.

Supporting atomicity of actions in group editors requires addressing several problems. One problem is that transaction boundaries can sometimes be difficult to determine. The simplest solution is to treat each user's interaction that generates an update as a request for a transaction. However, consider a case where a user is doing a free-form drawing by pressing and moving a mouse. In such a case, the updates are generated continuously on every mouse-move event. However, the user may reasonably expect the entire action of drawing while the mouse is pressed to be a single action from the perspective of undo and atomicity. Another example is an interactive global find and replace string operation in a text editor. Find/replace commands are generated between every interaction, but the user may expect the entire sequence to be a single action for undo purposes. A good design principle is to normally treat each user's interaction that generates a command as a transaction, but if a different choice of transaction boundaries is made for the purpose of undo, to use the same choice for the purpose of defining atomicity.

Another problem in implementing atomicity is that the operations that constitute the transaction may have to be executed before the transaction is complete, for example, in order to provide feedback to a user who is doing free-form drawing in a graphical document or a text-search and replace operation throughout a text document. This can be a problem because the editor may not be able to determine in advance whether the transaction will successfully complete. An operation in a transaction could fail owing to the inability to acquire locks, for instance. A solution to the problem is to execute the transaction optimistically on the local copy first, determine all the locks that are needed as the transaction is executed, and then do a local undo in the normally rare case that the transaction fails for concurrency control reasons [Kni90]. The undo required for this is simpler than a group undo because it applies only to the user's local copy of the document.

5.9 FUTURE WORK

Group editors are likely to continue to evolve in the future. Many of the basic concepts in the design of group editors, such as doing concurrency control and undo, and providing collaboration awareness, have been explored in various editors. However, they have usually been explored in different editors, many of which are research prototypes. Group editors still have not yet evolved to the point where any single group editor provides all the features described in this chapter. Nevertheless, successful use has been reported from even prototype group editors, which indicates that group editors can become widely used, once they are available as standard tools on common computing platforms and sufficiently robust for everyday use.

Group editors need to better support both synchronous and asynchronous collaboration in the future. The support for persistence of shared objects and sessions in the DistView/CBE system [Lee96] and in the TeamRooms system [Ros96b] helps support asynchronous activity. For asynchronous collaboration, additional collaboration awareness may need to be provided to late joiners, so that they know what activities have taken place since they last participated. Providing support for on-line session recording and replay [Man95] are steps in that direction, but need to be abstracted out so that users can get a higher-level context about the work they have missed.

We believe that group editors will be much better integrated with other tools used by users. In particular, group collaboration environments are likely to consist of not only group editors, but also other groupware-oriented versions of applications such as Internet browsers, audio/video/text conferencing tools, data visualization tools, etc. The various groupware tools need to be provided in an integrated environment with a shared session management, global context information, and a seamless transfer of information from one tool to another. We are beginning to see some trends in that direction in several recent university projects such as wOrlds [Tol95], Collaboratory Builder's Environment at the University of Michigan [Lee96], and the GroupKit and TeamRooms work at the University of Calgary [Ros96a, Ros96b]. Commercial efforts by Microsoft and Netscape to integrate groupware tools in their browsers, by IBM/Lotus to extend Lotus Notes to support synchronous collaboration, and by JavaSoft to provide a collaboration toolkit based on Java, are steps in a similar direction.

REFERENCES

[Abd91] Abdel-Wahab, H.M. and Feit, M.A., XTV: A framework for sharing X window clients in remote synchronous collaboration. In *Proceedings, IEEE Tricomm '91: Communications for Distributed Applications and Systems*, April 1991.

[Abo92] Abowd, G. and Dix, A., Giving undo attention. *Interacting with Computers*, 4(3):317–342, 1992.

[Bae93] Baecker, R.M., Nastos, D., Posner, I.R. and Mawby, K.L., The user-centered iterative design of collaborative software. In *INTERCHI'93 Conference Proceedings*, pages 399–405. Addison-Wesley, 1993.

[Ben93] Benford, S.D. and Fahlén, L.E., A spatial model of interaction in large virtual environments. In *Proceedings of the European Conference on Computer-Supported Cooperative Work (EC-SCW'93)*, pages 109–124. Kluwer, 1993.

[Ber94] Berlage, T., A selective undo mechanism for graphical user interfaces based on command objects. *ACM Transactions on Computer-Human Interaction*, 1(3):269–294, 1994.

[Bir87] Birman, K.P. and Joseph, T.A., Reliable communication in the presence of failures. *ACM Transactions on Computer Systems*, pages 47–76, February 1987.

[Bir90] Birman, K. et al, *The ISIS System Manual, Version 2.0*, April 1990.

[Cha84] Chang, J.M. and Maxemchuck, N.F., Reliable broadcast protocols. *ACM Transactions on Computer Systems*, 2(3):251–273, Aug. 1984.

[Cho95] Choudhary, R. and Dewan, P., A general multi-user undo/redo model. In *Proceedings of the Fourth European Conference on Computer-Supported Cooperative Work*, pages 231–246. Kluwer Academic Publishers, September 1995.

[Dew91] Dewan, P., Flexible user interface coupling in collaborative systems. In *Proceedings of the ACM CHI'91 Conference on Human Factors in Computing Systems*, pages 41–48, April 1991.

[Dew99] Dewan, P., Architectures for collaborative applications. In Beaudouin-Lafon, M. (Ed.), *Computer Supported Cooperative Work*, Trends in Software Series 7:169–193. John Wiley & Sons, Chichester, 1999.

[Ell88] Ellis, C., Gibbs, S.J. and Rein, R., Design and use of a group editor. In G. Cockton (Ed.), *Engineering for Human–Computer Interaction*, pages 13–25. North-Holland, Amsterdam, September 1988.

[Ell89] Ellis, C., Gibbs, S.J. and Rein, R., Concurrency control in groupware systems. In *Proceedings of the ACM SIGMOD '89 Conference on Management of Data*, pages 399–407. ACM Press, 1989.

[Fis88] Fish, R., Kraut, R., Leland, M. and Cohen, M., Quilt: A collaborative tool for cooperative writing. In *Proceedings of ACM SIGOIS Conference*, pages 30–37, 1988.

[Fol74] Foley, J.D. and Wallace, V.L., The art of natural graphical man–machine conversion. *Proceedings of the IEEE*, 62(4):4622–471, April 1974.

[Gre94] Greenberg, S. and Marwood, D., Real-time groupware as a distributed system: concurrency control and its effect on the interface. In *Proceedings of the ACM Conference on Computer-Supported Cooperative Work*, pages 207–217, 1994.

[Gre99] Greenberg,S. and Roseman, M., Groupware toolkits for synchronous work. In Beaudouin-Lafon, M. (Ed.), *Computer Supported Cooperative Work*, Trends in Software Series 7:135–168. John Wiley & Sons, Chichester, 1999.

[Gri76] Grief, I., Seliger, R. and Weihl, W., Atomic data abstractions in a distributed collaborative editing system. In *Proceedings of the 13th Annual Symposium on Principles of Programming Languages*, pages 160–172, 1976.

[Han71] Hansen, W.J., User engineering principles for interactive systems. In *AFIPS Conference Proceedings*, Vol. 39, pages 523–532. AFIPS Press, 1971.

[Hay94] Hayne, S., Pendergast, M. and S. Greenberg, S., Implementing gesturing with cursors in group support systems. *Journal of Management Information Systems*, 10(3):43–61, 1994.

[Ish99] Ishii, H., Integration of shared workspace and interpersonal space for remote collaboration. In Beaudouin-Lafon, M. (Ed.), *Computer Supported Cooperative Work*, Trends in Software Series 7:83–102. John Wiley & Sons, Chichester, 1999.

[Kar93] Karsenty, A. and Beaudouin-Lafon, M., An algorithm for distributed groupware applications. In *Proceedings of the 13th International Conference on Distributed Computing Systems*, pages 195–202. IEEE Press, 1993.

[Kni90] Knister, M. and Prakash, A., DistEdit: A distributed toolkit for supporting multiple group editors. In *Proceedings of the Third Conference on Computer-Supported Cooperative Work*, pages 343–355, Los Angeles, California, October 1990.

[Kni93] Knister, M. and Prakash, A., Issues in the design of a toolkit for supporting multiple group editors. *Computing Systems – The Journal of the Usenix Association*, 6(2):135–166, Spring 1993.

[Lee96] Lee, J.H., Prakash, A., Jaeger, T. and Wu, G., Supporting multi-user, multi-applet workspaces in CBE. In *Proceedings of the ACM Conference on Computer-Supported Cooperative Work*, pages 344–353, 1996.

[Mac99] Mackay, W.E., Media Spaces: Environments for informal multimedia interaction In Beaudouin-Lafon, M. (Ed.), *Computer Supported Cooperative Work*, Trends in Software Series 7:55–82. John Wiley & Sons, Chichester, 1999.

[Man95] Manohar N.R. and Prakash, A., The session capture and replay paradigm for asynchronous collaboration. In *Proceedings of the Fourth European Conference on Computer-Supported Cooperative Work*, pages 149–164. Kluwer Academic Publishers, September 1995.

[McG92] McGuffin, L. and M. Olson, G., ShrEdit: A shared electronic workspace. Technical Report CSMIL No. 45, University of Michigan, Ann Arbor, 1992.

[Neu90]   Neuwirth, C.M., Kaufer, D.S., Chandhok, R. and Morris, J.H., Issues in the design of com-
          puter support for co-authoring and commenting. In *Proceedings of the Third Conference on
          Computer-Supported Cooperative Work*, pages 183–195, Los Angeles, California, October
          1990.
[New91]   Newman-Wolfe, R.E. and Pelimuhandiram, H.K., MACE: A fine-grained concurrent editor.
          In *Proceedings of the ACM/IEEE Conference on Organizational Computing Systems (COCS
          91)*, pages 240–254, Atlanta, Georgia, November 1991.
[Pra92]   Prakash, A. and Knister, M., Undoing actions in collaborative work. In *Proceedings of the
          Fourth ACM Conference on Computer-Supported Cooperative Work*, pages 273–280, Toronto,
          Canada, October 1992.
[Pra94a] Prakash, A. and Knister, M., A framework for undoing actions in collaborative work. *ACM
          Transactions on Computer–Human Interaction*, 1(4):295–330, December 1994.
[Pra94b] Prakash, A., and Shim, H., DistView: Support for building efficient collaborative applica-
          tions using replicated objects. In *Proceedings of the Fifth Conference on Computer Supported
          Cooperative Work*, pages 153–164, Toronto, Canada, October 1994. ACM Press.
[Rei91]   Rein, G.L. and Ellis, C.A., rIBIS: A real-time group hypertext system. *International Journal
          of Man–Machine Studies*, 34(3): 349–367, 1991.
[Res96]   Ressel, M., Nitsche-Ruhland, D. and Gunzenhäuser, R., An integrating, transformation-
          oriented approach to concurrency control and undo in group editors. In *Proceedings of the
          ACM Conference on Computer-Supported Cooperative Work*, pages 228–297, 1996.
[Rod96]   Rodden, T., Populating the application: A model of awareness for cooperative applications. In
          Proceedings of the ACM Conference on Computer-Supported Cooperative Work, pages 87–96,
          1996.
[Ros96a] Roseman, M. and Greenberg, S., Building real time groupware with GroupKit, a groupware
          toolkit. *ACM Transactions on Computer–Human Interaction*, 3(1):66–106, March 1996.
[Ros96b] Roseman, M. and Greenberg, S., TeamRooms: Network places for collaboration. In *Pro-
          ceedings of the ACM Conference on Computer-Supported Cooperative Work*, pages 325–333,
          1996.
[Sch96]   Schuckmann, C., Kirchner, L., Schümmer, J. and Haake, J.M., Designing object-oriented
          synchronous groupware with COAST. In *Proceedings of the ACM Conference on Computer-
          Supported Cooperative Work*, pages 30–38, 1996.
[Ste96]   Steinmetz, R., Human perception of jitter and media synchronization. *IEEE Journal of Se-
          lected Areas in Communications*, 14(1):61–72, January 1996.
[Str94]   Streitz, N.A., Geißler, J., Haake, J.M. and Hol, J., DOLPHIN: Integrated meeting support
          across local and remote desktop environments and liveboards. In *Proceedings of the ACM
          Conference on Computer-Supported Cooperative Work*, pages 345–357, Chapel Hill, North
          Carolina, October 1994.
[Str97]   Strom, R., Banavar, G., Miller, K., Prakash, A. and Ward, M., Concurrency control and view
          notification algorithms for collaborative replicated objects. In *Proceedings of the 17th Interna-
          tional Conference on Distributed Computing Systems*, pages 194–204, Baltimore, MD, USA.
          IEEE Computer Society Press, 1997.
[Tol95]   Tolone, W., Kaplan, S. and Fitzpatrick, G., Specifying dynamic support for collaborative work
          within wOrlds. In *Proceedings of the 1995 Conference on Organizational Computing Systems*,
          pages 55–65, August 1995.
[Tol96]   Tollmar, K., Sandor, O. and Schömer, A., Supporting social awareness @work: Design and ex-
          perience. In *Proceedings of the ACM Conference on Computer-Supported Cooperative Work*,
          pages 298–307, 1996.
[Vit84]   Vitter, J.S., US&R: A new framework for redoing. *IEEE Software*, pages 39–52, October
          1984.

6

Groupware Toolkits for Synchronous Work

SAUL GREENBERG and MARK ROSEMAN
University of Calgary

ABSTRACT

Groupware toolkits let developers build applications for synchronous and distributed computer-based conferencing. This chapter describes four components that we believe toolkits must provide. A *run-time architecture* automatically manages the creation, interconnection, and communications of both centralized and distributed processes that comprise conference sessions. A set of *groupware programming abstractions* allows developers to control the behavior of distributed processes, to take action on state changes, and to share relevant data. *Groupware widgets* let interface features of value to conference participants be added easily to groupware applications. *Session managers* let people create and manage their meetings and are built by developers to accommodate the group's working style. We illustrate the many ways these components can be designed by drawing on our own experiences with GroupKit, and by reviewing approaches taken by other toolkit developers.

6.1 INTRODUCTION

Building groupware for synchronous, distributed conferencing can be a frustrating experience. If only conventional single-user GUI toolkits are available, implementing even the simplest systems can be lengthy and error-prone. A programmer must spend much time on tedious but highly technical house-keeping tasks, and must recreate interface components to work in a multi-user setting. Aside from the normal load of developing a robust application, the programmer of groupware must also attend to the setup and management of distributed processes, inter-process communication, state management and process synchronization, design of groupware widgets, creation of session managers, concurrency control, security, and so on.

Computer Supported Cooperative Work, Edited by Beaudouin-Lafon
© 1999 John Wiley & Sons Ltd

Consequently, a variety of researchers have been exploring groupware toolkits. Their purpose is to provide tools and infrastructures powerful enough to let a programmer develop robust, high-quality groupware with reasonable effort. Some in-roads have been made, but we are far from a complete solution. Realistically, most of today's groupware toolkits are best seen as breakthrough research systems used either to explore particular architectural features of groupware toolkits, or as platforms to build experimental groupware prototypes. While they have not reached the maturity of single-user GUI toolkits, these pioneering efforts have laid a foundation for the next generation of toolkit design.

This chapter examines the technical foundations of groupware toolkits. The toolkits we consider are those that construct real-time distributed multi-point groupware applications, where two or more people in different locations would be able to visually share and manipulate their on-line work. Typical applications produced by these systems would be electronic whiteboards, games, multi-user text and graphics editors, distributed presentation software, textual chat systems, and so on. The discussion is heavily influenced by our experiences with our own groupware toolkit called GroupKit [Ros96a, Ros92, Gre94b] as well as the issues raised by other researchers doing similar work.

The chapter highlights four critical features that such toolkits should provide to reduce implementation complexity:

- *Run-time architectures* can automatically manage processes, their interconnections, and communications.
- *Groupware programming abstractions* can be used by a programmer to synchronize interaction events and the data model between processes as well as the views presented across displays.
- *Groupware widgets* can let programmers add generic groupware constructs of value to conference participants.
- *Session managers*, crafted by programmers, can let end-users create, join, leave and manage meetings.

An important omission from this list are the audio and video links necessary for the interpersonal communication channel between conference participants. This is a large area in itself. For simplicity, we will assume that audio and video are handled out of band, where toolkits can include hooks to bring up other audio/video systems. However, we do point the reader to Chapter 4 in this book [Ish99], which provides an excellent example of an integrated audio/video/computational space. It should go without saying that future toolkits must incorporate audio and video as first-class building blocks.

6.2   RUN-TIME ARCHITECTURES

Real-time distributed groupware systems are almost always composed of multiple processes communicating over a network. Because this can be complex to create, we feel strongly that toolkits should provide not only programming facilities for creating groupware, but also the run-time architecture for managing the run-time system. In this section, we will concentrate only on the tension between centralized vs. replicated architectures, and its impact on the design of toolkits. In Chapter 7 in this book [Dew99], Dewan continues this theme by revisiting the issues and by explaining further architectural differences possible in collaborative applications.

6.2.1   Centralized vs. Replicated Architectures

Groupware researchers have long argued the merits of centralized vs. replicated architectures [Ahu90, Gre90, Lau90a, Lau90b, Pat91, Gre94a, Wil95, Hil94, Pat94, Dou96, Gra96a].

- *Centralized* architectures use a single application program, residing on one central server machine, to control all input and output to the distributed participants. Client processes residing at each site are responsible only for passing requests to the central program, and for displaying any output sent to it from the central program. The advantage of a centralized scheme is that synchronization is easy — state information is consistent since it is all located in one place, and events are always handled from the client processes in the same order because it is serialized by the server.
- *Replicated* architectures, on the other hand, execute a copy of the program at every site. Thus each replica must coordinate explicitly both local and remote actions, and must attend to synchronizing all copies so they do not get out of step.

Because of their simplicity in handling concurrency and in maintaining a single state model, centralized architectures for groupware have had many advocates [Ahu90, Gre90, Lau90a, Wil95, Hil94, Gra96a], and one may wonder why a replicated approach would ever be considered. The main issues are latency, bottlenecks, and heterogeneous environments. First, a centralized scheme implies sequential processing, where user input is transmitted from the remote machine to the central application, which must handle it and update the displays (if necessary) before the next input request can be dealt with. If the system latency is low, this is not a problem. But if it is high, the entire system will become sluggish. While sluggishness is annoying when others' actions are delayed, it is devastating when the system is unresponsive to a person's own local actions, especially in highly interactive applications. Second, the central system can become a performance bottleneck. Highly interactive and graphical applications can push even the fastest CPUs to their limits when several screens must be updated. Similarly, the relaying of all activities to and from a single process can create a traffic jam in some environments. Third, centralized architectures will have problems dealing with heterogeneous environments, as it is unlikely that a single process can update properly remote clients running on (say) a Windows95 and a Macintosh environment, as they all have a different look and feel.

A replicated scheme, on the other hand, implies parallel processing, where the handling of interactions and screen updates can occur in parallel at each replication. If done properly, communication is efficient as replicas need only exchange critical state information to keep their models up to date. While remote activities may still be delayed, a person's local activities can be processed immediately. Process bottlenecks are less likely — each replica is responsible for drawing only the local view, unlike the central model which must update the graphics of all screens. Consequently, heterogeneous environments are easily handled, for the communication protocol can act as a device-independent graphics layer, and views can be drawn using the native look and feel.

The cost of replication is increased complexity. We are now programming and synchronizing a distributed system, and must handle issues such as concurrency control. Different replicated toolkits handle this in a variety of ways. For example, Share-Kit [Jah95] has no direct concurrency control, and it must be programmed in from scratch if a programmer requires it. Others do provide concurrency capabilities. DistEdit [Kni90] uses atomic broadcasts. ObjectWorld's shareable objects have the ability to detect messages that have arrived out of order, and allow programmers to do non-optimistic locking [Tou94]. GroupKit [Ros96a] can force serialization for some actions by funneling selected activities through one of the replicated processes.

Somewhere in-between are semi-replicated hybrid architectures that contain both centralized and replicated components. For example, Patterson [Pat96] advocates a centralized *notification server,* whose sole job is to maintain a shared state, to respond to state change requests by clients, and to notify others when the state has changed. It would be up to the replicas to decide what the view should look like, and to update the display accordingly.

6.2.2   Impact on Toolkit Design

System designers often argue that a good toolkit will hide implementation and architectural concerns, leaving the programmer to concentrate on the semantics of the task. Yet architectures cannot be completely hidden in groupware toolkits, for the type of architecture may have profound impacts on the way programmers code their systems, and on the system performance. For example, centralized systems often have performance limitations that must be well understood, so that they can be mitigated by the application programmer. Similarly, replicated architectures are distributed systems, and programmers must be concerned with issues such as concurrency control, communications, and fault tolerance.

The run-time architecture also affects the programming paradigm style. For example, many toolkits separate the underlying *data abstraction* (i.e. the data model) from the way a graphical *view* of that data is generated on the display [Kra88, Hil92] (discussed further in Section 6.3). Figure 6.1 illustrates this. The abstract data model here is an array with three numbers, and the view is generated separately from this abstraction. Views of the abstract model may differ. In this case, two participants view the data as a bar chart, and the third participant sees it as a pie chart. Whenever a value in the data model is changed, the views are regenerated to keep themselves consistent with it. In terms of the run-time architecture, the way the abstraction and views are dealt with depend upon how they are distributed across the system. For example, we could have the data abstraction and view generation done wholly by a central process. Alternatively, the abstraction may be centralized, and the mechanisms to create the views replicated. Or perhaps all components are replicated. Whichever variation is used, the abstract data model should be kept consistent across the entire groupware system, and synchronization must be maintained between the model and the individual views generated from it. This means that the infrastructure to support a separate abstraction and view, as well as the nature of the programming API provided by the toolkit, are highly dependent on the nuances of the run-time architecture.

A good toolkit will provide programmers with high-level constructs to deal with all the issues mentioned above, but not mask them [Dou95, Dou96, Gra96a, OGr96]. To illustrate this point, the rest of this section will show why programmers need to know about concurrency control, synchronization of abstract models and views, communications, and fault tolerance.

6.2.2.1   Concurrency Control

Greenberg and Marwood [Gre94a] argue that no generic concurrency control scheme can handle all groupware applications, simply because the user is an active part of the process. For example, conservative locking and serialization schemes that block processing until concurrency can be guaranteed can have deleterious effects on highly interactive user actions owing

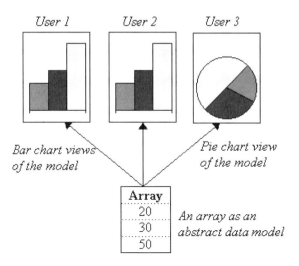

Figure 6.1   An example of an abstract data model, and views generated from the model

to processing delays and latency, while optimistic schemes have problems when on-going events have to be undone. They also argue that some conflicting interactions are best left to the users to solve by social means, implying that some feedback of conflicting actions be shown within the interface.

Because of this, toolkits should provide a variety of concurrency control schemes and feedback mechanisms, and programmers must explicitly decide which of them to deploy when designing the application. Note that this argument becomes moot when latency is not perceivable, since the users would not notice any effects of concurrency control. In this case, either a centralized approach and its implicit serialization of events, or a replicated approach using hidden concurrency control, would work well.

Many groupware researchers have investigated concurrency control. While it is beyond the scope of this chapter to do a comprehensive survey, readers are referred to the surveys by Greenberg and Marwood [Gre94a], and the earlier work of Ellis and Gibbs [Ell89]. Further discussions of consistency and concurrency control are found within Chapters 5, 8 and 7 in this book [Pra99, Dou99, Dew99].

6.2.2.2   Synchronization

As mentioned earlier, specific architectures usually lend themselves to particular ways of separating the underlying abstract data model from the graphical views generated from it. A centralized system keeps both model and view in the same place, so synchronization is easy. In contrast, replicated architectures maintain copies of both the data state and the view at all sites. In-between is Patterson's [Pat96] Notification Server, which keeps the abstract data model in a central server, with replicas deciding how to display the view of that information when state changes are transmitted to them.

At the toolkit level, this division of model and view as well as its distribution across processes is usually visible to the programmer — the programming abstractions provided are used by them to update the abstract model or the view, and to synchronize replicas when needed. Similarly, the way the toolkit provides the abstractions to process user events and to synchronize models and views often depends upon the way the model and the views are distributed in the architecture. This topic will be taken up again in more detail in Section 6.3: Programming Abstractions.

6.2.2.3   Communication

Inter-process communication can be a complex task, especially when efficiency is a concern. Centralized models are particularly vulnerable to communications bottlenecks, as the server must not only handle input from the client, but update all displays as well. Replicated architectures can be more efficient, for the events sent across the network can be short messages containing semantic changes to state. At the toolkit level, the programmer would rarely want to deal with all the annoyances of setting up communications connections. However, they should have the means to decide what to communicate between processes for efficiency purposes, and also the means to decide priorities.

For example, consider a drawing application containing telepointers, where the telepointers are not supplied as a widget. In terms of what to communicate, the complete telepointer graphics need not be shipped. Instead, a message can be sent specifying the pointer shape, with subsequent messages sending out a pointer id and its *x-y* coordinates. In terms of priority, when a pointer is moved the programmer should be able to specify that only that last pointer location need be transmitted if there is a communications bottleneck, and that this should have a lower priority than (say) a drawing message.

6.2.2.4   Fault Tolerance

Because almost all groupware systems are distributed in one way or another, fault tolerance becomes a concern. At the toolkit level, the programmer should be able to determine the system's response to particular faults. These include degradation or complete loss of communications between processes, excessive delays, and so on. This implies that the toolkit must have a notification mechanism that indicates faults to the program. It also implies that the programmer is aware of the faults that are inherent in the particular architectural design.

6.2.3   Examples

6.2.3.1   WScrawl: A Centralized Architecture that Leverages X Windows

WScrawl [Wil95] is a multi-user sketchpad built using the X Window System. While WScrawl is not a toolkit, the author describes how his program leverages the communications and display capabilites of X Windows, as well as its client/server architecture [Sch86]. X Windows allows a programmer to open several displays, to read input from each workstation, and to write graphics to the screen. Groupware such as WScrawl is created by tracking the display and input stream for each user, all within a single program. Each stream is monitored for input events. For every input event (such as a mouse move that initiates a draw line action), the event is processed, and all displays can be updated accordingly

For example, the pseudo-code below handles a trivial conference of two users, each using separate displays named Display1 and Display2, where the conference just draws a point on each display [Wil95]:

```
display[1] = XOpenDisplay ("Display1");
display[2] = XOpenDisplay ("Display2");
for (i=1; i<=2; i++) {
    XDrawPoint (display[i], 20, 100);
    XCloseDisplay(display[i]);
}
```

6.2.3.2   Rendezvous: A Centralized Architecture

The Rendezvous groupware toolkit [Hil94, Pat90, Pat91, Hil92] is heavily modeled on the idea of maintaining a single abstract data model that is shared by everyone. As mentioned earlier, multiple views of that model can be drawn differently on each person's display. Rendezvous places both the single abstraction and the view models on a single processor. Its developers claim that the single abstraction always contains the correct state of the application. Consequently, all copies or view updates derived from this abstraction will be correct. The problem is that Rendezvous is slow, because all views run off the same processor. Its designers suggest, but have not implemented, a semi-replicated approach that keeps that shared abstraction at a central site, with views being replicated at other sites.

6.2.3.3   The Notification Server: A Centralized Component of a Hybrid Architecture

Patterson, one of the authors of Rendezvous, revisited the idea of a semi-replicated hybrid architecture [Pat96]. He is now constructing a centralized "Notification Server" that could be provided as a toolkit component in an otherwise replicated architecture. Its job is to provide a central service for managing common state information, akin to the shared abstraction seen in Rendezvous. While the natural use of the server is to centralize the abstract data model, the choice of what state information to centralize is ultimately up to the designer.

The Notification Server contains two kinds of objects: Places and Things.

- *Places* identify what common states are accessed by which applications. Clients who enter a particular place are notified about any state changes in that place.
- *Things* are the actual objects that maintain state, and are essentially property–value pairs extended to contain attributes that specify access control and types of notifications triggered (e.g. on creation, change or deletion).

What is important here is that the server has no understanding of application semantics. Virtually any state can be represented, as long as it can be described as a property–value pair. It is left up to the replica how to deal with state changes upon notification. Patterson argues that this centralized Notification Server simplifies concurrency control because locking is done in one place through Thing's attributes, and that serialization is a natural consequence of centralization. He also argues that the availability of a consistent, centralized state makes it easier to update newcomers — participants who have just entered a conference that is already in progress. Finally, this dedicated server model implies that attention can be devoted to making it efficient and robust — in Patterson's words, "a lean, mean notification machine".

6.2.3.4   GroupKit: A Mostly Replicated Architecture

The GroupKit groupware toolkit [Ros96a, Gre94b] includes a mostly replicated run-time infrastructure. It actively manages the creation, location, interconnection, and teardown of

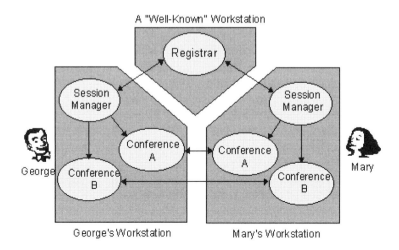

Figure 6.2   An example of GroupKit's run-time architecture and process model

distributed processes; communications setup, such as socket handling and multicasting; and groupware-specific features such as providing the infrastructure for session management and persistent conferences. Its infrastructure consists of a variety of distributed processes arranged across a number of machines. Figure 6.2 illustrates an example of the processes running when two people are communicating to each other through two conferences 'A' and 'B'. The three large boxes represent three different workstations, the ovals are instances of processes running on each machine, and the directed lines joining them indicate communication paths. Three types of GroupKit processes are shown: a single registrar, session managers, and conference applications.

- The *registrar* (top box in Figure 6.2) is a centralized process that acts as a connection point for a community of conference users. Its address is "well-known" in that other processes know how to reach it. This is the only centralized process required by GroupKit's run-time infrastructure.
- The *session manager* is a replicated process, one per participant (side boxes). It provides both a user interface and a policy dictating how conferences are created or deleted, how users are to enter and leave conferences, and how conference status is presented (see Section 6.5: Session Management). When session manager processes are created, they connect to the registrar. The registrar maintains a list of all conferences and the users in each conference. It thus serves as an initial contact point to locate existing conference processes and their addresses.
- Finally, a *conference application* is a GroupKit program (e.g. shared editor, game) invoked by the user through the session manager. Conference applications typically work together as replicated processes, in that a copy of the program runs on each participant's workstation. They are connected via peer to peer communication channels. Two conferences, each with two distributed replicas, are shown in Figure 6.2.

GroupKit programmers build both session managers and conference applications, and the two are separate from one another. Programmers are aware that they are building distributed applications, and must attend to issues such as concurrency control, fault-tolerance, and synchronization. The programming abstractions let the programmer choose and mix several styles of coding: view synchronization through multicast RPCs, or state synchronization of a replicated abstract data model (see Section 6.3: Programming Abstractions). The toolkit provides a few simple concurrency control schemes for the programmer to choose from, mostly available within the shared data model. Communications are mostly hidden away; while it is possible to massage communication events for efficiency, this is mostly done by working around the system rather than with it. Fault tolerance is done by primitive events that notify a programmer when participants have "left" the conference and when a conference has "died". However, they are not notified nor can they easily handle performance degradation.

This run-time infrastructure is maintained entirely by GroupKit. The conference application code does not need to take any explicit action in process creation or communication set-up. Instead, the application may just ask to be notified through an event when particular session activities occur. The conference processes that comprise a conference session can also coordinate with each other through the high-level programming abstractions provided by GroupKit, as discussed in Section 6.3.

6.2.3.5   Clock: A Flexible Architecture

The main goal of the Clock language and ClockWorks programming environment [Gra96] is to support the development of groupware applications at a very high-level, hiding all details of the underlying implementation architecture. This high level has two consequences. First, programmers do not need to be concerned with the details of distribution, networking and concurrency control. Second, implementations of Clock are free to use any implementation architecture, as long as the semantics of the Clock language are preserved. (Unlike other languages for groupware development, Clock has precisely defined semantics, independent of any implementation [Gra95].)

The *abstract architecture* of Clock programs is developed using the visual ClockWorks programming environment. This abstract architecture captures the structure of Clock programs, but does not specify how the program will be implemented in a distributed context. The abstract architecture language is based on separating the abstract model from its views, similar to Rendezvous [Hil92] and the Model–View–Controller (MVC) paradigm used in Smalltalk [Kra88]. Because of its high-level, the architecture language supports rapid development and easy modification of groupware programs [Gra96b].

Abstract architectures can be mapped into a variety of implementation architectures. By locating the complete architecture on a server machine and using the X Window System to post windows on different client machines, a centralized architecture can be obtained. By locating the shared components of the Clock architecture on a server machine and replicating private components on client machines, a semi-replicated hybrid architecture is obtained. By replicating both shared and private components, a replicated architecture can be obtained. Currently, Clock programs can be implemented as either centralized or semi-replicated.

There are several advantages with the Clock approach to flexible implementation architectures. Since the run-time system is completely responsible for implementing network communication and concurrency control, complex optimizations may be built into the system that would be too hard to develop on a per-application basis [Gra96a]. Also, programmers can easily experiment with what kind of architecture is most appropriate for their application without having to extensively modify the program. The primary disadvantage of the Clock approach is that programmers give up control over precisely how different components are going to communicate. For example, the Clock semantics demand that concurrency control be pessimistic, which is not practical over networks with very bad latency.

6.2.4 Discussion

There is no real answer to whether a centralized or replicated scheme works best for groupware. Rather, it is a set of tradeoffs that revolves around the way they handle latency, the ease of program startup and connection, programming complexity, synchronization requirements, processor speed, the number and location of participants expected, communication capacity and cost, and so on. For example, a centralized system would likely work just fine for a very small group of users (e.g. pairs), given a high-bandwidth, low-latency network and an application that makes only modest demands of the processor. Replicated systems are probably better for larger groups, for slower networks, and for applications that demand local responsiveness.

Because these situations are neither static or universal, no single solution will suffice. Perhaps what is required is a "dynamic and reactive" groupware architecture, where the decision of what parts of the architecture should be replicated or centralized can be adjusted to fit the needs of particular applications and site configurations. We have already seen that Clock components can be configured to run as centralized or semi-replicated objects [Gra96a]. O'Grady [OGr96] takes this one step further in his design of GEN, a prototype groupware toolkit based upon distributed objects that allows a high degree of run-time configuration. GEN not only allows application designers to chose whether individual objects are centralized or replicated, but also allows designers to create their own strategies for data distribution and concurrency control. For example, GEN was altered to allow for object migration, where centralized objects are automatically moved to the site that uses them the most frequently. In parallel work, Dourish's chapter in this book presents his design of Prospero, a groupware toolkit that also allows decisions on data distribution and other aspects to be made on the fly [Dou95, Dou96, Dou99]. Essentially, toolkits such as GEN and Prospero are designed to be highly flexible. Not only can developers choose between a variety of strategies, but they can also extend the toolkit to cover situations not envisaged by the original toolkit creators.

6.3 PROGRAMMING ABSTRACTIONS

Groupware toolkits must provide programmers with abstractions for coordinating multiple threads and distributed processes, for updating a common abstract data model, and for controlling the view derived from that model. The actual abstractions supplied usually depend upon the run-time architecture (as described in Section 6.2), as well as the schemes used to share state information.

Patterson [Pat94] argues that the degree to which abstract data models are separated from the views generated from them leads to several different shared state architectures, with consequences to the programming abstractions provided.

1. In an unshared system, neither data nor view model are shared. It is up to the programmer to maintain the underlying data models (if any exists), the graphical views, and the links between the views and the model (if any).

2. In a shared model, the data model is shared by the entire system. Programming abstractions allow one to access and change the shared model, and to specify how the (possibly different) unshared views are to be created from the shared model.

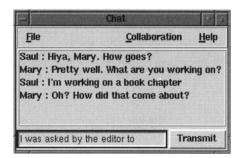

Figure 6.3   Using multicast RPCs for a simple chat application

3. In a shared view, both views and models are shared. Programming abstractions are available to change the view or the model, with changes automatically propagating from one to the other.

This section describes several programming abstractions that are now common: multicast remote procedure calls, events and notifiers, shared data, and shared data and views. Each lends itself to the three architectures mentioned above.

6.3.1   Multicast Remote Procedure Calls

With replicated processes, replicas can communicate, share information, and trigger common program execution through multicast *remote procedure calls* (RPCs). As with conventional RPCs, a programmer specifies the procedure and arguments that should be executed in remote processes. It is multicast because several processes can be designated in a single call.

Through this simple yet powerful abstraction, any unshared system can be synchronized. For example, traditional callbacks to a user's input can be replaced by a multicast RPC that causes the resulting action to be performed in all processes. The following pseudo-code illustrates this by showing how the simple text chat system shown in Figure 6.3 can be implemented. The main window contains the dialog transcript, and is common across all displays. Each participant types their text into their private text input field at the bottom. Whenever a person presses the "transmit" button, their name and the text they composed are sent to all others for insertion into the transcript.

```
Set this_user to the name of the local user
When transmit button is pressed
    Set message to the contents of the input field
    Multicast to everyone:
        Insert into your chat box "this_user: message"
    Clear the input field
```

In the above example, there is no data model. Only the view is synchronized by explicitly manipulating the widgets in the view. Data can be synchronized as well by multicast RPCs, although it is the programmer's responsibility to do all the housekeeping and to generate the view from the data model.

6.3.1.1 Examples

Several systems use multicast RPCs as their sole programming abstraction. Share-Kit [Jah95] uses C and the Unix RPC mechanism to build its multicast layer; its programmers must register a procedure and its argument formats as an RPC and use special keywords to invoke them. The Conference Toolkit [Bon89] uses a routing table to let developers specify the routing of data between application instances; that is, how commands from one replica are directed to other replicas. The Notification Server [Pat96] provides a "back door" that allows programmers to channel multicast messages between clients; these messages could be constructed in a way that simulates multicast RPCs.

GroupKit [Ros96a, Gre94b] simplifies multicast RPCs by allowing RPCs and arguments to be specified in the same way as normal procedure calls, and by hiding routing and communications details. To do this, GroupKit's run-time system tracks the addresses and existence of other application processes, and decides how to multicast the RPCs to some or all conference processes. This means that the programmer does not have to track details such as the file descriptors, socket management, and so on. GroupKit provides three forms of RPCs, and each differs in who the messages are sent to. The first, called gk_toAll, multicasts the procedure to all conference processes in the session, including the local user. This results in the same procedure being executed everywhere. The second, called gk_toOthers, multicasts a command execution to all other remote conference processes in the session except the local process that generated the call, which is useful when local actions differ somewhat from remote ones. The third form directs the command to a particular conference process. This is valuable for handling special cases, such as updating a new arrival to an on-going conference about the current state of the application. Additionally, GroupKit's RPCs are non-blocking. Once the request for an RPC invocation is made, the local program continues its execution without waiting for a reply from remote processes. This ensures that conference processes are not delayed or blocked in the event of network latency or crashes on remote machines.

As an example, we implemented the simple text chat system shown in Figure 6.3 in GroupKit (which extends the Tcl/Tk scripting language by John Ousterhaut [Ous94]) using the gk_toAll RPC. The complete code is shown below, excluding a few minor bits that format the widgets on the display. What is important to realize is that only a few lines of code are required to make this program group-aware: gk_initConf initializes the runtime architecture for the conference; gk_defaultMenu includes GroupKit's menu widget, [users local.username] retrieves the name of the local user, and gk_toAll multicasts the RPC to insert the user's name and text into the chat box. All other lines are just the standard Tcl/Tk code necessary to create the interface.

```
gk_initConf $argv                 # Initialize the conference

#== Create widgets
gk_defaultMenu .menubar           # Add the default groupkit pulldown menu bar
listbox .chat                     # The shared chat box is actually a listbox
entry .input                      # Users type their text into this entry box
button .b -text Transmit \        # Create a button labelled 'Transmit'
    -command "broadcastLine"      #  and attach a callback to it

#== Not shown: code to format widgets on the display

#== This callback multicasts an RPC to all replicas (using gk_toAll)
#== along with this user's name and text
proc broadcastLine {} {
   gk_toAll doAddLine \                    # Multicast the doAddLine RPC + arguments
```

```
        [users local.username] \    #    1st argument: the user's name
        [.input get]                #    2nd argument: the text
    .input delete 0 end             # Now clear the input field
}

#==This is executed as an RPC at all sites.
#==It inserts the name and text into the chat box
proc doAddLine {name text} {
    .chat insert end [concat $name ": " $text]
}
```

While simple, GroupKit's multicast RPC model provides a powerful yet flexible approach to distributed programming. The programmer does not have to know the addresses of other conference processes or track process creation and destruction as people enter and leave the session. The calls work the same way whether one user or twenty users are in the conference session.

6.3.2   Events and Notifiers

A second programming abstraction allows a programmer to synchronize changes to either views or models by specifying interesting events and how others are notified when these events occur. Because events can be tied to anything, they can serve both unshared and shared systems.

An *event* provides a way for conference applications to track when various things happen. Events can be generated automatically by the run-time architecture, such as when participants join or leave the conference session, or from (say) communications failures. They can also be generated directly from the programmer in application-specific circumstances. Either way, the programmer can take action on a specific event by attaching a *notifier* to it, which typically executes a callback whenever the event occurs (notifiers are also known as handlers in some systems).

6.3.2.1   Examples

Patterson's Notification Server [Pat96], described previously in Section 6.2, illustrated an architecture that supports notification. Here, events are simply changes in the state of the underlying data ("Things"). Notification is controlled by the attribute field of the Thing, and occurs automatically whenever a state changes.

GroupKit contains an event/notifier mechanism as well as events automatically maintained and generated by the run-time infrastructure [Ros96a]. Events are typically used to handle arriving and departing participants, updating latecomers, synchronizing distributed processes, and noticing changes to shared data. Events consist of an event type and a set of attribute/value pairs that provide information about the event. While in some ways similar to Patterson's Notification Server, state information is replicated rather than centralized. Programmers trap particular events by attaching a notifier, with desired actions specified through callbacks that are automatically executed when the event occurs.

GroupKit's run-time infrastructure automatically sends three different event types to conference processes. The first two event types are generated when users join and leave the session, as a conference process may want to take special action when this happens. For example, the code fragment below tells everyone that a new participant has arrived by printing a message on all screens. The first line attaches a notifier to a "newUserArrived" event, which is automatically generated by GroupKit when a new user joins the conference. This will trigger execution of the subsequent lines.

```
gk_bind newUserArrived {                              # Attach code to this event
  set new_user_name [users remote.%U.username]        # Get the new person's name
  puts "$new_user_name just arrived!"}                 # Print message to the screen
```

The third event automatically generated by GroupKit is used to handle latecomers to conferences that are already in progress. When a latecomer arrives, its conference process is brought up to date by one of the other conference processes in the session, usually by sending it the existing state of the conference. Details of how to update the newcomer is left up to the programmer by having them create an appropriate callback.

Finally, application developers can generate their own custom events. This can be useful in more complex applications, where a change being handled in one part of the program can generate an event to notify other parts of the program (or other processes) of the change. For example, a programmer can create a shared data model and use events to generate views from it. Changes to the model's state can be attached to events, with notifiers created to update the view accordingly. Different views are handled by attaching different callbacks to the notifiers.

A variety of other toolkits use some type of event/notification scheme; e.g. Rendezvous [Hil92], Chiron-1 [Tay95], and Weasel [Gra92]. However, these are typically tied to directly linking the shared views with a data model, discussed next.

6.3.3   Shared Models and Views

While multicast RPCs and events can be used to coordinate conference replicas, they do demand more housekeeping as the application becomes complex. Consequently, several groupware toolkits provide programming abstractions to maintain and update a shared data model, and some means for attaching a view to the model.

The idea of separating a data model from its view originated in Smalltalk's Model–View–Controller [Kra88], later extended to groupware [Pat91, Hil92, Gra92, Tou94]. In most implementations, the system maintains a consistent shared data model (i.e. by handling concurrency and synchronization), and either notifies processes of changes to the data or automatically updates views whenever changes occur.

6.3.3.1   Examples

GroupKit provides a shared data model called an *environment*, a dictionary-style data structure containing *keys* and associated *values* [Ros96a]. While instances of environments run on different processes, the run-time system makes sure that changes to one instance are propagated to other instances. What makes GroupKit's environments powerful are that changes to an environment's state can be tracked as events that trigger notifiers (as discussed previously). The programmer can bind callbacks to an environment, and receive notification when a new piece of information is added to it, when information is changed, or when information is removed. Corresponding actions are then triggered at all sites.

This scheme can generate different views from the same data abstraction. Events can be monitored by the interface code, and the view adjusted to reflect the state of the data model contained in the environment. For example, the code fragment below creates a shared environment called "data", which contains a field called "number". A groupware button is displayed that shows the current value of the number, incremented whenever any user presses the button.

```
gk_newenv -bind -share data              # "Data" is a shared environment
button .button -command \                # Create a button. Whenever it is
  [data number [expr [data number]+1]    #   pressed, increment "number", a
                                         #   key in the "data" environment
data bind changeEnvInfo  {               # Update the view of the number in the
  .button configure -text [data number]}#   button whenever its value changes
data number 0                            # Initialize "number" to 0
```

A programmer uses GroupKit's environments to implement synchronized views and models. In contrast, the Rendezvous toolkit treats views, models and the links between them as first-class citizens [Hil94]. The system encourages developers to create groupware applications using its powerful *abstraction–link–view* (ALV) model [Hil92], whose constructs are:

- a shared underlying data abstraction,
- a view of the abstracted entity that may differ for each user,
- a constraint (called a link) that automatically adjusts the view when the data abstraction is changed.

Rendezvous differs architecturally from GroupKit, in that the data model and the propagation of constraints are centralized. As well, constraints are more powerful than the event/notifier scheme, because complex relationships are automatically maintained by the system through a one-way constraint solver. The Clock system [Gra96b] also uses constraints to link views with the underlying model.

A variety of other systems also have a strong notion of maintaining the relation between a model and a view. The Chiron-1 user interface system has abstract data types (abstractions), dispatchers (links) and views; however, a simpler event-based architecture rather than constraints are used to propagate changes [Tay95]. While Chiron-1 was not explicitly designed to be a groupware toolkit, a multi-user Tetris game was developed to show the flexibility of its architecture. In Weasel [Gra92], programmers use a special declarative language called RVL to specify the relations between abstractions and views, how views are customized, and the coordination required.

Populated virtual environments also use an abstract model/view paradigm. The model is the 3-D abstraction, while the rendered views of the model are perspectives generated from a particular (x, y, z) viewpoint into the model. The model is typically spatial. People enter the spatial environment, where they are represented as "avatars" to others (icons or even video images of themselves). They can move through the space and manipulate artifacts within it. They are usually aware of the presence and (perhaps pseudo-) identity of others, can see where others are attending, and can begin text or voice based communications with them. Examples are DIVE [Car93] and Moondo [Intel].

6.3.4 Discussion

Programming abstractions such as the ones described above ease considerably a programmer's task of building groupware. For example, since multicast RPCs are a natural extension of the way normal callbacks are used, novice GroupKit programmers were able to create simple groupware applications with minimal training. The event/notifier and shared data abstractions are more elegant, but demand that the programmer learn a new coding style, for it usually takes more planning and initial coding to separate the data model from its view.

However, groupware programming abstractions do not eliminate all coding complexity. The programmer must consider the interaction between the processes that are being coordinated by multicast RPCs, by events, and by shared data; unconsidered side effects can cause the unexpected to happen. There is also a craft to using the programming constructs effectively. For example, multicast RPCs usually demand that the programmer consider what local actions should be taken and what variables should be set before the procedure and arguments are multicast. The shared data abstractions have their own problems. When data model and views are separated, the programmer has to handle exceptions that often occur when most, but not all of the view is identical. When views intentionally differ (such as when one person sees an array as a bar chart and the other as a pie chart, as in Figure 6.1), the programmer has to make difficult interface design decisions that will allow people to interact over disjoint views. In all cases, debugging can be hard when problems do occur, because the interaction between conference processes can be non-deterministic and difficult to envisage.

6.4   GROUPWARE WIDGETS

Perhaps the greatest benefit of today's graphical user interface toolkits is their provision of tried and tested interface widgets. Programmers can typically configure and position them in a few lines of code, perhaps with the help of an interface builder. When done properly, pre-packaged widget sets provide a consistent look and feel to the interface. Because widgets are often designed by interface experts, the everyday programmer can insert them into the application with some assurance that they are usable.

Because many groupware applications will be graphical, groupware programmers have the same need for widgets. The toolkit should therefore make it easy for programmers to add groupware features to applications that conference participants will find valuable. However, groupware widgets differ from normal widgets. They have different semantics; actions performed on them must be reflected across displays; and novel widgets have to be designed that address needs specific to groupware. In this section, we consider two classes of groupware widgets: groupware versions of single-user widgets, and group-specific widgets that support activities found only in group work.

6.4.1   Groupware Versions of Single-User Widgets

Some researchers have created multi-user analogs of conventional single-user widgets, such as buttons, menus and simple text editors, and investigated how to make the sharing of widgets between conference participants flexible enough to fit different applications and group situations.

To highlight several issues, let us consider the problems we face when redesigning a button widget to fit groupware. Buttons are simple devices in conventional interfaces. When a user presses the button, its look changes to reflect that it is being selected. Upon release, the button shape returns to normal and an action is executed. If the cursor is moved off the button during a mouse press, the button reverts back to its original appearance and the release will have no effect.

When the button is redesigned as groupware, several issues arise.

1. When should feedback of one user's actions be shown to their partners as *feedthrough*? Should feedthrough be shown for every interface action (e.g. highlighting that matches button presses and releases), or only for the final action (that the button press resulted in an action)? Should feedthrough appear graphically identical to the local user's feedback, or should it be stylized to communicate only the essence of the other's actions?

2. How does the button handle multiple and simultaneous access? Does it contain an idea of ownership, so only one person is allowed to press it? If so, how is access control handled? Or does the button implement turn-taking so that only one person can press it at a time, and if so, how does it show other users that they cannot press the button? If simultaneous access is allowed, what are the semantics of simultaneous presses, and how is feedthrough displayed?

3. How are resulting actions handled? For example, are attached callbacks automatically invoked in all replicas on one person's button press, or must the programmer distribute its effects explicitly?

4. What happens when people are viewing different parts of the display? If one person cannot see the button because they have scrolled to another area, is feedthrough shown in a different manner, and if so, how?

5. If different representations are used (e.g. two differing native look and feels because groupware is running across two different platforms), how can the interface syntax of one button be translated to the perhaps different syntax of the other button?

These issues become much more problematic when we move to multi-user equivalents of complex widgets that have a high interaction component, such as list boxes, text entry fields, graphical canvases and so on. None of these problems has a trivial solution, and designers of groupware toolkits have to make hard decisions on what to do in each case. Part of the design space includes how much flexibility they can provide the programmer to allow them to make their own application-specific decisions.

A few researchers have begun to address these issues by creating generic programming attributes for groupware widgets. Several have concentrated on a widget's coupling level and access control. Others have tried to redesign conventional widgets to make them more appropriate to groupware settings.

6.4.1.1 Coupling

Dewan [Dew91, Dew92] defines coupling as the means by which interface components share interaction state across different users. In tight coupling, state is shared by all aspects of the interface component, and a person's actions in one display results in immediate update on another display. In loose coupling, one person's actions propagate over to another display only when a critical event is performed; the final state is the same, but intermediate states are not seen. For example, a tightly coupled button would appear identical on all displays as it was being pressed, moved across, and released. A loosely coupled button would only show the release action, with intermediate feedthrough eliminated.

Dewan and Choudhary [Dew92] argue that flexible coupling is important for a variety of reasons. First, groupware programs range from fully synchronous, to nearly synchronous, to asynchronous; coupling is just another way of setting synchronicity. For example, we can argue that the only difference between a real-time text program that shows characters as they are being typed (text chat), vs. complete messages (e-mail) is their coupling level! Second, tightly coupled actions showing intermediary steps may be annoying to users in situations where they are pursuing their own individual work. Alternatively, tightly coupled systems are critical during highly-interactive exchanges between people [Tat91]. Third, loosely coupled systems exchange state less frequently, which means there are less performance demands on the system. Finally, coupling can control the degree that people work in private spaces, and how and when they wish to make that space public.

Dewan and Choudhary [Dew92] implemented coupling in their Suite groupware toolkit by allowing programmers and users to set *coupling attributes* that are associated with individual interaction entities (although these can be arranged in a multiple inheritance structure). Attributes indicate the level of coupling, as well as how they should be applied selectively to members of a group. Suite also divides interaction entities into disjoint coupling sets. For example, the data state, the view state, and a format state can be coupled independently (the latter allows the view of the data to be formatted in different ways across displays). Furthermore, action coupling can be set to determine how the commands (or callbacks) attached to user actions are executed at other sites.

Reconsider the button example. The coupling levels can define: the way button presses are tied to underlying data models by coupling data state; the level of feedthrough desired in the view by coupling views; and how callbacks are invoked by coupling actions. Ideally, the groupware programmer would consider coupling levels to be just another set of attributes that can be configured when creating the button. The same idea can be applied to more complex widgets, and Suite has several examples of how coupling can be applied to complex editing and form-filling systems.

Coupling is available in other toolkits as well. The Rendezvous toolkit [Hil94] allows flexible coupling because of the way views are separated from data. Because the links in Rendezvous' ALV model specify how views and models are synchronized [Hil92], different levels of coupling can be specified by the programmer. The difference is that the programmer has to code the way coupling is achieved, rather than simply set the attributes of a widget.

6.4.1.2   Access Control

Access control determines who can access a widget and when. Access control may be required for several reasons. First, people may wish to have their own "private" widgets, where only they can manipulate (or even view) them. An example is a text field in a groupware outliner, where the person editing the field wishes to maintain ownership of it, perhaps just for the duration of the edit or for the length of the session. Second, it may not make sense for users to simultaneously manipulate some widgets. Perhaps only one person at a time should be able to press a button, manipulate a scroll bar (to prevent "scroll wars"), or insert text into a field. As with coupling, the demands for access control may be highly dependent on the particular interface being constructed, and groupware programmers need to be able to control this.

Few groupware toolkits let programmers manipulate access control in a light-weight, fine-grained fashion. If anything, they group it into concurrency control, with access being mediated by locks and other tedious mechanisms. The notable exception is again Suite. In it, Shen and Dewan [She92] associate the fine-grained data displayed by a groupware application with a set of "collaboration rights", where the rights are specified by either programmer or user through a multi-dimensional, inheritance-based structure. Collaboration rights include read and write privileges, viewing privileges, and coupling. Through the inheritance structure,

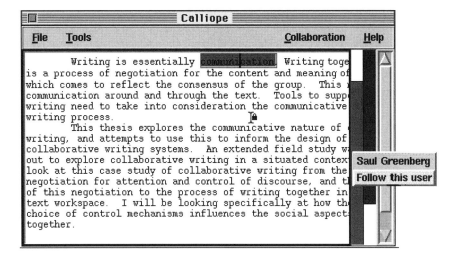

Figure 6.4   The Calliope multi-user editor, with permission from Alex Mitchell

access control can be specified at both a group and individual level. Sets of objects can be clustered together, with specific access definitions overriding general ones.

Smith and Rodden's [Smi93] "shared interface object layer" SOL, an architectural layer rather than a toolkit, considers how shareable versions of single-user widgets such as buttons and text entry fields can be created. They provide a set of generic access control mechanisms that determine what people could do with these shareable objects. Settable options include who can see the widget, who can use it, who can move it, and so on. The same group has created a more generalized shared object service called COLA [Tre94].

6.4.1.3 Widget Redesigns

Most single-user widgets should be completely redesigned to fit their groupware settings, because they would otherwise be too limiting. While there is no recipe for doing this, we can illustrate by example several groupware redesigns of single-user widgets.

Our first example is the *multi-user scrollbar*, first seen in the SASSE text editor [Bae93]. It differed from conventional scrollbars in that two thumbs (the selectable box) are displayed. Participants are allowed to scroll independently, and the thumbs' positions would reflect each person's relative position in the document. While SASSE's scrollbar was hard-wired into the editor, GroupKit developers turned it into a real multi-user widget that can be attached to any scrollable object in one or two lines of code [Ros96a, Gre94b]. As shown on the right side of Figure 6.4, the right half of the scrollbar is a normal single-user scrollbar, allowing the user to move within the document. To its left are vertical bars showing the relative locations of each conference user, identified by a unique colour. The bar's position and size is continuously updated as participants scroll through the document or change their window size. Additionally, the name of the bar's owner is displayed as a popup by mousing over it, and a "Follow this user" option allows participants to toggle the coupling status from independent scrolling to linked scrolling.

Our second example is a multi-user text widget. Single-user text widgets are simple text editors, while a true multi-user text editor should have features that allow simultaneous editing.

Mitchell [Mit96] used GroupKit [Ros96a] to create Calliope, a multi-user text editor. While not packaged as a widget, Calliope does indicate how such a widget could behave. As seen in Figure 6.4, Calliope provides a window displaying a shared text editor, and people can scroll independently through the text through GroupKit's multi-user scrollbars. Access control is user-selectable via a "sharing" menu option, and can range from the selection, word, line, paragraph or document level. As a region is selected, the lock request is automatically made. When another person attempts to select a locked region, the cursor changes to show conflict (the lock icon in Figure 6.4). Calliope also has extra tools, such as the ability to attach external notes to text for commentary that can be seen by others, to create private text which is added to the shared view only when desired, and access to a shared whiteboard for brainstorming activities. Text can also be queried to find who wrote it and when it was written, and colour-coded to show authorship.

6.4.2   Group-Specific Widgets

While group-aware versions of single-user widgets should be a part of any groupware toolkit, they are not enough. Toolkits should strive to provide novel widgets that support particular aspects of group work. In this section, we show several examples of group-specific widgets that are implemented or prototyped in GroupKit [Ros96a, Gre94b]. These include widgets for participant status, telepointers, and awareness.

6.4.2.1   Participant Status

As people enter and leave a conference, other participants should be able to see their comings and goings, much in the same way that we can see people arrive into a room. Because these people may be strangers, it can be useful to find out some information about them. GroupKit provides a rudimentary *participants widget*, illustrated in Figure 6.5, that can be included in any application. It lists all participants in the current conference session (left side), and the list is automatically updated as people enter and leave. When a participant is selected, a "business card" containing further information about them is displayed. This could include contact information (as shown), a picture of the person, and any other material that person wished to pass on about themselves.

An experimental variation of this widget displays participants in several ways, dependent on the information available about them: charicatures, still photos, and (if available) video snapshots whose images are updated every ten to twenty seconds. The video snapshots implement our version of the Portholes system [Dou92b]. These widgets also include the ability to monitor the activity of participants, such as whether they are actively using their computer. This is useful for facilitating contact between partners [Coc93, Gut96a].

6.4.2.2   Telepointers

Studies of small face-to-face groups working together over a shared work surface reveal that gesturing comprises about 35% of the group's activities [Tan91]. Gestures are a rich communication mechanism. Through them, participants indicate relations between the artifacts on the display, draw attention to particular artifacts, show intentions about what they are about to do, suggest emotional reactions, and so on. Many groupware systems now use telepointers (also known as multiple cursors) to provide a simple but reasonably effective mechanism

Figure 6.5   GroupKit's Participants widget

for communicating gestures [Hay94]. Unfortunately, modern window systems are tied to the notion of a single cursor, and application developers must go to great lengths (and suffer performance penalties) to implement multiple cursors. By supplying telepointers as widgets that can be attached to a view with a few lines of code, a programmer's burden is decreased significantly, and they are more likely to include this important feature within their application. For example, GroupKit programmers can add telepointers to an application with two lines of code:

```
gk_initializeTelepointers
gk_specializeWidgetTreeTelepointer .canvas
```

GroupKit's telepointers can partially handle displays where people may not see exactly the same thing because widgets are laid out in different locations. Instead of tying a telepointer to a window, a programmer can attach it to particular widgets and their children (this is the purpose of line 2, which adds telepointers only to the "canvas" widget). The telepointer is always drawn relative to the widget, rather than the application window. Similarly, we have applied telepointers to groupware text widgets that may format their contents differently on different displays. The telepointer in this case is tied to the position of the underlying text, rather than the Cartesian coordinates of the window. To illustrate the value of this approach, we applied these techniques to GroupWeb, a groupware web browser [Gre96e]. Because people have different sized windows, the HTML text and images can be laid out quite differently across participant's displays. However, their telepointers are always on top of the correct character or image.

An experimental version of GroupKit's telepointers allows them to be overloaded with semantic information to provide participants a stronger sense of awareness of what is going on, with little consumption of screen real-estate. Because telepointers tend to focus participants' attention, any information attached to them is probably noticed quickly. For example, we allow programmers to overload telepointers to indicate identity information (such as people's names), state information (such as what mode each participant is in), and action information (such as what action a person is taking). Figure 6.6 illustrates an example of how a telepointer can be overloaded with both action and identity information. The left window shows participant Carl's display, where he is navigating through a pop-up menu. We see a second cursor on the bottom of the display, which identifies its owner "Saul". The right window shows Saul's

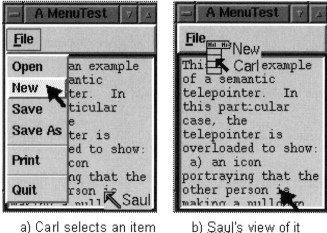

a) Carl selects an item   b) Saul's view of it

Figure 6.6   Overloaded telepointers, showing both action and identity information

display. Showing the complete menu that Carl has popped up on Saul's display could be annoying, especially if Saul were working in the area immediately underneath it. Instead, Carl's telepointer image and labels are altered to indicate a menu selection is being made (the mode), and what item is being selected (the action). In this case, the same semantic information of a menu action is shown on other displays concisely and with little loss of meaning.

6.4.2.3   Workspace Awareness

In real-life working situations, we are kept aware of what others are doing, sometimes by speech, and sometimes by seeing what others are working on through our peripheral vision and through glances. This helps us coordinate our work. These cues may not be available in the groupware channel, especially when people are allowed to have different viewports into a large workspace. Consequently, *workspace awareness* widgets must be provided that inform a participant about where other people are working in the shared work-surface and what they are doing [Dou92a, Gut96a, Gut95, Gut96b]. We should mention that workspace awareness does not have the same meaning as collaboration awareness (mentioned in this book in Chapter 7 by Dewan [Dew99] and in Chapter 5 by Prakash [Pra99]): workspace awareness concentrates on how a person's up to-the-moment awareness of what others are doing can be supported by representations and extensions of the actual shared workspace, which is a more restrictive definition.

An example of awareness widgets are radar overviews [Smi89, Bae93]. These displays present a miniature overview of the document overlaid by colored areas that show the actual viewport of each participant in the session. GroupKit contains several widget prototypes based on this idea [Gut96a, Gut95, Gut96b]. The radar overview shown in Figure 6.7 is one example. It includes an overview of a large shared workspace containing a concept map (a graph of ideas). Viewport outlines, one for each participant, contain portraits identifying their owners, and indicates what each can see. In addition, telepointers are displayed. The overview is tightly coupled to the main view of the document (not shown), and any changes are immediately reflected. A usability study has shown radar overviews to be an effective way for people to

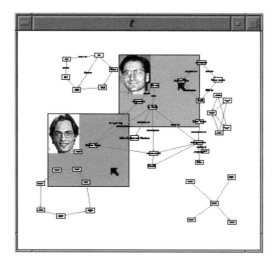

Figure 6.7 A miniature overview of a concept mapping system built in GroupKit, showing other's viewports, portraits, and telepointers. System created by Carl Gutwin, used with permission

maintain awareness of others in a spatial layout task [Gut96d]. They see changes as they occur, they know where others are working, and telepointers in the overview are used for deictic references.

We have developed a variety of other prototype widgets supporting workspace awareness. Detail views are miniatures showing exactly what another can see [Gut95, Gut96b]. The Headup Lens combines an overview with a person's main viewing area as transparent layers, one on top of the other [Gre96c]. The Fisheye Lens uses a fisheye view with multiple focal points to show where others are in the global context, and to magnify their area of work on all displays [Gre96b]. These and other awareness widgets are illustrated in two videos [Gre96a, Gut96c].

6.4.3 Discussion

The design of groupware widgets is still a young area. While many interface components exist in groupware applications that have potential as widgets, much work remains to be done in generalizing and packaging them as self contained widgets that are easily added to any application. We need strong programming abstractions, such as the notions of coupling and access control, to provide a programmer with the flexibility to specify a widget's behavior in different groupware settings. We need to redesign today's single-user widgets into reasonable yet powerful groupware counterparts. Finally, we need to create the next generation of groupware widgets, which includes refining their design and testing their worth through usability testing.

On the technical side, there is the issue of how widgets can be created by toolkit developers. Current tools are poor or non-existent. Rendezvous and Clock creators, for example, had to build all their widgets from scratch from graphical primitives [Hil94, Gra96]. GroupKit creators constructed a rudimentary "class builder" and were thus able to use and extend the existing GUI widgets supplied by the Tcl/Tk toolkit [Ros96a]. However, the class builder is awkward to use, and suffers run-time efficiency problems which can affect the performance of highly interactive widgets.

Finally, programmers of groupware could still benefit from interface builders as found in conventional GUI toolkits, which greatly eases the task of widget placement and attribute setting. Unfortunately, most groupware toolkits now available do not provide interface builders, with the exception of Visual Obliq [Bha94]. Similar to most modern conventional toolkits, groupware applications in Visual Obliq are created by designing the interface with an interface builder and then embedding callback code in an interpreted language. The resulting application can be run from within the interface builder for rapid turnaround time.

6.5   SESSION MANAGEMENT

Groupware developers often concentrate on building applications, such as multi-user sketchpads, games, and text editors. While it is important for developers to provide good groupware once people are connected and working together, it is just as important to provide a community with "session managers" for actually establishing their groupware connections. We firmly believe that toolkits must allow developers to construct or select from a large library of session management interfaces in a flexible enough fashion to accommodate the diverse requirements of different communities. Unfortunately, most of today's toolkits force a single, often rudimentary, session management interface onto its applications.

A session manager typically controls and presents an interface to the following tasks [Ros94]:

- creating new conferences
- naming conferences
- deleting conferences
- locating existing conferences
- finding out who is in a conference
- joining people to conferences
- controlling access to conferences
- allowing latecomers
- allowing people to leave conferences, and
- deciding whether conferences persist when all users exit.

For example, the interface of the session manager could present these as explicit steps that a user takes to begin and maintain the collaboration. These could also be implicit actions, where (say) the act of jointly editing an artifact automatically initiates the collaboration [Edw94].

Being able to provide different interfaces for session management is an important aspect of supporting the working patterns of a group. We believe that one of the obstacles to groupware use is the difficulty of starting up a groupware session [Coc93]. The obstacle may be in terms of usability (e.g. the system is difficult to initiate) or social (e.g. the policy the system imposes is not acceptable to the group). Session management must be more than an afterthought added to the applications, and should be tuned to the needs and collaboration patterns of the target user group.

6.5.1   Policies and Metaphors for Session Management

Session managers can implement and provide a broad variety of policies to users, as illustrated by the examples in this section.

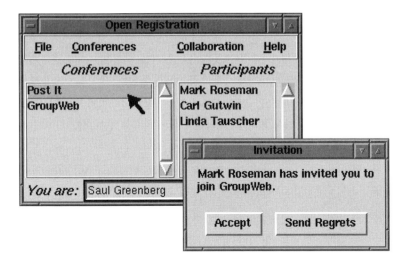

Figure 6.8 The Open Door session manager. Two conference sessions are shown, with three participants present in the "Post-It" conference

6.5.1.1 Rudimentary Policy

When session managers are not attended to, users are forced to handle session manager aspects themselves. That is, it is entirely up to the user to decide who to connect to, often by specifying low-level addressing such as Internet host names and TCP/IP port numbers. An example of this is the session manager for early versions of the NCSA Collage groupware system, which presents a form asking the user to supply one's login name, the IP address of the Collage server, and the server port number.

6.5.1.2 Open Door

The basic session manager provided by GroupKit [Ros96a, Gre94b] offers an "Open Door" permissive policy of creating and joining conferences, where people think in terms of conferences and participants instead of IP addresses. Figure 6.8 shows an example. Each conference contains a single groupware application (the application windows are not shown in the figure). In the "Conferences" pane, the local person (Saul Greenberg) sees that two conferences are in progress: "Post-It" and "Design Session". By selecting one of them, he can then see who is in a particular conference (the list in the "Participants" pane).

Conferences are entered in several ways: joins, invitations, and creation. First, Saul can *join* a conference by double clicking any conference name. This adds him to the list of participants and causes the particular application to appear on the display. Second, a person already in a conference can *invite* Saul into the session via a menu option, and a dialog will appear on the screen asking him if he wishes to join in. An example of this is shown in the figure. Third, Saul can *create* a new conference via the Conference menu: when he selects from a list of applications, a window running the application appears on the display and others are informed of its availability through the Conferences pane. This session manager also handles departure, and exiting attendees disappear from the Participants pane. When the last one leaves, that person is asked if the conference application should persist; i.e. that its state should be saved so it can be re-entered later with its contents intact.

6.5.1.3   Rendezvous Points

A quite different policy provides common rendezvous points. People go to a "place", and are automatically connected to all others in that place. The best known example of these are the popular Multi-User Dungeons (MUDs). When a person connects to a MUD via a well-known Internet address, they enter one of several rooms where they can engage in a text-based chat dialog with all others in the room. TeamRooms [Ros96b] carries the ideas of MUDs to graphical groupware by a rooms-based metaphor. Users of a community can create virtual meeting rooms, and stock them with groupware meeting tools. To create opportunities for collaboration, anyone can see what rooms are available, who is around, what rooms they are in, and how active they are. People can freely move between rooms. When they enter a room they are joined to all the conferencing tools located in the room; when they leave the room, any tools used in the room are left behind. If only one person is in a room, then it behaves as a single-user system. If no one is in a room, the tools and groupware artifacts remain available as they are treated as persistent conference sessions. This system could serve the needs of collaborators working on many tasks over a period of time, allowing them to easily move between tasks. It also serves as a meeting place, where people can see who is around in what room, and converse with them after entering the room. We expect place-based systems such as TeamRooms to have wide appeal, and other researchers are also pursuing this policy [Tol95]. For example, Lee et al [Lee96] are developing a general software architecture and API to such systems.

6.5.1.4   Other Policies

Many other session managers are possible. For example, a facilitated meeting session manager has been implemented in GroupKit, where a chairperson has complete control over what applications are part of a meeting, and who can participate. Other policy examples follow the model of telephone calls, or the way conference calls are established through a central switching point. A session manager can also be document-centric. For example, if a person opens a file that is currently being edited by someone else, the groupware connection can be made automatically. The point is that a developer requires the tools to modify packaged session managers or create new ones that fit the community.

6.5.2   Building Blocks for Session Managers

Most toolkits provide only rudimentary and hard-wired session management facilities. Share-Kit, for example, provides only basic connection facilities, although it does allow information about participants and about the session to be transmitted to others upon connection. Similarly, Rendezvous has a built-in session manager which they call a startup architecture [Pat90]. There have been a few investigations into architectures for flexible session management (e.g. Intermezzo [Edw94, Lee96]) but these are not really toolkits. Excepting GroupKit, most toolkits do not let programmers build both applications and session managers, or do not separate the two concepts.

Because few toolkits support session management as a first-class entity, we are a long way from knowing exactly what primitives and API should be provided to the developer. In our own experiences with GroupKit, we have developed flexible session management facilities around the idea of *open protocols* [Ros93]. Briefly, the Registrar central server (Figure 6.2) provides a replicated data structure that tracks meetings and attendees, but specifies no policy for how the data structure is to be used. Session managers are clients to the Registrar, and specify the policy by the selection of operations they perform. Maximum flexibility is achieved by providing open access to the Registrar's data structure via a protocol or interface of small but powerful operations (e.g. add or delete conference). Clients may be different, as long as they are well behaved with respect to each other and to the policy.

In terms of programming session managers, programmers can trap session manager events and take actions upon them via callbacks. Different session managers will use these in different ways to create their policy. To ease the programmer's chore, GroupKit also provides default callbacks to handle routine operations. The programmer can override these when necessary. Using these events, the programmer can create different access control mechanisms, start new applications or end existing ones, and build the interface in a way that shows the user what is going on. Examples of some of the events are described below:

- *userRequestNewConf:* the user has requested that a new conference be created
- *newConfApproved* and *deleteConfApproved*: the request for a new conference or termination of an existing one has been approved
- *foundNewConf* and *foundDeletedConf:* a new conference has been created, or an existing one has been removed
- *foundNewUser* and *foundDeletedUser:* a user has entered or left a conference
- *newUserApproved*: the user's admittance into the conference has been approved
- *lastUserLeftConf*: the last user in a conference has left
- *conferenceDied:* a conference process we created has terminated.

6.5.3   Discussion

Both good groupware applications and good session managers are needed for groupware to succeed. Without good session managers, it is hard to make electronic contact and get groupware started; many opportunities for collaboration will likely fall by the wayside. We believe that next-generation toolkits will, like GroupKit, include session management as an important building block. At the very least, the toolkit should provide a reasonable set of stock session managers that implement a broad range of policies. If adequate primitives are provided, the programmer should be able to modify existing session managers and create new ones to fit the particular needs of a work community.

It is even possible that session management toolkits can be developed that are completely independent from the application component and its run-time architecture. As evidence, the GroupKit session manager was recently repackaged as a stand-alone toolkit. Since then, it has been adapted to work with the Clock groupware development tool [Gra96] to manage both centralized and semi-replicated sessions. While minor code changes were required, it works well in spite of the radical differences between the run-time system and underlying language of Clock and GroupKit.

6.6   CONCLUSION

This chapter has presented four components that we believe toolkits must provide to groupware programmers. A run-time infrastructure automatically manages the creation, interconnection, and communications of the distributed processes that comprise conference sessions, greatly simplifying a programmer's job of managing a distributed system. Groupware programming abstractions allow developers to control the behavior of distributed processes, to take action on state changes, to share relevant data, and to generate views. Groupware widgets let a programmer quickly add interface features of value to conference participants. Session managers that let users create and manage their meetings are built by developers to accommodate the group's working style. Examples were taken from a variety of different toolkits to illustrate how these components can be provided in practice.

The class of groupware toolkits considered in this chapter consider only real-time distributed applications. This is just a subset of groupware, and many groupware toolkits address disparate application domains. For example, ConversationBuilder [Kap92] and Strudel [She90] are used for constructing speech act protocols. Oval is used to build semi-structured messaging and information management systems [Mal92]. Lotus Notes, although not a programming toolkit, lets people develop and tailor a wide variety of asynchronous applications (Lotus Inc.). Even toolkits within the domain of real-time interaction handle different niche problems. Dewan and Choudhary's Suite toolkit [Dew92] applies only to highly structured text objects and investigates how flexible access control mechanisms are incorporated into them. Knister and Prakash's [Kni90] DistEdit provides groupware primitives that could be added to existing single-user text editors to make them group-aware. DistView, produced by the same group, is oriented towards a fairly strict view-sharing approach to sharing window components and underlying data via an object replication scheme [Pra94]. Smith and Rodden's SOL considers design features for making single-user widgets shareable [Smi93].

The chapter also limited its discussion to four components. While we believe these are fundamental building blocks, there are certainly other components that must be included in a commercial, robust groupware toolkit. A few examples follow (see Urnes and Nejabi [Urn94] for a further list of features).

- *Security and privacy.* Groupware could be a large security hole unless great care is taken in determining that only the right people are allowed in a meeting, and that permissions to execute actions at sites other than their own does not compromise the system. Similarly, communication channels should be encrypted in case the conference deals with sensitive information. These should all be supplied as part of the stock toolkit.

- *Audio and video support.* Most of the toolkits mentioned do not directly support audio and video. Yet almost all real-time groupware requires at least audio. These can be provided out of band, through telephones, videoconferencing systems, and media spaces (see Chapter 3 in this book [Mac99]). Still, there is a trend in application design to integrate audio, video, and computational groupware. The ClearBoard system described in Chapter 4 [Ish99], for example, allows participants to see through their computational space to a video image that portrays correct eye gaze position and hand gestures relative to the surface (see also [Ish92]). There is also the problem of synchronizing audio/video with actions in the computational space, for even a few seconds of delay between the two can be disconcerting to the group members. A further discussion on multimedia in groupware can be found in this book in Chapter 8 [Dou99].

- *Communication channel and networks.* All groupware systems depend upon communication channels. Ideally, the underlying network will be tuned to support the performance demands of groupware, and the API should reflect the programmer's needs. Example extensions to standard networks are MBone [Mac94], an Internet multicast backbone that lets one send multimedia on wide-area networks such as the Internet, and Isis [Bir93], which guarantees correct serialization of events over the network.

- *Fault tolerance.* As network loads increase and connections become less reliable, fault tolerance becomes increasingly important. Groupware toolkits must include facilities to allow the application to degrade gracefully, to checkpoint failed conferences for later resumption, and to seek alternate communication paths when a channel fails. Dourish also addresses some of these issues in this book in Chapter 8 [Dou99].

- *Versioning and downloading.* In replicated architectures, problems arise when one site is missing software or has a different version of it. The system should be able to check versions, and download software when necessary.

- *Session capture and replay.* Records of meetings are sometimes crucial. While capturing video is straightforward, capturing computational actions is more difficult [Man95]. The challenge remains on how to capture automatically the highlights of lengthy meetings in a concise manner.

- *Multi-user undo.* Many single-user systems contain undo facilities. Yet undo in groupware is a hard problem. While a few researchers have been working in this area [Pra92, Ber94], we still have a long way to go before we can package undo facilities so that groupware programmers can include it easily within their application. Chapter 5 in this book contains a detailed discussion of the role of undo in a group editor [Pra99].

- *Concurrency control.* While mentioned as part of the run-time architecture, concurrency control in groupware is a sub-field in its own right. Much work remains to be done crafting appropriate tools, architectures, and abstractions that make concurrency control easy for the programmer, while minimizing its impact on the end-user's interface.

- *Application domains.* In all probability, some groupware toolkits will have to be specialized to handle the nuances of particular real-time applications domains. DistEdit, for example, concerns itself only with text editing [Kni90]. Others will deal with the structured meetings found in group support systems [Pen95], or with extending capabilities of existing single-user systems; e.g. primitives to make the *emacs* text editor group-aware [Pat95].

- *Alternate models.* The separation of model and view is only one of the many ways that groupware can be configured. For example, Karsenty and Beaudouin-Lafon [Kar95] have defined the seven-layer SLICE model. Some of these layers are: an abstract document (the model), a document layer (the displayed view), a direct manipulation layer (the means to interact with the view); a view representation layer (to control how views are displayed); and a cursor layer that tracks the mouse and shows telepointers. In Chapter 7 in this book, Dewan considers other architectural models as well [Dew99].

- *Development environments.* All the toolkits mentioned have inadequate development environments. For example, debugging groupware is hard because it is a distributed system, and we need appropriate debuggers. Interface builders are lacking. Appropriate tools for testing are non-existent.

- *The Web.* The recent popularity of the World Wide Web, as well as the network and multi-platform properties of the Java programming language, implies that the Web could become *the* delivery vehicle for real-time groupware. While the Web, Java and the Internet itself have particular features that lend themselves towards groupware (e.g. its ubiquity, its client/server model, its telecommunications constructs), it also includes constraints that may challenge the design of groupware toolkits (e.g. security, performance, session management styles). While the Web does provide incredible opportunities for groupware (some are surveyed in this book in Chapter 8 [Dou99]), we may find ourselves compromised by its technical constraints and by the way it is commonly used.

While the next generation of toolkits are now being built, groupware systems still have a long way to go to catch up to their single-user counterparts. We look forward to the day when all toolkits will incorporate multi-user features. When that day comes, the artificial distinction between constructing single and collaborative systems will disappear.

ACKNOWLEDGEMENTS

Carl Gutwin and Ted O'Grady participated in many discussions about what is required for groupware toolkits, and helped influence the contents of this chapter. Prasun Dewan, Nicholas Graham, and John Patterson reviewed versions of this manuscript. They contributed both constructive comments and further system description. Comments by anonymous referees helped improve this document. Funding by the National Science and Engineering Research Council of Canada and by Intel Corporation are gratefully appreciated.

REFERENCES

[Ahu90] Ahuja, S.R., Ensor, J.R. and Lucco, S.E., A comparison of applications sharing mechanisms in real-time desktop conferencing systems. In *Proceedings of the ACM COIS Conference on Office Information Systems*, pages 238–248, Boston, April 25–27, 1990.

[Bae93] Baecker, R., Nastos, D., Posner, I. and Mawby, K., The user-centered iterative design of collaborative writing software. In *Proceedings of ACM InterCHI'93 Conference on Human Factors in Computing Systems*, pages 399–405, Amsterdam, the Netherlands, April 24–29, 1993.

[Ber94] Berlage, T., A selective undo mechanism for graphical user interfaces based on command objects. *ACM Transactions on Computer-Human Interaction,* 1(3):269–294, September 1994.

[Bha94] Bharat, K. and Brown, M., Building distributed, multi-user applications by direct manipulation. In *Proceedings of the ACM UIST'94 Symposium on User Interface Software and Technology*, pages 71–80, Marina del Rey, California, November 2–4, 1994.

[Bir93] Birman, K.P., The process group approach to reliable distributed computing. *Communications of the ACM*, 36(12):37–53, December 1993.

[Bon89] Bonfiglio, A., Malatesta, G. and Tisato, F., Conference Toolkit: A framework for real-time conferencing. In *Proceedings of the EC-CSCW '89 First European Conference on Computer Supported Cooperative Work*, pages 303–316, Gatwick, London, UK, September 13–15, 1989.

[Car93] Carlsson, C. and Hagsand, O., DIVE – A platform for multi-user virtual environments. *Computers and Graphics*, 17(6), 1993.

[Coc93] Cockburn, A. and Greenberg, S., Making contact: Getting the group communicating with groupware. In *Proceedings of the ACM COOCS'93 Conference on Organizational Computing Systems,*, pages 31–41 Milpitas, California, November 1–4, 1993.

[Dew91] Dewan, P., Flexible user interface coupling in collaborative systems. In *Proceedings of the ACM CHI'91 Conference on Human Factors in Computing Systems*, pages 41–48, New Orleans, Louisiana, April 28–May 2, 1991.

[Dew92] Dewan, P. and Choudhary, R., A high-level and flexible framework for implementing multi-user user interfaces. *ACM Transaction on Information Systems*. 10(4):345–380, 1992.

[Dew99] Dewan, P., Architectures for collaborative applications. In Beaudouin-Lafon, M. (Ed.), *Computer Supported Cooperative Work*, Trends in Software Series 7:169–193. John Wiley & Sons, Chichester, 1999.

[Dou92a] Dourish, P. and Bellotti, V., Awareness and coordination in shared workspaces. In *Proceedings of the ACM CSCW'92 Conference on Computer Supported Cooperative Work*, pages 107–114, Toronto, Canada, October 31–November 4, 1992.

[Dou92b] Dourish, P. and Bly, S., Portholes: Supporting awareness in a distributed work group. In *Proceedings of the ACM CHI'92 Conference on Human Factors in Computing Systems*, pages 541–547, Monterey, California, May 3–7, 1992.

[Dou95] Dourish, P., Developing a reflective model of collaborative systems. *ACM Transactions on Computer–Human Interaction.* 2(1):40-63, March 1995.

[Dou96] Dourish, P., Consistency guarantees: Exploiting application semantics for consistency management in a collaboration toolkit. In *Proceedings of the ACM CSCW'96 Conference on Computer Supported Cooperative Work,*, Boston, Mass., November 16–20, 1996.

[Dou99] Dourish, P., Software infrastructures. In Beaudouin-Lafon, M. (Ed.), *Computer Supported Cooperative Work*, Trends in Software Series 7:195–219. John Wiley & Sons, Chichester, 1999.

[Edw94] Edwards, W.K., Session management for collaborative applications. In *Proceedings of the ACM CSCW'94 Conference on Computer Supported Cooperative Work*, pages 323–330, Chapel Hill, North Carolina, October 22–26, 1994.

[Ell89] Ellis, C.A. and Gibbs, S.J., Concurrency control in groupware systems. In *Proceedings of the ACM SIGMOD International Conference on the Management of Data*, pages 399–407, Seattle, Washington, 1989.

[Gra92] Graham, T.C.N. and Urnes, T., Relational views as a model for automatic distributed implementation of multi-user applications. In *Proceedings of the ACM CSCW'92 Conference on Computer Supported Cooperative Work*, pages 59–66, Toronto, Canada, October 31–November 4, 1992.

[Gra95] Graham, T.C.N., *Declarative development of interactive systems.* Volume 243 of *Berichte der GMD*, R. Oldenbourg Verlag, Munich, July 1995.

[Gra96] Graham, T.C.N., Morton, C.A. and Urnes, T.. ClockWorks: Visual programming of component-based software architectures. *Journal of Visual Languages and Computing*, Academic Press, July 1996.

[Gra96a] Graham, T.C.N., Urnes, T. and Nejabi, R. Efficient distributed implementation of semi-replicated synchronous groupware. In *Proceedings of the ACM UIST '96 User Interface Software and Technology*, Seattle, Washington, November 6-8, 1996.

[Gra96b] Graham, T.C.N. and Urnes, T., Linguistic support for the evolutionary design of software architectures. In *Proceedings of the ICSE'18 Eighteenth International Conference on Software Engineering*, pages 418–427, IEEE Press, March 1996.

[Gre90] Greenberg, S., Sharing views and interactions with single-user applications. In *Proceedings of the ACM COIS Conference on Office Information Systems*, pages 227–237, Boston, Mass., April 25–27, 1990.

[Gre94a] Greenberg, S. and Marwood, D., Real time groupware as a distributed system: Concurrency control and its effect on the interface. In *Proceedings of the ACM CSCW'94 Conference on Computer Supported Cooperative Work*, pages 207–217, Chapel Hill, North Carolina, October 22–26, 1994.

[Gre94b] Greenberg, S. and Roseman, M., GroupKit. In *ACM SIGGRAPH Video Review*, Issue 108, Videotape available from ACM Press, 1994.

[Gre96a] Greenberg, S. and Gutwin, C., Applying distortion-oriented displays to groupware. In *Video Proceedings of the ACM CSCW'96 Conference on Computer Supported Cooperative Work*, Boston, Mass., November 16–20, 1996. Videotape available from ACM Press.

[Gre96b] Greenberg, S., Gutwin, C. and Cockburn, A., Awareness through fisheye views in relaxed-WYSIWIS groupware. In *Proceedings of Graphics Interface'96*, pages 28–38, Toronto, Ontario, May 1996. Distributed by Morgan-Kaufmann.

[Gre96c] Greenberg, S., Gutwin, C. and Cockburn, A., Using distortion-oriented displays to support workspace awareness. In A. Sasse, R.J. Cunningham, and R. Winder, (Eds.), *People and Computers XI (Proceedings of the HCI'96)*, pages 299–314, Springer-Verlag, 1996.

[Gre96d] Greenberg, S. Gutwin, C. and Roseman, M., Semantic telepointers for groupware. In *Proceedings of OZCHI '96: The Sixth Australian Conference on Computer–Human Interaction*, Hamilton, New Zealand, November 24–27, 1996.

[Gre96e]   Greenberg, S. and Roseman, M., GroupWeb: A WWW browser as real time groupware. In *ACM SIGCHI'96 Conference on Human Factors in Computing System, Companion Proceedings*, pages 271–272, Vancouver, Canada, April 13–18, 1996.

[Gut95]   Gutwin, C., Stark, G. and Greenberg, S., Support for workspace awareness in educational groupware. In *Proceedings of the CSCL'95 Conference on Computer Supported Collaborative Learning*, pages 147–156, Bloomington, Indiana, October 17–20, 1995. Distributed by Lawrence Erlbaum Associates.

[Gut96a]   Gutwin, C., Greenberg, S. and Roseman, R., Supporting awareness of others in groupware. In *ACM SIGCHI'96 Conference on Human Factors in Computing System, Companion Proceedings*, pages 205–215, Vancouver, Canada, April 13–18, 1996.

[Gut96b]   Gutwin, C., Greenberg, S. and Roseman, M. (1996) Workspace awareness in real-time distributed groupware: Framework, widgets, and evaluation. In A. Sasse, R.J. Cunningham, and R. Winder, (Eds.), *People and Computers XI (Proceedings of the HCI'96)*, pages 281–298, Springer-Verlag, 1996.

[Gut96c]   Gutwin, C., Greenberg, S. and Roseman, M., Staying aware in groupware workspaces. In *Video Proceedings of the ACM CSCW'96 Conference on Computer Supported Cooperative Work*, Boston, Mass., November 16–20, 1996. Videotape available from ACM Press.

[Gut96d]   Gutwin, C., Roseman, M., and Greenberg, S., A usability study of awareness widgets in a shared workspace groupware system. In *Proceedings of the ACM CSCW'96 Conference on Computer Supported Cooperative Work*, Boston, Mass., November 16–20, 1996.

[Hay94]   Hayne, S., Pendergast, M. and Greenberg, S., Implementing gesturing with cursors in Group Support Systems. *Journal of Management Information Systems*, 10(3):43–61, 1994.

[Hil92]   Hill, R.D., The Abstraction-Link-View paradigm: Using constraints to connect user interfaces to applications. In *Proceedings of the ACM SIGCHI'92 Conference on Human Factors in Computing Systems*, pages 335–342, Monterey, California, May 3–7, 1992.

[Hil94]   Hill, R.D., Brinck, T., Rohall, S.L., Patterson, J.F. and Wilner, W., The Rendezvous architecture and language for constructing multi-user applications. *ACM Transactions on Computer–Human Interaction*, 1(2):81–125, June 1994.

[Intel]   Intel Corporation, Software available through the World Wide Web, http://www.intel.com/iaweb/moondo/index.html.

[Ish92]   Ishii, H. and Kobayashi, M., ClearBoard: A seamless medium for shared drawing and conversation with eye contact. In *Proceedings of the ACM CHI'92 Conference on Human Factors in Computing Systems*, pages 525–532, Monterey, California, May 3–7, 1992.

[Ish99]   Ishii, H., Integration of Shared Workspace and interpersonal space for remote collaboration. In Beaudouin-Lafon, M. (Ed.), *Computer Supported Cooperative Work*, Trends in Software Series 7:83–102. John Wiley & Sons, Chichester, 1999.

[Jah95]   Jahn, P., *Getting started with Share-Kit*. Tutorial manual distributed with Share-Kit version 2.0. Communications and Operating Systems Research Group, Department of Computer Science, Technische Universitat, Berlin, Germany, 1995. Available via anonymous ftp from ftp.inf.fu-berlin.de/pub/misc/share-kit.

[Kap92]   Kaplan, S.M., Tolone, W.J., Bogia, D.P. and Bignoli, C., Flexible, active support for collaborative work with conversation builder. In *Proceedings of the ACM CSCW'92 Conference on Computer Supported Cooperative Work*, pages 378–385, Toronto, Canada, October 31– November 4, 1992.

[Kar95]   Karsenty, A. and Beaudouin-Lafon, M., Slice: A logical model for shared editors. In S. Greenberg, S. Hayne and R. Rada, Editors, *Groupware for Real Time Drawing, A Designer's Guide*, pages 156–173, McGraw-Hill Europe, 1995.

[Kni90]   Knister, M.J. and Prakash, A., DistEdit: A distributed toolkit for supporting multiple group editors. In *Proceedings of ACM CSCW'90 Conference on Computer Supported Cooperative Work*, pages 343–355, Los Angeles, California, October 7–10, 1990.

[Kra88]   Krasner, G.E. and Pope, S.T. (1988), A cookbook for using the model-view-controller user interface paradigm in Smalltalk-80. *Journal of Object Oriented Programming*, 1(3):26–49, August/September 1988.

[Lau90a]   Lauwers, J.C. and Lantz, K.A., Collaboration awareness in support of collaboration transparency. In *Proceedings of the ACM SIGCHI'90 Conference on Human Factors in Computing Systems*, pages 303–211, Seattle, Washington, April 1–5, 1990.

[Lau90b] Lauwers, J.C., Joseph, T.A., Lantz, K.A. and Romanow, A.L., Replicated architectures for shared window systems: A critique. In *Proceedings of the ACM COIS'90 Conference on Office Information Systems*, pages 249–260, Boston, Mass., April 25–27, 1990.

[Lee96] Lee, J.H., Prakash, A., Jaeger, T. and Wu, G., Supporting multi-user, multi-applet workspaces in CBE. In *Proceedings of the ACM CSCW'96 Conference on Computer Supported Cooperative Work,*, Boston, Mass., November 16–20, 1996.

[Mac94] Macedonia, M.R. and Brutzman, D.P., MBone provides audio and video across the Internet. *IEEE Computer*, 27(4):30–36, IEEE Press, 1994.

[Mac99] Mackay, W.E., Media spaces: Environments for informal multimedia interaction In Beaudouin-Lafon, M. (Ed.), *Computer Supported Cooperative Work*, Trends in Software Series 7:55–82. John Wiley & Sons, Chichester, 1999.

[Mal92] Malone, T.W., Lai, K.Y. and Fry, C., Experiments with Oval: A radically tailorable tool for cooperative work. In *Proceedings of the ACM CSCW'92 Conference on Computer Supported Cooperative Work*, pages 289–297, Toronto, Canada, October 31–November 4, 1992.

[Man95] Manohar, N.R. and Prakash, A., The session capture and replay paradigm for asynchronous collaboration. In *Proceedings of the ECSCW'95 Fourth European Conference on Computer Supported Cooperative Work,* pages 149–164, September 1995.

[Mit96] Mitchell, A., Communications and shared understanding in collaborative writing. M.Sc. Thesis, Department of Computer Science, University of Toronto, Canada, 1996.

[OGr96] O'Grady, T., Flexible data sharing in a groupware toolkit. M.Sc. Thesis, Department of Computer Science, University of Calgary, Calgary, Alberta, Canada. November 1996.

[Ous94] Ousterhout, J., *Tcl and the Tk Toolkit*. Addison Wesley, Reading, Mass., 1994.

[Pat90] Patterson, J. F., Hill, R. D., Rohall, S. L. and Meeks, W. S., RendezVous: An architecture for synchronous multi-user applications. In *Proceedings of the CSCW'90 Conference on Computer Supported Cooperative Work*, pages 317–328, Los Angeles, California, October 7–10, 1990.

[Pat91] Patterson, J.F., Comparing the programming demands of single-user and multi-user applications. In *Proceedings of the UIST'92 Symposium on User Interface Software and Technology*, pages 87–94, Hilton Head, South Carolina, November 11–13, 1991.

[Pat94] Patterson, J.F., A taxonomy of architectures for synchronous groupware applications. Paper presented at the *Workshop on Software Architectures for Cooperative Systems*, held as part of the ACM CSCW'94 Conference on Computer Supported Cooperative Work, 1994.

[Pat95] Patel, D. and Kalter, S.D., Commercializing a real-time collaborative toolkit. In S. Greenberg, S. Hayne and R. Rada (Eds.), *Groupware for Real Time Drawing, A Designer's Guide*, pages 198–208, McGraw-Hill Europe, 1995.

[Pat96] Patterson, J.F., Day, M. and Kucan, J., Notification servers for synchronous groupware. In *Proceedings of the ACM CSCW'96 Conference on Computer Supported Cooperative Work,* Boston, Mass., November 16–20, 1996.

[Pen95] Pendergast, M., GroupGraphics: Prototype to product. In S. Greenberg, S. Hayne and R. Rada (Eds.), *Groupware for Real Time Drawing, A Designer's Guide*, pages 209–227, McGraw-Hill Europe, 1995.

[Pra92] Prakash, A. and Knister, M.J., Undoing actions in collaborative Work. In *Proceedings of the ACM CSCW'92 Conference on Computer-Supported Cooperative Work*, pages 273–280, Toronto, Canada, October 31–November 4, 1992.

[Pra94] Prakash, A. and Shim, H.S., DistView: Support for building efficient collaborative applications using replicated objects. In *Proceedings of the ACM CSCW'94 Conference on Computer-Supported Cooperative Work*, pages 153–164, Chapel Hill, North Carolina, October 22–26, 1994.

[Pra99] Prakash, A., Group editors. In Beaudouin-Lafon, M. (Ed.), *Computer Supported Cooperative Work*, Trends in Software Series 7:103–133. John Wiley & Sons, Chichester, 1999.

[Ros92] Roseman, M. and Greenberg, S., GroupKit: A groupware toolkit for building real-time conferencing applications. In *Proceedings of the ACM CSCW'92 Conference on Computer Supported Cooperative Work*, pages 43–50, Toronto, Canada, October 31–November 4, 1992.

[Ros93] Roseman, M. and Greenberg, S., Building flexible groupware through open protocols. In *Proceedings of the ACM COOCS'93 Conference on Organizational Computing Systems*, pages 279–288, Milpitas, California, November 1–4, 1993.

[Ros94]   Roseman, M. and Greenberg, S., *Registration for real time groupware*. Research Report 94/533/02, Department of Computer Science, University of Calgary, Alberta, Canada, 1994.

[Ros96a]   Roseman, M. and Greenberg, S., Building real time groupware with GroupKit, a groupware toolkit. *ACM Transactions on Computer–Human Interaction*, 3(1):66–106, March 1996.

[Ros96b]   Roseman, M. and Greenberg, S., TeamRooms: Network places for collaboration. In *Proceedings of the ACM CSCW'96 Conference on Computer Supported Cooperative Work,* Boston, Mass., November 16–20, 1996.

[Sch86]   Scheiffler, R.W. and Gettys, J., The X-Windows system. *ACM Transactions on Computer Graphics*, 5:79–109, 1986.

[She92]   Shen, H. and Dewan, P., Access control for collaborative environments. In *Proceedings of the ACM CSCW'92 Conference on Computer Supported Cooperative Work*, pages 51–58, Toronto, Canada, October 31–November 4, 1992.

[She90]   Shepherd, A., Mayer, N. and Kuchinsky, A., Strudel — an extensible electronic conversation toolkit. In *Proceedings of ACM CSCW'90 Conference on Computer-Supported Cooperative Work*, pages 93–104, Los Angeles, California, October 7–10, 1990.

[Smi89]   Smith R. B., O'Shea T., O'Malley C., Scanlon E. and Taylor, J., Preliminary experiences with a distributed, multi-media, problem environment. In *Proceedings of the EC-CSCW '89 1st European Conference on Computer Supported Cooperative Work*, Gatwick, UK, September 13–15, 1989.

[Smi93]   Smith, G. and Rodden T., Using an access model to configure multi-user interfaces. In *Proceedings of the ACM COOCS '93 Conference on Organizational Computing System,* pages 289–298, Milpitas, California, November 1–4, 1993.

[Tan91]   Tang, J.C., Findings from observational studies of collaborative work. *International Journal of Man–Machine Studies*, 34(2):143–160, 1991. Republished under the same title in Saul Greenberg, editor, *Computer Supported Cooperative Work and Groupware*, Academic Press.

[Tat91]   Tatar D. G., Foster G., and Bobrow D. G., Design for conversation: Lessons from Cognoter. *International Journal of Man–Machine Studies*, 34(2):185–210, February 1991. Republished under the same title in Saul Greenberg, editor, *Computer Supported Cooperative Work and Groupware*, Academic Press.

[Tay95]   Taylor, R.N., Nies, K.A., Bolcer, G.A., MacFarlane, C.A., Anderson, K.M. and Johnson, G.F., Chiron-1: A software architecture for user interface development, maintenance, and run-time support. *ACM Transactions on Computer-Human Interaction*, 2(2):105–144, June 1995.

[Tol95]   Tolone, W., Kaplan, S. and Fitzpatrick, G., Specifying dynamic support for collaborative work within wOrlds. In *Proceedings of the ACM COOCS '95 Conference on Organizational Computing System*, pages 55–67, Mipitas, California, August 13–16, 1995.

[Tou94]   Tou, I., Berson, S., Estrin, G., Eterovic, Y. and Wu, E., Prototyping synchronous group applications. *IEEE Computer*, 27(5):48–56, May 1994.

[Tre94]   Trevor, J., Rodden, T. and Mariani, J., The use of adaptors to support cooperative sharing. In *Proceedings of the ACM CSCW'94 Conference on Computer Supported Cooperative Work*, pages 219–230, Chapel Hill, North Carolina, October 22–26, 1994.

[Urn94]   Urnes, T. and Nejabi, R., *Tools for Implementing Groupware: A Survey and Evaluation*. Technical report CS-94-03, Department of Computer Science, York University, Toronto, Canada, 1994.

[Wil95]   Wilson, B., WSCRAWL 2.0: A shared whiteboard based on X-Windows. In S. Greenberg, S. Hayne and R. Rada (Eds.), *Groupware for Real Time Drawing, A Designer's Guide*, pages 129–141, McGraw-Hill Europe, 1995.

7

Architectures for Collaborative Applications

PRASUN DEWAN
University of North Carolina

ABSTRACT

The architecture of a collaborative application is characterized by the modules, layers, replicas, threads, and processes into which the application is decomposed; the awareness in these components of collaboration functions; and the interaction among these components. It influences the function, fairness, fault tolerance, ease of modification, and performance of the application, the amount of programming effort required to implement the application, and the reuse of existing single-user code. This chapter presents a design space of existing and potential collaboration architectures and discusses the consequences of choosing different points in this space.

7.1 INTRODUCTION

The architecture of a software application characterizes the components of the application, the function implemented by each component, and the interaction among these components [ShaG96, Kaz94]. It is an important issue in the design of the application since it influences the performance, ease of modification, and other properties desired by users and programmers of the application. It is also a difficult issue to resolve since decomposing a large problem into smaller parts is a challenging task: there are a number of different ways in which this decomposition can be done, and the consequences of choosing different decompositions are not always apparent.

For these reasons, a new discipline of computer science has emerged to help programmers choose architectures for software applications [ShaG96]. The architectural techniques developed so far either apply to general software applications or are tied to specific functionality such as database management [ShaG96] and user-interface support [ShaG96, Bas93]. This chapter addresses the domain of collaborative applications by describing the influence of collaboration support on the architecture of an application.

Five kinds of components of a collaborative application are considered: modules, layers, threads, processes, and replicas. These components occur in both collaborative and non-collaborative applications but the collaboration domain introduces special techniques for decomposing an application into these components. The exact functionality of these components is not identified, since it depends on application semantics. Instead, they are classified according to whether or not they implement collaboration-specific functionality. Similarly, the exact events communicated among these components are not identified. Instead, they are distinguished only by whether or not they carry collaboration-specific information.

The design space of collaboration architectures is characterized by presenting a generic architecture that captures properties common to the points in this design space, and a set of dimensions that represent the differences among these points. Different choices along each of these dimensions are identified and evaluated by discussing their influence on properties desired by programmers/users. Several generic properties are considered such as ease-of-modification and performance that have been identified by previous work on software architectures. In addition, the special case of reuse of existing single-user code, an important goal in the design of collaborative applications, is considered.

To better explain the scope of this work, it is useful to identify what we are not addressing here. We are not considering the functionality of a collaborative system, which is covered in [Dew94a, Ols93] and the accompanying discussion on shared editors in Chapter 5 of this book [Pra99]. Moreover, we are not describing tools/infrastructures for implementing collaborative applications, some of which are surveyed in the accompanying discussions on toolkits and infrastructures in Chapters 6 and 8 in this book [Gre99, Dou99]. The process of developing a collaborative application is considered to consist of three main steps: 1) design the functionality, 2) decompose the application into components, and 3) use tools for implementing the components. We shall be looking at only step 2 of this process. Naturally, these steps are not independent. For instance, the choice of the architecture may depend on the functionality desired, and a tool is typically tied to a particular architecture. We will look at these relationships but will not examine in depth the functionality and tools issues, *per se*. A preliminary discussion of these concepts was presented at a conference [Dew95].

The remainder of this discussion is organized as follows. I first present a model of collaboration that defines the kind of collaborative applications considered. Next I describe the generic collaboration architecture for implementing these applications. I then present the various dimensions along which collaboration architectures differ and discuss the tradeoffs to be made in choosing different points along these dimensions. These dimensions are used to classify architectures supported by several existing collaboration tools, and I distill the discussion about the tradeoffs by giving a set of architectural design rules that should be followed when implementing collaborative applications, which are in the spirit of those given in [ShaG96] for user-interface support. Conclusions and directions for future work complete the chapter.

7.2   COLLABORATION MODEL

To identify architectures of collaborative applications, we first need a model of collaboration that characterizes the functionality supported by these applications. We use a collaboration model based on the notion of generalized editing [Dew90, Dew92, Dew94a]. Figure 7.1

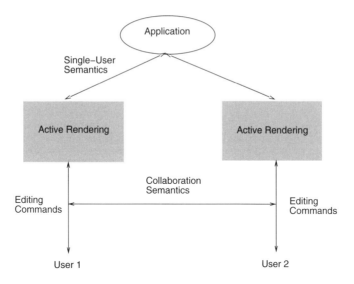

Figure 7.1   Editing-based collaboration model

illustrates the model. According to this model, an application can be considered an editor of semantic objects defined by it. A user interacts with the application by editing a rendering [1] of these objects using text/graphics/multimedia editing commands. Thus, interaction with an interactive application is similar to interaction with a text or graphics editor. The difference is that a rendering is "active" that is, changes to it can trigger computations in the application and conversely, it can be modified in response to computations invoked by the application.

As shown in Figure 7.1, each user perceives a different rendering of the semantic objects. However, the actions of the users are not isolated — they are linked by the application to facilitate and control collaboration among them. For the purposes of this discussion, we will divide the semantics of a collaborative application into *single-user semantics*, which define the feedback users receive in response to commands entered by them or actions taken by the application autonomously (in response to internal state changes or messages from other applications); and *collaboration semantics*, which define the feedback users receive in response to commands entered by others.

This is a simple but general model of collaboration. It models the single-user semantics of a variety of contemporary single-user and collaborative applications. A text/graphics editor can be considered an editor of a text/graphics file; a language-oriented editor can be considered an editor of a program syntax tree; a spreadsheet can be considered an editor of a matrix that responds to an editing of an entry in the matrix by updating related entries; and a debugger can be considered an editor of a debugging history that responds to the insertion of a new command in the history by computing the command and appending the output to the history.

It also models the collaboration semantics of a variety of contemporary collaborative applications. A "same-time" ("different-time") application is an editor that links (does not link) its renderings in real-time; a "same-place" ("different-place") application is an editor that creates (does not create) all renderings at the same site; a WYSIWIS [2] (non-WYSIWIS) application is

---

[1] On the suggestion of one of the referees, I use the term "rendering" here instead of "display" in order to include non textual/graphical presentations of objects such as audio/video renderings of data.

[2] What You See Is What I See [Ste87].

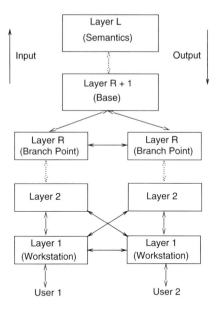

Figure 7.2   Generic architecture

an editor that ensures that the renderings are identical (different); and a workflow application is an editor that responds to editing commands by initiating the next step in the workflow.

Thus, at some level of abstraction, any collaborative application can be considered a generalized editor. [3]

7.3   GENERIC ARCHITECTURE

Figure 7.2 shows a generic collaboration architecture for implementing the model described above. It is a generalization of the architecture Patterson proposed at the CSCW'94 workshop on "distributed systems, multimedia and infrastructure support in CSCW" [Dew94b] that makes fewer assumptions about collaborative applications. As we shall see later, this architecture can be instantiated to multiple specific architectures.

The architecture assumes that a user's input/output is processed by a hierarchy of layers. A lower-level layer (that is, a layer closer to the user) manages objects that are *interactors* of objects in the immediately higher-level layer. I will refer to the latter as *abstractions* of the former. An interactor of an abstraction creates a *presentation* of the abstraction, which contains a transformation of the information in the abstraction (e.g. a text field representing an integer, or a bitmap representing a text field) plus some additional information serving as "syntactic sugar" (e.g. a label field or a window scrollbar). Thus, perceptible renderings of abstractions are created by applying the presentation operator successively to their interactors, and the interactors of these interactors, and so on. An abstraction can have a variable number of interactors, which may change dynamically as users create or delete renderings of the abstraction.

---

[3] We refer to generalized editors that perform editing commands without computing additional application-specific side effects as simply *editors*. These applications are addressed in depth in Chapter 5 of this book [Pra99].

The layers communicate with each other using *events*. Often, this term implies that the communication is sent asynchronously by the sender to the receiver. However, we will use it here in a more general sense and allow the information to be retrieved synchronously from the sender by the receiver. We divide events of a collaboration application into *interaction events* and *collaboration events* based on whether they support single-user or collaboration semantics. An interaction event may be an *output event* or an *input event* depending on whether it is sent to a lower- or upper-level layer.

Abstractions send output events to their interactors and receive input events from the latter. Output events received by objects from their abstractions may be transformed into lower-level events before they are sent to their interactors. Conversely, input events received by objects from their interactors may be transformed into higher-level events before they are sent to their abstractions. Not all input events received by interactors need to be sent to their abstractions — in particular, events that request manipulation of local syntactic sugar. Moreover, not all output events transmitted down by interactors are triggered by output events received from their abstractions. These include not only those events that change local syntactic sugar but also those that generate local echo/feedback in response to requests for changing the higher-level state in the abstraction.

A collaboration event may be a copy or extension of an interaction event or it may be an entirely new kind of event. It may be sent not only to a lower-level and upper-level layer but also a cross layer, that is a layer in an another branch, as shown in the figure.

Some levels in this architecture are *shared* while others are *versioned* or *replicated*. A shared level is associated with a single, shared layer that processes the input/output of multiple users of the application, while a versioned or replicated level is associated with a private layer for each user of the application, which processes the input/output of only that user and collaboration events concerning the user. An object in a private layer is private while an object in a shared layer is shared by multiple users. We refer to the collection of all private objects of a user and the shared objects accessible to the user as the *interaction state* of that user. All levels below a private level are constrained to be private levels and all levels above a shared level are constrained to be shared levels. Thus, the architecture defines a tree of layers rather than a general graph. We refer to this tree as a *protocol tree* in analogy with the related networking concept of a protocol stack. We refer to the lowest shared layer as the *base*, the highest versioned layers as *branch points*, the base and all layers above it as the *stem*, and a branch point and all the layers below it as a *branch* of the architecture. Moreover, we refer to all private layers at a certain level as *peers* or *replicas* of each other.

An abstraction may have interactors in zero or more replicated layers. We refer to the different interactors of an abstraction as replicas, peers, or versions. In general, they can create different logical presentations of the abstraction. However, in most current collaboration architectures, they create different physical replicas (for different users) of the same logical presentation. It is for this reason, we have used the term "replica" for a peer interactor and layer, though strictly speaking, the term "version" is more general. In the rest of the discussion, we will use these terms interchangeably. It is important to note that an interactor in a layer may not have a peer interactor in a peer layer, since not every layer creates an interactor for an abstraction in the layer above.

Abstractions and interactors may not only transform interaction events but also control the interaction by checking access rights, consistency, and other constraints. Unlike the Smalltalk Model–View–Controller paradigm [Kra88] but like the abstraction-view paradigms supported by InterViews [Lin89], Rendezvous [Hil94], PAC [Cou87], and several other frameworks, we do not treat the transformation and control components as separate objects. Similarly, unlike the Clover model [Sal95], we do not differentiate among the different collaboration functions implemented by an abstraction or interactor, clubbing them all in one multi-function object. Furthermore, unlike the PAC model, we do not capture the structure of a hierarchical abstraction or interactor, modelling it as a single unit. We do not assume that an abstraction or interactor is actually implemented as a programming language object. Similarly, we do not assume that an architectural event is actually implemented as a programming event. It may be sent in response to the evaluation of a programming constraint or some other higher-level computation that is not explicitly aware of events. Programming issues are beyond the scope of this discussion since we are focusing here only on architectural issues.

The bottom-most layers in this architecture are the workstation (operating system and hardware) layers managing the screen and input devices attached to a workstation. The workstation layers are usually replicated to allow the collaborators to use different workstations. A notable exception is MMM [Bie91], which allows a single workstation layer to be shared by multiple users concurrently manipulating the same screen using different input devices. We refer to the topmost layer in the architecture as the *semantic layer* and the abstractions in this layer as *semantic objects*. Unlike a lower-level object, a semantic object is not itself an interactor for another object. However, like an interactor, a semantic object in a replicated layer may have peers or replicas in peer layers. Peer semantic objects are (the highest-level) computer representations of the same user-level abstract object.

Not all application modules are layered in the protocol tree shown in the figure. We refer to such modules as *external modules*. The layers and modules in a collaboration architecture include both *application components* implemented by the application programmer, and *system components* provided by an infrastructure or tool. When characterizing the "architecture" of a collaboration tool, we will, in fact, be characterizing those aspects of the architectures of clients of the tool that are defined by the tool. An individual client may refine this architecture by adding further layers and modules.

7.4 DESIGN SPACE

The generic architecture given above defines a design space of collaboration architectures that differ in the way they resolve several important issues:

- *Single-User Architecture:* What is the architecture for implementing single-user semantics?
- *Concurrency:* Which components of the application can execute concurrently?
- *Distribution:* Which of these components can execute on separate hosts?
- *Versioning/Replication:* Which of these components are replicated?
- *Collaboration Awareness:* Which of these components are collaboration aware, that is, implement collaboration semantics?

Specific answers to these questions cannot be given here, since they would depend on particulars of the application. Instead, general constraints or approaches for resolving these issues are presented along with the consequences of using these approaches.

In the discussion, we consider two decompositions of a collaborative application: by computation and concurrency unit. The first one, used in Figure 7.2, assumes that an application is divided into one or communicating modules, a module may be composed of one or more lev-

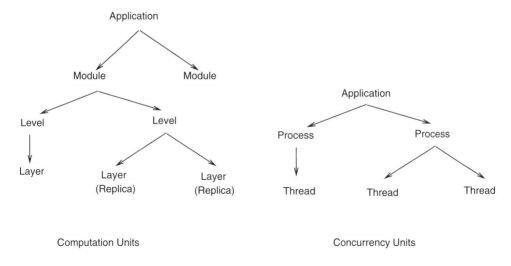

Figure 7.3 Decomposing an application by computation and concurrency units

els, and each level consists of one or more replicated layers. In the rest of the discussion, we shall often use the terms "level" and "layer" interchangeably, especially when a level consists of a single layer. The second one assumes that an application is decomposed into one or more distributable processes, and each process forks one or more concurrent threads. The difference between a process and a thread is that the former is a heavyweight unit of concurrency, associated with its own address space, which can be created on different hosts. In contrast, all threads within a process share a common address space and host, though they may execute on different processors on the host. Figure 7.3 shows the two decompositions of an application. As shown later, these two kinds of decompositions are not independent in the architectures presented below.

7.4.1 Single-User Architecture

The single-user architecture or *basis* of a multiuser architecture describes those aspects of the latter that implement single-user semantics. In this discussion, of course, we are concerned mainly with those aspects that influence/are influenced by collaboration semantics. We consider single-user architectures here because the design of the collaborative aspects is often dependent on the basis.

Strictly speaking, the basis is a view of a collaboration architecture that may not have an independent existence. In practice, however, collaboration architectures are designed by extending existing single-user architectures. A large variety of single-user architectures have been devised in the context of single-user user-interface software. We will focus here only on those that are known to have formed the bases of existing collaboration architectures. Our architectural descriptions are a set of assumptions regarding the nature of a single-user architecture. Thus, they apply to a family of architectures rather than a specific architecture.

The most general architecture is one that makes no assumption about the nature or number of application layers. By making no assumptions about an application, we can cover arbitrary applications, but cannot reason about any of them. The architecture of these applications can be described as a single level of Figure 7.2 that contains arbitrary abstractions/interactors.

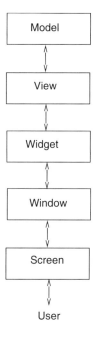

Figure 7.4   Common user-interface layers

It is possible to subclass this architecture in several ways depending on the assumptions we make about the kinds of user-interface layers used. Four main kinds of general layers have been identified so far: window, widget, view, and model [Mye95, Kra88], which would have increasing levels in a layered architecture that includes them (Figure 7.4).

An architecture that supports one of these levels does not necessarily have all the potential levels below it. For instance, a view layer may be implemented directly on top of the workstation without defining a widget layer. We can distinguish among these architectures by defining a layering degree, L, which gives the number of software layers in the architecture. For instance, TeamWorkStation [Ish90] has a layering degree of 2, since it assumes workstation and application layers (see also Chapter 4 in this book [Ish99]); XTV [Abd94], Rapport [Ens88], Shared X [Gar94], and MMConf [Cro89] have layering degrees of 3, since they assume an additional window layer; GroupKit [Ros96] has a layering degree of 4, since it assumes an additional widget layer (see also Chapter 6 in this book [Gre99]); and Suite [Dew92], Weasel [Gra92], and Clock [Gra96] have a layering degree of 5, since they assume an additional view layer. The application layers in all cases may be further subdivided into other layers. The layering and other degrees we associate with a tool (infrastructure) give the minimum degrees of client applications that use the tool. As we shall see later, the layering degree of an architecture bounds its awareness, replication, concurrency, and distribution degrees.

It is possible to further specialize these architectures by classifying them according to the specific instances of the abstract layers used in their implementation. For instance, an early version of GroupKit was based on InterViews widgets [Lin89] while the current one is based on Tk widgets [Ous94]. However, we will not distinguish among these specific instances, since from the architectural point of view, these differences are not important.

7.4.2 Collaboration Awareness

We discuss now different approaches to transforming a single-user layering to a multiuser one.

One approach is to keep the exact same set of layers and add collaboration functionality to one or more of these layers. This approach is used in many existing architectures including Shared X, which extends the X Window server, and Suite, which extends the view layer. However, it supports limited reuse of existing software since it requires changes to the layers that are made collaboration-aware. Moreover, all implementations of a layer must be changed even if they provide the same interface. It also supports limited modifiability in that a single-layer implements both the single-user and collaboration semantics. (These problems may be reduced, but not eliminated, if these layers are coded in an object-oriented programming language, since the changes may be localized in high-level classes and automatically inherited by unchanged lower-level classes.) Finally, it is not viable if the source code of the layer to be changed is not available.

Another approach is to put a *pseudo-layer* between two existing layers of the single-user architecture. To each of these two layers, the pseudo-layer provides an extension of the interface the other one provided. As a result, it accepts all of the input and output events sent to it by the layers below and above it, respectively. Depending on the nature of the interface between the two existing layers, the addition of the pseudo-layer may require recompiling and/or relinking of the existing layers. However, unlike other approaches, it does not require changes to the original layers. Moreover, it allows the same pseudo-layer to be added between multiple implementations of the two layers, as long as these implementations provide the same interface. It also supports increased modifiability since a pseudo-layer does not have to be changed in response to changes in the implementations of the original single-user layers. This approach is supported in XTV, which inserts a pseudo-layer between an X server and client, and COLA [Tre94] and DistView [Pra94], which add pseudo-layers at higher-levels (see also Chapter 5 in this book [Pra99]).

The pseudo-layer approach has two main drawbacks: First, all communication between the two layers of the original architecture must now pass through an extra layer, which may reside in a separate address space. For instance, in XTV, all communication between an X server and client must pass through a pseudo X server. Second, a pseudo-layer may need to duplicate the data structures and code of the original layers. For instance, an X pseudo-server that allows only certain windows to be shared must recreate the window tree hierarchy maintained by the X server.

Adding a pseudo-layer does not change the layering degree of the architecture, since the layer is not a "real" layer in that it does not transform its input or output. A pseudo-layer can be considered as logically belonging to the next lower layer, and should be replicated, threaded, or distributed with this layer.

Which levels of the architecture should be made collaboration-aware; that is, at which levels must collaboration-awareness be added to existing layers or new pseudo-layers introduced? One approach is to localize these modules at a single level. Assuming this approach is used, we need to choose the collaboration-aware level. There are several advantages of choosing a lower level. First, a lower level is typically common to a larger number of applications. [4] For instance, the X Window System is used by both Suite and non-Suite applications, while the Suite view layer is used only by the subset of X applications that are Suite applications.

---

[4] This is not always the case since a higher-level layer might be ported to multiple lower-level layers.

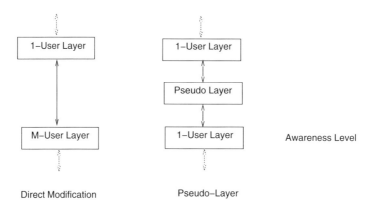

Figure 7.5   Modifying a 1-user layer vs. adding a new pseudo-layer

As a result, adding collaboration-awareness at a lower level typically provides collaboration support for a larger number of applications, since it is available not only to direct clients of the layer but also clients of higher-level layers implemented on top of this layer. Second, a lower-level layer can give users earlier feedback than higher-level layers. In general, there is a delay between the time information is received by a lower-level layer and the time it is transmitted to a higher-level layer. For instance, a widget layer may transmit edits to a form item to the higher-level layer only when the user completes the item. Hence, the lower-level a collaboration-aware layer is, the earlier it can distribute a user's edits to others and point out access and concurrency control violations. Earlier feedback allows users to collaborate more synchronously and reduces the amount of work that may have to be undone. Finally, under this approach higher-level layers are not required to process interaction events from lower-level layers (see below), which makes them more modular and portable since they are dependent on handling fewer kinds of events from lower levels.

On the other hand, there are two important, related advantages of adding collaboration support at higher-levels. First, coupling, locking, access control, and other collaboration functions can operate on units that are more meaningful to the user/programmer. For instance, unlike a window layer, a view layer can separately lock the different views displayed in a window. Second, a higher collaboration-aware level can, if it is replicated, typically, provide more degrees of sharing among peers at that level. To explain why, we make the following two observations. The sharing of peer interactor objects implies the sharing of the next-level abstraction objects, assuming that abstractions are kept consistent with their interactors. However, the sharing of an abstraction does not imply sharing of its interactors, since the peer interactors may transform the shared abstraction in different ways and add different kinds of syntactic sugar. Thus, a collaboration-aware layer can allow a) no sharing between peer abstractions, b) sharing of peer abstractions without sharing of lower-level interactors, and c) sharing of lower-level interactors if appropriate input events can be solicited from the lower-level layers. For instance, Suite can allow a) no sharing between peer views, b) sharing of peer views without sharing of the windows displaying them, and c) sharing of peer windows by soliciting all X events. In contrast, a lower collaboration-aware level cannot allow sharing of higher-level abstractions without sharing of their interactors at this level.

In the higher-level case, sharing of lower-level interactors is achieved, at the cost of increasing the *interaction awareness* in the higher-level layer; that is, the awareness of interac-

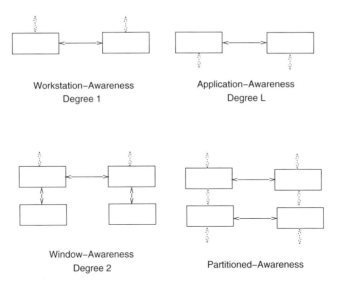

Figure 7.6   Approaches to collaboration-awareness

tion events of lower-level layers. For instance, to allow sharing of lower-level interactors such as windows, multi-user Suite is forced to handle several low-level X events such as window movement and resize events, which single-user Suite was unaware of.

We associate a collaboration architecture with an *awareness degree*, which is the level of the highest layer that is collaboration-aware. The value of this degree ranges from 1 in TeamWorkStation, which provides all collaboration support at the workstation level; to 5 in DistView, which requires the model layer to be collaboration-aware.

Since there are benefits of adding collaboration-awareness at both lower and upper levels, it is useful to consider an approach that partitions this awareness among multiple layers. Such an approach could offer the benefits of both the lower-level and higher-level approaches. In particular, it can offer logical collaboration units, flexible sharing, and low interaction awareness. However, unlike the localized approach, this approach would require providers of multiple modules to address collaboration, coordinate their activities, and often implement similar functionality (such as remote invocation) multiple times. This approach is offered in MMConf by making both the window and application layers collaboration-aware, and in Suite, by allowing both the view and application layers to be collaboration-aware. Figure 7.6 illustrates the various approaches to collaboration awareness.

7.4.3   Versioning and Replication

The versioning/replication architectural dimension determines the base and branch points in the generic architecture of Figure 7.2. As mentioned before, all layers below a base are replicated. We can thus associate an architecture with a *replication degree*, which is the level of the branch point. Two extreme approaches to replication are the *centralized* and *replicated* approaches. The former creates no replicated level while the latter creates no base level. In between these two approaches, several *semi-replicated* approaches are possible, which choose different levels for the base layer. Thus, the replication degree of an architecture with L levels is in the range 0 to L (Figure 7.7).

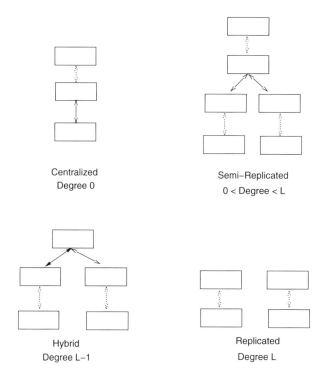

Figure 7.7   Replication approaches

There are important advantages of choosing a higher replication degree. As we shall see later, the replication degree of an architecture bounds its distribution and concurrency degrees. Thus, a higher replication degrees allows more distribution and concurrency benefits (discussed later). Moreover, a higher replication degree allows more divergence in the interaction states of the users since fewer levels are shared. For instance, if the view level is shared, then all users are constrained to see the same views of models. A higher degree of replication allows but does not force more divergence since it is possible for peer objects to share state via collaboration events, as mentioned in the previous section.

On the other hand, replicating a level requires a mechanism for keeping the peer layers at that level consistent. If these layers are meant to be exact replicas, then often a tool can automatically provide this mechanism. Automatic consistency among the objects in exact replicas is typically achieved by executing the same set of operations on these objects (see Chapter 5 in this book [Pra99]). For instance, if a user presses a button widget, then this operation is also invoked on all peers of the widget that are meant to be exact replicas. However, multiple invocations of an operation lead to several problems:

- *Inefficiency:* They can lead to serious efficiency problems if the operation is an expensive one.
- *Access bottleneck:* They may try to simultaneously access a central resource (such as a file) thereby causing an access bottleneck.
- *Incorrect writes:* They may modify the same central resource, thereby causing the same value to be written multiple times. The access and write problems would be eliminated in a system that replicated all resources.

- *Incorrect side effects:* They may send mail, print documents, and perform other side effects multiple times.

The last two problems can be averted in collaboration-aware peer layers that ensure (based, for instance, on user identities) that only one of these layers performs the write and other side effects.

Not all layers perform operations with one or more of these properties. Typically, it is the topmost layer — the one containing semantic objects — that performs such operations. Therefore, several systems adopt a special case of the semi-replicated architecture that keeps the semantic layer centralized and the lower-level layers replicated. We refer to this architecture as the *hybrid* architecture. Given an application with L levels, the replication degree of the hybrid architecture for this application is $L - 1$.

Since replication has both important advantages and disadvantages, there is substantial variation in the replication degrees of collaborative applications. Another cause for this variation is the variation in the level of the collaboration tools used for automatically implementing replication. A collaboration tool can either replicate all or none of the layers in its client. Since there are important disadvantages of replicating the topmost layer, typically the tool will replicate its layers but not those of its client. As a result, tools at different levels will offer different replication degrees.

Systems supporting the hybrid architecture include Rendezvous, Suite, Weasel and Clock. Systems that offer full replication include GroupKit and GroupDesign [Kar93], while the only one known to offer pure centralization is MMM. TeamWorkStation supports a replication degree of 1. A window-based architecture such as XTV and Rapport that centralizes its client has been traditionally called a *centralized architecture* [Lau90]. However, under our terminology, it is a semi-replicated architecture with degree 2, since the workstation and window layers are replicated. Because of the replication degree supported by them, MMM/Team Workstation/XTV/Suite cannot allow screen/windows/views/models to diverge. GroupKit and GroupDesign allow all of these layers to diverge, but require collaboration-awareness to solve the problems with invoking the same operation on multiple replicas.

7.4.4 Concurrency

Decomposing an application into multiple threads is important in single-user applications since it allows these threads to execute simultaneously on a multiprocessor system. It is particularly important in multimodal applications where the devices for different I/O modes such as audio, video, mouse, and keyboard can be managed by different threads. The multi-user case offers additional opportunities and reasons for creating multiple threads. Typically, the users of a collaborative application can input and output data concurrently. Thus, the different branches created for these users are potential concurrency units that can be executed simultaneously by different processors of a multiprocessor system. Even in a single-processor system, creating separate threads for these branches is important. It supports fair (preemptive) scheduling among these threads by ensuring that a computation triggered in a branch by the actions of a user does not lock out other users for an unbounded time.

However, there are reasons why a complete branch may not be associated with its own thread. The system support needed to create threads may not be available to programmers. Moreover, programmers may not be willing to put the effort required to create and synchronize threads. A collaboration tool can automate this task for the layers it knows about but not those in its clients. Similarly, it may not be possible to assign a thread to a layer without requiring

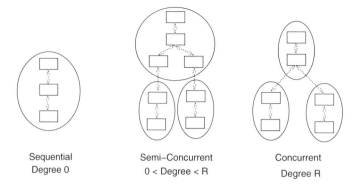

Figure 7.8   Concurrency approaches. The rectangular boxes are layers and the ellipses are threads

changes to the layer since the syntax and semantics of an invocation in the same or different thread may be different. Thus, the goal of increasing the concurrency may conflict with the goal of reuse since the former may require changes to source code of an existing layer.

As a result, different architectures may take different approaches to concurrency depending on how they tradeoff the benefits of concurrency with its drawbacks. To capture differences among these architectures, we associate them with a *concurrency degree*, which is a measure of how many layers in a branch execute in their own thread. An architecture has concurrency degree, C, if no layer at or below level C shares a thread with a stem layer or a layer in a different branch. Different layers in a branch may, and typically do, share a common thread. The concurrency degree of a collaboration architecture ranges from 0 to R, where R is its replication degree. We refer to architectures with concurrency degree 0 and R as *sequential* and *concurrent* architectures, respectively, and the remaining architectures as *semi-concurrent* architectures (Figure 7.8). A sequential architecture must be a centralized architecture. In a non-centralized architecture, the workstation level is guaranteed to be replicated. A replicated workstation level (but not other levels) must be distributed, by definition, since a level is distributed if it resides on multiple workstations. Furthermore, we assume that distributed layers execute concurrently. Hence no non-centralized architecture is sequential.

All collaboration tools known to the author offer the concurrent approach. Of course, the replication degrees in these systems may be different, as mentioned before, which causes variations in the concurrency offered by them. For instance, the concurrency degree in Rendezvous and Suite is 4 and in XTV it is 2. In all existing replicated architectures it is the same as the layering — and hence replication — degree.

The above discussion identifies a simple approach to introducing concurrency in a collaborative application: assign all branch layers below some level C to a separate thread. A concurrent architecture created using this approach does not necessarily offer the maximum possible concurrency, which would require an approach that identifies all portions of the application that could potentially execute concurrently and assigns each of these to a separate thread. We refer to such an approach as the *maximal-concurrent* approach. This approach is highly application dependent and either requires the programmer to identify the threads, which has proven to be a tedious, error-prone, and difficult task in general, or the system to automatically perform this task, which in general is impossible. Unlike the maximal-concurrent approach, our approach does not process concurrently the actions in a branch or stem invoked by a single-user (such as concurrent mouse and key clicks by the same user), or the actions in the stem invoked by different users (such as concurrent key clicks by two independent users handled by a central layer). However, it does allow the computation of the local feedback in the branches of different users to be performed concurrently.

Note that the notion of the concurrency degree applies to all collaboration architectures including those that assign threads based on approaches other than the one given above. However, it does not capture all concurrency differences among these architectures. For instance, as mentioned above, a concurrent architecture may or may not be a maximal concurrent architecture.

7.4.5 Distribution

Once the threads of an application have been identified, they must be assigned to process address spaces, which in turn must then be assigned to hosts. Assigning different threads to multiple address spaces increases fault tolerance since fatal errors in one thread do not necessarily cause the whole application to fail. This is particularly important in the multi-user case, since users would like to be protected from the errors of others. If the replicas created for different users are assigned to different address spaces, then a fatal error in one replica would not necessarily cause the other replicas to crash.

Distributing different processes to different hosts also allows an address space to be close to the resources it is accessing the most. Again, this is particularly important in the multi-user case, since the replicas created for different users need to access different and possibly widely separated workstations. By executing replicated layers on a local workstation, no remote communication is required to generate the local feedback computed by these layers. Moreover, events transmitted from these workstations are high-level events generated by the local layers rather than low-level events generated by the workstation. Typically, a higher-level I/O event contains less data and is communicated less frequently than a lower-level one, and thus generates less traffic on the network. For instance, communicating committed changes to an integer value communicates less data than communicating incremental changes to a slider representation of it.

On the other hand, distributing portions of an application on different workstations is not without drawbacks. The distributed parts of the application are not guaranteed to see the same environment, which can cause problems. For instance, problems would occur if the application uses a file name that is not valid at all sites unless the application is site-aware. Moreover, synchronizing distributed replicas is a difficult problem. Often an event received by a layer must also be sent to remote replicas to satisfy consistency constraints among them. To ensure good response times for the local users, such events must be processed immediately by the local layers without trying to ensure a global ordering among them. As a result, the distributed replicas may get inconsistent unless application-specific techniques [EllG89] are used to transform or abort received events, or the events are guaranteed to commute.

As a result, different architectures take different approaches to distribution depending on how they tradeoff its communication benefits with its drawbacks. To capture differences among these architectures, we associate an architecture with a *distribution degree*, which is analogous to its concurrency degree. It is a measure of how many layers in a branch can execute on the local host. An architecture has distribution degree, D, if no layer at or below level D shares an address space with a stem layer or a layer in a different branch. Different layers in a branch may, and typically do, share a common address space. The concurrency degree of a system is always higher than its distribution degree since distributed modules execute

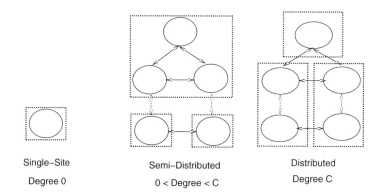

Single–Site   Semi–Distributed   Distributed
Degree 0   0 < Degree < C   Degree C

Figure 7.9 Distribution approaches. Ellipses are threads and rectangles are hosts

concurrently. However, it is not the same, since a particular address space can execute multiple threads concurrently. Thus, the distribution degree of a collaboration architecture ranges from 0 to C, where C is its concurrency degree. We refer to architectures with distribution degree 0 and C as *single-site* and *distributed* architectures, respectively, and the remaining architectures as *semi-distributed* architectures (Figure 7.9). A single-site architecture must be a sequential architecture since distributed modules execute concurrently. Like the maximal-concurrent approach, it is possible to imagine a *maximal-distributed* approach that dynamically assigns each application module to the workstation accessing it the 'most'. However, such an approach [Jul88] is still a subject of research and requires application-specific support. Our notion of a distribution degree does not distinguish between those distributed architecture that offer maximal distribution and those that do not.

The distributed approach determines only how the application is decomposed into processes and not how these processes are assigned to hosts. Depending on the workstation and network speed, it may, in fact, be sometimes beneficial to execute branch layers on a fast remote workstation. The higher the distribution degree of an architecture, the more the flexibility in reducing the communication costs.

Not all communication costs go down when a replica is executed on a local host. In particular, the cost of communicating with remote higher-level and peer layers goes up. However, assuming that information gets abstracted as it flows upwards and that a collaboration or input event received by a layer triggers a lower-level output event, the overall communication cost is reduced. To better understand the logic behind this conclusion, consider Figure 7.10, which shows the difference between placing replicas, A and A$'$, on local and central hosts. Consider how an input IA, to layer A, is processed by the various layers in the architecture. Layer A produces some local feedback, OAL, sends a collaboration event, CA, to its peer, and an input event, IB, to the higher-level layer. The higher-level layer, in turn, produces feedback TOB (which is the total feedback consisting of feedback of B and all of the layers above), which, in turn, is transformed to TOA by layer A. On receiving CA, layer A$'$ produces coupling feedback CAO, and sends an input event IB$'$ to B$'$. Layer B$'$, in turn, produces total feedback TOB$'$, which, in turn, is transformed by A$'$ to TOA$'$.

Consider the local and central placement schemes shown in Figure 7.10. The difference between them is in the placement of the replicas — under local placement, replicas A and A$'$ are placed on the local workstations, while under central placement, they are placed on the central site. In the local case, events IA, TOA, CAO, TOA$'$, OAL are transmitted locally, and

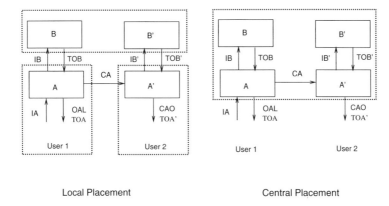

Figure 7.10 Local and central placement of replicated layers

events IB, TOB, CA, TOB′, and IB′ are transmitted across the network, while in the central case, the converse is true. If we assume that information gets condensed when it is processed by a higher-level layer, then the following relationships hold among the size of these events: IA > IB, TOA > TOB, CAO > CA, TOA′ > TOB′. Also, if we assume that a higher-level event triggered by an input event is smaller than any lower-level event also triggered by the same input, then OAL > IB′. These relationships imply that more information is transmitted locally in the first case.

We have ignored, above, peer collaboration events sent to B′ and other layers above A′. In both cases, such events will be communicated locally. However, under local placement, the resulting output sent to the remote user will be higher level — the output of B′ rather than A′ — thereby further reducing the communication cost. We have also ignored collaboration events sent to cross layers. For similar reasons, they also favor local placement of modules.

Most existing architectures offer the distributed approach, that is, distribute all of their concurrent threads. A notable exception is the Rendezvous architecture, which offers a distribution of degree of 2 but a concurrency degree of 4. In this architecture, all layers except the X Window layers execute at a central site. However, at the central site, the layers in different branches execute in separate threads. The Clock system provides a hybrid approach, allowing the same application program to have degrees 2 to 4, depending on whether it centralizes the replicated widget and view layers.

We have assumed that every collaboration event sent to a peer layer results in an output event. This may not be true for constraint-based systems such as Rendezvous, Weasel, and Clock, which may need several collaboration events to be exchanged before the constraint evaluation can fire the output events. It is perhaps for this reason that Rendezvous does not use a distributed architecture, though preliminary performance results from Weasel and Clock show advantages of using such an architecture even in a constraint-based environment.

7.5 EXTERNAL MODULES

Not all collaboration modules can be added to existing single-user layers or new pseudo-layers. It may also be necessary to create new external modules that do not belong in the protocol tree, for several reasons (Figure 7.11):

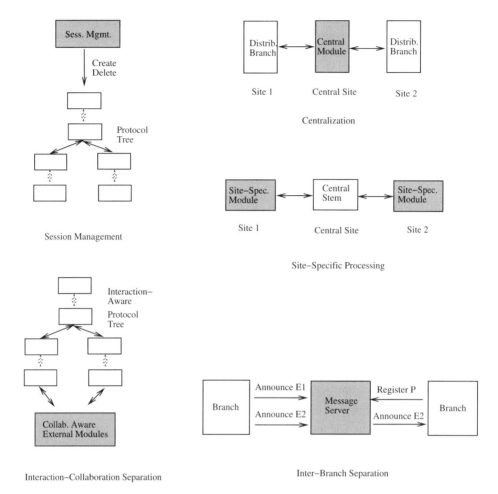

Figure 7.11   Reasons for adding external modules

- *Session Management:* In a collaborative system, session management modules are needed to create/delete the protocol tree of an application when a session with an application is started/terminated. In the single-user case, the operating system is responsible for creating/deleting interactive sessions, but in the multi-user case, special, possibly application-specific, protocols are necessary for session management [Ros96]. Since these protocols create/delete protocol trees, they cannot be implemented within the tree itself, and thus must be provided by external modules.
- *Centralization:* Replicated collaboration-aware layers may need to communicate with central modules to keep central resources such as locks or ensure global ordering of messages communicated among these layers. These modules can be implemented in the stem of the protocol tree, which is the approach taken in Suite. However, this approach cannot be taken if the architecture is fully replicated or if it cannot have any collaboration-aware stem layers. In these cases, the central modules must be external to the protocol tree.
- *Site-Specific Processing:* Centralized collaboration-aware layers may need to communicate with modules that must be located at a particular site for efficiency or other reasons.

Examples of such modules are those that access files, devices, or processes at a particular site or keep information about the active users or sessions at a site. These modules can be implemented in collaboration-aware branch layers at that site if such layers exist; otherwise they must be modules external to the protocol tree. Systems that distribute replicas create a site-specific server for creating and terminating processes at that site. Similarly, Suite creates an audio server at each site to access the audio devices at that site [Rie93].

- *Collaboration and Interaction Independence:* For modularity reasons, it may be desirable to separate the processing of interaction and collaboration events. As mentioned before, pseudo-layers can be used to increase this separation since such layers are responsible only for transmitting interaction events and not for transforming them. However, these layers have the performance disadvantages mentioned before and support limited separation since they must process both kinds of events. Similarly, within a layer, encapsulation may be used to separate the interaction-aware and collaboration-aware objects. An approach providing more separation is to process collaboration events in external modules, which can be shared by multiple layers and branches.

- *Inter-Branch Independence:* It is useful to reduce the awareness a branch has about branches created for other users. This increases the modularity of the system, and more important, reduces the cost of connecting a branch to other branches. If every branch kept track of every other branch it may need to communicate with, then branch awareness and interaction awareness would be implemented by the same layers, and more important, a branch would need to be informed each time a new branch is created that may need to communicate with it. It may be more attractive to implement one or more (possibly replicated) external message servers [Rei90], responsible for linking the replicated branches. A message server receives message *patterns* from information clients indicating the kind of messages they are interested in receiving, and *announcements* from information servers announcing events in which information clients may be interested. The message server forwards an announcement from an information server to all information clients who have registered an interest in the announcement. This is essentially the approach taken in [Bon89]. A message server leads to more modularity and reduced connection cost, but increases the "hop count" of inter-branch messages; that is, it increases the number of modules responsible for processing inter-branch messages. The increased hop count is a serious problem if the message server is centralized and the branches are distributed, since the message server can become a central bottleneck. On the other hand, as mentioned before, such a central agent may be necessary in any case to implement global ordering of distributed operations.

In many of the cases above, we have not defined the specifics of how the external modules are connected to each other, threaded, distributed, or replicated. These issues can be resolved in the same way they were resolved for the original modules. In fact, it is possible to create a hierarchy of replicated, distributed, concurrent external modules. For instance, GroupKit creates a central registrar that acts as a connection point and name server, with replicated local session managers at all sites deciding the policy for how people enter groupware sessions.

7.6 RULES

Ideally, we would like to identify universal principles that should be followed in the design of all collaboration architectures. However, as explained in the sections above, there are no absolute rules in the design of these architectures. Therefore, what we offer, instead, is a set of qualified rules summarizing the advantages/disadvantages of different architectural approaches. These can be used by developers of an application/tool to optimize the set of properties that are important for that application/tool.

- *Layering:* A higher degree of layering can support higher degrees of awareness and replication.
- *Awareness:* A higher degree of awareness leads to more flexible sharing and higher-level units of collaboration, but supports less reuse, delays feedback, and increases interaction awareness (if the partitioned approach is not taken).
- *Replication:* A higher degree of replication supports more divergence and a higher degree of concurrency; but requires more layers to be kept consistent, and results in inefficiency, access bottlenecks, and incorrect writes and other side effects.
- *Concurrency:* A higher degree of concurrency increases fairness, performance, and the maximum degree of distribution; but reduces reuse, requires special system support, and increases programming overhead.
- *Distribution:* A higher degree of distribution increases fault tolerance and reduces communication costs, but introduces problems of synchronization and heterogeneity.
- *Partitioning:* Partitioned collaboration awareness reduces interaction awareness; but requires more programming effort and supports less reuse.
- *Pseudo-Layer:* The pseudo-layer approach supports more reuse and modularity; but offers less performance and can result in duplication of effort.
- *External Modules:* External modules are necessary for supporting session management, centralization, site-specific processing, collaboration and interaction independence, and inter-branch independence; but increase the complexity of the system and can reduce performance.

7.7   CLASSIFYING EXISTING SYSTEMS

Tables 7.1 and 7.2 describe architectures of several existing collaboration systems. Table 7.1 gives the layering and associated degrees supported by them. Since all of these systems are collaboration tools, these values refer to the minimum values of these degrees, since some clients may create additional layers, replicas, processes, and threads in the application. We have assumed above that all view layers are built on top of widget layers so that a comparison of the various degrees is more meaningful. Table 7.2 indicates the other properties supported by them: pseudo-modules, partitioned awareness, and external modules to support session management, centralization, site-specific computing, collaboration awareness, and message servers. These tables show the similarities and differences among these tools. All systems except MMM support multi-workstation collaboration. Among these systems, TeamWorkStation is workstation-based; XTV, Shared X, and MMConf are window-based; and Rendezvous, Suite, Weasel, and DistView are view-based. MMM offers the pure centralized architecture; MMConf, GroupKit, and DistView the replicated architecture; and TeamWorkStation, XTV, Rendezvous, Weasel, and DistView the semi-replicated architecture. In all systems except Rendezvous, the distribution degree is the same as the concurrency degree. From an architectural point of view, there are no differences between Suite and Weasel.

Table 7.1   Layering and associated degrees of existing architectures

System	Layers	Lyr. Deg.	Awr. Deg.	Rep. Deg.	Conc. Deg.	Dist. Deg.
MMM [Bie91]	app/workst	2	2	0	0	0
TeamWorkStation[Ish90]	app/workst	2	1	1	1	1
XTV [Abd94]	app/win/workst	3	2	2	2	2
Shared X [Gar94]	app/win/workst	3	2	2	2	2
MMConf [Cro89]	app/win/workst	3	3	3	3	3
GroupKit [Ros96]	app/wid/win/workst	4	4	4	4	4
Rendezvous [Hil94]	app/view/wid/win/workst	5	5	4	4	2
Suite [Dew92]	app/view/wid/win/workst	5	5	4	4	4
Weasel [Gra92]	app/view/wid/win/workst	5	5	4	4	4
Clock [Gra96]	app/view/wid/win/workst	5	5	4	4	2–4
DistView [Pra94]	app/view/wid/win/workst	5	5	5	5	5

Table 7.2   Pseudo-layers, partioned awareness, and different kinds of external modules

System	Pseudo	Part.	Sess. M.	Central	Site-Spec.	Colab. Awr.	Msg. Serv.
MMM	N	Y	N	N	N	N	N
TeamWorkStation	N	N	Y	N	N	N	N
XTV	Y	N	Y	N	Y	N	N
Shared X	N	N	Y	N	N	N	N
MMConf	N	Y	Y	N	Y	N	N
GroupKit	N	Y	Y	N	Y	N	N
Rendezvous	N	Y	Y	N	N	N	N
Suite	N	Y	Y	N	Y	N	N
Weasel	N	Y	Y	N	N	N	N
Clock	N	Y	Y	N	N	N	N
DistView	Y	Y	Y	N	N	N	N

7.8   CONCLUSIONS AND FUTURE WORK

This work makes several contributions. It motivates the need for studying software architectures of collaborative systems, describes a generic architecture that encapsulates architectural properties common to a wide range of collaborative systems, identifies a set of issues that a designer of a specific architecture must face, discusses and evaluates competing approaches to addressing these issues, classifies existing systems according to the approaches they have taken, and gives a set of architectural rules.

This work is related to the SAAM model for describing architectures of software systems [Kaz94]. This model advocates:

1. a canonical decomposition of the functionality of the system
2. identification of the structure of the system, that is, the set of components of the system and the communication among these components
3. identification of the functions performed by each component
4. selection of a set of abstract properties for evaluating the architecture
5. selection of a set of concrete tasks that have these properties, and

6. evaluation of the extent to which the architecture supports the abstract properties and concrete tasks.

This work has applied several of these steps. In particular, it has applied step 1 by decomposing the functionality of a collaborative application into interaction functions and collaboration functions, 2 by identifying the layers, threads, and processes of a collaborative system, 3 by distinguishing between collaboration-aware and unaware layers, 4 by selecting functionality, performance, programming effort, reusability, and modularity as evaluation properties, and 6 by evaluating how well each of these abstract properties are satisfied by an architecture. It would be useful to extend this work by :

- identifying concrete tasks that have the evaluation properties and evaluating how well the architecture supports these tasks
- doing a finer structural decomposition that identifies the components of the layers and the external modules of the architecture, and
- doing a finer task assignment that distinguishes among layers based not only on whether they perform interaction or collaboration functions but also on the set of collaboration functions they perform.

The framework and associated terminology can be used for understanding, comparing, and classifying existing collaboration systems. It can also be used to varying degrees to design new systems. One method would be to take the set of approaches supported in an existing system to develop a new system that addresses details not covered here differently. For instance, the set of approaches used in XTV can be used to develop a shared window system based on a different network single-user window system such as the Plan 9 window system [Pik90]. A more novel use of the framework would be to choose a new combination of the set of the approaches described here. For instance, a new version of Suite can be developed that supports a fully replicated architecture. This framework makes these tasks easier by telling the designers which questions they have to answer, what choices are available, and what the consequences of these choices are.

This work can be extended in many other ways. It would be useful to decompose a layer by structure, as in the PAC model, and function, as in the Clover model. A first-cut at combining this architecture with PAC and Clover has been published recently [Cal97]. It is also necessary to identify other assumptions, issues, approaches, and criteria for comparing architectures. In particular, it is useful to relax the assumption that all levels above a central level are also centralized. In a single-workstation collaborative system such as MMM, it may be useful to create different branches for different users. Moreover, in such a system, it would be useful to capture, in the concurrency degree, the notion of assigning different devices to different threads. This architecture was developed based on experiences with implementing multi-user textual/graphical user-interfaces. It would be useful to test its applicability for multi-user audio/video and 3-D virtual reality user-interfaces. It may also be useful to relax the assumption that a layer is replicated/threaded/distributed as a whole, which does not apply to Shastra [Anu93]. In Shastra, the semantic layer consists of two parts: one performs expensive computations while the other performs relatively inexpensive ones. The expensive part is centralized but the inexpensive one is replicated and distributed since computation costs dominate in one case and communication costs in the other. It would also be useful to consider migration and caching of centralized components of collaborative applications [Gra96, Chu96] and their impact on performance.

ACKNOWLEDGEMENTS

I am grateful for the in-depth comments of the referees. This research was supported in part by National Science Foundation Grants IRI-9408708, IRI-9508514, IRI-9627619, and CDA-9624662, and DARPA/ONR Grant N 66001-96-C-8507.

REFERENCES

[Abd94]   Abdel-Wahab, H. and Jeffay, K., Issues, problems and solutions in sharing clients on multiple displays. *Internetworking: Research and Experience*, 5:1–15, 94.

[Anu93]   Anupam, V. and Bajaj, C., Collaborative multimedia scientific design. In *Proceedings of ACM Conference on Multimedia*, pages 447–456, 1993.

[Bas93]   Bass, L., Architectures for interactive software system: Rationale and design. *Trends in Software: Issue on User Interface Software*, 1:31–44, 1993.

[Bie91]   A. Bier, E.A. and Freeman, S., MMM: A user interface architecture for shared editors on a single screen. In *Proceedings of the ACM Symposium on User Interface Software and Technology, UIST'91*, pages 79–87, November 1991.

[Bon89]   Bonfiglio, A., Malatesta, G. and Tisato, F., Conference toolkit: Framework for real-time conferencing. In *Proceedings European Conference on Computer-Supported Cooperative Work, ECSCW'89*, pages 303–316, 1989.

[Cal97]   Calvary, G., Coutaz, J. and Nigay, L., From single-user architectural design to PAC*: a generic software architecture model for CSCW. In *Proceedings Human Factors in Computing Systems, '97*, pages 242–249, ACM Press, March 1997.

[Chu96]   Chung G. and Dewan, P., A mechanism for supporting client migration in a shared window system. In *Proceedings of the ACM Symposium on User Interface Software and Technology, UIST'96*, pages 11–20, October 1996.

[Cou87]   Coutaz, J., PAC, an object oriented model for dialog design. In *Proceedings of Interact'87*, pages 431–436. North Holland, 1987.

[Cro89]   Crowley, T. and Forsdick, H., MMConf: The diamond multimedia conferencing system. In *Proceedings of the IFIP WG8.4 Groupware Technology Workshop*, August 1989.

[Dew90]   Dewan, P. and Solomon, M., An approach to support automatic generation of user interfaces. *ACM Transactions on Programming Languages and Systems*, 12(4):566–609, October 1990.

[Dew92]   Dewan, P. and Choudhary, R., A high-level and flexible framework for implementing multi-user user interfaces. *ACM Transactions on Information Systems*, 10(4):345–380, October 1992.

[Dew94a] Dewan, P., Choudhary, R. and Shen, H., An editing-based characterization of the design space of collaborative applications. *Journal of Organizational Computing*, 4(3):219–240, 1994.

[Dew94b] Dewan, P., CSCW'94 workshops. In *Proceedings of the ACM Conference on Computer Supported Cooperative Work, CSCW'94*, pages 1–4, October 1994.

[Dew95]   Dewan, P., Multiuser architectures. In *Proceedings of IFIP WG2.7 Working Conference on Engineering for Human–Computer Communication, EHCI'95*, pages 43–70, August 1995.

[Dou99]   Dourish, P., Software infrastructures. In Beaudouin-Lafon, M. (Ed.), *Computer Supported Cooperative Work*, Trends in Software Series 7:195–219. John Wiley & Sons, Chichester, 1999.

[EllG89] Ellis, C.A. and Gibbs, S.J., Concurrency control in groupware systems. In *Proceedings of the ACM SIGMOD '89 Conference in Groupware Systems*, May, 1989.

[Ens88]   Ensor, J.R., Ahuja, S.R., Horn, D.N. and Lucco, S.E., The Rapport multimedia conferencing system: A software overview. In *Proceedings of the 2nd IEEE Conference on Computer Workstations*, pages 52–58, March 1988.

[Gar94]   Garfinkel, D., Welti, W. and Yip, T., Shared X: A tool for real-time collaboration. *Hewlett-Packard Journal*, pages 23–24, April 1994.

[Gra92]   Graham, T.C.N. and Tore Urnes, T., Relational views as a model for automatic distributed implementation of multi-user applications. In *Proceedings of the ACM Conference on Computer*

Supported Cooperative Work, CSCW'92, pages 59–66, November 1992.

[Gra96]   Graham, T.C.N., Urnes, T. and Nejabi, R.,   Efficient distributed implementation of semi-replicated synchronous groupware. In *Proceedings of the ACM Symposium on User Interface Software and Technology*, pages 1–10, October 1996.

[Gre99]   Greenberg, S. and Roseman, M., Groupware toolkits for synchronous work. In Beaudouin-Lafon, M. (Ed.), *Computer Supported Cooperative Work*, Trends in Software Series 7:135–168. John Wiley & Sons, Chichester, 1999.

[Hil94]   Hill, H., Brinck, T., Rohall, S., Patterson, J. and Wilner, W., The RendezVous architecture and language for constructing multiuser applications. *ACM Transactions on Computer Human Interaction*, 1(2), June 1994.

[Ish90]   Ishii, H. and Ohkubo, M., Design of a team workstation. *Multi-User Interfaces and Applications*, pages 131–142, 1990.

[Ish99]   Ishii, H., Integration of shared workspace and interpersonal space for remote collaboration. In Beaudouin-Lafon, M. (Ed.), *Computer Supported Cooperative Work*, Trends in Software Series 7:83–102. John Wiley & Sons, Chichester, 1999.

[Jul88]   Jul, E., Levy, H., Hutchinson, N. and Black, A., Fine-grained mobility in the emerald system. *ACM Transactions on Computer Systems*, 1988.

[Kar93]   Karsenty, A., Tronche, T. and Beaudouin-Lafon, M., GroupDesign: Shared editing in a heterogeneous environment. *Usenix Computing Systems*, 6(2):167–195, Spring 1993.

[Kaz94]   Kazman, R., Bass, L., Abowd, G. and Webb, M., SAAM: A method for analyzing the properties of software architectures. In *Proceeding of International Conference on Software Engineering, ICSE'94*, pages 81–90, May 1994.

[Kra88]   Krasner, G.E. and Pope, S.T., A cookbook for using the model-view-controller user interface paradigm in Smalltalk-80. *Journal of Object-Oriented Programming*, 1(3):26–49, August/September 1988.

[Lau90]   Lauwers, J.C. and Lantz, K.A., Collaboration awareness in support of collaboration transparency: Requirements for the next generation of shared window systems. In *Proceedings of Human Factors in Computing Systems, CHI'90*, pages 303–312, ACM Press, April 1990.

[Lin89]   Linton, M.A., Vlissides, J.M. and Calder, P.R., Composing user interfaces with interviews. *IEEE Computer*, pages 8–24, February 1989.

[Mye95]   Myers, B., User interface software tools. *ACM Transactions on Computer–Human Interaction*, 2(1):64–103, March 1995.

[Ols93]   Olson, G.M., McGuffin, L.J., Kuwana, E. and Olson, J.S., Designing software for a group's needs: A functional analysis of synchronous groupware. *Trends in Software: Special Issue on User Interface Software*, 1:129–148, 1993.

[Ous94]   Ousterhout, J.K., *Tcl and the Tk Toolkit*. Addison-Wesley, Reading, MA, 1994.

[Pik90]   Pike, R., Presotto, D., Thompson, K. and Trickey, H., Plan 9 from Bell Labs. In *Proceedings of the Summer UKUUG Conf.*, pages 1–9, July 1990.

[Pra94]   Prakash A. and Shim, H.S., DistView: Support for building efficient collaborative applications using replicated active objects. In *Proceedings of the ACM Conference on Computer Supported Cooperative Work, CSCW'94*, pages 153–162, October 1994.

[Pra99]   Prakash, A., Group editors. In Beaudouin-Lafon, M. (Ed.), *Computer Supported Cooperative Work*, Trends in Software Series 7:103–133. John Wiley & Sons, Chichester, 1999.

[Rei90]   Reiss, S.P., Connecting tools using message passing in the Field environment. *IEEE Software*, 7(4):57–66, July 1990.

[Rie93]   Riedl, J., Mashayekhi, V., Schnepf, J., Claypool, M. and Frankowski, D., SuiteSound: System for distributed collaborative multimedia. *IEEE Transactions on Knowledge and Data Engineering*, 5(4):600–609, August 1993.

[Ros96]   Roseman M., and Greenberg, S., Building real-time groupware with GroupKit, a groupware toolkit. *ACM Transactions on Computer–Human Interaction*, 3(1):66–106, 1996.

[Sal95]   Salber, S., *De l'interaction individuelle aux systèmes multi-utilisateurs. L'exemple de la communication homme-homme-médiatisée*. Thèse de doctorat, Université de Grenoble, France. September 1995.

[ShaG96] Shaw, M. and Garlan, D., *Software Architecture: Perspectives on an Emerging Discipline*. Prentice Hall, New Jersey, 1996.

[Ste87]   Stefik, M., Foster, G., Bobrow, D.G., Kahn, K., Lanning, S. and Suchman, L., Beyond the chalkboard: Computer support for collaboration and problem solving in meetings. *Communications of the ACM*, 30(1):32–47, January 1987.

[Tre94]   Trevor, J., Rodden, T. and Mariani, J., The use of adapters to support cooperative sharing. In *Proceedings of the ACM Conference on Computer Supported Cooperative Work, CSCW'94*, pages 219–230, October 1994.

8

Software Infrastructures

PAUL DOURISH
Xerox PARC

ABSTRACT

Increasingly, personal computers and workstations come ready "out of the box" to participate as nodes of a distributed computing network. Elements of distributed computing infrastructure, from network file systems and shared printers to high-speed connection back-
bones, are part of our everyday experiences as users of computers. This chapter discusses
software infrastructures for the design of CSCW applications. In particular, it is concerned
with how developments in distributed computing and user interface architecture can be exploited in applications that support collaborative activity. The chapter considers a variety
of currently-available infrastructure components and discusses how they can be used in
collaboration, before going on to suggest a new approach which revises the nature of the
relationship between infrastructure and applications.

8.1 INTRODUCTION

CSCW is a highly diverse discipline. From its very beginnings, it has drawn from psychology
and sociology as much as from computer science. In turn, within computer science, issues
from the areas of network communication and distributed systems have been as important as
those from user interface design and usability.

The focus of this chapter is software infrastructure in the design of CSCW systems. By
"infrastructure", I mean those elements which lie below the level of the collaborative systems
themselves, but which can be exploited in the design of those systems. Explicitly collaborative
infrastructures, or collaboration toolkits, are discussed in Chapter 6 of this book [Gre99]. So,
many of the infrastructure components that will be discussed here have been (or are being)
designed outside the CSCW domain itself. This chapter will take a CSCW perspective on
these non-CSCW technologies, and discuss how they can be used in CSCW applications.

Computer Supported Cooperative Work, Edited by Beaudouin-Lafon
© 1999 John Wiley & Sons Ltd

Later on, we will also consider implications both for the design of CSCW technologies and the future development of software infrastructures.

8.1.1   Overview

This chapter is organized into two main parts.

First, in Sections 8.3–8.5, we will consider software technologies that provide infrastructure services which can be used in CSCW systems. This will cover both the general use of particular types of infrastructure system, as well as discussing particular tools applicable to CSCW.

The second part (Section 8.6 onwards) will outline new work on CSCW support based on *computational reflection*. This approach provides a way for applications to become involved in aspects of infrastructure, so that the infrastructure can be tailored to the specific needs of particular applications. I have been developing this approach in the design of a prototype CSCW toolkit called Prospero.

8.2   INFRASTRUCTURE ELEMENTS IN CSCW

The nature of CSCW software lends itself to the appropriation of other technological bases as an infrastructure for collaboration. We will consider three particular areas here: first, distributed systems, which support network-wide computation; second, database systems and related concerns in storage and replication; and third, user interfaces to distributed, network-wide applications.

8.2.1   CSCW and Distributed Systems

CSCW software is inherently distributed, and so a variety of techniques and systems developed within the distributed systems community can be fruitfully adopted in CSCW. Aspects of distributed systems technology which are relevant include shared distributed objects, mobile services, replication mechanisms, global coordination, distributed naming schemes and architectural considerations in data and application distribution.

As with most other elements of infrastructure discussed in this chapter, distributed system technologies can be deployed as infrastructure at a variety of levels. On one level, distributed system components can be used to provide a basic set of services *on top of which* CSCW systems will be built. In these cases, the CSCW system is seen as an application of the distributed system infrastructure. Implemented at a different level, the CSCW system can be seen as *being itself a distributed system*. In this approach, the distributed system technologies can be directly incorporated into the collaborative application or environment.

8.2.1.1   Transparency in Distributed Systems

However, the observation that CSCW systems are distributed, and hence potentially amenable to distributed system solutions, can be a misleading one. Whether CSCW applications are implemented as distributed services or clients of those services, designers must take care not to confuse the goals of distribution with those of collaboration.

Many distributed systems set out to achieve some form of *transparency*. Typically, the goal of transparency takes the form of attempting to hide from the user the consequence of some aspect of distribution, while still realizing the benefits. Consider some examples below:

- *Location transparency* refers to isolating the application or client from the effects introduced by the *location* of the computation.
- *Concurrency transparency* refers to isolating the application or client from the effects introduced by the fact that their computation might, in fact, consist of multiple concurrently-executing subprocedures which, together, can be regarded as a single computation.
- *Replication transparency* refers to attempts to hide the fact that what appears to be a single data item may, in fact, be copied and reproduced at different points in a network.
- *Failure transparency* refers to attempts to hide from applications the consequences of a potential failure at one point in the network, by attempting to recover using other resources available in the distributed system.

In different settings, different forms of transparency can be invaluable in providing users and applications with seamless access to an apparently unified large computational resource which is, in fact, made up of discrete, connected units. However, these same features can become problematic in the CSCW setting, since the goals of CSCW are different. For instance, issues such as location and replication, which might be hidden by a traditional distributed system, can often turn out to be significant for the ways in which a group will work, or even for the nature of the work which they attempt to perform. Greenberg and Marwood [Gre94] discuss the ways in which concurrency management, for example, can interfere with the smooth and natural flow of user interaction when a distributed systems layer makes concurrency control "transparent" to the CSCW application. They point out that the details which distributed systems hide (by making them transparent) are ones which are highly significant for the coordination of group tasks.

Distributed system techniques *are* important elements of CSCW infrastructure, and extremely valuable. Data replication allows fast, concurrent access in cases where it would otherwise be impossible, and location transparency allows users to interact in mobile or fluid settings. However, before these techniques are applied directly to collaborative systems, the designer must develop a more detailed understanding of potential interactions between the behavior of users and the action of the system. Certainly, collaborative activity is often distributed; but this does not imply that collaborative applications and distributed applications are one and the same.

8.2.2   CSCW and Databases

Many features of CSCW applications make database technology an attractive candidate for infrastructure. Most programs are data-based, of course, but in particular CSCW systems often involve sets of computations over an explicit data store (or collaborative workspace). Similarly, database technologies have evolved to provide the means to coordinate and share data across time and space. As such, many collaborative systems can benefit from techniques developed in database management, and the persistence which databases offer may be exploited in supporting asynchonous working styles.

Most database systems support multiple users, but mapping the needs of collaborating groups onto the multi-user facilities of an existing database technology can be problematic. Multi-user databases are generally constructed so that they hide the activities of multiple users. Database systems erect walls between simultaneous users, in order to render each user impervious to the actions (or even the presence) of others. The goal is to present each user with the illusion of a dedicated system. This is not simply an issue in how their interfaces are constructed, but reaches down to the basic conceptual model. Even the transaction execution model, for example, is explicitly designed to shield users from the effects of each other's actions, and to maintain the idea of a dedicated resource for each user.

The activities of others, then, are hidden and may become visible only through activity within the data store itself; and that activity is organized as essentially single-user, so that database consistency constraints can be maintained. However, a wide range of research studies in CSCW (typically going under the general term "awareness") have emphasized the importance of the *visibility of others' work* as a resource for coordination. In Heath and Luff's seminal study of the activities in the control rooms of the London Underground, for instance, they uncover a range of practices by which the controllers not only monitor each other's actions in order to coordinate the work as a whole, but also ways that they explicitly *make* their work visible to each other [Hea92]. Dourish and Bellotti [Dou92] observe similar issues at work in experimental collaborative design tasks. This sort of mutual visibility of action is hard to achieve in traditional databases. So while the database model might *enable* cooperative work by allowing multi-user data access, it generally doesn't *support* a collaborative model of data management.

However, some database research work has focused on extending the database model in ways which extend to collaborative settings. Extended transaction models such as nested transactions (originally introduced by Davies [Dav73]) or multiple granularity concurrency control [Gra75] have been developed. These extended models were driven by the requirements of domains such as computer-aided design or software development environments, where transactions may last much longer, involve multiple participants, or be transferred from one participant to another before being committed. At the same time, new techniques for semantics-based concurrency control in database applications (such as those of Herlihy [Her90] or Farran and Ozsu [Far89]) allow for greater parallelism in transaction execution, and hence more flexibility in mapping collaborative actions onto a database kernel. In the same way, aspects of database infrastructure may have to be extended for collaborative settings. (A semantics-based technique, similar to those cited above but specifically designed for CSCW applications, will be described in Section 8.6.4.2.) Barghouti and Kaiser [Bar91] provide a comprehensive overview of these developments, which hold considerable promise for the future role of database technologies in CSCW.

8.2.3   CSCW and User Interfaces

CSCW systems are generally interactive, and so the design of the user interface is critical to their acceptibility and use. However, as in the domains discussed above, CSCW introduces new challenges for user interface design.

In a single-user system, the user interface is responsible for presenting representations of the system's activity. For instance, the "hourglass" cursor indicates that the system is currently performing some time-consuming operation in response to a user request; dialog boxes may appear, asking for confirmation for requested actions (especially ones with potentially severe consequences); user-initiated changes in system state are reflected in changes to the display state of user interface objects (e.g. reversing black and white to indicate object selection).

Although these same mechanisms can be exploited in collaborative systems, we must, once again, consider the implications of moving into a multi-user setting. There's an important piece of context which allows these kinds of behaviors to make sense in traditional inter-active systems; the fact that there's *only one user*. This is particularly important because it implies that there is a straightforward relationship between the user's request and the system's response. Objects do not highlight themselves, but do so because they have been selected; dia-log boxes asking for action confirmations do not appear at random, but in response to specific user actions. By and large, the system need not explain why (for example) a dialog box has appeared, because the user knows that it is in response to their recent activity. If something happens in the interface, it must be as a result of either the user's action or the system's.

However, in collaborative systems, this assumption may no longer hold. There are now multiple users to be considered, and actions which are observable in the interface may well be the result of *someone else's* activity, which may or may not be visible to other users. The direct connection between the user's activity and the system's has been broken, and with it, many of the assumptions on which user-interface design rests. So, as in the previous cases, the needs of CSCW applications often force us to re-think the elements and functionality of the traditional user interface.

That said, there *have* been cases where elements of current user interface systems have been fruitfully exploited in collaborative systems. One particular line of work has been with network-based interface architectures such as the X Window System and NeWS. These sys-tems separate window clients (programs which use the window system to display results) from window servers (which provide windowing functionality for particular screens or displays), potentially across a network, using a hardware-independent protocol for drawing and window-ing actions. This network independence immediately leads to the potential for multiplexing the windowing protocol, and hence sharing a single client between a number of displays. A number of systems of this sort have been developed, of which the best-known is probably Shared X [Gar89]. Application replication via window sharing allows previously single-user applications to be operated in a multi-user environment, albeit with certain restrictions to man-age input streams. This is an extremely powerful approach, especially since it allows users to carry on working with familiar, everyday applications.[1]

Other user interface toolkits, widgets and mechanisms have been extended to support col-laborative working. This work has typically been done in groupware toolkits, which are dis-cussed in Chapter 6 of this book [Gre99] and so will not be discussed further here.

We will now go on to look at some particular technologies which can be valuably exploited as infrastructure for CSCW systems. For clarity, they will be addressed in three different areas: communication; coordination; and storage.

8.3 COMMUNICATION

Most CSCW technologies depend critically on digital communication infrastructures. Indeed, there have been claims that the most successful CSCW products are those which we might think of as simply being communication systems (such as electronic mail, networked file ser-vices or the World Wide Web). This section will explore the communication facilities which underpin CSCW applications development, and recent advances in communication facilities which are particularly relevant to collaboration.

---

[1] The sad truth about many collaborative editors which have been developed by CSCW researchers is that, while they might well be *collaborative*, they are rarely very good *editors*. This is another reason to value application-sharing approaches.

8.3.1   Internet Multicast and the MBone

One infrastructure advance of the past few years which is particularly relevant for CSCW is the development and widespread deployment of Multicast Internet Protocols, and the emergence of the multicast backbone or "MBone", a virtual Internet backbone for the distribution of multicast data.

The original Internet Protocol (IP) [Pos81] is a unicast protocol. That is, it supports one-to-one communication; each packet identifies a single receiver, and IP routes it precisely to that host. Receivers are named by IP addresses, which identify particular hosts. (Actually, IP addresses identify particular network connections, so that "multi-homed" machines with multiple network connections will actually have multiple addresses, but the fiction that IP addresses name hosts will be convenient here.)

In his thesis work at Stanford, Steve Deering developed mechanisms for IP multicast which could be layered on top of the existing unicast internet architecture [Dee88]. In his model, a set of addresses are recognized as naming "multicast groups" rather than single hosts. Using a low-level protocol called the Internet Group Multicast Protocol (IGMP), hosts can add themselves to multicast groups, essentially declaring an interest in the data sent to that group.[2] Any packets sent to a group (by using the group address as the packet destination address) will be routed to all hosts which have added themselves to the group. The IP multicast implementation is responsible for finding efficient distribution patterns for multicast data, so that packets sent to multicast groups will traverse any particular network connection at most once.

Multicast IP is managed by extending the routing mechanism of the traditional IP mechanism. IP packets sent to unicast addresses are handled normally, but packets sent to the multicast addresses will be processed specially. However, existing IP routing software and hardware were developed without support for Deering's new multicast model. The solution to this bootstrap problem was to develop, along with the new multicast routing mechanism, a way for multicast-aware routers to communicate with each other over traditional unicast channels. This approach — called IP tunnelling — treats unicast connections (the "tunnels") as simple network links between multicast routers. The unicast channels that distribute multicast data between multicast routers form a virtual internet over the existing Internet infrastructure. This is the so-called MBone, and it allows experiments with internet-wide multicasting to proceed before support for multicast protocols has migrated into the standard internet routing hardware and software.

Deering's original work was based on a multicast routing mechanism called DVMRP (Distance Vector Multicast Reverse Path). More recently, new routing mechanisms, such as MO-SPF (Multicast Open Shortest Path First) [Moy94] and CBT (Core Based Trees) [Bal93] have emerged as possible internet-wide routing mechanisms. However, the choice of routing protocol does not affect the basic multicast service model.

Multicast extends the one-to-one model of unicast routing to a many-to-many model. Any member of a group can send data to the group, and any data sent to the group will be distributed to all participants. A multicast group can be thought of as a "software bus" allowing arbitrary communication between all connected components (group members). Multicast IP, then, provides a natural model for group communication in CSCW applications, and a number of widely-used multicast applications — the so-called "MBone Tools" — are collaborative applications.

---

[2] IGMP occupies roughly the same place in the IP multicast stack as ICMP (the Internet Control Message Protocol) plays for unicast IP.

8.3.1.1   Audio and Video Communication: vat, rat, nv and vic

The best known MBone tools are those which support the most common MBone activity — videoconferencing. While videoconferencing is rarely classed as a collaborative technology in itself, the long tradition of research in media spaces and video-mediated interaction (e.g. [Bly93] and Chapter 3 in this book [Mac99]) mean that it could certainly be regarded as a CSCW infrastructure component in its own right; but more pertinently here, it illustrates the use of multicast mechanisms in supporting cooperative work.

Early MBone tools, *vat* and *nv*, support audio- and videoconferencing respectively using multicast protocols. Audio and video sessions are made available as multicast groups, so that any MBone-connected host can subscribe to the group and "tune in". Since multicast is a many-to-many (rather than one-to-many) distribution model, this allows any member of the group to send multimedia data to all others.

However, the current Internet is a harsh environment for reliably delivering real-time data such as audio and video. Different participants may be connected by different means, have different levels of bandwidth available to them, and different latencies; and activity elsewhere on the network can introduce congestion at different points in the network. Factors like these make it difficult to provide continuous, timely streams of multimedia data uniformly across a multicast group. To address these problems, many MBone tools support a model called *lightweight sessions* [Flo95].

In TCP, reliable delivery is the responsibility of the sender. However, this approach does not work in multicast situations for a variety of reasons. One of these is the scaling problem; in a sender-based approach, the sender would be responsible for the different timeouts and resends for hundreds or thousands of receivers. Another is the danger of "ACK implosion", as all the receivers acknowledge receipt of a packet. Instead, in the *lightweight sessions* approach, receivers are made responsible for managing reliable streams. In addition to the data components, "session messages" are used to maintain a view of session membership, as well as to provide other checkpointing mechanisms around which the data protocols can operate. This approach to managing multicast sessions applies not only to the audio and video tools, but also to artifact-based collaborative tools described in the next section.

In addition to the problem of reliability in multicast streams, there is also a need to ensure timely delivery of temporal streams such as audio and video. The network itself provides no support for timely delivery. Instead, in the lightweight sessions model, incoming data is buffered in the receiver, which then attempts to deliver it to the user in a timely manner. The "playback point", corresponding to buffering delay, is continually adapted to current network conditions; closer to packet arrival time in the case of good network connectivity and performance, and further from packet arrival time if network response is poor (thus allowing more time for misordered packets to arrive and fill holes in the buffer).

Two newer tools, *vic* [McC95] and *rat* [Har95], are improved tools for video and audio respectively, incorporating lessons gleaned from the widespread deployment and use of tools like *vat* and *nv* over the MBone since 1990. They reflect greater understandings of network-friendly approaches to compression and encoding, architectures for real-time streams management on the Internet, and the integration of user interface and network level concerns.

8.3.1.2   Collaboration Tools: wb and nte

The first widespread MBone tools, discussed above, were for audio- and videoconferencing. More recently, tools directly supporting artifact-based collaborative work have appeared.

Wb [Flo95] is a shared whiteboard application from Lawrence Berkeley Labs (where vat and vic were developed). *Wb* is commonly used not only for collaborative interaction, but also as a presentation medium for Internet-broadcast talks. It presents a collaborative whiteboard with multiple pages. Any multicast group member can create a page, and any can draw on any page. *Wb* has been designed with a concern for scalability which is somewhat unusual in real-time CSCW design, with the result that it can support hundreds of receivers distributed across the Internet in a single session.

One particularly interesting aspect of *wb*, which emphasizes the way in which it combines networking and CSCW technologies, is the mechanism used for late joining (allowing clients to join a session which is already in progress). In general, *wb* uses a retransmission request mechanism for *wb* clients (or trees of clients) to ask for lost packets to be delivered again. *Wb* uses this same retransmission request mechanism to allow clients which join sessions in progress to catch up with the session state. Essentially, a client which joins a session in progress can be thought of as a client which has not successfully received *any* packets in the session so far. So the standard retransmission request mechanism provides a way for late arrivals to be brought up-to-date.

Wb provides collaborative access to drawings, and while text can be added to pages, it does not provide a way to collaboratively edit that text. *Nte* [Han97] is a collaborative text editor which uses multicast to support group collaboration over the Internet and MBone. Like *wb*, *nte* employs the techniques of lightweight sessions and Application Layer Framing [Cla90] to provide a high degree of scalability. Reliability and resilience to transient network failures in the face of this scalability is achieved through a loose consistency model, and the exploitation of natural redundancy; *nte* uses text lines as its basic data unit, but most characters are entered on the same line as the previously-entered character, so successive data transmissions involve inherent redundancy, which reduces the need for retransmissions.

8.4   COORDINATION

Along with communication, simply getting the data from one point to another or a set of others, a critical concern for CSCW technologies is the *coordination* of distributed action. While communication and coordination are two sides of the same coin, in this section we look at approaches which focus more on the management of concerted action, rather than on data transfer.

8.4.1   Group Communication: ISIS and Horus

Isis is a group communication system developed at Cornell University (and subsequently at Isis Distributed Systems) [Bir94a]. Its design was originally aimed at the production of reliable, fault-tolerant systems. Isis provides a *process group* abstraction in which inter-process communication can be directed towards groups rather than individual processes, as in the internet multicast model described above.

The basis for group communication in Isis is a model called *virtual synchrony* [Bir87]. Message deliveries to the members of a group are virtually synchronous. In this approach, message delivery is controlled so that there are no observable differences in the message arrivals at process group members. The motivation behind this model is support for replication-based fault-tolerance in distributed applications. Critical services are replicated as members of process groups rather than individual components. The system can continue to function even though the individual members of a process group may fail; *every* member of the group must fail before the group as a whole fails. Virtual synchrony ensures that all members of a process group see the same pattern of network activity; in turn, this ensures that their state is accurately replicated, so that they are each maintained in equivalence.

Although replication for fault-tolerance was the original motivation behind the development of group communication in Isis, it has been used by a number of researchers as the basis for the development of CSCW systems, including the DistEdit toolkit [Pra99] (see Chapter 5 in this book), the collaborative virtual reality system DIVE [Car93] and the COLA application platform [Tre95].

Horus [Ren96] is a more recent group communication system designed by the researchers who previously developed Isis. The primary research focus behind the development of Horus is flexibility through *micro-protocol configuration*. Rather than providing group communication mechanisms as a monolithic protocol, Horus allows programmers to compose a series of microprotocols which provide different functional elements, such as total ordering, reliable delivery, encryption and fragmentation and reassembly. In this way, the programmer can configure the protocol stack to the specific needs of any particular application, eliminating potentially costly features not needed in particular circumstances. These issues of configuration and customization will be addressed in more detail later in this chapter (Section 8.6).

8.4.2 Coordination Languages

One particularly interesting set of coordination technologies which can be exploited in developing CSCW applications is coordination languages. The earliest explicit coordination language is Linda [Gel85], originally developed at Yale in the mid-1980s. Linda comprises a set of programming language extensions which provide coordination facilities for distributed programming. Gelernter explicitly draws a distinction between the coordination language — provided by the Linda facilities — and the computation language — a standard programming language within which the Linda primitives are embedded. Early versions of Linda were embedded in a variety of languages, including C and Lisp.

A number of other languages have emerged for explicitly distributed programming, in which coordination mechanisms become programming language features, rather than library extensions for process communication, and so on. Obliq is a simple but powerful language of this sort, developed by Luca Cardelli at DEC's System Research Center. Obliq is of particular interest here, since it has been used as the basis of a graphical builder for collaborative applications, Visual Obliq [Bha94].

8.4.2.1 Linda

Linda was originally developed for parallel programming applications, although the loose coupling of components which it provides also makes it suitable for styles of programming more readily classed as "distributed" than as "parallel". Linda comprises a set of programming language extensions embedded in a traditional "computational" programming language in order to provide the coordination facilities needed for distributed programming. Linda's coordination model is explicitly designed independently of underlying connection models and topology, making it suitable for a wide range of parallel programming environments, from distributed processing on a LAN to tightly-coupled shared memory parallel computers.

The Linda model augments the base language with access to an associatively-matched shared tuple space. Any process can place data objects into the tuple space, and retrieve them by associative pattern-matching. Tuples are added to the space using the `out` primitive, which creates a tuple of its arguments and enters it into the space. Tuples can be retrieved using the `in` primitive. Arguments to `in` can be marked as *formals* — that is, variables which should be bound by the primitive, rather than used to specify patterns.

For example, consider the situation in which some process or processes have executed the following statements:

```
out(5, i, ''foo'');
out(6, i, ''bar'');
out(7, ''baz'');
```

These place three tuples into the tuple-space. The first two are 3-element tuples in which the second element has been initialized to the value of the variable i in the running process. Some other process can now execute the primitive `in(5, ?j, ''foo'')`. The question mark before the variable j marks it as a formal. The Linda system will then search the tuple-space for any 3-tuple with first element 5 and third element "foo". If there are multiple matches, then one will be selected at random and the variable j will be bound to its second element. If there are no matches, then the primitive will block until one becomes available.[3]

The blocking behavior of `in` can be used to coordinate the activity of different processes. A third Linda primitive, `in?`, is a non-blocking equivalent which returns true if there is currently some tuple in the tuple space which matches, and false if there is none (rather than blocking until it becomes available).

The fourth Linda primitive is `eval`. The argument to `eval` is a computational which, when complete, returns a tuple which will be added to the tuple space. The computation is spawned in parallel, and the original process continues immediately. For instance, in a "task farm" approach, a single process might spawn a whole set of computations using `eval` and then use `in` to wait for and collect the results.

Unlike the multicast mechanisms described earlier, Linda's basic (in/out) communication model transmits data to a single recipient (unless `in?` is used to read data without removing it from the tuple space). However, the senders need not name recipients; instead, data are simply placed in the tuple space and then retrieved by pattern matching. This feature makes Linda an interesting basis for CSCW implementation, since it abstracts away from details such as group membership, group naming and connectedness, as well as away from the topology and communication mechanism which supports the Linda model itself. Like the multicast model, Linda's abstract communication model supports a receiver-independent "software bus" architecture, distributed across multiple machines; but unlike multicast (or at least, current multicast applications such as *wb* and *nte*), it provides a framework for CSCW application programming which is independent of the underlying network service model.

8.4.2.2 Obliq

Obliq is not a coordination language in the same sense as Linda — that is, it is not a language dealing simply with coordination issues and which can then be embedded in an existing language for computation. Instead, it is a fully-functional object-oriented programming language

---

[3] In statically typed base languages, type information may also be used as input to the tuple matching process.

in its own right. However, it is a language specifically design for *distributed* object-oriented computation, and one which has been used as the basis not only for collaborative applications, but for a graphical builder for collaborative applications. As such, it merits attention here.

Obliq takes the basic object/message model of object-oriented programming and uses this as a means to distribute communication across a network. Objects in Obliq are implemented using the "Network Objects" mechanism of Modula-3 [Bir94b], and inter-object communication across a network becomes a natural expansion of the message-passing model of object-oriented programming.

Obliq objects have state, and in the presence of network communication this raises a set of potentially complex issues to do with the replication of objects and the consequent replication of state. Obliq deals with this through a *distributed scoping* mechanism. First, it makes objects static, and local to their own sites. Objects cannot move across network connections. Instead, object references are made available to be communicated across network links. In combination with other language facilities, such as aliasing and object cloning, this allows object migration facilities (for example) to be built up out of the state-safe primitives which Obliq provides. In general, then, it is not objects which move around the network, but *computations*. Computations run across the network either through invocations or through the transmission of procedures and closures. Since Obliq is lexically scoped, all free variables in closures are bound to references at their original site (using the network reference model).

8.4.2.3 Obliq as CSCW Infrastructure: Visual Obliq

One reason that it is particularly interesting to look at Obliq from the perspective of CSCW infrastructure is that it has been used as the basis for a research project on the development of CSCW technologies. The goal of the Visual Obliq project [Bha94] was to develop a direct manipulation graphical interface builder for collaborative applications which was no more complicated to use than familiar equivalent tools for single-user interfaces (such as NeXT's "Interface Builder", or Sun's "Guide").

To the application developer, the Visual Obliq interface builder looks like a traditional direct-manipulation interface builder. It provides a canvas, onto which the user can drag interface components, which can be laid out according to the needs of the particular application. Dialog boxes provide controls over the attributes of each component, so that aspects of their appearance or behavior can be changed. Interfaces can be tested from within the builder, or the builder can be used to generate code which implements the created design.

The interface designer can associate callback code, written in Obliq, corresponding to the actions of the various components (e.g. pressing a button, or selecting a menu item). However, in addition to the pure Obliq language (which, of course, already embodies a model of distributed programming), facilities are also provided which support collaborative activity. The basic Obliq mechanisms — in particular, distributed lexical scope and network object references — provide a rich but simple model of distributed processing which can be used to support data migration, remote object access and distributed state.

8.5 STORAGE

Given the phenomenal growth of the World Wide Web (WWW) over the past few years, the use of WWW as a basic infrastructure for CSCW development is clearly something to investigate. The combination of platform independence and Internet accessibility makes WWW technology a clear infrastructure candidate.

8.5.1   CSCW and WWW

A variety of systems have exploited WWW in different ways. At GMD, the BSCW (Basic Support for Cooperative Work) system [Ben95] uses WWW as a means to provide Internet-accessible shared workspaces supporting group work. Projects such as Freeflow [Dou96c] use WWW to provide platform-independent interfaces to network-based collaborative services such as workflow systems. Mushroom [Kin95] uses WWW to provide a virtual shared space for group interaction, while systems such as America On-Line's "Virtual Places" augment WWW with collaborative access over existing WWW-based document repositories.

The emergence and increasing interest in CSCW systems based on WWW technology raises a number of questions for the future development of WWW, which is undergoing considerable change. There are three components of WWW technology which are exploited in the development of CSCW systems.

1. *Shared document access*. The basic hypertext access model provided by HTTP (the HyperText Transmission Protocol for communication between WWW clients and servers) provides for access to distributed document repositories across the Internet. Unified access to a shared document repository can in turn support collaborative activities.
2. *User interface management*. HTML extends the basic document markup model with support for user interfaces constructed from basic widget components. It provides a platform-independent basis for user interface management.
3. *Unified access to services*. Through the CGI mechanism, which makes external programs accessible as WWW documents, WWW technology provides distributed access to network services to participants across the Internet, independent of platform and location.

These mechanisms, independently and collectively, provide significant support for the creation of collaborative applications and, perhaps even more significantly, for their deployment.

8.5.1.1   BSCW

BSCW (Basic Support for Cooperative Work) is a Web-based collaborative system [Ben95]. BSCW maintains workspaces accessible to multiple participants over the Internet. Documents can be stored in the workspace, making them available to other participants, and retrieved by others. The workspace is a coordination point for the multiple users, as well as providing a simple visualization of the document store.

BSCW provides an access control mechanism to maintain control over who can read and write documents in the workspace. It also uses a general event mechanism to maintain users' awareness of activities in the shared space. These mechanisms are all part of the BSCW server. The Web is used to provide a network-accessible user interface and visualization environment, as well as access to the document repository (workspace) itself.

8.5.2   SEPIA and CoVer

The World Wide Web is, of course, a distributed hypertext system. However, as suggested in the previous section, most uses of WWW as CSCW infrastructure have not focused on it as a distributed hypertext system, but rather have exploited its facilities for shared access to documents and platform-independent interface functionality. A number of other projects have used hypertext more generally as a means to support collaborative working.

SEPIA [Str92, Haa92] is a collaborative authoring system developed at GMD which uses hypertext and hypermedia to support collaboration in various ways. The basic hypertext model provides a means to structure interactions. One component of SEPIA — the *argumentation space* — is a collaborative argumentation system, similar to models such as IBIS. Argumentation structures allow users to post issues (as hypertext nodes) and then annotate them with argumentation (backing, agreements, comments, disagreements, and supportive argumentation). The various relationships between pieces of argumentation (such as "supports" or "refutes") can be modeled as different forms of hypertext link. As the collaboration progresses, the argumentation structure emerges as a hypertext document. In this way, then, the basic hypertext model directly supports this form of collaboration.

Another component, the *rhetorical space*, exploits hypertext to represent and manipulate the structure of the document being produced. Document sections are unpacked as hypertext nodes, with the rhetorical organization of the document made visible as hypertext relationships. Again, the basic hypertext model provides a decomposition of the task, and so supports visualization of the collaborative process.

SEPIA uses a collaborative versioning system called CoVer [Haa93] which is also specialized to the need of collaboration. Activity over hypertext nodes causes new versions to be created, and CoVer maintains the relationships between new and old versions. The version mechanism provides a historical record of the actions of individuals and the evolution of the document. It also allows concurrent versions to be created in the presence of simultaneous work by multiple participants, as well as providing for their subsequent integration into a single, unified document.

8.6   INFRASTRUCTURE AND SPECIALIZATION

In the first part of this chapter, we have seen a number of elements of CSCW infrastructure, and technologies which can be used to provide infrastructure services to collaborative applications. In this second part, I want to take a different tack. Here, we will step back to consider the issue of infrastructure provision more generally.

The focus in this section will be on what it means to provide infrastructure services, and what is demanded of them by applications and application programmers. I will outline a set of systematic problems introduced by conventional approaches to system structure, and introduce a solution which has been developed and demonstrated by a prototype CSCW toolkit called Prospero.

8.6.1   Layered Models

A critical assumption underlying the discussion of CSCW and infrastructure in the discussion above concerns the separation of system components. At some point or other, we have discussed a large number of components — networking services, distributed object services, hypertext storage services, CSCW support, user interface and applications. We have relied, implicitly, upon a standard model of the relationship between these components in which the operating services assume the "lowest level", the applications the "highest", and other components are ranged in between, organized in a "stack" separated into different "levels" each using facilities offered by components lower in the stack, and offering services to the components above.

This approach to structuring large software systerms is familiar, even commonplace — so much so, in fact, that it can remain implicit in discussions such as those above without causing confusion. Perhaps one of the best-known layered models of this sort is the seven-layer ISO Reference Model (ISORM) created as part of the Open Systems Interconnection standardization effort [Zim80]. The ISORM defines seven different levels of network processing (Physical, Data, Network, Transport, Session, Presentation, and Application) layered on top of each other and each depending on the services provided by the layers below. It is perhaps because this influential model was developed in the context of data networking that, while the layered approach is very common in all sorts of systems, it is particularly common in describing networked and other distributed systems, including CSCW systems.

8.6.2   Abstraction and Mapping Dilemmas

The development of models such as the ISORM described above arises directly from the notion of abstraction in software design. Abstraction is a basic tool which we use to manage system problems — to break them down into components, to compose them into larger systems, and to separate issues of concern for independent analysis and solution. Abstraction allows us to separate the details of an implementation from the means by which it will provide its functionality or set of services to other system components. It allows for a separation of (and hence an independence between) the *implementation* of a system and the *interface* it provides. Abstraction allows us to tackle large problems, to organize the work of large software teams, and to reuse software. Our concern here is on the place of abstraction in CSCW infrastructure.

A module, or system component, offers an abstraction at its interface, which sets the terms in which other system components can make use of its services. The responsibility of a component is to allow other components to talk in terms of that abstraction, while the implementation itself talks in other terms (perhaps those terms offered to it as a client of other system components). For example, a window system provides abstractions such as windows and scroll bars, while internally it deals with screen areas and pixels; a statistical package offers abstractions such as distributions and means, while internally it deals with data arrays and functions; and a programming language compiler offers abstractions such as function calls and arrays, while internally it deals with stack frames and memory blocks. The job of the implementation (or the job of the implementor) is to map these higher-level structures of the abstraction into the lower-level structures available at the implementation. Since there are frequently a range of ways in which some higher-level feature can be implemented, the implementor makes a set of *mapping decisions* from higher to lower level. For instance, in implementing a simple records system, an implementor might choose whether to store records as an array or a linked list. Decisions like these — normally quite simple — occur throughout an implementation. They are the work of programming.

However, these decisions — such as between arrays and linked lists — carry with thcm consequences for the usc of the abstraction by clients. Linked lists favor particular sorts of access patterns at reduced storage cost, while arrays represent a different approach to the same trade-offs. The programmer is, then, making a set of decisions which are informed by expectations of likely access patterns; that is, expectations of the need of clients of the abstraction.

The problems begin to emerge when multiple clients (different programs or system modules) wish to make use of the same abstraction and implementation. This is a common — indeed, desirable — state of affairs. We would hardly exert much effort developing a window system unless we expected it to be able to support more than one windowing application. However, consider the case where the two applications wish to make quite different use of the abstraction. One wishes fast access to any record, in unitary time; the other favors sequential access to large, sparse sets of records. This is a *mapping dilemma* — the implementor must make one decision or the other, but in doing so, favors one style of client over the other.

So the mapping decisions which the implementor makes can affect the performance and behavior of clients. What's more, these decisions are invisible to the clients. Locked away behind opaque abstraction barriers, mapping decisions cannot be seen by the client. This combination of opacity and mapping dilemmas leads to *mapping conflicts* — occasions on which the client code encounters problems because it presumed that a mapping decision has been made one way, while in fact it has been made another.

These problems are endemic to the way abstraction is used in system design, and occur in all areas of system development. Dealing with them is part of the daily experience of programming, and mechanisms to cope with them are familiar to any programmer. For example, the way in which some systems — such as databases and graphics systems — have to be written carefully so as not to cause excessive paging behavior in the virtual memory system is an example of the efforts which programmers have to exert in the face of mapping dilemmas. However, rather than developing new programming strategies to cope with these situations, the approach we will explore here takes a deeper look at the source of the problems and opportunities for avoiding the mapping dilemmas altogether.

8.6.3   Open Implementation and Reflection

The problems with abstraction encountered in the previous section have been the motivation for recent work in *Open Implementations* [Kic96]. An open implementation is one which reveals aspects of its internal design in a principled way, so that these aspects can be examined and controlled by clients of the abstraction. The clients can adjust their behavior according to the details of the implementation which lies below the abstraction or, more radically, can adjust the abstraction, tailoring it to their own particular needs.

One technique which has been particularly useful in open implementation is *Computational Reflection* [Smi84]. The reflective approach was originally developed in the area of programming language design, but it has much wider potential applications. The principle behind computational reflection is that a system can embody a representation of its own behavior which is "causally connected" to the behavior it describes. This causal connection defines a *two-way relationship* between the representation and the behavior. Changes in the system's behavior will result in changes in the representation (so that the representation always provides an accurate view of the system's behavior at any time); and, at the same time, any change made to the representation will result in a change to the system's behavior.

Early work with reflection took place in the domain of programming language design and implementation. A reflective programming language might give programs access to a runtime model of the language's execution model. Programs written in that language have access to, and control over, an operational model of the language's semantics, portable across implementations of that language. This can be used to extend language semantics (adding new language features, such as procedure parameter mechanisms), or to adjust implementation decisions to suit the needs of the client (specializing internal language implementation features, such as data representation procedures). From the problems identified with abstraction in the previous section, the argument is that this access can be used to see and control the mapping decisions which have been made, and so avoid mapping dilemmas, where the needs of the client and the (hidden) details of the implementation are in opposition.

Open implementations provide not only an implementation of a core set of abstractions, but also an abstract view onto the inherent structure of the implementation. The interface to the core abstraction is called the "base level interface" (or just the base interface), while access to the abstract view of the implementation is provided through the "metalevel interface" (or just meta-interface). The meta-interface provides the means to view and control the way in which mapping decisions are made, so that applications can customize how the abstractions which the system offers are provided. The separation of base and meta-interfaces results in a clean separation between base code (which uses the base interface and implements the system) and the meta-code (which uses the meta-interface to customize the implementation). This separation results in more easily maintainable systems.

8.6.3.1 Reflection in CLOS

Let's consider a more detailed example. One of the best-developed and most widespread reflective systems is the Common Lisp Object System (CLOS). CLOS is an object system for Common Lisp, which is directly incorporated into the language (and which is now included in the ANSI language specification). CLOS programmers can write object-oriented programs using familiar object-oriented mechanisms such as classes, objects and methods (as well as a few less familiar ones, such as multi-methods and method combination). These basic components of the programming language constitute CLOS's base level.

CLOS also offers a metalevel, which allows the internal details of the programming language and its implementation to be tailored to the needs of specific applications. The CLOS implementation offers a view of its own internal mechanisms — for instance, the creation of new instances, or the search for method code when a generic function is invoked.[4] This model of internal action is structured as a CLOS progam; essentially, CLOS is defined as if it, itself, were a CLOS program. Representations of the internal structures of CLOS, such as classes and methods themselves, are presented as CLOS objects. So, any particular class is available in CLOS as an instance of the predefined class `standard-class`. Newly defined classes are, by default, instances of `standard-class` (that is, `standard-class` is their *metaclass*); and operations over classes (such as finding their superclasses, allocating instances or adding methods) are represented as methods on `standard-class`.

This metalevel arrangement allows CLOS programmers to "reach into" the implementation and change aspects of it to suit their own needs. Since `standard-class` is a normal CLOS class, it can be subclassed like any other. New methods defined on the subclass will override those already defined. Since the methods defined on `standard-class` are the internal behaviors of the object system, those internal behaviors will be replaced for any class whose metaclass is the new programmer-supplied metaclass, rather than `standard-class`. The programmer has changed how aspects of the language behave.

This mechanism can be used for a wide range of purposes:

1. The reflective mechanism can be used to make *efficiency* improvements for particular cases.

---

[4] A generic function occupies the place in CLOS of a virtual function in C++ or a message in Smalltalk.

For instance, a programmer might wish to make changes to the way the language implements instance allocation and slot lookup, perhaps to support "sparse" objects which define
many slots (instance variables) but only use a small number.

2. The reflective mechanism can be used to effect *compatibility* changes, such as how the
   conflict resolution mechanism works for multiple inheritance. This can be used so that
   legacy code from a different object system can still be supported.

3. The reflective mechanism can be used to *extend* the base language's functionality. For
   instance, we might wish to provide a constraint mechanism which looks to the programmer
   like normal slot lookup.

The reflective approach allows these sorts of modifications to be done *within* the scope of
the language, rather than being performed on a particular implementation, which would be
inherently non-portable.

It is important to note that what CLOS offers at the metalevel is a *representation* of its internals, in terms of a CLOS program. In other words, there is a level of interpretation between
the representation at the metalevel and the details of the actual implementation which lie below. After all, the structure of the CLOS metalevel is part of the definition of CLOS, and must
be portable across different implementations. The details and performance optimizations of
specific implementations, such as the uses of partial evaluation in the PCL implementation
[Kic90], play no part in the metalevel representation. So while *aspects* of the implementation
— or views of specific mapping decisions — are offered at the metalevel, this is at least one
step removed from the details of the implementation code itself. The essence of open implementation design is to give *principled* access to aspects of the implementation; access that is
organized around the metalevel designer's expectations of future needs.

Open implementation techniques developed largely in the domain of programming languages, although recently they have been applied to other systems, including window systems
[Rao91], distributed systems [Oka94] and databases [Bar96]. My own recent work has focused on the use of these same principles and techniques in the CSCW context, leading to the
development of a reflective CSCW toolkit called Prospero.

8.6.4   Prospero: Open Implementation and CSCW

The problems described above, problems of opaque interfaces, abstractions and mapping conflicts, are endemic to the way we use abstraction in systems design. As a result, they occur in
all the various domains to which system design principles are applied. In CSCW, we can see
a number of manifestations.

For instance, consider the problem of data replication. Toolkits for building collaborative
applications will often provide a "shared data object" abstraction, which allows different
clients to process and manipulate data, with the effects being propagated across a network
to other interfaces. This is clearly an extremely valuable abstraction for collaborative applications, and one which we would certainly wish to exploit and build upon. However, we have to
consider what implementation decisions are being masked by the shared data abstraction.

One set of decisions focus on data replication. Is the user data object to be replicated, so
that copies of it exist at each likely access site, or is there one central copy on which actions
are performed? If there is a single copy, where is it located? If there are multiple copies, how
are conflicts managed? The goal of the abstraction is to hide exactly these sorts of decisions
— ones which are unnecessary for the maintenance of the abstraction itself. However, these
decisions are critical when it comes to *using* the abstraction. Data replication and conflict

management decisions have significant implications for the ways in which the abstraction can be used to support collaboration. For instance, if there is a single copy of the data item, then the access latency for widely distributed users may increase beyond the level necessary for fast interactive response. On the other hand, if there are multiple copies, then conflict management and resolution strategies may begin to have effects which are reflected at the interface. Users may have to obtain locks on data, for instance, and there may be pauses while these are obtained; or actions may be subsequently "undone" in order to maintain overall consistency. (These issues are discussed in detail by Greenberg and Marwood [Gre94] and in Chapter 5 of this book [Pra99].)

Prospero is a prototype toolkit for collaborative applications which uses open implementation to give the application developer control over how the toolkit will provide its support [Dou95a, Dou96a]. In particular, Prospero provides mechanisms for data distribution and concurrency control which not only support particular styles of CSCW application, but also allows application programmers to reach into the toolkit and customize those mechanisms to the needs of specific applications.

8.6.4.1   Data Distribution and Divergence

Traditional approaches to data distribution in CSCW are concerned with issues such as centralization versus replication, or supporting synchronous versus asynchronous working. However, as discussed earlier, distinctions like these begin to affect the ways in which applications can be built on top of toolkits, and in which those applications can be used in collaborative working.

The standard approach is to manage access over potentially distributed data by mapping the activities of multiple users onto a single stream of activity. Techniques such as dividing access across asynchronous sessions, establishing total orderings over simultaneous distributed activities, or serializing access at a single central data store, are all ways of mapping the activities of multiple users into a single, unified stream.

The establishment of a single stream out of multiple, potentially simultaneous sources of activity is the focus for a number of mapping decisions critical of significance to collaborative activity. The distribution mechanism which Prospero offers is explicitly based on multiple streams of activity, around which it manages distributed data and distributed action in terms of *divergence* and *synchronization* [Dou95b].

Actions which arise in the course of collaboration — creating objects, editing them, changing attributes, or whatever — are each associated with some particular stream. Streams normally correspond to different individuals in each collaborative session, although this is not a requirement of the model. Streams might represent session recorders, for instance, or be proxies for remote groups, etc. When an action is added to a stream, the effect is to cause a *divergence* between that stream's view of the data store and the views of other streams, since those streams have not yet seen the action take place. Periodically, streams are *synchronized* to re-establish a shared view of the data store.

The model is defined independently of any particular period of synchronization, so that the period can be varied in different applications. With a small period of synchronization, streams will be synchronized frequently, after only small changes have been made. For instance, when the period is fractions of a second, then the effect will be similar to that of traditional "synchronous" applications, in which the activities of one user are reflected quickly in the views or interfaces of others. However, when the period of synchronization is large, perhaps of the order of hours or days, then the effect is similar to that of traditional "asynchronous" applications, in which individuals work separately, coordinating their work and exchanging changes less frequently.

Divergence and synchronization are made explicit in this model so as to open them up for examination and change within the toolkit. Application programmers can gain control over the means for adding actions to streams, and for establishing divergence. Similarly, the programmer can gain control over the conditions under which synchronization takes place, as well as the extent of synchronization required.

8.6.4.2 Consistency Guarantees

One traditional way of managing exclusion and hence maintaining data consistency in the face of parallel user activity is the use of *locks*. Prospero extends the basic locking approach with a new abstraction called *consistency guarantees* [Dou96b]. Consistency guarantees provide a more flexible approach to managing data consistency, as well as supporting customization by application programmers to define new models of consistency management specialized to the semantics of individual applications.

The basis of the traditional locking mechanism is that the server (or lock-granting authority) gives a guarantee of data consistency (the lock) in exchange for a characterization that the client provides of upcoming activity (commonly, a description of the area over which the lock should operate). The lock can be regarded as a guarantee of future consistency for two reasons: first, because inconsistency could arise due to simultaneous activity if the locking mechanism was not used; and second, because the server will grant the lock to only one client, ensuring serial access.

The consistency guarantees mechanism which Prospero provides generalizes the locking mechanism in two ways. First, clients can provide richer descriptions of upcoming activity. These are called *promises*, specified in terms of the semantics of operations. Clients create promises from sets of semantic properties (idempotency, monotonicity, destructiveness, etc). These promises contain more useful information than the traditional read/write distinctions, which allow the server to make more informed decisions.

The second generalization is in the form of the locks. Rather than returning normal locks, Prospero servers return guarantees of achievable consistency when synchronization occurs. (Although this discussion is framed in terms of client/server for familiarity, Prospero uses a peer-to-peer model.)

A traditional lock guarantees absolute consistency. Prospero consistency guarantees, on the other hand, may offer more limited forms of consistency (such as "syntactic consistency", in which multiple possible values for data items are collected together so that all participants share a common view, although more work must be done later to resolve the situation).

Although the consistency guarantees approach loosens various restrictions of traditional locking, there is still a significant problem with the promise/guarantee model. Because promises must be given before action, there is a need to predict what user action will take place, and then to restrict action to precisely what was promised. Especially in asynchronous (or, rather, infrequently synchronized) working, this restriction can prove a serious limitation to the styles of work which users can perform. To avoid this, Prospero allows clients to break their promises. If a user "breaks a promise" — that is, engages in activity other than that which was promised — then the guarantee no longer holds, although the system may still attempt to incorporate the changes made. Particular client applications may or may not offer this facility to their users; they may insist upon keeping to plan, or they may choose to warn users when a promise may be broken. The framework as a whole, however, is designed to deal with these sorts of situations.

8.6.4.3   Configuring Infrastructure in Prospero

Like other open implementations, there are two aspects to Prospero. The first is the default or base level behavior — the basic mechanisms which programmers can use to develop applications. Programmers can use Prospero to develop CSCW applications in which user actions are associated with streams of activity which are periodically synchronized with each other. The default stream type, `bounded-stream`, allows a certain number of actions to be accumulated before it automatically forces synchronization with peer streams in the system. Concurrency control is optimistic by default.

The second aspect is the metalevel control which the open implementation provides. In Prospero, the relationships between actions, streams, divergence and synchronization mechanisms is made available through the provision of the system's meta-objects and the generic functions which relate them within a programming structure. So programmers can reach in and modify the ways in which divergence is observed, or the triggers to synchronization, or the nature of synchronization which will be performed. Similarly, the consistency guarantees mechanism provides a programmatic way for application developers to express semantic features of their programs, so that these can be incorporated into the consistency management mechanism, effectively specializing internal toolkit behaviors to the characteristics and requirements of particular applications.

Just as in the CLOS example provided earlier, this metalevel programming takes place largely through the subclassing and specialization of the metaobject classes which the toolkit reveals. This allows programmers to precisely direct their adjustments, in two ways. First, it reduces the amount of metalevel programming they need to perform; most behaviors can simply be inherited, rather than rewritten, and only the new behaviors must be described. Second, it narrows their focus to the particular areas of the system requiring modification; the generic dispatch mechanism of object-oriented programming allows multiple behaviors to exist side-by-side.

These mechanisms have supported the development of widely different applications in Prospero; synchronous and asynchronous, graphical and data-based, with centralized and replicated data, and loose and strict consistency policies. These applications demonstrate the way in which Prospero's open implementation design allows application programmers to avoid the mapping conflicts which emerge in traditional designs, and take control of the infrastructure which supports them.

8.6.4.4   Example: The Bibliographic Database

Let's consider a brief example to illustrate how Prospero is used to create collaborative applications and, at the same time, illustrate the new role of infrastructure under a reflective approach. Longer and more detailed examples are provided in [Dou96a].

Consider creating a shared application for managing bibliographical entries. You might read the store of references to browse them, look up specific entries, or to generate a set of formatted references from the citations in a document. You might update the store to correct an error in an existing entry or to add new publications as they become available. The application is shared amongst a number of users, perhaps the members of a research group who share a set of common interests (and, therefore, are likely to refer to the same set of publications).

The first step is to organize the actions around streams. Updates, changes, lookups and retrievals are separate operations which are captured in streams of activity associated with each user. The critical issue is the set of circumstances under which streams will be synchronized. Prospero offers a number of pre-defined streams with different synchronization characteristics; `bounded-stream` is a stream which will synchronize with its peers whenever a certain number of operations have been performed on it, or an `explicit-synch-stream` will accumulate actions until one particular synchronization action occurs. Alternatively, at the metalevel, a new stream class can be constructed with specialized behaviors for any given setting. However, in this case, let's take `explicit-synch-stream`.

To encode the application's behavior in Prospero, the programmer creates new application action classes which corresspond to the different sorts of activities in which clients can engage (`lookup`, `new-record`, `change-record`). Objects corressponding to each application action are generated as the actions are performed, and are added to the stream. Prospero handles the synchronization between streams.

Prospero's behavior can be further specialized by using semantic properties of the application actions to increase parallelism. As described earlier, the idea here is that we can use the detailed semantics of the application domain as the basis for consistency management, rather than simply using the generic "read" and "write" of the database infrastructure. In this example, the major opportunity is in the two conditions in which data might be written — correcting a record or adding a new record. Three observations are critical:

1. Updates are far more common than corrections.
2. Updates do not conflict with lookups.
3. Two parallel updates are unlikely to conflict. Even if they are for the same publication, then they should contain the same information, and so either one can be executed and the other discarded.

These observations allow us to encode application semantics in the consistency management mechanism. First, we adjust the definitions of the application actions defined above, so that they are now defined in terms of a set of *application semantic properties* — in this case, whether or not they introduce potentially conflicting changes into the data store. This is only true of corrections, so only the `correct-record` action class will inherit from the property class `changes-data`.

Now that actions are specified in terms of semantic properties, the consistency management mechanism is updated in terms of these properties. The programmer can choose how to make use of the properties and what sorts of consistency guarantees to use. This is specified by providing methods for the compatibility testing methods which compare specific operations and return an indication of compatibility. In some cases, this might involve consulting recent execution history, or combining a set of compatibility predicates over a number of operations. In this case, however, we can solve the problem with only two operations — one method which says that any two generic application actions are compatible, and a second overriding method which says that no action is compatible with one which inherits the property `changes-data`.

As with the streams mechanism, once the action of the application has been specified in these terms, the Prospero mechanisms will handle synchronization and consistency management independently. However, in much the same way as these mechanisms have provided the means for the programmer to specialize the toolkit's mechanisms for particular settings, so these automatic mechanisms may themselves be further appropriated and specialized. This example, however, does not require further specialization.

8.6.5   Reconsidering Infrastructure

The reflective approach opens up a new view of infrastructure. Instead of having to map the functionality required of an application into the generic facilities which the infrastructure provides, this approach instead allows programmers to specialize the infrastructure components so that they match the needs of particular settings.

This radically changes the nature of infrastructure, which takes a much more active role in the applications we might develop. Further, the relationship between application and infrastructure is changed, since the infrastructure no longer stands alone, unchanging, against the backdrop of different uses. Instead, it provides a framework within which each application can gain access to resources, but deploy them differently, reflecting the different needs, requirements and expectations for different applications or domains.

Prospero is a demonstration and exploration of these ideas as applied to CSCW. As was explored in the first half of this chapter, collaborative applications and settings can require significant flexibility in the underlying infrastructure. Prospero shows how the reflective/open implementation approach can recast this relationship and so provide a means to creating much more flexible levels of infrastructure.

8.7   SUMMARY

Since the design and implementation of CSCW applications draws on a number of areas of system design, such as data communication, distributed systems and user interfaces, there are a range of technologies and techniques which can be employed as infrastructure for CSCW systems design. This chapter has provided an overview of some of these areas, as well as discussing particular components which have been, or can be, used as infrastructure supporting CSCW systems development.

However, there are some important considerations to be borne in mind when evaluating infrastructures for CSCW systems. Experience has demonstrated that the needs and goals of CSCW design are often at odds with the design goals of these infrastructural components, and in particular, the way in which infrastructure services are implemented and combined can systematically introduce problems for the design and use of CSCW systems. For example, the management of distributed or replicated data, and subsequently the mechanisms which are used to maintain consistency in the face of potentially simultaneous action by multiple individuals, can interfere with patterns of collaborative activity. To support the rich forms of interaction which we observe in studies of cooperative work, applications need to be able to configure the way in which infrastructure services are offered to them.

In the final section of this chapter, I outlined an approach to this problem. The solution uses an architectural technique called Open Implementation, which provides clients of an abstraction with a principled form of access to a model of internal operations. The clients can use this mechanism to examine the way in which internal mapping decisions have been made, and to adjust those to suit particular application requirements. This approach has been exploited in Prospero, a prototype toolkit for CSCW applications, based on the open implementation approach.

CSCW is a young and rapidly expanding field; and at the same time, many of the infrastructures on which we base our technologies are changing even faster. As we learn more about how these infrastructures can be deployed, and more about how CSCW applications are designed and used, then we can expect to see not only new opportunities for infrastructure support, but also new models of the integration and mutual adaptation of infrastructure and CSCW applications programming.

ACKNOWLEDGEMENTS

Jim Holmes provided useful feedback on an earlier draft of this chapter, and Jon Crowcroft and Mark Handley useful pointers for the section on internet multicast. Prospero was developed while I was working at the Rank Xerox Research Centre, Cambridge Laboratory (formerly EuroPARC) and at University College, London.

REFERENCES

[Bal93]   Ballardie, A., Francis, P. and Crowcroft, J., Core Based Trees (CBT): A scalable inter-domain multicast routing architecture. *Proc. ACM Symposium on Computer Communications SIG-COMM'93*, San Francisco, California. ACM, New York, 1993.

[Bar96]   Barga, R. and Pu, C., Reflection on a legacy transaction processing monitor. *Proc. Reflection'96*, San Francisco, California, 1996.

[Bar91]   Barghouti, N. and Kaiser, G., Concurrency control in advanced database applications. *ACM Computing Surveys*, 23(3):269–317, 1991.

[Ben95]   Bentley, R., Horstman, T., Sikkel, K. and Trevor, J., Supporting collaborative information sharing with the World-Wide Web: The BSCW Shared Workspace System. *Proc. Fourth International World Wide Web Conference*, Boston, Mass. O'Reilly and Associates, Cambridge, Mass., 1995.

[Bha94]   Bharat, K. and Brown, M., Building distributed, multi-user applications by direct manipulation. *Proc. ACM Symposium on User Interface Software and Technology UIST'94*. ACM, New York, 1994.

[Bir87]   Birman, K. and Joseph, T., Exploiting Virtual Synchrony in Distributed Systems. *ACM Operating Systems Review*, 22(1):123–138, 1987.

[Bir94a]   Birman, K. and van Raneese, R., *Reliable Distributed Computing with the Isis Toolkit*. IEEE Computer Society Press, Los Alamitos, California, 1994.

[Bir94b]   Birrell, A., Nelson, G., Owicki, S. and Wobber, E., *Network Objects*. Systems Research Center Research Report 115, Digital Equipment Corporation, Palo Alto, California, 1994.

[Bly93]   Bly, S., Harrison, S. and Irwin, S., Media spaces: Bringing people together in a video, audio and computing environment. *Communications of the ACM*, 36(1), 1993.

[Car95]   Cardelli, L., A language with distributed scope. *Proc. ACM Symposium on Principles of Programming Languages*. ACM, New York, 1995.

[Car93]   Carlsson, C. and Hagsand, O., DIVE: A platform for multi-user virtual environments. *Computer Graphics*, 17(6):663–669, 1993.

[Cla90]   Clark, D. and Tennenhouse, D., Architectural considerations for a new generation of protocols. *ACM Communications Review*, 20(4):200–208, 1990.

[Dav73]   Davies, C., Recovery semantics for a DB/DC system. *Proc. ACM National Conference*. ACM, New York, 1973.

[Dee88]   Deering, S., Multicast routing in internetworks and extended LANs. *Proc. ACM Symposium on Computer Networks SIGCOMM'88*. ACM, New York, 1988.

[Dou92]   Dourish, P. and Bellotti, V., Awareness and coordination in shared workspaces. *Proc. ACM Conference on Computer-Supported Cooperative Work CSCW'92*, Toronto, Canada. ACM, New York, 1992.

[Dou95a]   Dourish, P., Developing a reflective model of collaborative systems. *ACM Transactions on Computer–Human Interaction*, 2(1):40–65, 1995.

[Dou95b]   Dourish, P., The parting of the ways: Divergence, data management and collaborative work. *Proc. European Conference on Computer-Supported Cooperative Work ECSCW'95*, Stockholm, Sweden. Kluwer, Dordrecht, 1995.

[Dou96a]   Dourish, P., *Open Implementation and Flexibility in CSCW Toolkits*. Ph.D. dissertation, Department of Computer Science, University College, London, UK, 1996.

[Dou96b]   Dourish, P., Consistency guarantees: Exploiting application semantics for consistency management in CSCW toolkits. *Proc. ACM Conference on Computer-Supported Cooperative Work CSCW'96*, Cambridge, Mass. ACM, New York, 1996.

[Dou96c]   Dourish, P., Holmes, J., Maclean, A., Marqvardsen, P. and Zbyslaw, A.,   Freeflow: Mediating between representation and action in workflow systems. *Proc. ACM Conference on Computer-Supported Cooperative Work CSCW'96*, Cambridge, Mass. ACM, New York, 1996.

[Far89]   Farran, A. and Ozsu, M.T., Using semantic knowledge of transactions to increase concurrency. *ACM Transactions on Database Systems*, 14(4):503–525, 1989.

[Flo95]   Floyd, S., Jacobson, V., McCanne, S., Lui, C-H. and Zhang, L., A reliable multicast framework for light-weight sessions and application level framing. *Proc. ACM Symposium on Computer Communications SIGCOMM'95*, Boston, Mass. ACM, New York, 1995.

[Gar89]   Garfinkel, D., Gust, P., Lemon, M. and Lowder, S., *The SharedX Multi-User Interface User's Guide, Version 2.0.* Software Technology Lab Report STL-TM-89-07, Hewlett-Packard Laboratories, Palo Alto, California, 1989.

[Gel85]   Gelernter, D., Generative communication in Linda. *ACM Transactions on Programming Languages and Systems*, 7(1), 1985.

[Gra75]   Gray, J., Lorie, R. and Putzolu, G., *Granularity of Locks and Degrees of Consistency in a Shared Database.* Research Report RJ1665, IBM, San Jose, California, 1975.

[Gre94]   Greenberg, S. and Marwood, D., Real-time groupware as a distributed system: Concurrency control and its effect on the interface. *Proc. ACM Confeerence on Computer-Supported Cooperative Work CSCW'94*, Chapel Hill, North Carolina. ACM, New York, 1994.

[Gre99]   Greenberg, S. and Roseman, M., Groupware toolkits for synchronous work. In Beaudouin-Lafon, M. (Ed.), *Computer Supported Cooperative Work*, Trends in Software Series 7:135–168. John Wiley & Sons, Chichester, 1999.

[Haa93]   Haake, A. and Haake, J., Take CoVer: exploiting version support in cooperative systems. *Proc. InterCHI'93*, Amsterdam, Netherlands. ACM, New York, 1993.

[Haa92]   Haake, J. and Wilson, B., Supporting collaborative writing of hyperdocuments in SEPIA. *Proc. ACM Conference on Computer-Supported Cooperative Work CSCW'92*, Toronto, Canada. ACM, New York, 1992.

[Han97]   Handley, M. and Crowcroft, J., Network Text Editor (NTE): A scalable shared text editor for the MBone. *Proc. ACM Symposium on Computer Communications SIGCOMM'97*, Cannes, France. ACM, New York, 1997.

[Har95]   Hardman, V., Sasse, A., Handley, M. and Watson, A., Reliable audio for use over the internet. *Proc. INET'95*, Hawaii. 1995.

[Hea92]   Heath, C. and Luff, P., Collaboration and control: Crisis management and multimedia technology in london underground control rooms. *Computer Supported Cooperative Work*, 1(1), 69–94, 1992.

[Her90]   Herlihy, M., Apologizing versus asking permission: Optimistic concurrency control for abstract data types. *ACM Transactions on Database Systems*, 15(1):96–124, 1990.

[Kic90]   Kiczales, G. and Rodriguez, L., Efficient method dispatch in PCL. *ACM Symposium on Lisp and Functional Programming LFP'90*, Nice, France. ACM, New York, 1990.

[Kic96]   Kiczales, G., Beyond the black box: Open implementation. *IEEE Software*, 8–11, January 1996.

[Kin95]   Kindberg, T., Mushroom: a framework for collaboration and interaction across the Internet. *Proc. ERCIM Workshop on CSCW and the Web*, Sankt Augustin, Germany, 1995.

[Mac99]   Mackay, W.E., Media spaces: Environments for informal multimedia interaction In Beaudouin-Lafon, M. (Ed.), *Computer Supported Cooperative Work*, Trends in Software Series 7:55–82. John Wiley & Sons, Chichester, 1999.

[McC95]   McCanne, S. and Jacobson, V., Vic: A flexible framework for packet video. *Proc. ACM Multimedia'95*, San Francisco, California. ACM, New York, 1995.

[Moy94]   Moy, J., *Multicast Extensions to OSPF*. RFC 1584, SRI Network Information Center, Menlo Park, California, 1994.

[Oka94]   Okamura, H. and Ishikawa, Y., Object location control using meta-level programming. *Proc. European Conference on Object-Oriented Programming ECOOP'94*, Bologna, Italy. Springer-Verlag, Heidelberg, 1994.

[Pos81]   Postel, J., *Internet Protocol*. RFC 791, SRI Network Information Center, Menlo Park, California, 1981.

[Pra99]   Prakash, A., Group editors. In Beaudouin-Lafon, M. (Ed.), *Computer Supported Cooperative Work*, Trends in Software Series 7:103–133. John Wiley & Sons, Chichester, 1999.

[Rao91]   Rao, R., Implementational reflection in Silica. *Proc. European Conference on Object-Oriented Programming ECOOP'91*, Geneva, Switzerland. Springer-Verlag, Heidelberg, 1991.

[Ren96]   van Reneese, R., Birman, K. and Maffeis, S., Horus: A flexible group communication system. *Communications of the ACM*, 39(4):76–83, 1996.

[Smi84]   Smith, B.C., Reflection and semantics in Lisp. *Proc. ACM Symposium on Principles of Programming Languages*, Salt Lake City, Utah. ACM, New York, 1984.

[Str92]   Streitz, N., Haake, J., Hanneman, J., Lemke, A., Shutt, W. and Thuring, M., SEPIA: A cooperative hypermedia authoring environment. *Proc. ACM Conference on Hypertext*, Milano, Italy. ACM, New York, 1992.

[Tre95]   Trevor, J., Rodden, T. and Blair, G., COLA: A lightweight platform for CSCW. *Computer-Supported Cooperative Work*, 3:197–224, 1995.

[Zim80]   Zimmerman, H., OSI Reference Model — The ISO model of architecture for open systems interconnection. *IEEE Transactions on Communications* 28(4):425–432, 1980.

9

Expanding the Role of Formal Methods in CSCW

CHRIS JOHNSON
University of Glasgow

ABSTRACT

Before we can build CSCW systems it is important to have a clear idea of the requirements that they must satisfy. This chapter argues that formal methods can be used to help represent and reason about these requirements. Unfortunately, the formal notations that support the development of single-user interfaces cannot easily be used to support the design of multi-user applications. Traditional approaches abstract away from the temporal properties that characterize interaction with distributed systems. They often neglect the input and output details that have a profound impact upon multi-user interfaces. The following pages argue that these details can be integrated into formal specifications. For the first time, it is shown how mathematical specification techniques can be enhanced to capture physical properties of working environments. This provides a link between the physiological studies of ergonomics and the interface design techniques of HCI. Such links have been completely neglected within previous work on design notations. In all of this, the intention is to fight against a narrow, myopic, view of formal methods. These notations need not simply be used to focus in upon a relatively small number of software engineering principles. The aim is to show that formal methods can be used creatively to solve a vast range of design problems within complex multi-user interfaces.

9.1 INTRODUCTION

The term "formal method" is used to refer to a variety of notations and development techniques that support the rigorous development of complex systems. By the term rigorous, we mean that they have a mathematical basis which can be used to determine whether a particular description of a complex system is in some sense correct. At first sight, the use of

Computer Supported Cooperative Work, Edited by Beaudouin-Lafon
© 1999 John Wiley & Sons Ltd

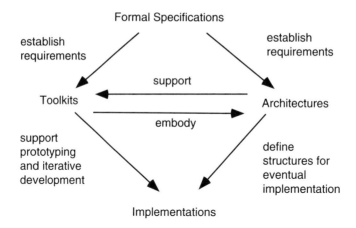

Figure 9.1   Formal methods and the development of CSCW systems

abstract mathematics may seem to have little connection with the previous chapters in this collection. These have focused upon particular CSCW interfaces, development architectures or multi-user toolkits. In contrast, this chapter argues that formal methods offer considerable benefits for the development of CSCW systems. Figure 9.1 illustrates how they might guide the different approaches described in the previous chapters of this book. Before designers can select appropriate architectures, they must have a clear idea of the requirements that their system must satisfy. Before development teams can identify potential toolkits, they must first establish the constraints that their interface must satisfy.

9.1.1   Why Use Formal Methods In CSCW Systems?

There are a number of additional, commercial reasons why formal methods are being recruited to support the design of CSCW systems. Mathematical notations are increasingly being used in the development of large-scale applications. Craigen, Gerhart and Ralston's survey for the US Department of Commerce cites projects ranging from nuclear reactor control systems to French rapid transport applications [Cra93]. Formal methods have also been used to support the development of interactive systems [Joh96b]. A number of authors have extended these techniques to support the design of multi-user interfaces. For instance, Palanque and Bastide have developed a graphical notation to represent simultaneous transactions by multiple users on shared interaction objects [Pal95]. The applications, cited above, all focus upon CSCW interfaces for office-based applications. Safety-critical systems, perhaps, represent the greatest potential for the application of formal methods. Johnson, McCarthy and Wright have exploited a range of graphical formalisms to identify human factors problems amongst the aircrews in several major accidents [Joh94a]. A common motivation behind all of this work has been a concern to avoid some of the weaknesses that natural language presents for the development of multi-user systems [Joh95a].

9.1.2   The Limitations of Natural Language

What is a formal method? In one sense, a formal method is any notation that has a clear syntax and a well-understood semantics. By syntax, we mean that there are rules for building up sentences out of simpler components. For instance, the sentence "all users can quit the system at any time" follows the established grammatical rules for the English language. "Time users all any system the quit can at the" breaks the rules. The term semantics is used to refer to the meaning of a sentence. We can all hopefully agree upon the intended meaning of the first example. If we break the syntactic rules, as in the second example, then it is more difficult to extract the meaning of a sentence.

According to our definition, natural language is a formal method. The previous paragraph has shown that it has both a syntax and semantics. Without these underlying properties it could not be used to support the development of multi-user systems. Designers and engineers would not be able to interpret phrases such as "all users can quit the system at any time". Unfortunately, there are a number of problems. The intended meaning of an English sentence is not always clear. For instance, the previous example does not describe the input devices and command sequences that each user might exploit to quit the system. Such ambiguity may cause irritation and inconvenience in the design of collaborative working environments. In safety-critical applications, the consequences can be much more profound. For example, the following recommendation was published by the United Kingdom's Department of Energy in the aftermath of the Piper Alpha accident:

> "There should be a system of emergency exercises which provides Offshore Installations Managers with practice in decision-making in emergency situations, including decisions on evacuation. All of the Offshore Installations Managers and their deputies should participate regularly in such exercises" [Cul90, page 399, para 20.61].

These natural language requirements cannot easily be used to support the detailed development of CSCW systems. They do not provide enough information about the "emergency exercises" for designers to review existing practice. It is ambiguous in the sense that any two individuals might disagree about what is meant by an "emergency situation". These problems provide real barriers to the use of natural language in the team-based development of CSCW systems.

9.1.3 The State of the Art

Formal notations help to reduce the ambiguity and imprecision that characterize natural language. This is, typically, done by imposing constraints upon the sentences that are valid within a language. For example, syntactic rules can be used to define a structure or format for natural language clauses. Within this general approach, there are a range of different ways in which formal notations can support the development of CSCW systems.

9.1.3.1 Formal Methods for Principled Design

An important benefit of formal methods is that they enable designers to express important properties of CSCW systems at an extremely high level of abstraction. By stripping out low-level implementation details, it is possible to focus in upon common properties that affect a large number of multi-user systems. For example, Dix, Rodden and Somerville use the following formulae to specify the notion of fidelity in a multi-user version control system [Dix97]. By fidelity, they intend that the version history for any object should accurately reflect the transactions that have been performed upon it. In the following, @(context) is an actual context corresponding to a context label in a version manager:

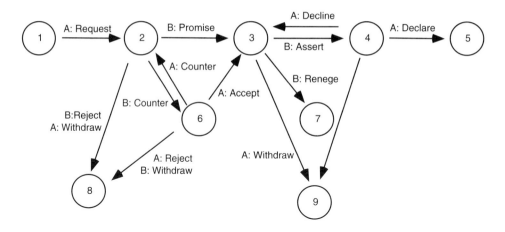

Figure 9.2 Conversation for action (from Winograd and Flores)

$$\forall context \in Contexts, context' \in dom\ world\ context(entity') :$$
$$world\ context(entity')(context') = world@(context')(entity) \qquad (9.1)$$

The important point here is that mathematical abstractions, such as the set of $Contexts$, can be used to represent the concept of fidelity without referring to the particular details that must be considered during a full implementation. The use of mathematics encourages designers to carefully formulate an explicit expression or representation for such properties. This avoids the misunderstandings that can arise when such high-level goals are left as implicit objectives for design teams.

9.1.3.2   Formal Methods for Interaction Architectures

The previous section briefly argued that formal notations can be used to represent high-level design objectives. They can, however, also be used to direct the implementation of particular systems. Winograd and Flores exploited this approach when using state transition diagrams to develop a high-level architecture for their Coordinator application [Win87]. Figure 9.2 shows how the states, denoted by circles, are used to represent critical points in a "conversation for action". The transitions between states, denoted by arcs, are used to represent communication between the participants. The key point here is that the syntactic structures of the notation help designers to strip aside the mass of irrelevant detail that can obscure critical properties of CSCW systems. By focusing on states and the transitions between them, the previous diagram clearly illustrates the various opportunities that face each participant at each stage of an interaction. Figure 9.2 also illustrates some of the weaknesses of this approach. State transition diagrams provide a very sequential view of interaction with CSCW systems. It can also be difficult to capture some of the detailed cognitive and system factors that affect interaction with multi-user applications.

	User 1			User 2			Computer/communications infrastructure	
location	internal actions	user (articulatory) actions	location	internal actions	user (articulatory) actions	perceivable computer actions	internal actions
Sector A	locate button	select button				button hilited on 1	user 1's request sent
						user 2's machine shows request pending	
			Sector B	observe request pending symbol	select view request menu item	"re-connecting" message on 1	dispatch transfer request from 2
Sector C							

Figure 9.3   UAN showing interaction over a mobile network

9.1.3.3   Formal Methods for Task Analysis in Traces of Interaction

The semi-formal User Action Notation (UAN) avoids some of the limitations of state transition diagrams [Hix93]. UAN organizes the actions comprising a task into categories based on the agent that executes them and their function in the task. These categories define the syntax of the notation and are represented as the columns of a tabular format. For example, Figure 9.3 shows how an extended form of UAN can be used to analyze mobile communication between concurrent users of a multiple computer system [Joh97]. Initially, user 1 is in cell A and requests information from user 2. The communications infrastructure forwards the request to user 2 who views it before dispatch. In the meantime, user 1 has moved into another cell and the system must reestablish their connection through another transceiver. It is important to emphasize that Figure 9.3 represents a different application of formal methods from that shown in Figure 9.2. Rather than representing a high-level architecture for interaction, as in the case of Coordinator, the UAN diagram is being used to represent and reason about particular user tasks during a particular trace of interaction. Unfortunately, a number of problems limit the utility of this notation. It provides no means of reasoning about temporal properties. This is important because the handover delay in Figure 9.3 might have a minimal effect if it lasted a few seconds. If it took several minutes then the "re-connecting" message might have to be reworded to provide more information about the cause of the delay. Temporal information can be represented using the extended XUAN notation [Gra95]. The more general point here is again that the restricted syntax of formal notations helps designers to focus in on critical properties of a CSCW system. In Figure 9.3, those properties include the physical locations of the users and their observable actions. However, this is only achieved at the cost of other properties, such as temporal relationships, that cannot be so easily captured within the syntactic structures.

9.1.3.4   Formal Methods for Accident Analysis

In contrast to the tabular form of UAN, Petri Nets provide a graphical notation that has long been used to represent temporal properties of interactive systems [Kra91]. Bastide and Palanque [Bas90] exploit Petri Nets to derive formal specifications of interactive systems at a very high level of abstraction. Johnson et al [Joh94a] have shown that Petri Nets can be used to represent the operator–system interaction which can lead to accidents in safety-critical sys-

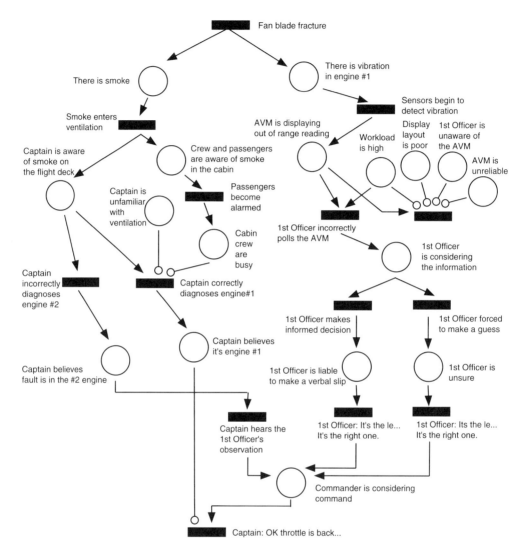

Figure 9.4   A high-level Petri net

tems. Timing properties are represented by sequences of places. These are denoted by a circle and can be used to show states of interaction. Places are linked by transitions. These are denoted by rectangles and can be used to represent events during interaction. Figure 9.4 illustrates this approach. It also shows how Petri Nets can be used to analyze relatively complex traces of group interaction. Once again, it is important to emphasize that the previous diagram represents a different style of application for formal methods. Previous examples have used state transition diagrams to analyze high-level architectures for CSCW systems, UAN was used to analyze user tasks during a potential trace of interaction. Here, Petri Nets are being used to analyse crew interaction prior to the Kegworth air crash. This more situated use of a notation helps to focus in upon critical features of a previous failure as a means of establishing requirements for future systems. There are, however, a number of limitations that restrict the utility of Petri Nets for the design of CSCW systems. For example multi-user undo cannot easily be represented using this notation [Gra95]. Similarly, the associated proof techniques that support this approach can be surprisingly complex given the intuitive appeal of the graphical representation.

9.1.3.5   Formal Methods for Proof

The ability to prove properties of a system, prior to implementation, is a key benefit of formal methods. Proof is essentially a form of reasoning or argument that uses the syntactic rules of a notation to determine the validity of a theorem or hypothesis. This can be illustrated by the following example using first-order logic. Designers might specify that a system should be shut down if two users issue input to that effect:

$$shut\_down \Leftarrow$$
$$input(user\_1, stop) \wedge input(user\_2, stop). \tag{9.2}$$

The system is shut down if $user\_1$ and user_2 issues input to stop the system.

First-order logic provides a proof rule which states that if we know that some fact P is implied by some other fact Q and we know Q then it is safe to conclude P:

$$P \Leftarrow Q, Q \vdash P. \tag{9.3}$$

Given that P is true if Q is true and we know Q then it is safe to conclude that P is true.

Given the two previous clauses we can now establish whether or not the system will ever be shut down. In a model checking approach to theorem proving, this would be achieved by generating possible states of the system and inspecting those states to determine whether or not both users had issued the appropriate input. This illustrates an important weaknesses of theorem proving for interactive systems. There is no automatic means of determining whether or not users will actually provide the anticipated *input* in any state of the system. On the other hand, this approach does force designers to consider the assumptions that they make about operator behavior. For instance, the proof process outlined in (9.3) forces designers to consider those situations in which users might be expected to cooperate in the manner described by (9.2).

A range of tools support the application of formal methods. For example, theorem proving tools provide designers with a semi-automatic means of checking whether certain properties do or do not hold for a particular design [Har95]. Similarly, model checking tools can be used to search for particular situations that may or may not arise during the course of interaction. These tools increase the level of automation provided by theorem proving systems and provide direct means of searching for particular scenarios of interaction. Other tools can also be recruited to aid the formal development of multi-user systems. For example, Figure 9.5 illustrates the user interface to Logica's commercial Z tool, called Formaliser. This automatically helps designers to construct syntactically correct specifications through structure editing. Other tools can be used to "directly" develop prototype implementations from formal specifications [Joh92]. This is important because mathematical specification techniques provide an extremely poor impression of what it would be like to interact with a potential interface.

Figure 9.5 The Formaliser syntax editing tool

The remainder of this chapter focuses upon the application of logic to support the design of CSCW systems. This decision is justified by a number of arguments. Firstly, logic forms a key component of most undergraduate degrees in computing science and engineering. This supports the skill base that is necessary for the pragmatic application of these techniques within commercial development practices. Secondly, there exist a range of relatively simple transformations between other formalisms, such as Petri Nets, and first-order logic. This offers designers the possibility of recruiting different notations during different stages of the development process. Finally, logic programming environments, such as that supported by PROLOG, offer a means of deriving prototype implementations from abstract specifications. As mentioned, this is vital if designers are to validate the products of formal analysis.

9.2 STARTING FROM THE GROUND UP: THE APPLICATION OF FORMAL METHODS TO CSCW

The limitations of natural language stem from the fact that it is difficult to write down the exact syntactic rules which guide its use. Similarly, it can be difficult to agree upon the semantics of particular words. Dictionaries provide many different definitions for common words and phrases. Even human factors experts disagree about the meaning of terms such as "workload" [Kan88]. Given such ambiguity and inconsistency, people have long sought to strip away the clutter of everyday language to focus in upon the essentials of communication. Much of this work has built upon the use of mathematics to define syntactic rules for the development of valid sentences. The same mathematical constructs can also be used to specify an exact semantics for these phrases. For example, the designers of a CSCW interface must consider the commands that can be issued by system operators. The following clause might be used to

specify that $user\_1$ issues input to quit the application. The intention is to express requirements in a clear and simple manner without the elaborate syntax of natural language:

$$input(user\_1, quit). \qquad (9.4)$$

$User\_1$ issues input to quit the system.

Even with such simple beginnings it is possible to reason about the design of a potential
interface. For example, the previous clause does not state that other operators, $user\_2$, $user\_3$
etc., also issue input to quit the system. In other words, clause (9.4) does not require agreement
between multiple operators. Designers must identify such collaborative requirements if they
are to provide the additional cues and prompts that are necessary to achieve coordination.
A further benefit is that additional requirements can be gradually introduced as development
progresses. For example, the following clause states that the application is shut down if $user\_1$
or $user\_2$ issues input to quit the system:

$$shut\_down(system) \Leftarrow input(user\_1, quit) \lor input(user\_2, quit). \qquad (9.5)$$

The application is shut down if user one or user two issues input to quit the system.

This clause relies upon logic operators, $\lor$ (read as "or") and $\Leftarrow$ (read as "if"). These provide
the syntax that is needed to construct more complex requirements out of basic relationships
such as $input(user\_1, quit)$. We have previously argued that natural language cannot easily be used to support the large-scale development of CSCW systems because it may have
ambiguous semantics. We face a similar problem here. What is the meaning of $\lor$ or of $\Leftarrow$?
Fortunately, there are a number of techniques that can be used to capture the meaning of such
operators. For example, the following truth table provides the semantics for the $\lor$ operator.
The first line states that whenever we know that P is true and we know that Q is true then
it is safe to conclude that $P \lor Q$ is true. The second line states that whenever we know that
P is true and Q is false then it is safe to conclude that $P \lor Q$ is true. The rest of the table
can be read in a similar fashion. It is important to emphasize, however, that the formal development of software requires more complex tools than truth tables. The following table is
included to reinforce the central idea behind formal specifications. Mathematical structures
restrict and focus the components of requirements documents so that they have a precise and
concise meaning:

P	Q	$P \lor Q$
true	true	true
true	false	true
false	true	true
false	false	false

Rather than present a complete introduction to first-order logic, the remainder of this chapter focuses upon the application of formal methods to support the design of CSCW systems.
Hodges provides a fuller description of the underlying mathematics [Hod77]. Natural language annotations will be provided in the following pages to help readers who are more interested in the application of the logic rather than its theoretical foundations.

9.2.1   An Example Application

We are concerned that a real-world example is used to illustrate our approach. The following pages, therefore, investigate the design of a control room for an oil production facility. These systems have posed a significant challenge for both systems designers and human factors specialists [War89]. Oil production facilities are complex applications. For instance, operators must monitor the extraction of oil from geological structures under the sea-bed. They must also control the extraction and purification of any gas which is recovered with the oil. The UK Government's Gas Conservation Policy prevents these gas products from being "flared" or burnt on the rig. Operators must also monitor repair activities and maintenance schedules. This involves the coordination of many different teams. These properties of the application help to ensure that oil production control systems exhibit many of the problems that frustrate the design of CSCW applications. Groups of operators must monitor computer displays in order to identify faults in many different processes. Users must detect and coordinate their responses to a range of potential errors. Information systems present their operators with information about the extraction of oil products from geological structures deep beneath the sea-bed. Not only must users monitor the rate of extraction but they must also maintain a constant watch for problems that threaten the safety of the rig. For instance, gas leaks pose a considerable risk of fire. If gas is detected then control-room personnel must investigate the cause and identify potential solutions.

9.3   DIALOGUE SEQUENCES

First-order logic provides a means of focusing in upon critical properties of interfaces to applications such as the oil production control system. Designers can represent and reason about a design without being forced to consider the low-level details of device polling and event handling. An important point in all of this is that the elements of a specification should provide a common focus for multi-disciplinary design teams. For instance, it might be stated that a fault monitoring system is ready to start logging failures if a user issues a command to start. In order to satisfy such a requirement, interface designers must enable users to easily issue such high-frequency commands. Application engineers must support the functionality that lies behind these commands. A key issue here is that the use of the formal notation does not bias or pre-judge the work of these groups. For instance, the designer is not forced to consider which devices will be used to issue the $start$ command. The choice of presentation strategies can profoundly affect the usability of the final interface. Formal methods can be used to construct a design without forcing commitment to a particular implementation early in the development process:

$$start\_logging \Leftarrow$$
$$input(user\_1, start) \wedge effect(start, off, logging). \tag{9.6}$$

The monitoring system starts logging faults if $user\_1$ issues input to start the application and the effect of that input is to transform the state of the system from one in which it is off to one in which it is logging faults.

First-order logic can be recruited to reason about the complexity of concurrent interaction between multiple users. Contention is a frequent problem in multi-user systems which allow two or more operators to access the same resources. For example, one user might attempt to quit the application while another attempts to log a fault:

$$log\_contention \Leftarrow$$
$$input(user\_1, quit) \wedge input(user\_2, log\_pump\_A\_error). \tag{9.7}$$

Contention arises in the logging system if $user\_1$ issues input to quit the system and $user\_2$ issues input to log a fault.

This conflict could be resolved by always giving priority to commands from a particular user [Pen90]. Alternatively, priority might be associated with certain commands [Ell91]. Input with a lower priority may be disregarded. The input $quit$ does not affect the state of the system:

$$resolve\_contention \Leftarrow log\_contention \wedge$$
$$effect(quit, on, on) \wedge effect(log\_pump\_A\_error, on, pump\_A\_error). \tag{9.8}$$

Contention is resolved if the logging command takes effect but input to quit the system does not change the state of the application.

Unfortunately, a number of problems must be resolved before first-order logic can be used to support the design of concurrent multi-user systems. In particular, there is no notion of ordering in first-order logic. This creates problems because many critical issues in the development of CSCW systems arise from the sequencing of events. In our example, no conflict need arise if the system were closed down after the fault had been recorded. As there is no notion of sequence in first-order logic, the previous clause would still specify that contention occurs even if $quit$ were issued some time after $log\_pump\_A\_error$. Temporal sequencing must be introduced if such concurrency requirements are to be made explicit within logic specifications of interactive systems.

9.3.1   Time and First-Order Logic

The lack of sequencing in first-order logic has important consequences for the design of CSCW systems. Delays in receiving information, from systems and other users, can lead to breakdown and referential failure [McC91]. Concurrent input can lead to contention and interference. The following section describes how the temporal properties of an interface can be made explicit within logic specifications. This provides the designer with a medium in which to reason about the possible impact of timing properties upon the users of CSCW applications.

9.3.1.1   Fixed Time-Stamps

Fixed time-stamps provide one means of avoiding the limitations of first-order logic. This approach associates a particular instant of time with each clause in a specification. For example, it might be specified that $quit$ and $log\_pump\_A\_error$ should be input at twenty seconds past midday. An additional requirement might also be that the command to quit the system should not take effect when the fault is being logged at twenty-five seconds past midday. An important point here is that time-stamps help to build a standard time-line for critical requirements. This provides a means of explicitly representing synchronization requirements:

$$
\begin{aligned}
fixed\_solution \; &\Leftarrow \\
&log\_contention(120020) \wedge effect(quit, on, on, 120025) \wedge \\
&effect(log\_pump\_A\_error, on, pump\_A\_error, 120025). \qquad (9.9)
\end{aligned}
$$

Contention is resolved if $quit$ and $log\_pump\_A\_error$ are input at twenty seconds past midday and five seconds later the monitoring system logs the fault.

There are a number of limitations which restrict the utility of fixed time-stamps within a specification. Considerable burdens are imposed upon the designer who must provide and maintain the temporal parameters in each clause. A further problem is that it is difficult to represent persistent properties of CSCW interfaces. For instance, a designer might wish to ensure that $quit$ does not take effect before $log\_pump\_A\_error$:

$$
\begin{aligned}
persistent\_solution \; &\Leftarrow log\_contention(120020) \wedge \\
&not(effect(quit, on, off, 120021)) \wedge not(effect(quit, on, off, 120022)) \wedge \\
&not(effect(quit, on, off, 120023)) \wedge not(effect(quit, on, off, 120024)) \wedge \\
&effect(log\_pump\_A\_error, on, pump\_A\_error, 120025). \qquad (9.10)
\end{aligned}
$$

Contention is resolved if $quit$ and $log\_pump\_A\_error$ are input at twenty seconds past midday and the input to quit the system does not take effect at twenty-one seconds past midday, twenty-two seconds past midday, twenty-three seconds past midday, twenty-four seconds past midday and the monitoring system logs the fault at twenty-five seconds past midday.

Fixed time-stamps also introduce a high degree of temporal determinism into a specification. In order to fulfill the previous specification both users must provide concurrent input at exactly twenty seconds past midday. If designers wished to represent means of avoiding contention at twenty seconds before midday, at twenty seconds to one, at half past four or at any other time, they would be forced to repeat previous clauses for each of these points.

9.3.1.2 Time Variables

The limitations of fixed time-stamps can be avoided by using time variables. For example, $fixed\_solution$ (9.9) might be re-expressed as follows:

$$
\begin{aligned}
variable\_solution \; &\Leftarrow log\_contention(T) \wedge effect(quit, on, on, T1) \wedge \\
&effect(log\_pump\_A\_error, on, pump\_A\_error, T1) \wedge after(T, T1). \; (9.11)
\end{aligned}
$$

Contention is resolved if $user\_1$ and $user\_2$ issue input at time T and the command to $quit$ the system is ineffective at some subsequent time, $T1$, when $user\_2$'s fault is logged.

The time variables, T and $T1$, could be instantiated at a number of points during interaction and the temporal ordering is made explicit by the predicate *after*. Unfortunately, the use of such variables still imposes considerable burdens upon the interface designer. It is particularly important that a clear semantics is maintained for predicates, such as *after*, which define an ordering over variables. These can radically effect the properties of any specification. For example, the following clause specifies that $user\_1$'s input does take effect after the fault has been logged:

$$circular\_solution \Leftarrow$$

$$log\_contention(T) \wedge effect(quit, on, on, T1) \wedge$$

$$effect(log\_pump\_A\_error, on, pump\_A\_error, T1) \wedge$$

$$effect(quit, pump\_A\_error, off, T2) \wedge after(T, T1)$$

$$\wedge after(T1, T2) \wedge after(T2, T). \tag{9.12}$$

Contention is resolved if $user\_1$ and $user\_2$ issue input at time T and the command to $quit$ the system is ineffective at some subsequent time, $T1$, when $user\_2$'s fault is logged but the input to $quit$ the system does take effect at time $T2$.

The previous clause illustrates some of the problems that can arise in large-scale specifications of CSCW systems. In particular, time $T2$ occurs both after and before time T. This circular model of time makes little sense. Unfortunately, there is a high risk of such considerable problems occurring if designers are forced to construct complex sequences in terms of the *after* relation. Temporal ambiguities may easily occur in specifications that contain hundreds or thousands of clauses, especially if they must be constructed and maintained by many different development teams.

9.3.1.3 Temporal Logic

Temporal logic extends first-order logic by supporting the following operators: $\Diamond$ (read as "eventually"); $\bigcirc$ (read as "next"); $\square$ (read as "always") and $\mathcal{U}$ (read as "until") [Man81]. This notation relieves the designer from the burdens of maintaining an explicit ordering in terms of predicates such as *after*. The ordering is captured within the definition of temporal operators. For example, $\Diamond$ may be defined using a set of time-stamps T, $|w|_t$ denotes the truth value of the formula w at time t. It is important to note, however, that designers can simply introduce temporal operators into a specification. They are not forced to explicitly represent the *after* sequences that are embedded within the definitions of temporal operators. Nor are they obliged to explicitly deal with the underlying model represented in the following definition:

$$|\Diamond(w)|_t \equiv \exists t1 \in T[after(t, t1) \wedge |w|_{t1}] \tag{9.13}$$

The $\Diamond$ operator is defined such that any formula w is eventually true at time t if there exists some later time, $t1$, when w is true.

Prior provides complete definitions for the various temporal operators mentioned above [Pri67]. In contrast, our focus is upon the application of the notation. The following section, therefore, shows how temporal logic can be used to analyse solutions for the problem of interference within our CSCW application.

9.3.1.4   Input Priorities Revisited

Contention can be resolved by associating priorities with commands. Scarce resources can be allocated to input with a high priority, input with a low priority may be disregarded. In terms of our oil production system, a command to switch off the fault monitoring application might be assigned a relatively low priority. The systems should continue to log faults whenever possible and input to disable the system might, therefore, be ignored if users continue to report problems in their equipment. Unfortunately, this solution suffers from a number of limitations. There is no guarantee of fairness, some users may be "frozen" out of interaction if their commands always receive low priority. In particular, a user could not predict the success or failure of a quit command unless they could determine the priority of concurrent input from all other users. A designer might reduce this uncertainty by ensuring that low-priority input is eventually effective:

$$
\begin{aligned}
priority\_solution \Leftarrow\ &log\_contention \wedge \\
&effect(log\_pump\_A\_error, on, pump\_A\_error)\ \wedge \\
&\Diamond\ effect(quit, pump\_A\_error, off).
\end{aligned}
\tag{9.14}
$$

Contention is reduced if input to log a fault takes effect in the present interval and eventually the input to quit the system takes effect.

This approach can be used to develop sophisticated priority structures. For example, a command to close the system might be assigned a lower priority than input to log a fault in the emergency deluge equipment for fire-fighting on the rig. This, in turn, might be assigned a higher priority than the input to log a pump fault. The following clause formalizes this requirement. It is clearly important to explicitly represent these priorities if critical input is not to be delayed:

$$
\begin{aligned}
ranking\_solution \Leftarrow\ &input(user\_1, quit) \wedge \\
&input(user\_2, log\_pump\_A\_error)\ \wedge \\
&input(user\_3, log\_deluge\_failure)\ \wedge \\
&effect(log\_deluge\_failure, on, deluge\_failure)\ \wedge \\
&\Diamond(effect(log\_pump\_A\_error, deluge\_failure, fire\_risk\_alert)\ \wedge \\
&\Diamond\ effect(quit, on, off)).
\end{aligned}
\tag{9.15}
$$

Contention is reduced if three users issue input at the same time to close down the system, to log a pump fault and to log a fault in the emergency deluge system. The input to log the deluge fault takes effect immediately and eventually the pump failure is recorded. This changes the state of the system into one in which there is a fire risk and eventually at some point after this the input to close down the system will have the effect of turning the system off, providing the state has returned to normal.

Unfortunately, postponing the effect of low-priority input can cause a number of problems for the users of groupware applications. The previous clause does not specify when the $\diamond$ (read as "eventually") clause will be true. Delays in system responses can lead to frustration and error [Kuh89]. Unpredictable behavior is likely to occur when periods of quiescence allow the system to process a backlog of low-priority input [Ell89]. Delayed commands might take effect at inappropriate moments during an interaction. The presentation of a large amount of contextual information is required before a user can resolve such instances of unpredictability.

9.3.1.5   Locking

Interference can occur even if input priority mechanisms are adopted. Low-priority input to halt the system might take effect before another user has finished logging a fault. This interference can be avoided by assigning priorities to transactions rather than single commands. For example, transaction locking restricts input from other users until an operation has been terminated. Input priority, user priority or first-come first-served mechanisms provide a means of determining the identity of the next user to "gain the floor":

$$transaction\_lock \Leftarrow input(user\_2, log\_pump\_A\_error) \wedge$$
$$(not(input(user\_1, I)) \; \mathcal{U} \; input(user\_2, end\_pump\_A\_error)). \quad (9.16)$$

Contention is reduced through the imposition of a lock if $user\_1$ cannot enter any input, I, until $user\_2$ has cleared the fault.

Unfortunately, single-entry transaction locking resolves contention by restricting multi-user systems to sequential interaction. There are a number of reasons why such an approach is often unacceptable. Users may not relinquish control if transactions are not terminated. Opportunism and negotiation may provide more fruitful grounds for cooperation than prescription. In contrast to transaction locking, data locking avoids contention by restricting the ability of operators to make modifications to shared resources. For instance, $user\_1$ might continue to interact with the fault monitoring system even though $user\_2$ is logging a fault on $pump\_A$. Designers may only choose to prevent $user\_1$ from also logging a fault on that component while $user\_2$ is accessing it:

$$logging\_lock \Leftarrow input(user\_2, log\_pump\_A\_error) \wedge$$
$$(not(input(user\_1, log\_pump\_A\_error)) \mathcal{U}$$
$$input(user\_2, end\_pump\_A\_error)). \quad (9.17)$$

Contention is reduced if $user\_1$ cannot log a fault until $user\_2$ has finished logging their fault.

It is important to notice that this solution has been expressed without reference to device primitives or particular polling strategies. Later sections will describe tools which have been developed to directly execute such abstract specifications. This provides a means of evaluating the consequences of placing restrictive locks upon the group process. For example, this approach can prove unnecessarily restrictive if locks are placed upon entire systems. Interference need not occur if users make concurrent updates to different processes. Alternatively, as we have seen, data locks may be imposed at the level of individual systems or sub-components. This introduces considerable complexity into the design of an interface [Gre87]. For instance, logging knock-on faults can involve the acquisition of a large number of locks. The process by which a user requests and relinquishes a shared resource can impose a large overhead on the times necessary to perform even simple operations.

9.4   FORMALIZING THE PRESENTATION OF CSCW SYSTEMS

The second way in which formal methods can be applied to support CSCW systems is in display design. This poses significant challenges because the presentation of multi-user applications is qualitatively different from that of single-user systems. Some displays are shared amongst the members of a group while others are not. For example, the task of monitoring oil production will require different information from that of gas extraction. This, in turn, will require different information from the task of fire prevention and detection. CSCW designers must consider the composition of displays that support these different activities. This development problem is complicated because the individual elements of a display will change over time. It is critical that development teams have some means of representing and reasoning about these common and private contexts if they are to provide adequate support for group activities and individual tasks.

9.4.1   Unstructured Graphics

Unstructured graphical representations do not distinguish between the images of display components, such as menus and icons. For instance, bitmaps represent the image of pixels as bits in a data structure. Designers might use these representations to specify the images that are presented to the multiple users of CSCW systems, such as the oil production application:

```
DeclareBitmap(logging_display.bit, 42, 49, logging_display.bits);
short on_display.bits[] =
/* Abbreviated for the sake of brevity */
{
  0x0000, 0x0000, 0x0000, 0x000f, 0xff00, 0x0000, 0x007f, 0xffc0,
  0x0000, 0x00ff, 0xfff0, 0x0000, 0x00ff, 0xfff0, 0x0000, 0x00ff,
  0x001f, 0x0000, 0x0340, 0x006f, 0x0000, 0x03b0, 0x0a97, 0x0000,
  0x037d, 0x3fef, 0x0000, 0x03ee, 0x0a1b, 0x0000, 0x03d7, 0x3ff7,
  0x0000, 0x03fd, 0x87ca, 0x0000, 0x03f7, 0x5616, 0x0000, 0x014b,
  0x0000, 0x0000, 0x0000,
};
```

It is extremely difficult to decompose data structures, such as the previous bitmap, into the components of a complex image. This hinders the development of multi-user computer systems because, typically, only part of a screen is shared by all system operators. The common parts of a display cannot easily be extracted from an unstructured representation.

9.4.2   Procedural Graphics

Procedural graphics systems construct pictures from sequences of instructions. Designers might use these systems to generate interface components without describing the entire appearance of a display. The shared images of CSCW systems can be represented and reasoned about in terms of the instructions necessary to create them. For instance, the following clauses show how the $\bigcirc$ (read as "next") operator can be used to describe the instructions that are necessary to draw part of a $pump\_A\_error\_icon$:

$$draw\_pump\_A\_error\_icon \Leftarrow$$

$$pen\_down \wedge \bigcirc(pen\_forward(10) \wedge$$

$$\bigcirc(pen\_rotate(90) \wedge \bigcirc(pen\_forward(20) \wedge$$

$$\bigcirc(pen\_rotate(90) \wedge \bigcirc(pen\_forward(10) \wedge ...)))) \qquad (9.18)$$

The error icon for $pump\_A$ is drawn if in the present interval the pen is lowered to the paper and in the next interval the pen is moved forward by ten units and in the next again interval the pen is rotated by ninety degrees and...

Procedural approaches offer only limited support for the prototyping of multi-user CSCW systems. Designers would be forced to write many thousands of instructions in order to create complex images. This burden is greatly increased because different sequences of instructions must simultaneously be executed on a range of different devices in order to present displays to a number of different users. If one instruction were omitted or placed out of sequence then the final image might be corrupted. Szekely and Myers identify a further limitation of procedural graphics systems [Sze88]. If users select part of a display, using a mouse or some cursor keys, then there is no means of identifying the target of their selection using the instructions that generated the image. Designers must, therefore, maintain additional data structures in order to determine which images are selected by operator input. This is a considerable overhead for prototype CSCW systems whose users may concurrently select many different parts of many different images.

9.4.3 Structured Graphics

Logic can be used to represent the images presented by a CSCW system at an extremely high level of abstraction. For instance, the following clause specifies that $user\_1$ is presented with a $condensate\_display$, $user\_2$ is presented with a $deluge\_display$. Similar clauses might be introduced to represent the images presented to $user\_3$, $user\_4$, $user\_5$ etc:

$$display(user\_1, condensate\_display). \qquad (9.19)$$

$$display(user\_2, deluge\_display). \qquad (9.20)$$

The first clause states that $user\_1$ is presented with the $condensate\_display$. The second clause states that $user\_2$ is presented with the $deluge\_display$.

Display abstractions can be decomposed into their component parts. For instance, the $condensate\_display$ presented to $user\_1$ might show that the pneumatic valves, the centrifuges and the non-return valves are all functioning correctly but that there is an error with pump A. This image is illustrated in Figure 9.6. The structure of the $user\_1$'s $condensate\_display$ is represented by the following clauses:

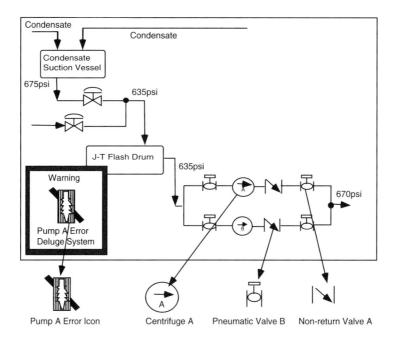

Figure 9.6 The graphical decomposition of the *condensate_display*

$$part(user\_1, condensate\_display, centrifuge\_A). \qquad (9.21)$$

$$part(user\_1, condensate\_display, pneumatic\_valve\_B). \qquad (9.22)$$

$$part(user\_1, condensate\_display, pump\_A\_error\_icon). \qquad (9.23)$$

$$part(user\_1, condensate\_display, non\_return\_valve\_A). \qquad (9.24)$$

The first clause states that the *centrifuge_A* icon is part of the *condensate_display* presented to *user_1*. The second clause states that the *pneumatic_valve_B* icon is part of the *condensate_display* presented to *user_1*. The third clause states that the *pump_A_error* icon is part of the *condensate_display* presented to *user_1* and so on.

Figure 9.7 illustrates how the *deluge_display* presented to *user_2* can be decomposed in a similar fashion. The structure of this image can be represented by the following clauses:

$$part(user\_2, deluge\_display, pump\_A\_error\_icon). \qquad (9.25)$$

$$part(user\_2, deluge\_display, inlet\_B\_capacity). \qquad (9.26)$$

$$part(user\_2, deluge\_display, pump\_C\_icon). \qquad (9.27)$$

$$part(user\_2, deluge\_display, protection\_cage\_C). \qquad (9.28)$$

The first clause states that the *pump_A_error* icon is part of the *deluge_display* presented to *user_2*. The second clause states that the *inlet_B_capacity* is part of the *deluge_display* presented to *user_2*. The third clause states that the *pump_C_icon* icon is part of the *deluge_display* presented to *user_2* and so on.

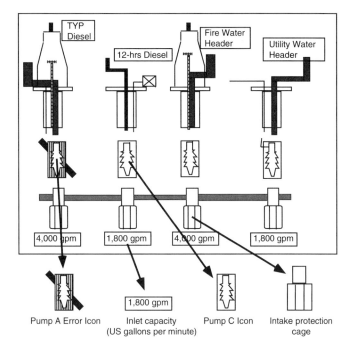

Figure 9.7   The graphical decomposition of the *deluge_display*

Designers can use logic clauses to identify those images, such as $pump\_A\_error\_icon$, which form the common context of operations performed by $user\_1$ and $user\_2$. This supports the detailed development of CSCW systems. For instance, designers might specify that the deluge pumping equipment is closed if $user\_1$ and $user\_2$ are presented with an error for pump A and both provide input to close off the pump. Such an agreement would be appropriate because closing-off fire-safety equipment has important consequences for the oil and gas extraction processes. The display requirement that they both see the error icon for $pump\_A$ is intended to ensure that both operators are presented with sufficient contextual information in order for them to coordinate their response:

$$voting\_close\_pump\_A \Leftarrow$$
$$display(user\_1, condensate\_display) \wedge$$
$$display(user\_2, deluge\_display) \wedge$$
$$part(user\_1, condensate\_display, pump\_A\_error\_icon) \wedge$$
$$part(user\_2, deluge\_display, pump\_A\_error\_icon) \wedge$$
$$\Diamond(input(user\_1, close\_pump\_A) \wedge$$
$$input(user\_2, close\_pump\_A)). \tag{9.29}$$

This states that a voting system is used to close $pump\_A$ if $user\_1$ is presented with the $condensate\_display$ and $user\_2$ is presented with the $deluge\_display$ and $pump\_A\_error$ icon is part of both displays and eventually both $user\_1$ and $user\_2$ provide input to close the $pump$.

Such clauses support further stages in the development of CSCW systems. For instance, it has not been specified that the $deluge\_display$ presents detailed information about the centrifuges that are used during gas extraction from the oil. It would not, therefore, be appropriate to expect $user\_2$ to resolve problems with these components without access to additional data. Contention might occur if they did attempt to operate a centrifuge.

For example, $user\_1$ might $close$ it while $user\_1$ tried to $open$ it. The display abstractions introduced in the previous paragraphs might be integrated with the temporal operators from the first part of this chapter to specify solutions for such problems. Designers might require that a lock is imposed to resolve contention if $user\_2$ is not presented with information about a particular centrifuge:

$$lock\_out\_centrifuge\_contention \Leftarrow$$
$$input(user\_1, close\_centrifuge\_A) \land$$
$$display(user\_2, deluge\_display) \land$$
$$not(part(user\_2, deluge\_display, centrifuge\_A)) \land$$
$$not(input(user\_2, I) \; \mathcal{U} \; input(user\_1, end\_centrifuge\_A\_error)). \quad (9.30)$$

This states that a lock is imposed to prevent contention over $centrifuge\_A$ if $user\_1$ provides input to close it and $user\_1$ is presented with the $deluge\_display$ and the $centrifuge\_A$ icon is not part of that display and $user\_2$ does not provide input until $user\_1$ has issued input to state that the error in the centrifuge is over.

We have argued that problems such as contention and deadlock make it necessary to consider the "look and feel" of a potential interface during the early stages of CSCW systems development. It is, therefore, important that designers can refine high-level clauses, such as $condensate\_display$, into the primitive images which are presented to users. One means of doing this is to describe images in terms of lines:

$$line(user\_1, centrifuge\_A, 0.1, 0.2, 0.6, 0.2). \quad (9.31)$$

This states that the image of the $centrifuge$ icon presented to $user\_1$ includes a line from coordinates (0.1,0.2) to (0.6, 0.2).

A limitation with this approach is that operator input is not usually directed towards lines but towards areas of the screen. A user selecting an icon does not, necessarily, expect to select a particular line of its image. In order to support such interaction, designers must exploit more sophisticated graphical "building-blocks". Figure 9.8 illustrates how the image of the $condensate\_display$ can be described in terms of a number of regions: a background region, a text region and a centrifuge region. Regions can be further decomposed into sub-regions. Each region has properties, such as size and position, attributes, such as font and pattern, and a behavior, such as whether or not it is selectable. For instance, the $centrifuge\_A$ icon could be presented to $user\_1$ as a region with a blank background and dimensions that occupy one-twentieth of the screen:

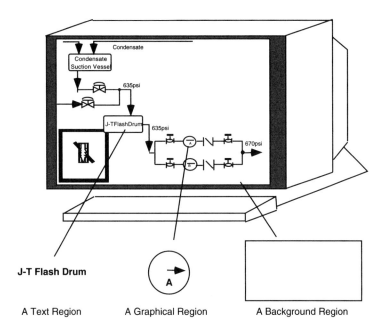

J-T Flash Drum

A Text Region   A Graphical Region   A Background Region

Figure 9.8   The region decomposition for part of the *condensate_display*

$$dimension(user\_1, centrifuge\_A, 0.05, 0.05). \qquad (9.32)$$

$$pattern(user\_1, centrifuge\_A, blank). \qquad (9.33)$$

The first clause states that the image of the *centrifuge_A* icon presented to *user_1* has dimension that occupy one twentieth of the screen. The second clause states that the image of the *centrifuge_A* icon presented to *user_1* has a blank background.

These clauses can represent the ways in which CSCW displays must be tailored in order to support group tasks. For instance, designers might require that *user_2* can monitor the effects of *user_1*'s intervention on the *centrifuge* while performing other duties. Under such circumstances, the centrifuge might be introduced into the *deluge_display*. The dimensions of the centrifuge icon could also be reduced in order to free display resources for the presentation of *user_2*'s primary activities. Although both users must be presented with information about the centrifuge, the size of this image is used to reflect the relative importance of the component for each user's task. The following clause illustrates how logic abstractions can be used to represent and reason about CSCW systems which support semi-independent views [Ell91] of application processes :

$$part(user\_2, deluge\_display, centrifuge\_A). \qquad (9.34)$$

$$dimension(user\_2, centrifuge\_A, 0.02, 0.02). \qquad (9.35)$$

The first clause states that the *centrifuge_A* icon is part of the *deluge_display* presented to *user_2*. The second clause states that the image of the icon presented to *user_2* has dimension that occupy one-fiftieth of the screen.

The choice of input media has a profound affect upon the usability of CSCW systems. For instance, Galer and Yap have used prototypes to investigate the costs and benefits of different input devices for the users of intensive care systems [Gal80]. Some operators suffered from high error rates when using thumb wheels, mice were difficult to use in cluttered clinical environments. In order to evaluate the tradeoffs that exist between tracker-balls, mice, joysticks and keyboards, the designers of CSCW systems must be able to represent a variety of input devices.

9.4.4   Introducing Input Information

Input can be represented by introducing device drivers into formal specifications. For instance, the following routine "blinks" the caret when a mouse is moved over a text region in an Apple Macintosh [App86]:

```
CLR.L           -SP         ;event code for null event is 0
PEA             2(SP)       ;pass null event
CLR.L           -SP         ;pass NIL dialogue pointer
CLR.L           -SP         ;pass NIL pointer
DialogueSelect              ;invoke DialogueSelect
ADDQ.L          #4,SP       ;pop off result and null event
```

Burton et al show how designers might formalize similar code in order to specify single-user graphical interfaces built from the Apple Macintosh Toolbox [Bur89]. Such descriptions provide an appropriate level of detail for many stages in development. They are, however, extremely device dependent. The complexity of accessing input at this level of detail might dissuade designers from assessing the costs and benefits of a range of devices for the many different users of CSCW systems. Like bitmaps, this approach provides a one-step refinement between abstract, formal representations of graphical interfaces and device specific implementations. This would have important consequences for the development of embedded control systems, such as our oil rig application. In these environments, CSCW applications must frequently be developed to run on a range of existing hardware. It would not be acceptable to rebuild a control room because its input devices could not be formalized in terms of their device drivers.

Input from a range of physical devices, such as mice or tracker balls, can be represented by generic events, such as *on_select* and *on_move*. Events can be introduced into formal specifications by associating them with graphical regions. For example, the following clause shows how designers might specify that *pump_A* is closed if *user_1* and *user_2* are presented with an *pump_A_error_icon* and both operators use a mouse to select this image. This clause can also be used to describe control rooms in which the operators had access to tracker-balls or cursor keys instead of mice. These devices could also generate *on_select* events. Such device independence helps to avoid premature commitment to particular hardware platforms. Implementation decisions can be postponed until late in the development cycle when the costs and benefits of a range of different input media have been considered. This encourages designers to identify those devices that are most appropriate to the particular tasks and environments of CSCW groups:

$event\_close\_pump\_A \Leftarrow$

$\quad display(user\_1, condensate\_display) \wedge$

$\quad display(user\_2, deluge\_display) \wedge$

$\quad part(user\_1, condensate\_display, pump\_A\_error\_icon) \wedge$

$\quad part(user\_2, deluge\_display, pump\_A\_error\_icon) \wedge$

$\quad \Diamond(input(user\_1, pump\_A\_error\_icon, on\_select) \wedge$

$\quad (not(effect(on\_select, pump\_A\_error\_icon, pump\_A\_off)\mathcal{U}$

$\quad input(user\_2, pump\_A\_error\_icon, on\_select)).$ \hfill (9.36)

This states that input events are used to close *pump_A* if *user_1* is presented with the *condensate_display* and *user_2* is presented with the *deluge_display* and the *pump_A_error* icon is part of the fault and line displays and eventually *user_1* issues a select event for the icon but this is not effective until *user_2* also issues a select event on the icon.

We have shown that formal notations can be used to represent the proportion and location of graphical images on a display. A limitation with this approach is that it does not consider the operators' physical and environmental surroundings. Specifying the size and position of an image is of little benefit if users cannot easily view the devices that are used to present the *condensate* and *deluge* displays. This is a weakness of almost all previous approaches to interface design. Few existing techniques consider the layout of particular working environments.

9.5   WORKING ENVIRONMENTS

The European Community Directive on work with Display Screen Equipment and the United Kingdom's Health and Safety Regulations provide guidelines on the correct layout of working environments for computer operators. Screens should be parallel to overhead fluorescent tubes, at right angles to windows etc. Unfortunately, many techniques in human–computer interaction completely ignore these issues. They provide ample support for screen layout and dialogue design but they provide no means of reasoning about the physical layout of work environments. Conversely, the empirical techniques and CAD tools that have been developed to analyse different operator postures do not address the concerns that dominate human–computer interaction [Mal89]. The lack of integration between user-interface design and environmental layout is not a serious problem in many contexts. Office workers can easily move keyboards, screens and telephones into positions that support their everyday tasks. This lack of integration is, however, a more serious problem for the development of safety-critical applications. The position of a display can determine whether operators will observe a warning within a particular time period [Wic84]. The physical location of buttons, keyboards and mice can affect the error rates for particular input sequences [Joh94b]. For example, the following clause states that *user_1* is responsible for observing and responding to the failure of a blowback valve. These devices ensure that material is not forced back up a line from which it is being pumped:

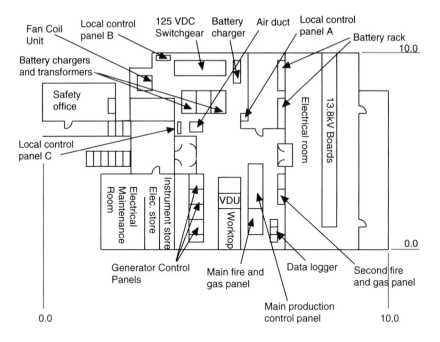

Figure 9.9   Control room module for North Sea oil production

$$user\_1\_responsible\_for\_closing\_valve\_A \Leftarrow$$
$$display(user\_1, condensate\_display) \wedge$$
$$display(user\_2, deluge\_display) \wedge$$
$$part(user\_1, condensate\_display, valve\_A\_error\_icon) \wedge$$
$$not(part(user\_2, deluge\_display, valve\_A\_error\_icon)) \wedge$$
$$input(user\_1, valve\_A\_error\_icon, on\_select). \tag{9.37}$$

This states that users agree to close $valve\_A$ if $user\_1$ is presented with the $condensate\_display$ and $user\_2$ is presented with the $deluge\_display$ and $valve\_A\_error\_icon$ is part of the condensate and but not of the deluge display and $user\_1$ provides input to close $valve\_A$.

Such dialogue requirements make implicit assumptions about the layout of a potential control room. Designers must ensure that $user\_1$ can view the $valve\_A\_error\_icon$ from their normal working position. Figure 9.9 illustrates that this may be a non-trivial problem. For instance, if the operator were routinely stationed behind the work surface at the bottom on the figure then it would be difficult for them to view a warning presented on the local control panels towards the top of the layout. Fortunately, logic abstractions can also be used to reason about the physical organization of complex working environments.

9.6   REPRESENTING WORKSTATION LAYOUT

Designers can exploit logic to represent the allocation of displays to the control panels that users must operate. For instance, clause (9.37) required that $user\_1$ should be presented with the $condensate\_display$. This could be presented through the local control panel next to the switchgear shown in Figure 9.9 rather than through the main VDU next to the worktop:

$$present(user\_1, condensate\_display, local\_panel\_A). \qquad (9.38)$$
$$location(local\_panel\_A, 6.0, 6.5). \qquad (9.39)$$
$$dimension(local\_panel\_A, 1.5, 0.9, 1.1). \qquad (9.40)$$

The first clause states that the condensate display is presented to $user\_1$ through local control panel A. The remaining clauses state that the control panel is located at Cartesian coordinates (6.0, 6.5) and is 1.5 meters in dimension along the X axis, 0.9 along the Y axis and 1.1 meters along the Z axis; this corresponds to the height of the panel.

Designers can use these clauses to guide the detailed layout of a control system. By introducing positional information into logic clauses it is possible to represent the likely working position of an operator performing a particular task. For instance, $user\_1$'s normal activity might be to coordinate the operation of the system from behind the worktop. This would place the user at a position close to $(6.0, 2.2)$. It would then be difficult for $user\_1$ to respond to warnings presented on local control panel A at the same time as monitoring a display on the fire and gas panel:

$$divided\_attention \Leftarrow$$
$$location(user\_1, 6.0, 2.2) \wedge$$
$$location(local\_panel\_A, 6.0, 6.5) \wedge$$
$$location(fire\_panel, 6.5, 1.5) \wedge$$
$$present(user\_1, Display\_1, local\_panel\_A) \wedge$$
$$present(user\_1, Display\_2, fire\_panel) \wedge$$
$$part(user\_1, Display\_1, valve\_A\_error\_icon) \wedge$$
$$part(user\_1, Display\_2, communications\_error) \wedge$$
$$input(user\_1, valve\_A\_error\_icon, on\_select) \wedge$$
$$input(user\_1, self\_test\_communications, on\_select). \qquad (9.41)$$

This states that $user\_1$ must divide their attention if they are at (6.0,2.2) and must monitor two different displays, one presented by local panel A at (6.0,6.5) and the other presented by the fire and gas console at (6.5,1.5). And that those displays contain warnings about a communications error and a fault with valve A and $user\_1$ must provide input to resolve those warnings.

Logic can be used to represent potential solutions to such problems. For instance, the position of the fire and gas console might be moved so that it could more easily be observed while $user\_1$ was monitoring the local control panel. This can be represented by altering one

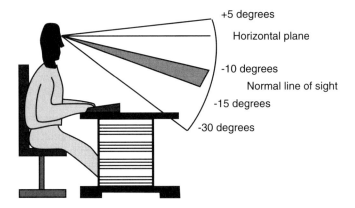

Figure 9.10   The relaxed viewing angle

of the *location* clauses. Alternatively, the task of monitoring and responding to the communications error might be allocated to another user. These two potential solutions again illustrate the close interaction between dialogue design and the layout of control rooms:

$$coordinated\_response \Leftarrow$$
$$part(user\_1, Display\_1, valve\_A\_error\_icon) \wedge$$
$$part(user\_2, Display\_2, communications\_error) \wedge$$
$$input(user\_1, valve\_A\_error\_icon, on\_select) \wedge$$
$$input(user\_2, self\_test\_communications, on\_select). \tag{9.42}$$

This states that there is a coordinated response if $user\_1$'s display contains a warning about a fault with valve A and $user\_2$'s display contains a warning about a communications problem and $user\_1$ must provide input to resolve the valve problem and $user\_2$ must resolve the communications error.

Such clauses illustrate the benefits of formal methods for the integration of interface design and environmental layout. It is not clear how the individual images shown to many different operators might be represented using the conventional sketches and two-dimensional plans of control rooms, such as that shown in Figure 9.9.

9.7   USING ERGONOMIC GUIDELINES TO INFORM CSCW DESIGN

Research in the field of human factors and ergonomics has developed a mass of information about suitable operator postures and working positions. For instance, Figure 9.10 illustrates Grandjean's [Gra88] guidelines for a relaxed viewing angle from an upright, seated posture. If operators are required to monitor displays outside of the -10 to -15 degree cone for long periods then static muscle overloading may occur. Until now, it has been difficult to envisage how such information can be used to *directly* inform the development of CSCW systems. In contrast, the previous clauses can be used to reason about the consequences of such figures for interactive dialogues in particular working environments. For example, assuming that $user\_1$ were at the worktop in the centre of the control room at (6.0,2.2,1.3) and that they were observing a point on local control panel A, mentioned in clause 9.41, at (6.0,6.5, 1.4) then the visual angle would be approximately 19 degrees below the horizontal. The panel would fall outside of the line of sight for comfortable eye rotation. This is derived from the following formula that relates the operator's seated eye height and the distance of a target on a control panel to the height of that target and the likely visual angle between the horizontal plane and that target:

$$\sqrt{seated\_height^2 + target\_distance^2}/sin\ 90 =$$
$$target\_height/sin\ visual\_angle \tag{9.43}$$

Such formulae can be used to guide interface development. In particular, it can be used to ensure that operators can actually monitor and use the multiple displays of CSCW systems. Designers should not place routinely monitored information for $user\_1$ on the local control panel. The operator would be forced to assume an undesirable posture to observe the display. This area might be used to present information for other operators who can more easily view this display. Similarly, $user\_1$ cannot be expected to observe high-priority error messages on the local control panel. Operators frequently fail to detect warnings on the edge of their vision [Wic84]. The identification of such "high-priority" errors is an important stage during the development of safety-critical interfaces. $User\_1$'s observation problem with local control panel A might be resolved by ensuring that such critical warnings are also presented closer to their normal line of sight. Equation (9.43) can be used to validate $user\_1$'s line of sight between various positions in the control room and these additional sources of information. These positions must, in turn, be checked to ensure that they do not obscure critical information for $user\_2$, $user\_3$ etc. Once an optimal position has been identified, logic can be used to represent the new position for the display:

$$resolve\_observation\_problem \Leftarrow$$
$$location(user\_1, 6.0, 2.2) \wedge$$
$$present(user\_1, Display\_1, local\_panel\_A) \wedge$$
$$part(user\_1, Display\_1, compressor\_failure) \wedge$$
$$present(user\_1, Display\_2, worktop\_panel) \wedge$$
$$part(user\_1, Display\_2, compressor\_failure). \tag{9.44}$$

This states that a potential observation problem can be resolved if $user\_1$ is located at (6.0, 2.2) and they are allocated a display, $Display\_1$, which includes a warning that a compressor is failing and that display is presented on the local control panel and they are allocated a display, $Display\_2$, which also includes a warning that the compressor is failing and that display is presented on the $worktop\_panel$.

Workstation layout not only affects the presentation of control information, it also has a profound impact upon input requirements. For example, Grandjean uses Figure 9.11 to illustrate the working distance from the elbow to the hand of an operator at table-top height [Gra88]. This applies to the fifth percentile of the male population. The inner arc represents the extent of the grasp from a relaxed, seated position. This analysis can be used to inform dialogue design. For example, in control systems it is important that certain input sequences are dif-

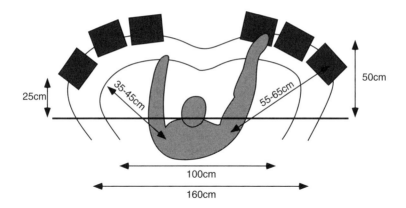

Figure 9.11   The horizontal reach limit

ficult to issue. The valve isolation switches might, therefore, be placed beyond the 55–65cm arc. Operators can make occasional stretches of 70–80cm without difficulty:

$$reach\_isolate\_valve\_A \Leftarrow$$
$$location(user\_1, 6.0, 2.2) \wedge$$
$$select(user\_1, close\_valve\_A\_switch) \wedge$$
$$component(close\_valve\_A\_switch, worktop\_panel) \wedge$$
$$location(close\_valve\_A\_switch, 6.0, 3.0, 0.9). \tag{9.45}$$

This states that the user must reach to close off valve A if they are at (2.0, 2.1) and they provide input to isolate the valve by selecting a button on the worktop control panel at (6.0,3.0,0.9).

The correct positioning of control panel components must reflect details of the operators' tasks. It should be hard to issue input sequences that cannot easily be reversed. Conversely, the input requirements that are implicit within dialogue designs must also take into account the physical demands that devices place upon their users. Operators should not routinely be expected to sustain postures that impose significant biomechanical strain.

9.8   PROTOTYPING

Mathematical specifications provide users with little idea of what it would be like to interact with a graphical interface. Prototypes provide a far better impression of the "look and feel" of a potential implementation. The experimental analysis of partial implementations can be used to inform the refinement of detailed specifications towards full implementation. They can be shown to members of concurrent design teams. They can be shown to operators and are amenable to experimental analysis. Logic programming environments, such as that supported by PROLOG, provide a convenient bridge between formal specifications and functioning prototypes. This environment has a well understood semantics based on that of first-order logic. This secton, therefore, provides a brief introduction to the design and implementation of the

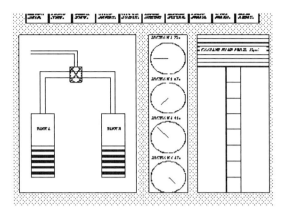

Figure 9.12 A Prelog prototype

Prelog system. This application has been specifically developed to implement CSCW prototypes. Prelog combines a temporal logic interpreter and a screen management system to directly execute the clauses that have been presented in this chapter.

9.8.1 Presenting Graphical Structures

A number of research groups have developed executable versions of the temporal logic notation that has been used in this chapter. For instance, the Tokio interpreter has been implemented using the PROLOG programming environment [Aoy86]. Clauses that contain temporal operators are re-written and are asserted over an appropriate interval. In other words, the Tokio interpreter maintains time-variables that are similar to those introduced in the earlier sections of this chapter. Unfortunately, Tokio only provides limited input and output facilities. The Prelog prototyping tool avoids this limitation by linking Tokio and Presenter [Too91]. Prelog uses the Presenter screen management system to provide facilities for manipulating region structures and for setting, clearing and interrogating properties of regions. Low-level implementation details, such as raster graphics operations, are isolated within the presentation system. This is a significant benefit for the development of CSCW system. Designers are not forced to consider low-level details for multiple presentation devices. Figure 9.12 shows a display that was generated using Prelog. In order to produce such an image, Prelog constructs a *part* hierarchy using clauses such as (9.21,9.22,9.23). The region properties, attributes and behaviors of each part, represented by clauses such as (9.33), are then recorded in a tree. This data structure is traversed. Information about each region is passed to Presenter. For designers, the net effect of linking Tokio and Presenter is to provide the impression of a graphical output channel.

9.8.2 Handling Device Input

Prelog must translate device primitives into input events. It is important that the complexity of handling input from many concurrent users should not frustrate the design of CSCW systems. Prelog reduces this complexity by isolating low-level device handling within Presenter. Current implementations support on_select, on_move and on_size to represent initial selection, move and scaling events. The on_select_up, on_move_up and on_size_up events represent terminating selection, move and scaling. Users may type input directly into editable regions.

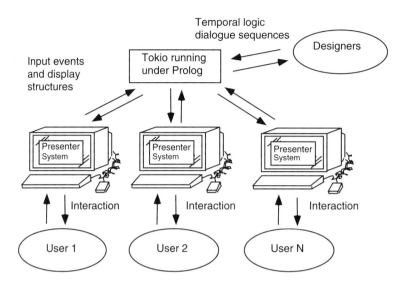

Figure 9.13   The distributed Prelog architecture

Such keyboard input is represented by an on_CR event which is generated each time a carriage return is pressed. If necessary, designers can then specify that Prelog should read the text which has been entered into an editable region.

It can be extremely computationally expensive to support fine-grained updates of shared objects in CSCW systems. Presenter provides means of reducing this cost; it implements Took's notion of surface interaction [Too91]. Some graphical operations, such as textual and geometric manipulations, have no "deep" semantic meaning for an application. They can, therefore, be handled by Presenter without reference to the logic specification. For instance, designers can specify that the image of the pump presented to $user\_1$ changes under selection. Presenter will then automatically highlight the region whenever $user\_1$ selects it. The designer is only forced to explicitly request this image update if it is to be presented to other users. Prelog also provides efficiency features which ensure that certain input events from particular operators can be discarded. For instance, on_move and on_move_up might be ignored by safety-critical CSCW systems in which users are prevented from altering the layout of their displays. All of these enhancements are optional and can be explicitly represented in the clauses of logic specifications.

Controlling event-based interfaces from within a logic programming envir
many practical and theoretical problems. In particular, it is unclear how async
current input from many different operators can be supported without sacrif
notion of execution as proof. If Prelog is interrupted with new input events, h
information be accommodated within an ongoing proof? For instance, if Prelo
to suspend a proof to handle a *move* event on an inlet icon, it might have
prior proof steps did not depend on previous information about the position
This would radically affect the nature of the programming environment provic
A large number of input events might stretch the resources of any implementati
ceptable level. An obvious alternative is to make Prelog responsible for sampling input. The
designer is free to specify when Prelog should poll Presenter. One drawback to this approach

is that important events from one user can be stored until Prelog has finished handling less important input from other users.

Tokio was intended to run on single-user, single-processor implementations. In contrast, our implementation of Prelog uses UNIX sockets [Lef90] to support interaction between a number of users communicating over local and wide area networks. Figure 9.13 illustrates the Prelog architecture. In the current implementation of Prelog, $graphics\_write(To\_client, Message)$ is evaluated as true if a $Message$ string is successfully sent to the client process running on the user's workstation. $graphics\_read(From\_client, Message)$ is evaluated as true if $Message$ unifies with input sent from a client process. For example, $event\_close\_pump\_A$ (9.36) can be implemented by the following clause. The $graphics\_read$ and $graphics\_write$ formats are used here to aid the exposition. Designers can re-name these clauses to increase the tractability of an executable specification:

$close\_pump\_A\_prototype \Leftarrow$

   $graphics\_write(user\_1, display(condensate\_display)),$

   $graphics\_write(user\_2, display(deluge\_display)),$

   $graphics\_write(user\_1, part(condensate\_display, pump\_A\_error\_icon)),$

   $graphics\_write(user\_2, part(deluge\_display, pump\_A\_error\_icon)),$

   $\Diamond(graphics\_read(user\_1, input(pump\_A\_error\_icon, on\_select),$

   $(not(effect(on\_select, pump\_A\_error\_icon, pump\_A\_off)\mathcal{U}$

   $graphics\_read(user\_2, input(pump\_A\_error\_icon, on\_select)).$ (9.46)

This states that there is a dialogue to close $pump\_A$ if a message is written to $user\_1$'s client to ensure that they are presented with the $condensate\_display$ and a message is written to $user\_2$'s client to ensure that they are presented with the $deluge\_display$ and messages are sent to ensure that the $pump\_A\_error$ icon is part of the displays and eventually a select event for that icon is read from the $user\_1$. This input is ineffective until a selection is also read from $user\_2$.

Prelog also supports the implementation of CSCW systems which provide multiple windows on each workstation. A stub process is created for each window, graphical clauses are easily parameterized by their intended destination; $user\_1\_window\_1$.

9.8.3 Environmental Animation

Prelog offers significant advantages over traditional prototyping tools. Previous systems help developers to quickly mock-up CSCW displays and animate dialogue sequences. There is a danger, however, that such tools may produce dialogues which cannot easily be integrated with their eventual working environment. Warnings may be obscured by other operators or pieces of equipment. On-line help may be abandoned if users cannot easily read particular displays. In contrast, the Prelog tool exploits $location$ clauses such as those in (9.45) to build up three-dimensional models of control rooms and offices. The same system can, therefore, be used to prototype dialogues as well as view the potential layout of working environments. These models can be shown to operators and to the members of concurrent design teams that are working on control room planning and display development. The term "environmental

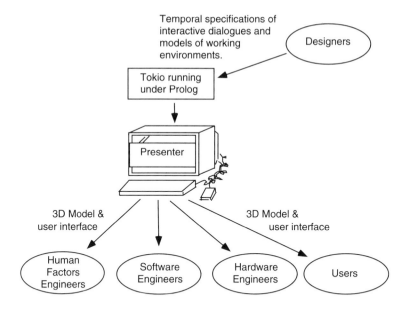

Figure 9.14   The application of Prelog for environmental animation

animation" has been used to refer to our integration of prototyping techniques and three-dimensional models. Figure 9.14 illustrates this aspect of the Prelog architecture. Further work intends to explore the more general use of formal notations to reason about the physical characteristics of working environments. For instance, logic can also be used to characterize acoustic properties. Layout information might then be recruited to represent appropriate sound levels within particular areas of a control room. Prelog might provide rudimentary simulations for these presentation techniques:

$$timbre(pump\_A\_error\_alarm, bell). \qquad (9.47)$$

$$amplitude(pump\_A\_error\_alarm, 60dBA). \qquad (9.48)$$

$$pitch(pump\_A\_error\_alarm, 260Hz). \qquad (9.49)$$

This states that the $pump\_A$ warning has the timbre of a bell, the amplitude of the warning is 60dB and its pitch is 260Hz.

In many human–machine interfaces, changes in the characteristics of acoustic signals are used to indicate changes in the underlying state of an application. For instance, a continuous tone might change into a bell in order to indicate a failure in the deluge system. Temporal logic offers one means of explicitly representing these dynamic properties [Joh91, Joh90].

9.9   CONCLUSION

This chapter has shown how mathematical specification techniques can support the design of CSCW systems. In particular I have argued that temporal logic can be used to represent

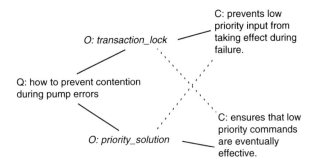

Figure 9.15   Literate specification for $transaction\_lock$

critical requirements for sychronization and locking. This approach is justified because temporal properties have a profound impact upon the nature of interaction in multi-user systems. It has also been argued that graphical information and input events must be explicitly represented within abstract models of CSCW applications. I have also shown how the application of formal methods can be extended to represent and reason about the physical dimensions of working environments. This is often neglected within the development of CSCW systems and represents an important extension to the application of formal methods. For CSCW systems, the layout of an office, factory or control room will have a critical impact on the operation and use of a human–computer interface. Finally, I have argued that prototyping tools must be provided if non-formalists are to assess the products of mathematical specification techniques. The Prelog system has been developed to address this concern. It can be used to directly derive partial implementations from temporal logic clauses, such as those introduced in this chapter. It can also be used to generate environmental animations, or 3-D models, of potential workstation layouts. This enables designers to view potential displays within their intended context of use.

Many questions remain to be addressed before formal methods can be widely applied to support the development of multi-user systems. In particular, there are problems in scaling up the approach to deal with very large-scale systems. Such applications raise a different set of CSCW problems. Not only do they raise issues about synchronizing multi-user access to computer resources, these design challenges also force designers to consider the synchronization of multiple development teams. This is difficult because many members of these teams will have no understanding of formal methods. In order to address this issue, we are developing literate specification techniques [Joh96a, Joh95b]. This approach provides clients and users with access to both formal and semi-formal documentation. In particular, design rationale is used to record the reasons *why* particular clauses were used during the development of a CSCW specification. For example, Figure 9.15 presents the arguments for and against locking out the user in the manner described by $transaction\_lock$ (9.16) and $priority\_solution$ (9.14). The problem of reducing contention during pump failures can either be satisfied by transaction locking or by the use of input priorities. These are labelled as alternative options, O. These options are linked to criteria, C, which represent the reasons for and against a particular approach. In the case of transaction locking this is supported by the criteria that it prevents low priority input from taking effect during the failure. Positive or supporting criteria are indicated by solid lines. In contrast, it is not supported by the argument that low-priority commands will eventually be effective. This is because they are literally locked-out of the system. The dotted lines indicate negative or weakening criteria. The intention here is that the QOC argumentation structures should enable designers to question the approaches that are embodied within formal specifications. It should be possible for non-formalists to ask *why* a system is designed the way it is.

The literate specification approach, described above, addresses a fundamental paradox in the formal design of CSCW systems. In order to obtain precise notations for reasoning about the complexity of multi-user communication, we may lose the ability to communicate within and between multiple design teams. Not everyone can be expected to learn and understand temporal logics. This re-iterates a key point for future work in this area. We will not be able to develop interfaces that support groupwork unless we provide techniques that can be used by groups of designers. This represents the greatest challenge to the continued application of formal methods for CSCW systems.

REFERENCES

[App86]   Rose, C. *Inside The Apple Macintosh*, Vol. I. Addison Wesley, Wokingham, UK, 1986.

[Aoy86]   Aoyagi, T., Fujita, M. and Moto-Oka, T., Temporal logic programming language -Tokio-programming in Tokio. In Wada, E. (Ed.), *Proceedings of the 4th Annual Conference - Logic Programming '85*, LNCS 221, pages 128–137. Springer-Verlag, Berlin, Germany, 1986.

[Bas90]   Bastide, R. and Palanque, P., Petri net objects for the design, validation and prototyping of user-driven interfaces. In Diaper, D., Gilmore, D., Cockton, G. and Shackel, B. (Eds.), *Human–Computer Interaction — INTERACT'90*, pages 625–631. Elsevier Science Publications, North Holland, Netherlands, 1990.

[Bur89]   Burton, C.T., Cook, S.J., Gikas, S., Rowson, J.R. and Sommerville, S.T., Specifying the Apple Macintosh Toolbox Event Manager. *Formal Aspects of Computing*, 1:147–171, 1989.

[Cra93]   Craigen, D., Gerhart, S. and Ralston, T., An international survey of industrial applications of formal methods. Technical Report NISTGCR 93/626, U.S. Department of Commerce, National Institute of Standards and Technology, Githersburg, USA, 1993.

[Cul90]   Cullen, *Proceedings of the Public Enquiry into the Piper Alpha Disaster*. The Department of Energy, London, UK, 1990.

[Dix97]   Dix, A., Rodden, T. and Sommerville, I., Modelling versions in collaborative work. *IEE Proceedings in Software Engineering*, 14(4):195–205, 1997.

[Ell89]   Ellis, C.A. and Gibbs, S.J., Concurrency control in groupware systems. *ACM SIGMOD Record*, 18(2):399–407, 1989.

[Ell91]   Ellis, C.A., Gibbs, S.J. and Rein, G.L., Groupware: Some issues and experiences. *Communications of the ACM*, 34(1):35–58, January 1991.

[Gal80]   Galer, I.A.R. and Yap, B.L., Ergonomics in intensive care: Applying human factors to the design and evaluation of a patient monitoring system. *Ergonomics*, 23(8):763–779, 1980.

[Gra88]   Grandjean, E., *Fitting the Man to the Task: Occupational Ergonomics*. Taylor & Francis, London, UK, 1988.

[Gra95]   Gray, P.D. and Johnson, C.W., Requirements for interface design notations. In Palanque, P. and Bastide, R. (Eds.), *Design, Specification and Verification of Interactive Systems '95*, pages 113–133. Springer Verlag, Berlin, Germany, 1995.

[Gre87]   Greif, I. and Sarin, S., Data sharing in group work. *Communications of the ACM*, 5(2):197–211, 1987.

[Har95]   Harrison, M.D., The role of verification. In Palanque, P. and Bastide, R. (Eds.), *Design, Specification and Verification of Interactive Systems '95*, pages 342–344. Springer Verlag, Berlin, Germany, 1995.

[Hix93]   Hix, D. and Hartson, H.R., *Developing User Interfaces*. John Wiley & Sons, London, 1993.

[Hod77]   Hodges, W., *Logic*. Penguin Books, London, 1977.

[Joh90]   Johnson, C.W. and Harrison, M.D., Using temporal logic to support the specification and prototyping of interactive control systems. *International Journal of Man–Machine Studies*, 36:357–385, 1992.

[Joh91]   Johnson, C.W., Applying temporal logic to support the specification and prototyping of concurrent multi-user interfaces. In Diaper, D. and Hammond, N. (Eds.), *People And Computers VI: Usability Now*, pages 145–156. Cambridge University Press, Cambridge, UK, 1991.

[Joh92]   Johnson, C.W., Specifying and prototyping dynamic human-computer interfaces for stochastic applications. In Alty, J.L., Diaper, D. and Guest, S. (Eds.), *People And Computers VIII*, pages 233–248. Cambridge University Press, Cambridge, UK, 1993.

[Joh94a]   Johnson, C.W., McCarthy, J.C. and Wright, P.C., Using a formal language to support natural language in accident reports. *Ergonomics*, 38(6):1265–1283, 1995.

[Joh94b]   Johnson, C.W., Representing and reasoning about the impact of environmental layout upon human computer interaction. *Ergonomics*, 39(3):512–530, 1996.

[Joh95a]   Johnson, C.W., Using Z to support the design of interactive, safety-critical systems. *IEE Software Engineering Journal*, 10(2):49–60, 1995.

[Joh95b]   Johnson, C.W., Literate specification. *Software Engineering Journal*, 11(4):224–237, 1996.

[Joh96a]   Johnson, C.W., Documenting the design of safety-critical user interfaces. *Interacting With Computers*, 8(3):221–239, 1996.

[Joh96b]   Johnson, C.W. and Gray, P.D., Error driven design. In Harrison, M.D. and Vanderdonk, J. (Eds.), *Design, Specification and Verification of Interactive Systems'96*, Springer Verlag, Berlin, Germany, 1996.

[Joh97]   Johnson, C.W., The impact of time and place on the operation of mobile computing devices. In *People and Computers XII*, pages 175–190. Springer Verlag, Berlin, Germany, 1997.

[Kan88]   Kantowitz, B.H. and Casper, P.A., Human workload in aviation. In Wiener, E.L. and Nagel, D.C. (Eds.), *Human Factors In Aviation*, pages 157–187. Academic Press, London, UK, 1988.

[Kra91]   Kramer, B., Introducing the GRASPIN specification language SEGRAS. *Journal of Systems and Software*, 15(1):17–31, 1991.

[Kuh89]   Kuhmann, W., Stress inducing properties of system response times. *Ergonomics*, 32(3):271 – 280, 1989.

[Lef90]   Leffler, S.J., McKusick, M.K., Karels, M.J. and Quarterman, J.S., *The Design and Implementation of the 4.3BSD UNIX Operating System*. Addison Wesley, Reading, USA, 1990.

[Mal89]   Malone, T.B., MPTS methodology in the Navy: Enhanced HARDMAN. In Pettigrew, D.L. (Ed.), *Proceedings of the 33rd Annual Meeting of the Human Factors Society*, pages 1044–1048. Human Factors Society, Santa Monica, USA, 1989.

[Man81]   Manna, Z. and Pnueli, A., Verification of concurrent programs: The temporal framework. In Boyer, R.S. and Strother Moore, J. (Eds.), *The Correctness Problem In Computer Science*, pages 215–273. Academic Press, London, UK, 1981.

[McC91]   McCarthy, J.C., Miles, V. and Monk, A.F., An experimental study of common ground in text-based communication. *Proceedings of the CHI'91 Conference on Human Factors in Computing Systems*, pages 209–215. ACM, New York, USA, 1991.

[Pal95]   Palanque, P. and Bastide, R., Formal specification and verification of CSCW using interactive cooperative object formalism. In *People and Computers X*, pages 197–212. Springer Verlag, Berlin, Germany, 1995.

[Pen90]   Pendergast, M.O. and Vogel, D., Design and implementation of a P.C. based multi-user text editor. In Gibbs, S. and Verrijn-Stuart, A.A. (Eds.), *Multi-User Interfaces And Applications*, pages 195–206. Elsevier Science Publications, North Holland, Netherlands, 1990.

[Pri67]   Prior, A., *Past, Present, Future*. Oxford University Press, Oxford, UK, 1967.

[Sze88]   Szekely, P. and Myers, B., A user interface toolkit based on graphical objects and constraints. *ACM SIGPLAN Notices*, 23(11):36–45, 1988.

[Too91]   Took, R., Integrating inheritance and composition in an objective presentation model for multiple media. In Post, F.H. and Barth, W. (Eds.), *EUROGRAPHICS '91*, pages 291–303. Elsevier Science Publications, North Holland, Netherlands, 1991.

[War89]   Wardell, R.W., An ergonomics perspective on safety in the oilfield. In Pettigrew, D.L. (Ed.), *Proceedings of the 33rd Annual Meeting of the Human Factors Society*, pages 999–1003. Human Factors Society, Santa Monica, USA, 1989.

[Wic84]   Wicken, C.D., *Engineering Psychology And Human Performance*. C.E. Merrill Publishing Company, London, UK, 1984.

[Win87]   Winograd, T. and Flores, F., *Understanding Computers And Cognition*. Addison-Wesley, Reading, USA, 1987.

Index

This index includes the CSCW applications, tools and models that are referenced in this book.

Action Workflow, 44
Ariel, 70
Aspects, 84
Augmented Petri Nets, 38

Backtalk, 38
BDL, 37
BSCW, 206
Buttons, 60

Calliope, 154
CAVECAT, 67, 69, 70, 78, 84
CaveDraw, 84
CDO meta-model, 40
CES, 107
Chiron-1, 148, 149
ClearBoard, 86, 92, 95, 162
ClearFace, 89
Clock, 143, 144, 149, 157, 161, 176, 181, 185
ClockWorks, 143
Clover model, 174, 190
COAST, 110, 113, 127, 128
Cognoter, 84
COLA, 153, 177, 203
Collaborative Process Model, 37
Collaboratory Builder's Environment, 125, 131
Collage, 159
Commune, 84
Conference Toolkit, 146
ConversationBuilder, 162
Cooltalk, 106, 127
Coordinator, 224
CoVer, 207
Cruiser, 67, 78, 84

DECAF, 110
DEC@aGlance, 13
Dialogo, 84
DistEdit, 106, 108, 112, 118, 123, 124, 126, 127, 137, 162, 163, 203
DistView, 111, 125, 128, 131, 162, 177, 179, 188
DIVE, 149, 203

Dolphin, 11, 104, 113, 123, 125–127
Domino, 37

FlowMark, 43
FlowPath, 47
Freeflow, 206

GEN, 144
Godard, 62, 63
GroupDesign, 181
GroupDraw, 84
GroupKit, 131, 136, 138, 141, 146–148, 153, 154, 157, 160, 161, 176, 181, 187, 188
GroupSketch, 84
GroupWeb, 155
GROVE, 84, 106, 114

Habanero, 123
Hole-In-Space, 57
Horus, 203
Hydra, 68

IBIS, 104, 207
ICN, 37, 39, 49
iiif, 59, 62, 70, 85
Information Control Net (ICN), 38
Interface Builder, 125, 205
Intermezzo, 160
Isis, 109, 163, 202
IVS, 76

Java, 125, 131, 163

Kasmer, 68, 78
Khronika, 63

Linda, 203
LiveBoard, 13
Lotus Notes, 21, 131, 162
Lotus/Domino, 20

MACE, 106, 112

MBone, 106, 125, 162, 200
Media Space, 57, 67, 71, 78, 84, 86
Mediascape, 69, 78
MERMAID, 85, 92
MMConf, 176, 179, 188
MMM, 174, 181, 188, 190
Model–View–Controller, 128, 143, 148, 173
Montage, 15, 67
Moondo, 149
Multi-User Dungeons, 160
Mushroom, 206

NeWS, 199
Notification Server, 138, 139, 141, 146, 147
nte, 202, 204
nv, 201

OAM, 37
Obliq, 203, 204
Officetalk, 37, 38
OFS model, 38
OSSAD model, 37
Oval, 162

PAC model, 173, 190
Petri net, 37, 49, 225
PicturePhone, 57
PMTC, 85, 92
Polymer, 37, 45
Polyscope, 64
Portholes, 65, 70, 71, 154
Prelog, 249, 251
Prep, 107
Prominand, 37
ProShare, 106
Prospero, 144, 207, 211

Quilt, 107

Rapport, 176, 181
rat, 201
RAVE, 57, 58, 63, 65, 67, 69–71, 78, 84
Rendezvous, 67, 141, 143, 148, 149, 152, 157, 160, 173, 181, 182, 185, 188
Role Interaction Nets, 37

SAAM model, 189
SACT, 37
SASSE, 106, 125, 126, 153
SCOOP, 38
SEPIA, 85, 207
Share-Kit, 137, 146, 160
Shared X, 176, 177, 188, 199
Shastra, 190
ShowMe, 13
ShrEdit, 127

SLICE model, 163
Society model, 37
SOL, 153, 162
Strudel, 162
Suite, 124, 152, 162, 176–178, 181, 182, 186, 188, 190

TeamPaint, 84, 96
TeamRoom, 17, 20
TeamRooms, 125, 131, 160
TeamWorkStation, 84, 86, 89, 92, 176, 179, 181, 188
Telepresence, 68, 84
TEMPORA, 38
Timbuktu, 84
TUMS, 37

UBIK, 38
User Action Notation, 225

vat, 104, 125, 201
VConf, 84
vfctool, 76
vic, 201
VideoDraw, 84, 94
VideoWindow, 67, 84
Virtual Places, 206
Visual Obliq, 158, 203, 205

WAVE, 71, 78
wb, 106, 116, 127, 202, 204
We-Met, 84
Weasel, 148, 149, 176, 181, 185, 188
WooRKS, 37
World Wide Web, 24, 56, 70, 78, 163, 199, 205, 206
wOrlds, 125
WScrawl, 140

X Window System, 140, 143, 177, 199
Xedit, 128
XTV, 176, 177, 181, 182, 188, 190